Deaf Eyes on Interpreting

Deaf Eyes on Interpreting

Thomas K. Holcomb and David H. Smith,
Editors

Gallaudet University Press *Washington, D.C.*

Gallaudet University Press
Washington, DC 20002
gupress.gallaudet.edu

Library of Congress Cataloging-in-Publication Data
Names: Holcomb, Thomas K., 1959– editor. | Smith, David H., editor.
Title: Deaf eyes on interpreting / edited by Thomas K. Holcomb, David H. Smith.
Description: Washington : Gallaudet University Press, 2018.
Identifiers: LCCN 2018007814 | ISBN 9781944838270 (hardback) | ISBN 9781944838553 (paperback)
ISBN 9781944838287 (e-book)
Subjects: LCSH: Interpreters for the deaf. | Translating and interpreting. |
BISAC: LANGUAGE ARTS & DISCIPLINES / Translating & Interpreting. |
LANGUAGE ARTS & DISCIPLINES / Sign Language.
Classification: LCC HV2402 .D425 2018 | DDC 362.4/283—dc23
LC record available at https://lccn.loc.gov/2018007814

Cover art: "Artistry through Deaf Eyes," giclee canvas by Jon Savage, 2017; the artist.

∞This paper meets the requirements of ANSI/NISO Z39.48-1992 (Permanence of Paper).

Contents

Foreword

Shelley Lawrence, Patty Lessard, Anna Mindess, Christine Monikowski, and Michelle Swaney

THE TWENTY ESSAYS within this volume, written by Deaf individuals with a vast array of experiences, perspectives, challenges, and concerns, support the well-known research in our field. We are all aware of "diminished program involvement with the Deaf community" and the shift in how interpreters begin their careers—via institutions of higher education rather than developing trust and understanding reciprocity in the Deaf community.[1] Consistent themes within these essays are things that were lost, in part, with the professionalization of the ASL/English interpreting field. We certainly have made some gains, but issues that beg for more attention include trust, allyship, quality of work, teaming, and connection to the Deaf community. Several of these factors are missing in action for many of the recipients of our services. Consequently, Shelley found herself asking the following questions as she reviewed the chapters:

- How is trust established and maintained?
- What is an ally? How does one become an ally? What actions are required and what actions are best avoided?
- What does quality interpreting mean and who decides this?
- How does one team? Who is one's team? What serves the consumer best and who makes the decision?
- What is one's connection to the Deaf community? Can anyone become a qualified interpreter without community ties? Can one become an ally or establish trust without this connection?

As each of us read these chapters, we reflected on our own experiences and the errors we have made in our careers, as well as the power and privilege we hold as interpreters. With each essay, we at some point cringed while reading the material. And then we tried to think about our past missteps and how we learn from each experience and pass that learning along to our colleagues, students, and mentees in the hopes of changing and improving our field.

As editors of this volume, Tom and Dave personally solicited the authors of the chapters. They wanted to include some of the many experiences Deaf people have when they are in an interpreted situation. By presenting this collection of anecdotes and relevant research, they hope the experiences for both Deaf people and interpreters will be better in the future and we can avoid the mistakes and misjudgments that have plagued our relatively young profession. Tom said, "Over the years I've had conversations with various individuals about the challenges associated with surviving in the 'hearing' environment" (personal communication). This volume is a sample of those conversations.

There are some examples in the chapters that made us proud to be interpreters and some personal stories that brought us to tears. Many of the essays in this volume initially elicited shock and dismay at the unprofessional behaviors exhibited by some of the interpreters and their obvious disregard and disrespect for their Deaf clients' desires and stated preferences. You may experience these same emotions, but we ask you to read this book because it is important for you, for all of us, to know what Deaf people are thinking. Do not assume you know. Do not assume because they smile and thank you for your work that they are pleased with your work. They often are, but sometimes they are not. In this volume, Deaf people explain why they are—and are not—pleased with our work.

As we read each chapter, we also looked into ourselves to consider whether we had contributed to oppressing or disempowering Deaf people. For example, Anna is very well known for authoring *Reading Between the Signs*, the primary purpose of which is "to sensitize interpreters to the crucial effects that the differences between Deaf and hearing cultures have on our work and relationships with Deaf people." Yet she admits that while negotiating with a Deaf person for a recent assignment, she "forgot the sentiments contained in the very lines I had written," which include the following:

- Discounting the deeper reality of cultural differences can lead to misunderstanding and discord if we assume that everyone shares identical values.
- In the new interpreter-centric model, "rates and working conditions are based on the needs of the interpreter, not on meeting the needs of Deaf participants."
- The clear-cut right to self-determination may become a little harder for us to see objectively, however, when it touches upon our own livelihood and the agencies, policies, feedback, and decision-making power related to interpreters.[2]

Michelle reflected on how critical it is for us—interpreters, interpreter educators, and future interpreters—to take an honest look at where we have been, where the field has been, where we are now, and how we can move forward and improve our work to best support the community that we serve—Deaf individuals of all ages, backgrounds, ethnicities, and additional disabilities. We need to understand what Deaf people have to say about the experiences they have when working with interpreters. All interpreters make errors of judgment (certainly all of us have made our share), but before we take the position of "there's no way to be perfect," we must recognize that the authors of these essays are neither asking for nor expecting perfection. These essays are honest reflections of the vulnerability that we may never fully understand due to our own power and privilege.

We were all very honored that Tom and Dave invited us to review these chapters. Each of us has experience as an interpreter, interpreter educator, or author, and as a guest in the Deaf community—ranging from at least twenty-five years to more than forty years. We humbly reflected on our own fallibility as we saw such a variety of interpreting assignments through the pensive eyes of these Deaf contributors. We want to say that over the years, we have probably made every mistake addressed in this volume. Perhaps this is the reason we were sometimes so emotional upon reading the chapters. We can see ourselves, hard as it is to accept.

We want to share our reflections on a few of our challenging interpreting assignments because we want you, the reader, to see how these chapters impacted us. We know it is easier to accept our successes than to own our failures. Yet, if we want to call ourselves "professional interpreters" we must remember that the heart of interpreting, the heart of what we do, is centered in our genuine understanding of what it means to work with people and our role in creating connections.

One of us remembers a recent assignment involving an experienced and sophisticated Deaf consumer and an all-day assignment that came through an agency. The interpreter (who preferred to work with a team) and the Deaf person (who indicated a team would be awkward and inappropriate during the sensitive meetings, given there would be several breaks) each thought they knew best. A compromise was reached, but neither party felt satisfied and bad feelings resulted (frustration on the part of the interpreter and disempowerment on the part of the Deaf person). Fortunately, because the interpreter and the Deaf person had a previous relationship, they were interested in resolving the issue, but it required many follow-up conversations. After reading this volume and learning more from these Deaf authors, the interpreter realized that the Deaf consumer was the expert when it came to their life and needed to be accommodated, whether or not it fit the classic 20/20 model.

Another reviewer, during one of those chapters that made her cringe, found herself wondering about other Deaf people, typical folks in the community going about their lives and occasionally interacting with interpreters; she interprets for these people, not the Deaf people who wrote chapters for this volume. While not related to a specific assignment, she still wondered, given her position of power and privilege, what assumptions she makes during her assignments. When a Deaf person smiles and says "thank you," does she show she wants feedback or does she appear unavailable? Why did she cringe—because she, too, has not conducted herself as well as she should? Rather than turning the page, she took the conversation to a few trusted Deaf friends and they were amazed to hear about this upcoming volume. Maybe we should all try to share these chapters and begin some honest (albeit uncomfortable) conversations.

This volume offers valuable insights into Deaf people's experiences of being on the receiving end of our work; these insights would be hard to find elsewhere. It is a gift, an opportunity for us to look inward at our motivations for choosing this field and for us to understand how our work has a significant impact on the lives and livelihoods of the people with whom we work. It is with profound gratitude that we thank Tom Holcomb and Dave Smith for their work and all the contributors who candidly revealed their thoughts and feelings.

So what has changed? Why are Deaf people offering their views now? Perhaps it is the application of the social justice lens to interpreted situations (the discrimination and oppression of minority groups and the lack of power minority groups have to self-determination). Perhaps it is the evolving assertion of Deaf consumers' rights. Regardless, we must acknowledge we have often kowtowed to translation (with questionable results) and dominant culture rules over true communication access. What does it mean to have a level playing field? What does professionalism look like in our respective communities? Can interpreters work with Deaf people to create the kind of experience that empowers rather than disempowers? Are we even aware of our behaviors that disempower consumers?

We predict that reading the essays in this book will not be a comfortable experience for many interpreters. They contain criticisms of the work we do. The repeated litany of negative experiences may feel like a blanket criticism of our entire profession. Do not be offended; learn from the mistakes of others. Chris reminds us to focus on the array of excellent suggestions the Deaf authors offer and try to apply them to our interpreting interactions. Do not be indignant or feel intimidated. It is not a personal attack; it is not about you!

Patty suggests we think of this volume as a kind of "customer satisfaction survey" if you will, the kind of thing commonly used by service providers ranging from workshop presenters to physicians. We sometimes hesitate to give a low score when our experience was not a good one. But when comments are invited, Patty says she tends to be more direct and critical and offers areas that could be improved. She recommends we keep this in mind when reading these essays. The contributors express raw feelings and frustrations, and they offer insights and suggestions to help us improve our work. They highlight the unintended consequences that lead to frustration caused by our decision-making and present an almost unified plea for us to work as allies. They ask for collaboration, life-long learning, commitment to providing effective communication and ensuring Deaf people's active participation in interpreting assignments. As our field evolves, we need to evolve with it.

Do remember that in Deaf culture, as Hall (in this volume) reminds us, "feedback is a *gift*, reflecting trust and intimacy in the other person, and a willingness to put work into strengthening that relationship and clarifying the message together. Feedback given to an interpreter means that the Deaf person cares enough to try improving or even validating that interpreter's work and professional skills for both that interpreter's personal benefit and for the whole Deaf community." Let us take this precious gift of trust and be brave enough as individuals and as a profession to alter the course of our collective journey. Remember that we, too, cringed and found some of the narrative difficult to accept. We ask you to take a deep breath and continue reading, as we did.

It is our sincere hope that this volume will be shared far and wide, and that each reader will have multiple takeaways or "aha" moments that catapult us into a new era of interpreting, a new era that takes the past into account, learns from it, applies what has been learned, and works diligently toward allyship, language proficiency, and cross-cultural communication that supports Deaf individuals in any and every way possible. After all, isn't that really the reason that we've chosen this profession?

NOTES

1. Dennis Cokely, "Shifting positionality: A critical examination of the turning point in the relationship of interpreters and the Deaf community," in *Sign Language Interpreting and Interpreter*

Education: Directions for Research and Practice, eds. Marc Marschark, Rico Peterson, and Elizabeth A. Winston (New York: Oxford University Press, 2005): 3–28; National Interpreter Education Center (NIEC). Cathy Cogen and Dennis Cokely, *Preparing Interpreters for Tomorrow: Report on a Study of Emerging Trends in Interpreting and Implications for Interpreter Education* (Boston, MA: National Interpreter Education Center at Northeastern University, 2015). Retrieved July 12, 2017 from http://www.interpretereducation.org/wp-content/uploads/2016/02/NIEC_Trends_Report_2_2016.pdf

2. Anna Mindess, Thomas K. Holcomb, Daniel Langholtz, and Priscilla Moyers, *Reading Between the Signs: Intercultural Communication for Sign Language Interpreters*, 3rd Ed (Boston, MA: Intercultural Press, 2014), xii, 279, 281.

Preface

THERE IS A growing body of literature related to ASL/English interpreting. However, there is very little published that presents the views of Deaf people as they revolve around interpreting. This is unfortunate because Deaf people talk frequently about their experiences with interpreters and the services they provide. Both of the editors do this because they work with interpreters on a regular basis.

Thomas K. Holcomb comes from a multigenerational Deaf family. Both his parents and grandparents on the maternal side are Deaf, as are his children and grandchildren. Although ASL is his first language, he grew up in the 1960s when sign language was not allowed in schools with young children. However, as was common in many schools for the deaf during those days, its use was tolerated outside the classroom and in the dormitories at the Indiana School for the Deaf, but never in the classroom. This official policy of oral-only in the classroom was strictly enforced with the goal of providing deaf children with every opportunity to develop speech skills.

When the family moved to Southern California in 1968, the California School for the Deaf at Riverside (CSDR) had a long waiting list due to the 1960s rubella epidemic. Instead, Tom and his older brother attended a public school that housed the local regional program for deaf children. Because of his academic skills as compared to the other 100 deaf students there, it was decided that he would benefit from being in the regular classroom. However, he was "too deaf" to lipread and speak for himself; he needed some kind of support in order to make this placement work. It is believed that he was the very first deaf student in the nation to receive the services of a sign language interpreter in an elementary school.[1] With the interpreter playing a prominent role in bridging the linguistic and social gaps for him, he was able to transverse between the "two worlds" with relative ease. When he became a teenager, his family moved to the East Coast where he completed his high school years at Model Secondary School for the Deaf (MSSD) and matriculated at Gallaudet College. Tom's use of interpreting services was minimal during those years.

For all his professional life since graduating from Gallaudet in 1980, Tom has used interpreting services intensively and extensively for work at Rochester Institute of Technology (RIT), San Jose State University (SJSU), and Ohlone College; for his graduate studies at RIT and the University of Rochester; and for community involvement. Currently, he is a professor in Ohlone College's Deaf Studies division where the Interpreter Preparatory Program is housed. In this environment, he spends many hours discussing with his colleagues and friends, both Deaf and hearing, about the limitations of the current standard practice of interpreting. These discussions led him to this book project with the goal of improving the interpreting experience for both Deaf and hearing people.

David H. Smith is the only deaf member of his family. He was born hearing and slowly lost his hearing after a bout with measles at the age of three. He was profoundly deaf by the age of ten. The initial diagnosis was "he's either very deaf or very stubborn," and he was referred to an audiologist for hearing aids. Somewhere along the path of seeing doctors and audiologists, it was suggested that Dave start attending the New York State School for the Deaf in Rome, NY. His parents decided to keep him home and have him attend the local schools since he was still able to articulate speech and appeared to understand most people well enough with his hearing aids on. He did not know ASL, so the idea of an interpreter was not even feasible. Also this was before the passage of Public Law 94-142, the Education for All Handicapped Children Act. Dave remembers that kindergarten did not go too well, and he had to repeat it. Somehow he survived the next twelve years of his public school education. It was a struggle at times and looking back he realizes he missed a tremendous amount of information in school.

Dave's first steps toward the beginning of his healthy Deaf identity occurred during junior high when his progressive-thinking speech therapist mentioned National Technical Institute for the Deaf (NTID) and suggested a visit. This was the first time he had been exposed to a Deaf-friendly environment. Dave entered NTID in 1980 and soon encountered his first interpreters. Even though he was not yet fluent in ASL, he still found them mostly beneficial. The reason for the word "mostly" is that there were a good number of novice interpreters who had just completed the Basic Interpreter Training Program (BITP). Most of these novice interpreters evolved into excellent professionals. Some did not survive the evaluative environment and pressure there and wisely moved on to other things. Dave used the interpreting services at NTID extensively and credits them with helping him survive the rigorous bachelor's degree program in biology at RIT.

After leaving NTID/RIT, Dave became a teacher at the California School for the Deaf in Riverside, so his use of interpreters was minimal during the 1990s. When he began his doctoral studies at the University of Nebraska, he was blessed with an excellent team of interpreters. They set an exemplary standard for what he expects in interpreters to this day: conceptual clarity in signing and accuracy in voicing with the ability to work as a team. Continuing his career as an academic at Fresno State and later at the University of Tennessee, Dave was fortunate to have an experienced Deaf faculty member, Dr. Paul Ogden, as his mentor. Just like Tom and his colleagues and peers, Dave and Paul had many discussions about interpreters and how to work with them. The result of their combined shared experiences and discussions can be read in chapter 10 in this volume.

This book project is an "all-Deaf" effort involving thirty-two contributors and editors who are Deaf. However, because we anticipate many readers of this volume to be either working hearing interpreters or future interpreters, we asked five prominent interpreters and interpreter educators to read and critique each chapter. The goal was to minimize the possibility of confusion or misunderstanding of the points the contributors tried to make in their entries. A brief background of each reader follows.

Shelley Lawrence of Pleasanton, California, is a professor emeritus, having directed and taught in the Interpreter Preparation Program at Ohlone College for thirty-five years. She is recognized for her pioneering work in applying the ASL expansion techniques to the field of ASL/English interpreting.

Patty Lessard of Fremont, California, has been working as a professional interpreter and interpreter educator since 1979. She is in demand nationally and internationally to support academic conferences, both as an interpreter and as a presenter. She is the author of several publications including an interactive curriculum, *Classifiers: A Closer Look*, and a series of self-study CDs made for working interpreters. She's also on the board of the Conference of Interpreter Trainers (CIT).

Anna Mindess of Berkeley, California, is well known for her book, *Reading Between the Signs: Intercultural Communication for Sign Language Interpreters.* This book is based on her research as well as years of experience working as a professional interpreter and dealing with cultural misunderstandings between Deaf and hearing people.

Christine Monikowski of Rochester, New York, is a scholar in the field of ASL/English interpreting with many publications to her name. Her most recent release is *Conversations with Interpreter Educators: Exploring Best Practices.* She is considered a national leader in the areas of interpreting education and educational interpreting.

Michelle Swaney of Knoxville, Tennessee, is the Instructional and Information Technology Officer at the Tennessee School for the Deaf, and a former faculty member at the University of Tennessee, Knoxville, which has an interpreter education program. She was among the first to work as a designated interpreter, beginning her service long before the term was devised.

In addition to critiquing each chapter, we asked the readers to write the foreword for this book with the idea of setting the stage for what is to come in the volume. Because we hoped that some of the ideas presented in the book would be implemented in order to improve the interpreting experience for everyone involved, we also asked Dr. Carolyn Ball, a national leader in interpreting and interpreting education, to write the afterword. Dr. Ball is currently executive director of Sorenson's VRS Interpreting Institute. Her background and leadership in promoting the field of interpreting and interpreter education is extensive including twelve years on the board of the Conference of Interpreter Trainers (CIT), six years as the president. She is serving the Registry of Interpreters for the Deaf (RID) as its treasurer.

With more than thirty contributors involved in this book project, we found it necessary to observe several conventions for the sake of consistency. First, because this book is about ASL/English interpretation, it's safe to assume that most, if not all, of the Deaf people in the book use sign language and are culturally Deaf. For this reason, we capitalize the D in Deaf except when we refer to deaf people in general, regardless of their ability to use sign language or involvement in the Deaf community.

Over the years, the terms and their associated acronyms used to identify programs that educate future interpreters have evolved. In the beginning, Interpreter

Training Program, or ITP, was commonly used when such programs came into existence in the 1970s. Eventually, the leaders in the field felt that the term was a misnomer because future interpreters were not trained but prepared to enter the profession. As a result, a new label, Interpreter Preparation Program, or IPP, became increasingly popular at many colleges and universities. More recently, interpreter educators have started to advocate for what they think is an even more appropriate term, *Interpreter Education Program* or *IEP*.

However, it has been our experience that there is confusion in the use of these acronyms as they are identical to others used frequently in the Deaf community and, more specifically, in the field of Deaf Education; for example, IEP also means individualized education program. For this reason, we will *not* use the acronym IEP in this volume to avoid this type of confusion but instead will use the entire phrase, Interpreter Education Program, in recognition that the programs do educate future interpreters, more so than train or prepare them.

With the contributions coming from more than thirty authors, the presentations vary a great deal from one chapter to the next. Some entries are personal stories of experiences working with interpreters while others are research-based. This array serves the purpose of providing the reader with multiple perspectives on issues associated with interpreting. The goal, however, is to encourage out-of-the-box thinking as well as consideration of creative solutions to challenges that Deaf people encounter in their interpreted experience.

NOTE

1. Thomas K. Holcomb, "Paving the Way for Reform in Deaf Education" in *Deaf Epistemologies: Multiple Perspectives on the Acquisition of Knowledge,* ed. Peter V. Paul and Donald F. Moores (Washington, DC: Gallaudet University Press, 2012), 125–46.

Acknowledgments

FIRST, BOTH OF US want to express our sincere appreciation to our spouses and families for their patience and on-going support over the past two years while we worked on this publication. The high level of patience on their part was especially necessary as we dealt with 30 different authors with 30 different personalities, 30 different writing styles, and 30 different work ethics (which tested our own patience). We owe our wives BIG time, especially for those times when we needed to "drop everything" to meet deadlines. We also love that they share our interest, passion, and commitment to make the interpreting experience better for everyone involved. In the end, they probably knew that the time we devoted would result in a better home life for themselves with less frustrated husbands!

We also want to thank Gallaudet University Press (GUP) for taking on this project. They gave us the contract to produce this volume even though our proposal was somewhat unorthodox in several ways. First, it is an all-Deaf volume dealing with the delicate issue of interpreting and access. We recognized the initial concern that this volume could turn into merely an "interpreter bashing" exercise instead of an educational effort. We understand how a negative approach without constructive feedback could easily be detrimental to the burgeoning field of professional interpreting. Second, with the field shifting toward publications where evidence-based data are favored over anecdotal presentations of lived experiences, we appreciate GUP's willingness to entertain the idea that both data-driven evidence and anecdotes are equally valuable if we are to improve the interpreting experience for both Deaf people and interpreters. Ultimately, we believe we were successful in maintaining a balance in the book and presenting the issues in a way that is constructive. We believe the end product is much stronger because of this flexibility.

For some contributors, it was their first experience in preparing a formal manuscript for publication. This necessitated many rounds of revisions, which made it time-consuming and extremely difficult for us due to our other work responsibilities. We want to thank Deaf-owned TSWriting Services for stepping in and working with these authors in getting their submissions well-prepared and well-written.

And finally, we want to thank our friends and colleagues, both Deaf and hearing, for the ongoing discussions we've had about our experiences with interpreting services. From reading all of these essays it may seem that interpreters can't do anything right. In reality, both of us have been blessed by interpreters who *do* get it, those who *do* work hard alongside us to address the injustice that is constantly imposed on us as we seek to gain access to the public, and those who *will* go out of their way to support us. You know who you are! Thank you!!!! In addition, we are constantly inspired by our collective strength as Deaf individuals as we endure covert and overt discrimination in our effort to participate in society. May we stay united in our effort to make the world a truly accessible place for everyone.

Deaf Eyes on Interpreting

Introduction

WE ARE PLEASED to offer this book for both the Deaf and interpreting communities with the hope of elevating the interpreting experience for everyone involved. Deaf people often discuss among themselves their experiences with interpreters, what they like or dislike about them, and the effectiveness of their work. Interpreters do the same, albeit without using client names (we hope), exchanging information about the work, the frustrations associated with their job, and more. As regular users of interpreting services, as well as being involved in interpreting education, we see a huge disparity in the literature between the contributions made by interpreters and interpreter educators and those made by Deaf people themselves. We undertook this book project in order to bring Deaf people to the forefront of the discussions about what constitutes quality interpreting service.

In reviewing the literature, we discovered that very few authors of published journal articles or book chapters related to interpreting services were Deaf. Those writers who were Deaf, in almost every case, were Certified Deaf Interpreters and/or involved in interpreting education. Their contributions were usually limited to these two areas. We found relatively few pieces of writing that offered the perspectives of Deaf people as stakeholders.

Perhaps there are several reasons for this. One is that interpreting has evolved from a service mostly provided by people close to the Deaf community (such as family members and close friends) into a profession (akin to accounting, architecture, or real estate) with ever higher degree requirements and national tests and certifications. Accordingly, interpreters have provided themselves with platforms where they can exchange their professional perspectives, research, and ideas on what they consider to be optimal delivery of their work. Furthermore, workshops, courses, and degrees are designed to support interpreters in their pursuit of professionalism and the maintenance of their certifications. All of this has happened while the Deaf community slowly has been left behind.

While Deaf people are the consumers or clients of interpreting services, most do not engage in any aspect of interpreter education or the certification process. This is not unlike the medical field, financial services, or construction where customers and clients are not involved with the licensing and monitoring of those involved in the work. Yes, there are ways to file grievances and reports of unethical practices, but the decision making as to who is qualified has been mostly taken over by the professionals themselves with little Deaf stakeholder input.

There has been widespread criticism regarding this disconnect between professional service providers and people who receive services. Consumer surveys, focus groups, and quality-control systems have been established in response to this concern. More recently, crowd-sourced review sites such as Yelp and Angie's List provide consumers with direct and immediate feedback on the work rendered by the organizations and/or individuals who provide a variety of services.

Many professional organizations decry this trend, questioning the validity and wisdom of such influential (and often anonymous) feedback. Many experts object to the evaluations of their professional work made by ordinary citizens who, in most cases, do not have sufficient background to evaluate the work. For example, can lay people really assess the work of a dentist? Tom recalls his father being impressed with a new dentist because he came out of the appointment relatively pain-free. Never mind that the reason for the pain-free experience may have been substandard dental work to begin with.

Conversely, another trend has emerged that has also shaped the way business and research is conducted in many areas. Data-driven decisions are increasingly common among leaders in determining the best course of action. In that process, personal anecdotes are dismissed as unreliable and unsound in favor of quantitative scientific approaches to gain a clear and accurate understanding of the facts and truth.

As we well know, discovering "truths" depends on the design of the data collection procedure. For this reason, epistemologies, or the "ways of knowing," of ordinary people should not be dismissed, especially if they show common themes. If anything, these stories should drive the research agenda. Accordingly, real-life stories of Deaf people and their experiences with interpreters must be valued and treated as critical data in shaping future directions in the interpreting field. Research agendas must include areas that are important to Deaf people, not just those that interpreters and interpreter educators think are important. As an example, there have been studies on interpreter fatigue and its impact on accuracy in the interpreted work. Based on these studies, the twenty-minute model of switching interpreters has become the standard in the field. However, there has been no study on the impact of such switches on Deaf people's comprehension of the interpreted work. This example demonstrates how the research agenda is skewed toward interpreters' focus on technical accuracy rather than on Deaf people's desire for consistency and ease of understanding. This is but one example of why epistemologies of Deaf people should never be dismissed in favor of the data-driven agenda of the profession.

Most of the contributors to this volume are not interpreters themselves, nor are they directly involved in interpreter education. Rather, they use interpreting services on a regular basis, both on personal and professional levels. Frequently, they express a strong desire for better interpreting experiences that would allow them to represent themselves better to the hearing, nonsigning public as competent and intelligent individuals, that would make it easier for them to comprehend the interpreted work, and that would enable them to engage with their hearing counterparts more easily and successfully.

In this volume, the thirty-two Deaf authors freely share a wide range of encounters with the goal of generating dialogue on improving the interpreting experience for both Deaf people and interpreters. The contributions are organized into four parts: Seeing the Issues through Deaf Eyes; Understanding the Issues through Deaf

Eyes; Exploring the Specialized Areas of Interpreting through Deaf Eyes; and Moving Forward with Deaf Eyes. A summary of each chapter is also available in ASL. They can be accessed by typing on the computer the URL listed on the title page of each chapter. They all can be accessed at https://www.youtube.com/channel/UCVIbI5DOBbWvfeyOv1VmUkQ.

The first part, "Seeing the Issues through Deaf Eyes," serves as a primer for this volume. Trudy Suggs discusses the importance of storytelling in understanding the true picture of the plight of the disempowered. Indeed, storytelling has played an important role in so many disenfranchised communities, including the Deaf community, in their struggle for liberation and empowerment. In his chapter, Thomas Holcomb envisions a new term, DEAM—a play on three English words (*Deaf, Dream, Team*)—to encourage both Deaf people and interpreters to work closely together to move the interpreting experience to the next level of excellence and accessibility. Transparency and accountability are often missing in the business side of interpreting, leaving Deaf people in the dark and powerless. Chad Taylor, Ryan Shephard, and Justin "Bucky" Buckhold discuss how the current practice of providing interpreting services is antiquated. They argue that it is time for the interpreting world to catch up to the modern world where transparency and accountability are expected and accepted. Only then will both Deaf people and interpreters be empowered to provide satisfactory services.

The following section, "Understanding the Issues through Deaf Eyes," includes the work of several scholars who share their research and case studies related to effective interpreting support for Deaf people. John Pirone, Jonathan Henner, and Wyatte Hall present their findings from interviews with several students about their mainstreamed collegiate experiences. ASL fluency, professionalism, and intercultural skills were identified as three primary concerns related to interpreter competencies in providing Deaf people with the necessary support in mainstreamed settings. Because interpreters may not yet have developed the necessary skills to do their job effectively, their presence in the classroom does not always translate into equality or access for mainstreamed Deaf students. Deaf professionals face the same challenges. In their interviews with several Deaf professionals, Kim Kurz and Joseph Hill asked them to list the specific skills interpreters need to do a superior job. Linguistic competency in *both* English and ASL is essential, which is surprisingly lacking among many interpreters. With strong bilingual skills, other critical factors such as depiction, discourse, audience engagement, message equivalence, language register, and pragmatic enrichment are made possible, allowing for exceptional interpreting work to support Deaf professionals.

The need for advanced ASL skills among interpreters is reinforced by Keith Cagle, Sharon Lott, and Phyllis Wilcox in their study on head movements. They argue that by incorporating appropriate head movements, interpreters can make it easier for Deaf people to understand the interpreted message. The functions of specific head movements are outlined in their chapter.

Continuing with the needs of Deaf professionals, Tara Holcomb and Aracelia Aguilar present a case study where two completely different outcomes were a result of differing actions taken by interpreters. These actions had a drastic impact on the authors' ability to participate and function effectively in a professional conference setting. Their essay illuminates the importance of honoring Deaf people and listening to them in their attempt to create the most accessible situation possible. Unfortunately, these attempts are frequently suppressed by interpreters and interpreter coordinators. Leala Holcomb shares zir experiences trying to create an accessible environment at the university where ze began zir doctoral studies, only to have the concerns dismissed by the university's disability services officials. Leala turned to social media in a desperate effort to find solutions and support with positive results.

Part III, "Exploring the Specialized Areas of Interpreting through Deaf Eyes," allows the authors to discuss issues that are specific to their professional arenas—higher education, K–12 education, the corporate world, and health care. Tawny Holmes shares her legal expertise on deaf and disabled people's rights to accommodations to ensure a successful collegiate experience. She also recounts her struggle for equal access inside and outside the classroom while she attended law school.

David Smith and Paul Ogden hope to demystify the academic world for interpreters who seek to work with Deaf academics. In their chapter, they provide a clear picture of the challenges facing all college professors and the unique challenges of the growing numbers of Deaf academics. Along this line, Patrick Boudreault and Genie Gertz discuss their struggles to gain access to professional conferences and the disempowering actions taken by conference organizers that prevented them from benefitting fully from such conferences. In his chapter, Thomas Holcomb argues that Deaf professionals deserve more than just completely trusting their interpreters to represent them well in their ASL to spoken English interpreting work. He shares an experience in which he had a team of transliterators sign back to him the spoken words of the interpreters who were assigned to voice interpret his signed lecture.

Continuing with the educational setting focus, the next two chapters deal with interpreting concerns at the K–12 level. In their entries, based on their own experiences, both Amy June Rowley and Fallon Brizendine present their serious reservations about educational interpreters and their inability to meet the needs of Deaf children in the mainstream. Even though Amy June Rowley is considered a success story in mainstreamed education, she refuses to subject her own Deaf children to the same process. In her chapter, she explains why. As a faculty member in an Interpreter Education Program, Fallon Brizendine supervises interpreting students at their internship placements in public schools. Based on her observations, she shares her deep concerns about the poor quality of education that deaf children are receiving in the mainstream environment, partially due to the inability of educational interpreters to provide the kind of access Deaf children need.

Moving on to the corporate world, Sam Sepah recounts his efforts to orient his designated interpreters to the corporate world of Google. He emphasizes that interpreters needed to learn both the corporate culture and his particular needs as a Deaf person. This was necessary in order to make the relationship between him and his interpreters, and between him and his colleagues at Google, a success.

With healthcare access emerging as a critical issue within the Deaf community, Susan Gonzalez and Marta Ordaz teamed up with Lewis Lummer and Cynthia Plue to discuss how to meet the communication and language access needs of Deaf and DeafBlind people in healthcare settings. The authors argue that interpreters must be creative and flexible enough to ensure that Deaf and DeafBlind individuals, especially those who are foreign-born, comprehend what is happening in healthcare situations.

Finally, in the last section, "Moving Forward with Deaf Eyes," thoughts and ideas are shared on ways that interpreters can become more effective in meeting the needs of Deaf people in interpreted settings. Wyatte Hall presents the parameters of Deaf-centered interpreting, in which Deaf people are truly supported in their efforts to participate in interpreted sessions. He contrasts this approach to what he calls voice-activated interpreters, in which the interpreters' focus is primarily on interpreting the spoken words as accurately possible, without any real consideration that the message will be understood by Deaf people. He contrasts this with a Deaf-centered model of interpreting; outlines its specific aspects, including feedback, pace, partnership, visual orientation, and cultural competence; and provides examples for each. Interpreters who adopt a Deaf-centered model of interpreting are often the favorite of Deaf people.

Marika Kovacs-Houlihan explains in her chapter how a person can work to achieve the coveted "favorite interpreter" label. She shares her personal experiences of working with favorite interpreters at her university. Some of them eventually became her designated interpreters, allowing her to excel in her work as a university faculty member. In order to be a Deaf-centered or favorite interpreter, interpreters need to be cognizant of Deaf culture norms, including making appropriate self-introductions. In her chapter, Naomi Sheneman notes that many interpreters fail to do so. For this reason, she makes a strong case that interpreters need to learn how to introduce themselves appropriately.

Finally, Chris Kurz, Kim Kurz, and Raychelle Harris discuss how academic ASL strategies can assist interpreters in making their interpretation more accessible to mainstreamed Deaf students. They present several considerations for interpreters to improve their effectiveness in delivery of the interpreted message. These areas include register, cognition, lexicon and semantics, fingerspelling, ASL phonological patterns, and assessment translation and testing.

The volume concludes with an afterword by noted interpreter educator and past president of the Conference of Interpreter Trainers (CIT) Carolyn Ball, who reinforces our plea for interpreters, new and experienced, to listen to our stories and learn about the Deaf-centered, Deaf-friendly, and Deaf-focused skills they need to be able to work collaboratively in teams the DEAM way.

We hope this book, whether read as some individual chapters or as whole, with our stories as narratives or shared research, has a positive impact on the field of interpreting. We need to get back to sharing and understanding some of the good Deaf roots and connections that made interpreters great while embracing the increased and long-overdue recognition that interpreters are now real professionals. Please go forth and understand we know that some parts of this book may make those in the profession feel uncomfortable and/or realize that their actions have been unintentionally disempowering. These are not intended to be mean-spirited vignettes but rather just the way we see and feel about it. We also hope that readers have positive "Aha!" moments and either find they have already been doing things the Deaf way or will learn how to move forward while following the DEAM approach.

1

Seeing the Issues through Deaf Eyes

1

The Importance of Storytelling to Address Deaf Disempowerment

Trudy Suggs

For the ASL summary of this chapter, go to https://youtu.be/Y_taTQu2OqY

When my two-year-old son broke his leg, I took him along with my one-year-old to the orthopedic doctor for a follow-up. At the time, I lived in a small town that had a deaf school. What that meant was there were hundreds of Deaf residents and practically everyone in town knew how to sign or at least how to work with interpreters.

After an unusually extended wait time, I had the certified and certainly very qualified interpreter, who I had worked with in the past, accompany me to ask the receptionist about the delay. The receptionist, typing on her computer, said that the doctor's schedule was backed up. I asked if we could see the doctor sooner rather than later since my children were restless and hungry. On top of that, my son, in a body cast from chest to toe, needed his medicine at home. She refused, so I asked to speak with the doctor or nurse. She again refused.

Throughout this entire interaction, she never once looked at me. Frustrated, I said, "Could you please look at me?" She turned her head and looked at the interpreter, who quickly pointed at me. I then asked, "Could you please offer a resolution? We've been here an hour." At that very moment, my youngest began crying. The receptionist, sighing, called a nurse, who was far more courteous and apologetic. I asked to file a complaint about the receptionist's behavior, and the nurse nodded, saying she'd get back to me. The interpreter and I returned to our seats.

A few minutes later, the receptionist called the interpreter over for a phone call. The interpreter answered the phone, beckoned me over, and said it was the office manager. She interpreted as the office manager began asking questions. All the while, the receptionist was looking at me with dagger eyes. I asked the office manager if I could email her, since the receptionist was listening in. The office manager agreed, and we hung up. Walking to my seat, I looked back and saw the interpreter casually cover her mouth as she whispered to the receptionist. Once the interpreter returned to her seat directly across from me, I asked what she had said to the receptionist.

> "Nothing, why?" the interpreter said.
>
> "I saw you whisper to her. What did you say?" I asked.
>
> She again said, "Nothing."
>
> I was puzzled. "No, I saw you whisper. What was it about?"
>
> She relented. "Uh, she began apologizing to me for her behavior and said she didn't mean to talk to you like that. I told her it was okay."
>
> I was surprised. "But it isn't okay how she treated me. Why didn't you tell her to apologize directly to me?"
>
> As realization of what she had done dawned over her face, we were called into the examination room and the appointment was over fairly quickly.

Such a simple act of trying to mediate a situation—when the interpreter really didn't have the right to—became a disempowering experience for me. Had the interpreter been in my shoes, would she have told the receptionist this delay and behavior was okay? I don't know, but this was the start of my extensive work on understanding disempowerment and how we have become complacent with its role in our lives. And there's been one crucial thread throughout the hundreds of stories shared with me about disempowerment: the importance of storytelling, or autoethnography.

Autoethnography and the Importance of Storytelling

Rachel Freed said, "We tell our stories *to transform* ourselves; to learn about our history and tell our experiences to transcend them; to use our stories to make a difference in our world; to broaden our perspective *to see* further than normal; *to act* beyond a story that may have imprisoned or enslaved us; *to live* more of our spiritual and earthly potential."[1]

This is exactly why it's so important for Deaf people to share stories with each other and with others such as interpreters: to learn about the never-ending history of oppression, audism, and disempowerment. Yet, interpreter education often consists of academic, on-the-job, and formal, research-based learning about Deaf culture, linguistic aspects of American Sign Language (ASL), ethics, test preparation, and Deaf history—but very rarely does it involve Deaf people telling stories about life on a day-to-day basis. The few stories that *are* shared often come in the form of mass-produced videos, well-orchestrated interviews, and/or discussion panels focused on generic "What is it like to be Deaf?" discussions, each broad enough to cover the entire community but not quite capture the intricate experience of being Deaf. In "Being Scheherazade: The Importance of Storytelling in Academic Writing," authors Pollock and Bono stated, "One impediment to effective storytelling is the lack of a human face—actors acting and the human imbuing all of our experiences. All too often, academic writers remove the human elements from their storytelling in an effort to sound 'scholarly.' They engage in arid, context-free theorizing, of interest only to the most ardent specialists in their domains."[2]

As Pollock and Bono pointed out, it is the day-to-day stories that are so crucial to understanding the challenges that Deaf people face, particularly with interpreters—that is, the stories they share in the privacy of their homes and through vlogs. Deaf people's frustrations are often discarded by hearing people who say, "My gosh, I'd never do that, how horrible!" and then perform the very same disempowering behavior minutes later.

Many interpreter education courses and workshops pertain to stereotypes or "what if" situations, but very few actually focus on the countless examples of disempowerment, and the consequences, simply because the disempowerment is so deeply embedded into their mindset of "it's just how things are"—much like the example shared at the start of this chapter. Another factor is that many programs emphasize the positive aspects of the field rather than the nitty-gritty of what Deaf people experience at the hands of interpreters. On top of that is the severe lack of data, resources, and education available *for* Deaf people. Most of the money for training and data goes to hearing-led interpreting projects, programs, and studies geared toward hearing interpreters. Even if such projects, programs, and studies involve Deaf people at lower levels, they are still hearing-led and therefore hearing-influenced at the final decision-making level.

Therefore, this anecdotal discussion and the subsequent chapters center on personal narratives rather than statistics or research-driven evidence. "One of the main advantages of personal narratives is that they give us access into learners' private worlds and provide rich data."[3] The autoethnographic approach in this book, with each author contributing a personal experience, is "a useful qualitative research method used to analyse people's lives, a tool that Ellis and Bochner define as '. . . an autobiographical genre of writing that displays multiple layers of consciousness, connecting the personal to the cultural.' There are different uses of the term and it varies according to the relations between the researcher's personal experience and the phenomenon under investigation. Autoethnography can range from research about personal experiences of a research process to parallel exploration of the researcher's and the participants' experiences and about the experience of the researcher while conducting a specific piece of research."[4]

Researcher and popular speaker Brene Brown said, "Vulnerability is about sharing our feelings and experiences with people who have earned the right to hear them. Being vulnerable and open is mutual and an integral part of the trust-building process."[5] Since I first spoke on disempowerment some years ago, hundreds of stories about disempowerment have been shared with me to the point where I have felt overwhelmed, even drained, by the gravity of their experiences. So many Deaf people have told me of their discomfort in sharing their experiences with hearing people, preferring Deaf people like me who have been in the trenches of disempowerment. By sharing my vulnerability through my stories, both in my presentations and on my blog, Deaf people and quite a few hearing interpreters have hopefully come to trust that I understand and validate what they share.

It is my hope that by having Deaf people share their disempowerment stories through various channels such as this book, articles and blogs, workshops, social media, and in autoethnographic research, we can all recognize that sharing stories does not always imply anger, bitterness, or vengeance. Rather, it is a profound way to share experiences that are rarely told because of fear of so many things: denial, judgment, and worst of all, dismissal of their experiences. Deaf people also often hesitate to share such stories with outsiders for fear of being called militant, bothersome, complainers, or any other number of labels. Let us not forget that many have grown up being indoctrinated with feedback that they're expecting too much when they ask for equal treatment, that it's not important to know what was just spoken, or that they're not as valued as others. Talking about real-life instances of disempowerment, ordinary or extraordinary, can help challenge the status quo and create greater opportunities for increased societal equity among Deaf people.

Disempowerment and Hearing Privilege

The word *disempowerment* has quite a simple definition for such a powerful concept: to take away power. Disempowerment takes place on a daily basis for most deaf people and runs the gamut of seemingly meaningless incidents to life-changing situations. When we think of disempowerment among Deaf people, we usually think of things like being denied interpreters, watching films or TV shows that aren't captioned, being told not to sign, or seeing hearing actors in roles portraying Deaf people. Yet there are smaller, everyday acts (microaggressions, if you will) that hold just as much capacity, if not more, to disempower Deaf people. And these everyday acts are often performed by perhaps some of the most powerful allies of the Deaf community: interpreters.

A crucial element to understand before delving into disempowerment is hearing privilege. Much like "white privilege," hearing privilege is an emerging topic. Tiffany Tuccoli, in her master's thesis, described it as ". . . advantages or entitlements that are enjoyed by people who can hear which are denied to those who are Deaf. These advantages give hearing people *power and authority* to decide how society should be designed"[6] (emphasis added).

This power and authority of designing society is what is often taken away from Deaf people as we go about our daily lives. Worse yet, we often are not sure if it's because we're Deaf or not. This is often found among other minorities as well:

> To use a non-interpreting example, Oprah Winfrey was denied access to a store in Paris. She felt that she had been discriminated against because she was black. The store claimed that they were setting up for a private party and couldn't let her in. Tim Wise suggests that the reason doesn't matter. What is more significant is that "Oprah Winfrey, with all her money, all her power, and all her influence, *still* had to wonder, even if only for a moment, whether her race had trumped all that in the eyes of another person" (Wise, 2008, p. 72). Deaf people frequently have similar thoughts and experiences when encountering systems and institutions that favor the ability to hear, or hearing privilege. No matter how competent or powerful those individuals are, the risk of encountering doubt and insecurity is simply a part of living in a hearing-dominated society.[7]

Another example of hearing privilege is illustrated in a video by Roger Claussen,[8] who led a National Association of the Deaf committee disseminating a survey about open-captioned films. In his ten-minute video, Claussen shared a humorous, yet realistic, narrative about the annoying factors hearing people never have to deal with or even think about. He talks about how, with rearview captioning, Deaf people are required to leave their driver's licenses if they want to use the captioning equipment, struggle with holding refreshments because the device installs in the refreshment holder leaving no place to put drinks, fiddle constantly with placement of the device for optimal viewing, have to carry the device to and from the bathroom, and have to stay well after the movie's end just to retrieve their driver's licenses.

Hearing privilege is natural for most people, and although it is often automatically integrated into a hearing person's life, it needs to first be recognized and understood before addressing disempowerment. Yet even this seems to be fraught with resistance. In 2016, a social media campaign took place focusing on "#hearingprivilege," in which people posted their experiences and how they were affected by hearing privilege. Some expressed discomfort at seeing hearing people posting their own experiences with #hearingprivilege, commenting that this was yet another example of hearing people intruding upon Deaf people's safe space and not necessarily honoring this space or their experiences. What was more striking was that there were others who felt this #hearingprivilege campaign was simply another way for Deaf people to complain and even attack hearing people. This goes back to the aforementioned act of dismissing Deaf people's experiences, and the vulnerability they faced in posting their experiences, as Brown stated.

For another example of disempowerment, let's go back to when I was thirteen years old. I went to a public high school that had eighty deaf students and eight full-time interpreters. I took a theater course with three other deaf students and maybe twenty-five hearing students; it was interpreted by one of the better interpreters. She criticized my signing *every single day*, saying that I signed "too ASL." She even went as far as voicing gibberish if she didn't understand me—often causing the hearing students and teacher to break out in laughter.

For an extremely insecure teenager struggling with her identity, having attention called to her like this was beyond horrifying. This was humiliation, pure and simple. The interpreter, to compensate for her lack of fluency, purposefully disempowered me. Interpreters should be accountable for their lack of fluency and not put this on the Deaf person's shoulders. Unfortunately, this is an all-too-common scenario among mainstreamed students. As a Deaf person from a Deaf family surrounded by Deaf role models, I still didn't know what to do. So one morning, I simply refused to go to school, dreading the thought of dealing with such humiliation. When I explained what I had to endure every morning in what was the first class of the day for me, my mother immediately contacted the guidance counselor, who was a CODA and also the interpreter coordinator. The counselor brought the interpreter in for a meeting with my mother and me. He scolded the interpreter for what she had done, saying she had no right to demean my language and that she needed to respect my language. That was one of the first times I had ever seen someone advocate for my native language to be left alone. While the interpreter did stop mocking me, her disempowering acts as a whole did not cease for any of the students and still affect me to this day.

To take away a deaf person's power, whether intentionally or unintentionally, is unacceptable. One common response from hearing participants in my workshops and readers of my articles is that the disempowerment examples that I share—not only my experiences but also other people's experiences—are "extreme examples," or that there must be reasons or more details I didn't share. Unfortunately, they aren't extreme; every single time I've shared a story, there is a chorus of "I went through that, too!" from so many Deaf people. Simply because hearing people don't necessarily encounter disempowerment or recognize the rawness of the experience doesn't mean the examples are extreme, far-fetched, or explainable.

Knowledge Imbalance

Many people, both Deaf and hearing, have appropriately lauded the interpreting profession, namely the Registry of Interpreters for the Deaf (RID), in raising its standards especially within the past few years. Yet there is one act of disempowerment throughout this progress that has been deeply, and easily, overlooked: the knowledge imbalance, creating a major disadvantage among Deaf people.

RID now requires its interpreters to have bachelor's degrees, among other criteria; this is a fantastic requirement because it ensures that interpreters are educated even if not in interpreting. Yet this automatically places them in a more educated position than Deaf people who don't have bachelor's degrees. Add to that the fact that many Deaf people don't have the same access to education as hearing people.

Interpreters, to receive certification, must also have the necessary (even if minimal) training in all of the aspects involved with interpreting. Are Deaf people given interpreters with top-notch fluency in *both languages*? Frequently, the answer is no. This education and the lack of full ASL fluency create a major imbalance in knowledge and power. After all, do Deaf people have the same access to education as interpreters? No.

Are Deaf individuals generally trained to work with interpreters on advocating for interpreter quality and on how the interpreting process ideally works? No, absolutely not. Is there any training provided to Deaf people in elementary school through adulthood on how to work with interpreters in various settings, or on self-advocacy? The answer is no once again; any existent curriculum is typically very limited in its availability. Consider that many interpreters receive formal, professional training in everything from ASL to ethics to business practices. Interpreters are also tested on their knowledge and skills, and then maybe certified.

Meanwhile, Deaf people have had to constantly educate each other on a grassroots level on how to deal with interpreting dilemmas because there is simply no formal training for Deaf people of all ages in working with interpreters. It's a catch-22 situation for most Deaf people: they can't get access to the very education they should have for the employment they should gain. Yet, through educational programs, interpreters are given the knowledge that Deaf people so greatly need and deserve. When Deaf people do not receive this same knowledge about interpreting, linguistics, their rights, and everything else under the sun, there are deep-seated repercussions.

Like it or not, interpreters have an incredible amount of jurisdiction over Deaf people's access to people, medical appointments, education, employment, phone calls, and pretty much everything else. This isn't necessarily bad, as long as they use this power appropriately and without malice. But this so-called jurisdiction can create even further potential for conflict and division. Making things even harder is how this power imbalance can become magnified in small towns where interpreters might, by default, rule the roost because they know everyone, Deaf or hearing, in town. This has happened time after time to the point where Deaf people lose jobs, are rejected for jobs, are perceived as unintelligent, and so much more, all because they had conflicts with their local interpreters.

This, then, leads to incidents as shared by so many Deaf people, demonstrating how interpreters are often the most disempower-ers, even if unintentionally. Keep in mind that there certainly are many hearing people who take power away from Deaf people deliberately, and may believe they have the *right* to do this and express shock and disbelief when Deaf people react negatively.

Consider medical appointments as an example. Often, interpreters are trained and/or instructed to wait in the hallway whenever the nurse or doctor leaves instead of staying in the room with the Deaf patient. From the interpreter's perspective, this is necessary given the potential for ethical dilemmas. Suppose the Deaf patient says something to the interpreter that is medically relevant but then doesn't share this information with the doctor. Is the interpreter bound to tell the doctor? Yet, is it really fair to keep the patient isolated in a room with no visual access to all of the sounds and conversations that a hearing patient could overhear?

Anita Buel, a certified Deaf community health worker (DCHW) in Minnesota, has an ongoing frustration (personal communication). CHWs are certified, trained advocates who accompany patients in their own communities (in this case, the Deaf community) and provide advocacy, information, and clarification for patients who may feel overwhelmed by medical jargon, procedures, and the overall health system. DCHWs, however, are not certified deaf interpreters; they have as much of a need for interpreters as the Deaf patients. Buel said she gets frustrated when she knows interpreters are in the hallway waiting and then enter the room already deep in conversation with the doctor or nurse. This, to her, shows that the patient is already at a disadvantage because interpreters often build relationships with medical professionals and therefore aren't always perceived as neutral parties or allies. Interpreters, by doing this, also have a rapport established with the medical staff that Deaf patients themselves often want to have.

This is also true in many other settings, such as courtrooms, where interpreters often are on a first-name basis with the judges, bailiffs, stenographers, and clerks. Perception can have a major impact, and when a Deaf person sees that an interpreter has an already-established relationship with someone in a setting, it can create a power imbalance along with other challenges already in place.

So what's the solution to this imbalance? There must be some kind of education in place for Deaf people, starting at early ages in schools. Education, in the form of classroom lessons and children's workshops, could include how to work with interpreters as well as knowledge of rights to communication access (such as interpreters), of the interpreting process, of the opportunities to work with interpreters, and of the other aspects involved in working with interpreters.

There are continuously multimillion-dollar grants provided for interpreting projects, expansion of interpreter programs, increasing people of color and diversity in the interpreting field, curriculum development, and much more (and of course, the majority of such funded programs is hearing-led). However, very little, if any, of that money is devoted to educating Deaf people— especially young children who don't have deaf family members—on how to work with interpreters, knowing their rights, and how to act if their rights have been obstructed in any way. Numerous possible ways can make this happen, such as having curriculum in place at Deaf schools, having interpreter education programs teach students how to arrange such a training with Deaf community leaders, and so forth. The best way to accomplish this would be to work together as allies.

Creating Alliances

Interpreters have a very delicate line to walk on the job: they have to figure out how to mediate culture, conflicts, personalities, and so many other components all at the same time as interpreting. And they must balance all of that with respecting the culture, language, and community values they work in. At best, this is a difficult task for many. Robert Lee said in his keynote speech at the 1998 RID Region III conference, "As a hearing, late-second-language learner of ASL, I have been invited into the lives of Deaf people, and I could just as easily be invited out. I have no intrinsic 'right' to be an interpreter, just as no outsider can claim the right to be a member of another culture, like people don't have the right to be part of a Swahili [sic] or a Native American tribe."* So how can "outsiders" be allies to a community they might not feel they're allowed to be part of?

The best thing interpreters or hearing "outsiders" can do in their quest to respect the Deaf community while providing as much support as possible is to become cognizant of the many manifestations of their individual and collective power and privileges, and to know that Deaf people do not need saving. This can be rather difficult to embrace especially if one has entered the profession with the noblest of intentions. Deaf people also should understand their own roles in the relationship dynamics of disempowerment and that interpreters are not always trying to claim ownership.

Transactional Relationships

Martin Buber, an eighteenth-century philosopher, explored the concept of how people treat each other. He identified two types of relationships among people

*It should be noted that Swahili is a language, not a tribe.

engaged in transactions: the *I-It Relationship* and the *I-You Relationship*. The *I-It Relationship* is what we create when we are in transactions with people whom we treat like objects—people who are simply there to serve us or complete a task. An example of this would be when interpreters look at consumers (Deaf or hearing) as simply opportunities to earn money and go home, and/or when Deaf people look at interpreters as simply there to serve their every whim (such as during video relay service calls). The other relationship, the *I-You Relationship*, is characterized by human connection and empathy. Over the years, the interpreter profession has moved from the helper model to the machine model to a continuum of sorts.

Brene Brown, who often cites Buber's work, said, "When we treat people as objects, we dehumanize them. We do something really terrible to their souls and to our own. I am suggesting that we stop dehumanizing people and start looking them in the eye when we speak to them. If we don't have the energy or time to do that, we should stay at home."

Interpreters might also feel discouraged by what they perceive as constant negative opinions of the interpreting field (which are in actuality Deaf people's lived experiences, not necessarily personally about interpreters—prompting the need to separate the interpreting work from themselves). Interpreters can either become complacent and maintain the status quo, or they can recall their original passion for the community. This book contains many new ideas, approaches, and models that can help interpreters get out of this complacency.

Understand, Analyze, and Act

Brown says, "Trust is a product of vulnerability that grows over time and requires work, attention and full engagement."[9] Yet how can we come together to prevent disempowerment, especially if someone is mistrustful of interpreters (or hearing people)? It's easy to become discouraged, especially as an interpreting student or someone new in the field. As an outsider to the community, it quickly becomes overwhelming to realize that you, a hearing person, are entering a community so fraught with emotion, oppression, and triggers that were in place long before you were even born, and that you may perpetuate, knowingly or not, many of these triggers or stereotypes. This in itself is a daunting realization, but this awareness is the first wonderful step toward minimizing disempowerment.

Concluding Thoughts

To come together, we can first become aware of disempowerment of Deaf people in all of its many forms, especially situational, and how we contribute to this whether we're Deaf or hearing. By actively resisting the almost automatic temptation to empathize with hearing consumers, or even Deaf consumers, we can minimize, even eliminate, potential disempowerment. In addition to educating ourselves, it's crucial that we recognize that disempowerment doesn't always happen on purpose; it's often by accident. Still, as renowned vlogger and blogger Franchesca "Chescaleigh" Ramsey said, "It's not about intent. It's about impact."[10]

By refusing to engage in conscious disempowerment, deferring to the Deaf person whenever appropriate—especially when asked about anything relating to the Deaf community, and allowing Deaf people to be primary decision-makers when appropriate, we can take steps toward ensuring that Deaf people retain their power. Interpreters can also serve as allies by supporting Deaf leadership, businesses, and agencies, and by operating under the assumption that a qualified Deaf person should be the automatic choice—and if this isn't the case, be among the first to question why not.

It is also crucial to remember that if a deaf person expresses frustration about an experience of disempowerment, it doesn't necessarily mean she or he is angry, divisive, or separatist. Nor does it mean that an interpreter is the worst person in the world. Rather, take a look at the situation and figure out how, if at all, interpreters or hearing people might have contributed to the situation. More important, do not instinctively blame the frustration on the Deaf consumer or say that the Deaf person is pulling a person down or is working against someone. Instead, support each other, recognizing (and validating) frustrations and vulnerability, and possess cultural competency. Listen to Deaf people's stories, even if the emotions are raw and may sting for any number of reasons.

Even the seemingly small acts of disempowerment that deaf people have become so accustomed, almost immune, to have a major impact on their everyday lives. It is crucial we all become fully educated as early in our lives as possible about acts of disempowerment, the interpreting process, legal rights, and how to deal with conflict or oppression. In addition to reducing disempowerment, this education and the tools it would put in place for the Deaf person would help reduce the ingrained frustration that often comes from encountering such disempowerment.

By understanding the gravity of each situation, small or large, through a storytelling or autoethnographic approach, we can then come to identify the steps leading up to that situation. By analyzing all of the parties involved and their perceptions, and by figuring out what resources we have, we can then determine the best course of action. By embracing what may seem to be difficult ideas, opinions, and stories from Deaf people, we can move forward together.

This mindset of understanding, analyzing, and acting is precisely what this book strives to achieve through personal stories, along with academic and real-life knowledge. By sharing stories and working together to develop solutions addressing the constant disempowerment that Deaf people experience, Deaf people and interpreters can stand on a more level playing field with equal knowledge, access, and power.

Notes

1. Rachael Freed, "The Importance of Telling Our Stories," *The Blog: Huffington Post,* November 17, 2011. http://www.huffingtonpost.com/rachael-freed/legacy-telling-our-story_b_776195.html

2. Timothy G. Pollock and Joyce E. Bono, "Being Scheherazade: The Importance of Storytelling in Academic Writing," *Academy of Management Journal* 56, no. 3 (June 2013): 629.

3. Mariza Méndez, "Autoethnography as a Research Method: Advantages, Limitations and Criticisms," *Colombia Applied Linguist Journal* 15, no. 2 (June–December 2013): 282.

4. Méndez, "Autoethnography as a Research Method," 280–81.

5. Brene Brown, *Daring Greatly: How the Courage to Be Vulnerable Transforms the Way We Live, Love, Parent, and Lead* (New York City: Avery, 2012): 45.

6 Tiffany Tuccoli, *Exploring Hearing Privilege*, (Master's Thesis, Gallaudet University, 2008), 23.

7. Doug Bowen-Bailey and Trudy Suggs, "To Lead or Not to Lead: Sharing Power in the Field of Interpreting." *RID Views*, 31, no. 2 (Spring/Summer 2015): 28–29.

8. Roger Claussen, "Movie Caption Survey," YouTube video, 10:08, published March 18, 2013, https://www.youtube.com/watch?v=FQ1JHyP_jYE.

9. Brene Brown, *Daring Greatly: How the Courage to Be Vulnerable Transforms the Way We Live, Love, Parent, and Lead* (New York City: Avery, 2012): 45.

10. Franchesca [Chescaleigh] Ramsey, "5 Tips for Being an Ally," YouTube video, 3:31, https://www.youtube.com/watch?v=_dg86g-QlM0.

Deaf Dream Team

2

DEAM Approaches to Interpreting

Thomas K. Holcomb

For the ASL summary of this chapter, go to https://youtu.be/hNP0bcp5NwU

> In preparation for a meeting scheduled in a few minutes, two interpreters discuss the logistics in front of me (without involving me) and agree to the standard twenty-minute switch interval. Once the meeting starts, Interpreter A sits in the designated chair and begins to interpret. Interpreter B sits in the front row to support Interpreter A as needed. With ten hearing people extremely involved in the meeting and the rapid fire exchanges among the participants, Interpreter A works furiously to keep up, leaving almost no opportunity for me to jump in. Interpreter A tries his best to identify each speaker by stating the color of the person's shirt, hairstyle, or other distinguishing features. Regardless, I am overwhelmed trying to follow the discussion, let alone understanding the interpreted message. After ten or fifteen minutes of trying, I give up on any effort to participate, instead focusing on the interpreter. Twenty minutes into the meeting, Interpreter B relieves Interpreter A. It takes me a few minutes to become accustomed to the different signing style and I realize that Interpreter B is not as skilled as A. I become even more discouraged and decide to sit back, watching the interpreter move her hands and wishing that the meeting would end soon.

Deaf professionals and students frequently find it challenging to fully access information during meetings and classroom discussions predominately consisting of hearing people,* even with interpreters present.[1] They also often find it difficult to actively participate in discussions or function as equal members of the group.[2] Likewise, interpreters have found that Deaf people often act as passive participants during an interpreted meeting or class session.[3] Consequently, both Deaf people and interpreters may leave interpreted events feeling less than satisfied with the outcomes.[4] More specifically, Deaf participants often leave disappointed in themselves for failing to demonstrate their knowledge, worth, or even intelligence

*The term *hearing* identifies situations where the majority of the people do not sign (e.g., lectures or meetings comprised of hearing people).

because of this limited participation. Interpreters often leave with a diminished sense of accomplishment knowing that Deaf people had struggled to remain alert or involved during the meeting. Unfortunately, these less-than-adequate experiences have become the norm in many interpreted settings with no prognosis for improved outcomes.[5] This is not acceptable. As Marschark et al. state in the preface of their book, *Sign Language and Interpreter Education*, "Both deaf and hearing participants lose if an interpreter is not involved or not successful."[6]

New ideas and approaches should be formulated to level the playing field for Deaf people to function more effectively in hearing-dominated environments. This can happen by having interpreters explore new techniques and make it a priority to support fuller and richer participation of Deaf individuals in interpreted settings. By working together, Deaf people and interpreters can create DEAM approaches to improve the interpreted situations for everyone involved.

DEAM is a play on three English words—*deaf, dream*, and *team*—and it refers to Deaf-centered, Deaf-friendly, and Deaf-focused solutions that are also respectful of interpreters' needs. By thinking outside of the box, interpreted situations can be improved for all involved: Deaf people, hearing people, and interpreters. This chapter strives to serve as an impetus for such discussions and provides some ideas for these mutual examinations.

One example of a DEAM approach can be found in *Deaf Professionals and Designated Interpreters: A New Paradigm,* edited by Peter Hauser, Karen Finch, and Angela Hauser in 2008.[7] With contributions from 25 Deaf professionals and interpreters, the book spotlights the challenges experienced by Deaf professionals in interpreted situations and discusses working with designated interpreters as a viable solution. More specifically, a designated interpreter has a different role than a typical interpreter. For one, designated interpreters have been preselected by Deaf professionals to work closely with them and are considered members of the Deaf professional's team. As Hauser and Hauser explained, "The designated interpreter is a dynamic and active participant in the deaf professional's environment, and his or her actions influence communication outcomes and the deaf professional's work performance."[8] Cook described designated interpreting as diplomatic interpreting in which "the Deaf professional's goals become the interpreter's goals"[9] and that being impartial or neutral, while expected of typical interpreters, is not one of the designated interpreter's goals. In this sense, the designated interpreter functions as a teammate with the Deaf professional to empower themselves to work effectively at their tasks.[10]

Although the majority of Deaf people do not enjoy the luxury of having designated interpreters, this body of work is valuable in that it shows that Deaf professionals and the interpreters with whom they work are actively exploring innovative solutions. Additional discussions and exchanges on how to improve interpreted situations are needed to help bring the field of interpreting to the next level of excellence.[11] It also will allow for more positive experiences among Deaf people in dealing with interpreted settings. In this vein, Cokely advocates for a new direction for the interpreting profession, a shift from the interpreters' role as "service providers for the community into service agents of the community."[12] Several ideas on how to improve the interpreted experience for both Deaf people and interpreters are presented below for the purpose of generating such discussions.

Interpreting in Hearing Situations Where the Formal Register Is Used: A DEAM Approach

A DEAM approach can be used to address the challenges of interpreting academic presentations from Spoken English to ASL. For example, the formal register used in most hearing lectures usually relegates listeners to a passive role. In contrast, ASL discourse dictates an active listening style and often encourages robust interactions between the speaker and receivers throughout the session.[13]A comparison between a typical hearing classroom and a classroom full of Deaf students reveals a remarkable difference in how students respond to and interact with teachers.[14] Likewise, the style of Deaf presenters at Deaf-run conferences is often dramatically different from that of hearing presenters at typical hearing conferences. For instance, while reading one's paper verbatim is common at a conference for hearing academics, this is practically unheard of at conferences geared toward Deaf people.

Effective ASL presenters are successful in creating Deaf-friendly and Deaf-centered presentations, following academic ASL protocol.[15] Posing rhetorical questions, guiding listeners through the presentation by illuminating important points, effective pausing, and chunking information as boundary markers are hallmarks of effective presentations in ASL.[16] In addition, listeners are expected to lend support to the presentation through backchanneling devices, such as verbal or nonverbal responses or even a combination of both.[17] The support provided to the speakers includes active listening skills such as responding to rhetorical questions, making pertinent comments about what is being said, sharing relevant experiences, confirming information, and exhibiting backchanneling behaviors.[18] These include appropriate facial reactions (e.g., head nodding, puzzled look) and signed responses (e.g., WOW, REALLY, I KNOW).[19] Such active interactions between the presenter and the audience make it possible for the listeners to process and understand the delivered information and to indicate immediately to the presenter if something is unclear so that clarification may be provided.[20] Interpreters need to find ways to do the same.[21] Otherwise, Deaf people will continue to understand only a fraction of the interpreted message, which has been found to be as low as 50 percent.[22]

Herein lies the challenge for interpreters. How does one incorporate the ASL discourse structure that is so drastically different from the typical discourse of hearing classrooms and conferences in his or her work? Interpreters generally do not assume this kind of responsibility; instead, they follow the hearing discourse style, making it difficult for Deaf people to follow the presentation and process the information.[23]

However, the most successful and sought-after interpreters manage to present the information in a more Deaf-friendly and Deaf-centered manner, incorporating the ASL discourse structure in their interpreted work.[24] For example, in a study by Ressler, certified Deaf interpreters (CDI) were found to use culturally appropriate features such as pausing, eye gaze, and head nods more frequently than hearing interpreters.[25] Cokely makes a case for improved interpreted situations by observing and learning from CDIs as they often utilize key features in making interpreted messages clearer for Deaf people.[26] Clearly, effective interpreters are mindful of the differences between the discourse styles and are responsive to the needs of Deaf people.[27] In this sense, they are already utilizing the DEAM approach by modifying the stiff and formal presentation style typical of hearing people's formal register to suit the formal, yet interactive, register of ASL. This makes it possible for Deaf people to engage more fully and subsequently have a greater opportunity to absorb the information.

Specific applications of the DEAM approach to the formal register might include peppering the interpreted work with rhetorical questions to encourage appropriate responses, reinforcing the act of back-channeling, emphasizing the topic, separating the main points from secondary comments, and acknowledging the comments being made by the listeners. In academic settings, these strategies have the potential to increase comprehensibility of the interpreted work. Consulting with Deaf people is critical for ensuring successful interpreting outcome for both Deaf people and interpreters.[28] Further research into the benefits of these and other DEAM strategies is greatly needed.

The DEAM Approach in Team Interpreting

In addition to the constraints of the hearing discourse structure, Deaf people often experience a "monotone syndrome," in which their head and eyes are forcedly fixated on one interpreter, even with many hearing people participating in the meeting. This intense concentration on the interpreter often results in eye and mental fatigue and has been likened to watching a computer screen for a lengthy period of time.[29] Campbell, Rohan, and Woodcock described the physical strain of watching an interpreter for a long time as follows: "Even with adequate contrast and no glare—the ideal so rarely achieved—continuously watching the interpreter in one position creates static posture in the neck."[30] It can be difficult for Deaf people to remain alert, assert themselves, and process the information being presented all at once if they are intently watching one interpreter during a multi-participant meeting.

While the team interpreting concept provides two interpreters, the goal is primarily to support the interpreters, not necessarily the Deaf person.[31] In RID's standard practice paper on team interpreting, team interpreting is described as "the utilization of two or more interpreters who support each other to meet the needs of a particular communication situation." In this vein, Hoza provided a list of ways team interpreters support each other:[32]

1. Relieving each other by taking turns producing the target language output.
2. Backing up each other by monitoring the output.
3. Working interdependently during the interpreting work.
4. Working as a single unit by collaborating and making the same kinds of decisions that are made by an interpreter who is working alone.

Usually, a team interpreting arrangement revolves around interpreters alternating their turns every 20 minutes[33] to prevent physical and mental fatigue associated with the demanding tasks of interpreting and the number of interpreting errors corresponding with the time spent interpreting.[34] While this solution may protect the interpreters from long-term physical impairment and increase accuracy, it ignores the needs of Deaf customers.

For Deaf people, the 20-minute switch between interpreters is not conducive to their participation. In fact, Deaf people have long complained about the jarring effect of this switch, especially when the skill level of and styles of the two interpreters are not compatible. As discussed in a focus group interview conducted by the National Consortium of Interpreter Education Centers (NCIEC), Deaf Advocacy Training Work Team, in 2009 one informant explained:[35]

> In court when there's a trial with jury, there are two interpreters. They have a camera on the interpreters to make sure they aren't off the point. There are different styles of interpreters that caused a lot of confusion. When the interpreters switch, it takes time for me to get used to their style—sometimes frustrating!

Furthermore, the dread Deaf people may feel when it is time for the lesser-skilled interpreter to resume his or her rotation is often distracting and disturbing. In this case, they worry about how long the "good" interpreter will remain and how difficult it will be when the less skilled interpreter returns. This team model needs to be reconsidered, and a DEAM approach can ensure that both interpreters and Deaf people's needs are met.

One solution is to divide duties between the interpreters in a different manner. Instead of a rotation based on time intervals, the interpreters could be assigned to interpret for specific individuals involved in a meeting; this is possible in two fashions. In meetings in which hearing participants are actively participating, the interpreters could take turns by alternating between each speaker. This designation has several benefits. The Deaf person can see different "voices" as signed by the alternating interpreters, thus reducing the monotone syndrome. Another benefit is that the interpreters can avoid having to sign/interpret continuously for a long period of time; instead, they have opportunities to take physical and mental breaks more frequently, however short, throughout the assignment.

In situations during which one hearing person is doing the majority of the talking, the 20-minute rule can still apply. The primary interpreter could have the responsibility of interpreting the main speaker and the second interpreter could cover everyone else, switching roles after 20 minutes. Again, this allows for the Deaf person to benefit from seeing "different voices" as presented by the second interpreter whenever someone other than the main presenter participates in the discussion. This approach has several benefits for the Deaf person at different levels, such as minimizing or avoiding the monotone syndrome in which the Deaf person sees only one voice—the interpreter's—for the entire 20-minute interval. Also, when a switch between interpreters is made according to the speakers, rather than an allotted time, the Deaf person is more attuned to the dynamics of the session. This creates a better situation for the interpreters with a more interested, active, and motivated audience. In addition, the jarring jolt of the switch becomes less problematic as the turn-taking between interpreters occurs more naturally. An added bonus is that the challenge of trying to interpret highly charged meetings becomes less difficult. For example, quick turn-taking between two people could be interpreted more effectively with one interpreter covering one person and another covering the second person, making it possible to interpret overlapping exchanges. Likewise, in meetings where simultaneously more than one conversation is going on, the Deaf person could watch two interpreters working two different conversations at the same time through this approach, reducing the need for "one person at a time, please" interruptions by the interpreters.

It is also important to acknowledge that this approach requires interpreters to work constantly without the benefit of a 20-minute "off" period, which could result in mental and physical fatigue. However, it has been observed that, with frequent turn-taking switches throughout the assignment, the interpreters have much more down time, affording them critical, albeit shorter, rest periods. Although this observation has not been substantiated by research, it is possible that the physical strain on hands is reduced because of the more natural intervals that occur between conversations and turn-taking rather than the ongoing artificial, more physically and mentally taxing 20-minute rotation.

Another concern regarding this arrangement is that with both interpreters being "on" at all times, the support system via feeding is lost. However, the "hot seat" interpreter model, also known as the support/feed model or the off/on task model, with one interpreter being primarily responsible for producing the interpretation at the moment, could still apply in formal situations in which one main presenter has little or no interactions from the audience. Even so, as is true for other situations, there are trade-offs. One is the loss of support from the secondary interpreter and the potential subsequent increase in interpreting errors in favor of overall increased access for Deaf people in meetings. In this case, it is important to include Deaf people in a discussion about what is more important to them: accuracy in the interpreted message, or increased participation and engagement with the larger group.

Regardless, this DEAM approach of shifting from timed rotations to more frequent and natural turn-taking has the potential of producing better outcomes for both Deaf people and interpreters through improved interpreted situations and experiences. Clearly, the need is present for further experimentation and discussion to identify the appropriate balance that would support both Deaf people and interpreters.

The DEAM Approach to ASL-to-English Interpretation

Another challenge associated with Deaf people trying to engage more successfully and comfortably with their hearing peers in meetings or conferences is the interpreter's ability to voice-interpret from ASL to English accurately and fluently. This is especially true in light of the increasing number of Deaf professionals in the past few decades, with a corresponding growth in the need for skilled interpreters, especially for ASL-to-spoken English interpretation.[36] However, with current practices in place, it is nearly impossible for Deaf people to determine the effectiveness of the interpreted work. This lack of access to the interpreted work has created an uncomfortable feeling among many Deaf people, a discomfort that cannot and should not be dismissed for numerous reasons.

One reason for this discomfort is the awareness among Deaf people that there are discrepancies in how their signed words are being interpreted. Some deviations from the intended message may include inaccurate register and poor vocabulary choice.[37] Several studies on ASL-to-English interpretation have found that mismatches between ASL and English interpretation occur often due to interpreters' insufficient understanding of ASL discourse structure.[38] Yet, these deviations are basically inaccessible to Deaf presenters, leaving them in the dark as to exactly how their signed messages are conveyed. For example, Cerney discussed how "interpretation is done differently by different people who make decisions about the work that they are doing" and how "individual and personal style of an interpreter will influence and infuse every target text that interpreter creates."[39]

Deaf people have been known to vent their frustrations with each other regarding their limited access to the interpreted work. Bug elaborated on this discomfort in one of his blog entries,[40] commenting that a Deaf person often has no idea how the interpretation is proceeding, whether errors have been made, if there is a mismatch in the register usage, and so forth.[41] One solution is for the Deaf person to read the transcription, if available, at the end of a session to determine the interpreted work's effectiveness. However, this solution is effective only if a captioner is present at the event. While this provides excellent feedback on the work of the interpreter and can serve as a basis for the Deaf person to determine whether to work with the same interpreter in the future, it does not allow for immediate intervention and correction.

In such cases, intervention strategies usually involve allies in the audience pointing out the problems. If a glaring error is made, for example, some hearing people find it necessary to correct the interpreter on the spot sometimes in a loud voice from the back of the room, or by approaching the working interpreters and whispering to them. However, this often results in a hostile response from the working interpreters who view such an intrusion as an affront to their work and profession.[42] Others may be more diplomatic by asking clarifying questions during the presentation, which then alerts the Deaf presenter that the interpreter made an interpreting error. For example, if the Deaf presenter talks about his Berkeley days and the interpreter voices Boston instead, a hearing ally could ask a question related to Boston. This allows the Deaf presenter to recognize the error in interpretation and rectify the confusion. Unfortunately, without such strategies or audience members, Deaf people are left without effective tools to determine the accuracy of the interpretation. This means Deaf people are usually unable to protect the integrity of their work and correct any errors.

Frequently, Deaf people feel powerless in such situations, as if they have little or no control with no practical solutions. Some resort to lipreading the interpreters in order to gain some sense of how the work is being conducted.[43] One informant in Stuard's study explained, "I constantly have to monitor interpreters via speechreading to make sure my message is getting across the way I want it to be." Another reason for lipreading the interpreters is the concern about the interpreter's ability to do the job, as discussed by another study participant: "I am sometimes worried about the ability of the interpreter to voice for me . . . I often voice for myself because of this worry."

This practice of lipreading the interpreters was also reported during a focus group interview conducted in 2009 by the Deaf Advocacy Training Work Team:[44]

> During group meetings, I don't know what he is talking about—I don't understand. My parole officer gets all confused with the information and they put handcuffs on me. So I have to watch the interpreters' lips to make sure he is voicing me right. I have a hard time reading the interpreters' lips to make sure the words they say are right.

Clearly, lipreading is not an optimal solution. To make things worse, Deaf people often are told that they must learn to trust their interpreters and to let go of their worries.[45] While most interpreters are committed to the best work possible, Deaf people deserve more than just being told to trust the interpreters. A DEAM approach is needed for optimal solutions to this challenge.

A possible solution is to add a transliterator to the interpreting team to sign verbatim the spoken words of the interpreters.[46] This would enable the Deaf presenter to monitor the interpreter's work by seeing the English translation of his or her own ASL presentation by the transliterator. This makes it possible for the Deaf person to operate as part of the team with the interpreters and yet maintain the power to decide what to do should an error occur during the presentation. This also allows the Deaf person to assess the quality of the work and modify the presentation style as needed. For example, he or she could slow down to give the interpreters additional time to do the translation, fingerspell more often to aid the interpreters in vocabulary selection, or be more precise in the signed presentation to ensure that specific vocabulary or phrase is used by the interpreter. Conversely, the Deaf person could see that the interpretation is accurate and remain focused on the presentation. Ultimately, everyone benefits from this DEAM approach in which all parties work closely together as a team.

Interestingly, this idea of adding the transliterator to the mix emerged as a result of an increasing number of hearing signers delivering their presentations in ASL, rather than signing and speaking simultaneously or using spoken English only. They had the power to ensure that they were being represented accurately by listening to the interpreters' work while presenting in ASL. They also had the ability to remedy interpreter errors, protecting their integrity and making sure they were being projected appropriately. Deaf people deserve the same opportunity. However, some Deaf people find it distracting to see another set of hands signing while presenting. Another possible DEAM solution is for the Deaf presenter to designate an ally outside the assigned interpreting team to become the support person for the presentation. Usually, this person would be a co-worker, a close friend, or a family member. Here, this person takes on the responsibility of monitoring the interpreters' work and providing assistance or repairs as needed. For example, if the interpreter misunderstood the main point, did not understand the acronyms used, or used the inappropriate tone, this support person is available to rectify the error if the assigned interpreters are unable to recognize the mistake in interpretation.

To prevent confusion or negative reaction from the assigned interpreters during the presentation, it is important that the Deaf presenter takes the responsibility of communicating clearly to the interpreters about this DEAM arrangement at the pre-meeting/presentation and presenting the information in a non-threatening manner. Otherwise, this has the potential of creating hostility between the working (assigned) interpreters and the assigned support person. While this DEAM approach may feel threatening to some interpreters, ultimately, the goal is to create a win–win situation for everyone involved. The interpreters get the support they need in a non-threatening manner, the Deaf presenter gets to protect the integrity of the presentation, and the non-signers get the information in the most accurate manner. More creative solutions are needed.[47]

Molly Wilson's Open Process Model of Team Interpreting is yet another solution. This model requires that all interactions between the team interpreters, from the pre-assignment discussions to interpreting support in the form of feeding to post-assignment debriefing, be conducted in ASL.[48] This behavior is considered culturally sensitive, respectful, and cognizant of the Deaf community's collectivist nature. Furthermore, the importance of interpreters having the right attitude is discussed by Hoza in his book, *Team Interpreting as Collaboration and Interdependence.*

> So, while interpreters spend a lot of time focusing on the nuts and bolts of team interpreting (and interpreting itself), perhaps interpreters need to attend more to cultural sensitivity (sometimes called "good attitude"), and heed special notice to the behaviors that they as a team have with Deaf people. One way in which this is accomplished is by the modality the team chooses to use for feeds, support, and negotiation. The modality the team uses reflects how they see the interaction with Deaf participants; the positioning of the team to be more visibly accessible to Deaf participants can also make the team interpreting more collectivistic and collaborative.[49]

Hoza's words support the Open Process Model, which allows Deaf people to be partners in interpreting work: "Rather than having the interpreting process under the sole ownership/control of the interpreters, an open process extends/expands the opportunity for Deaf people to participate in, and influence the accuracy and integrity of, the interpretation delivered."[50]

Clearly, the work of ASL-to-English interpreters is crucial to the professional success of Deaf people. Rather than expecting Deaf people to completely trust their interpreters, DEAM-centered solutions create opportunities for teamwork to ensure that the most effective interpretation work is provided. This, in turn, increases Deaf people's confidence in the work interpreters do.

Conclusion

Deaf professionals and interpreters need to trust each other and be confident enough to work closely together as a team. The concept of "team" may be applied in different ways, such as Deaf people and interpreters working together to explore ways for better interpreted situations. Another application of the team concept is to find ways for Deaf individuals to be more involved in the group in which they belong, whether it be a hearing classroom, a hearing work place, or a hearing convention. The third level of the team concept is where interpreters, transliterators, and Deaf individuals align closely together to ensure accuracy in presentations by Deaf people. The overall goal is to create opportunities in which both Deaf individuals and interpreters come out winners with improved interpreted outcomes.

Notes

1. Mark Marschark, Rico Peterson, and Elizabeth Winston, *Sign Language Interpreting and Interpreter Education: Directions for Research and Practice* (New York: Oxford University Press, 2005); Jemina Napier, Andy Carmichael, and Andrew Wiltshire, "Look-Pause-Nod: A Linguistic Case Study of a Deaf Professional and Interpreters Working Together," in *Deaf Professionals and Designated Interpreters: A New Paradigm,* eds. Peter C. Hauser, Karen L. Finch, and Angela B. Hauser (Washington, DC: Gallaudet University Press, 2008): 22–42.

2. Hauser et al., *Deaf Professionals and Designated Interpreters.*

3. David Bar-Tzhur, "Is Anybody Home? Getting Deaf Feedback," *The Interpreter's Friend* website, posted February 23, 2004, http://theinterpretersfriend.org/misc/home.html.

4. Marc Marschark, Patricia Sapere, and Rosemarie Seewagen, "Preface," in *Sign Language Interpreting and Interpreter Education: Directions for Research and Practice*, eds. Marc Marschark, Rico Peterson, and Elizabeth Winston (New York: Oxford University Press, 2005): v–x.

5. Stephanie Jo Kent, "Deaf Voice and the Invention of Community Interpreting," *Journal of Interpretation* 22, no. 2 (2012): 3; Marc Marschark, Patricia Sapere, Carol M. Convertino, and Rosemarie Seewagen, "Educational Interpreting: Access and Outcomes," in *Sign Language Interpreting and Interpreter Education: Directions for Research and Practice*, eds. Marc Marschark, Rico Peterson, and Elizabeth Winston (New York: Oxford University Press, 2005); Marc Marschark et al., "Preface," in *Sign Language Interpreting and Interpreter Education.*

6. Marc Marschark et al., "Preface," in *Sign Language Interpreting and Interpreter Education.*

7. Hauser et al., *Deaf Professionals and Designated Interpreters.*

8. Angela Hauser and Peter Hauser, "The Deaf Professional-designated Interpreter Model," in *Deaf Professionals and Designated Interpreters: A New Paradigm*, eds. Peter C. Hauser, Karen L. Finch, and Angela B. Hauser (Washington, DC: Gallaudet University Press, 2008): 3–21.

9. Amy Cook, "Neutrality? No Thanks. Can a Biased Role be an Ethical One?"*Journal of Interpretation* (2004): 19–56.

10. Annette Miner, "Designated Interpreters: An Examination of Roles, Relationships, and Responsibilities" in *Signed Language Interpretation and Translation Research*, eds. Brenda Nicodemus and Keith Cagle (Washington, DC: Gallaudet University Press, 2015): 196–211.

11. Roberto R. Santiago and Lisa Frey Barrick, "Handling and Incorporation of Idioms in Interpretation," in *Translation, Sociolinguistic, and Consumer Issues in Interpreting*, eds. Melanie Metzger and Earl Fleetwood (Washington, DC: Gallaudet University Press, 2007): 3–44.

12. Dennis Cokely, "Shifting Positionality: A Critical Examination of the Turning Point in the Relationship of Interpreters and the Deaf Community," in *Sign Language Interpreting and Interpreter Education*, eds. Marc Marschark, Rico Peterson, and Elizabeth Winston (New York: Oxford University Press, 2005): 3–28.

13. See Wyatte Hall, this volume.

14. Thomas K. Holcomb and Anna Mindess, *See What I Mean: Differences Between Deaf and Hearing Cultures*, DVD (San Francisco: Eye2eye Productions, 2009).

15. See Christopher Kurz, Kim B. Kurz, and Raychelle Harris, this volume.

16. James Paul Gee and Judy Kegl, "Narrative/story Structure, Pausing, and American Sign Language," *Discourse Processes* 6 (1983): 243–58; Judith Labath, "Features at Discourse Boundaries in American Sign Language Narratives," *Journal of Interpretation* (2005): 65–78; Brenda Nicodemus, *Prosodic Markers and Utterance Boundaries in American Sign Language Interpretation* (Washington, DC: Gallaudet University Press, 2009); Cynthia B. Roy, "Features of Discourse in an American Sign Language Lecture," in Clayton Valli and Ceil Lucas, eds., *Linguistics of American Sign Language: An Introduction* (Washington, DC: Gallaudet University Press, 1995): 394–408.

17. See Keith Cagle, Sharon Lott, and Phyllis Wilcox, this volume; Peter Llewellyn-Jones and Robert Lee, "Getting to the Core of Role: Defining Interpreters' Role Space, *International Journal of Interpreter Education* 5, no. 2 (2013): 54–72.

18. Anna Mindess, Thomas K. Holcomb, Daniel Langholtz, and Priscilla Poyner, *Reading Between the Signs* (Boston: Intercultural Press, 2014).

19. MJ Bienvenu and Betty Colonomos, *The Face of ASL,* DVD (Burtonsville, MD: Sign Media Incorporated, 1991); Dennis Cokely and Charlotte Baker, *American Sign Language: A Teacher's Resource Text on Grammar and Culture* (Silver Spring, MD: T.J. Publishers, 1980); Thomas K. Holcomb and Anna Mindess, *A Sign of Respect: Strategies for Effective Deaf/hearing Interactions,* DVD/Workbook Set (San Francisco: Eye2eye Productions, 2016).

20. See Wyatte Hall, this volume.

21. See Kim Kurz and Joseph Hill, this volume; Silvia Del Vecchio, Marcello Cardarelli, Fabiana De Simone, and Giulia Petitta, "Interacting with Participants Outside of Interpretation," in *Signed Language Interpretation and Translation Research*, eds. Brenda Nicodemus and Keith Cagle (Washington, DC: Gallaudet University Press, 2015): 24–48.

22. Marc Marschark et al., "Educational Interpreting: Access and Outcomes."

23. See Wyatte Hall, this volume; Kent, "Deaf Voice and the Invention of Community Interpreting."

24. Roberto R. Santiago and Lisa Frey Barrick, "Handling and Incorporation of Idioms in Interpretation," in *Translation, Sociolinguistic, and Consumer Issues in Interpreting*, eds. Melanie Metzger and Earl Fleetwood (Washington, DC: Gallaudet University Press, 2007): 3–44; Stephanie Jo Kent, "Deaf Voice and the Invention of Community Interpreting."

25. Carolyn Ressler, "Comparative Analysis of a Direct Interpretation and an Intermediary Interpretation in American Sign Language," *Journal of Interpretation* (1999): 71–102.

26. Cokely, "Shifting Positionality."

27. Kent, "Deaf Voice and the Invention of Community Interpreting."

28. Santiago and Barrick, "Handling and Incorporation of Idioms in Interpretation."

29. Marschark et al., "Educational Interpreting: Access and Outcomes."

30. Linda Campbell, Meg J. Rohan, and Kathryn Woodcock, "Academic and Educational Interpreting from the Other Side of the Classroom: Working with Deaf Academics," in *Deaf Professionals and Designated Interpreters: A New Paradigm*, eds. Peter C. Hauser, Karen L. Finch, and Angela B. Hauser (Washington, DC: Gallaudet University Press, 2008): 81–105.

31. Dennis Cokely and Jennifer Hawkins, "Interpreting in Teams: A Pilot Study on Requesting and Offering Support," *Journal of Interpretation* (2003): 49–94; Napier, Carmichael, and Wiltshire, "Look-Pause-Nod: A Linguistic Case Study of a Deaf Professional and Interpreters Working Together."

32. Jack Hoza, *Team Interpreting as Collaboration and Interdependence* (Alexandria, VA: RID Press, 2010).

33. G. Carmel, "Team Interpreting: Does it really work?" *RIDViews* 25, no. 1 (2008): 7–13; Cokely and Hawkins, "Interpreting in Teams: A Pilot Study on Requesting and Offering Support."

34. Barbara Brasel, "The Effects of Fatigue on the Competence of Interpreters for the Deaf," in *Selected Readings in the Integration of Deaf Students at C.S.U.N.* (#1), ed. Harry J. Murphy (Northridge, CA: California State University, 1976); William L. Johnson and Michael Feuerstein, "An Interpreter's Interpretation: Sign Language Interpreters' View of Musculoskeletal Disorders," *Journal of Occupational Rehabilitation* 15, no. 3 (2005): 401–15; National Consortium of Interpreter Education Centers. *American Sign Language Interpreter Teams Fact Sheet*, accessed June 1, 2017, http://www.tiemcenter.org/wp-content/uploads/2012/02/Fact-Sheet-American-Sign-Language-Interpreter-Teams-Final.pdf.

35. The National Consortium of Interpreter Education Centers (NCIEC), Deaf Advocacy Training Work Team, 2009.

36. Jules Dickinson, *Sign Language Interpreting in the Workplace* (Washington, DC: Gallaudet University Press, 2017).

37. See Leala Holcomb, this volume.

38. Brian Cerney, *Relay Interpretation*, accessed June 1, 2017, http://www.handandmind.org/CerneyDissertation.pdf; Cynthia Roy, "Evaluating Performance: An Interpreted Lecture," in *New Directions in Interpreter Education: Curriculum & Instruction: Proceedings of the Sixth National Convention of the Conference of Interpreter Trainers*, ed. M. McIntire (Silver Spring, MD: RID Publications, 1987): 139–47; Risa Shaw, "Determining Register in Sign-to-English Interpreting," *Sign Language Studies* 57 (1987): 295–322; June Zimmer, "From ASL to English in Two Versions: An Analysis of Differences in Register," *Word* 41, no.1 (1990): 19–34.

39. Brian Cerney, *Relay Interpretation* (2005), accessed June 1, 2017, http://www.handandmind.org/CerneyDissertation.pdf.

40. Bug, "Should We Trust Interpreters?" *Fookem and Bug,* accessed June 1, 2017, http://fookembug.wordpress.com/2007/02/26/should-we-trust-interpreters.

41. See Thomas Holcomb on trust, Ch. 12 in this volume.

42. Ruann L. Wood, "Bingo! Dealing with the Audience Heckler," *RID Views* 28, no. 4 (2011): 14.

43. Victoria L. Stuard, "Perceptions of Interpreter Qualification by Deaf Consumers and Hearing Interpreters," Unpublished PhD diss., Pepperdine University, 2008.

44. Deaf Advocacy Training Work Team, 2009.

45. See Thomas Holcomb on trust, Ch. 12 in this volume.

46. For review on transliteration, see Elizabeth A. Winston, "Transliteration: What's the Message?" in *Sociolinguistics of the Deaf Community,* ed. Cecil Lucas (San Diego, CA: Academic Press, 1989): 147–64.

47. See Thomas Holcomb on trust, Ch. 12 in this volume.

48. Bill Moody, "What is a Faithful Interpretation?" *Journal of Interpretation* 21, no. 1 (2011): 4.

49. Hoza, *Team Interpreting as Collaboration and Interdependence.*

50. Hoza, *Team Interpreting as Collaboration and Interdependence.*

3

Accountability and Transparency: The Missing Link in Ensuring Quality in Interpreting

Chad W. Taylor, Ryan A. Shephard, and Justin "Bucky" Buckhold

For the ASL summary of this chapter, go to https://youtu.be/Dud6KEMLZJk

Chad's Story

For my recent doctor's appointment, I found myself full of anxiety as always. Not because I hated seeing the doctor. Not because I worried about the possible diagnosis. Not because of the scheduled shots I was due to receive. But because I didn't know who the assigned interpreter would be. Too often, the interpreter would be someone who could not understand my crystal-clear signing or someone whose personality did not match with mine, or someone who was a close friend of a friend of mine, or simply someone whom I would not choose. After one particular awkward session where the interpreter botched the job, I shared my frustrations with my friends, many of whom belong to the same medical group. To my surprise, they had similar encounters with this certain interpreter. Where is the accountability and transparency when it comes to interpreters and the work they do?

Ryan's Story

For the umpteenth time this week, I received an email from an interpreting/language agency inquiring if I was available to interpret a doctor's appointment. Such invitations usually come with a simple request . . . that an ASL interpreter is needed. Never mind that I'm Deaf and would not be appropriate in situations where interpreting between spoken English and ASL is called for, I continue to receive these inquiries on a regular basis. Never mind that practically everyone in the Deaf and interpreting communities knows me, I continue to receive these inquiries. Never mind that my membership with RID clearly indicates my hearing status, I continue to receive these inquiries. Never mind that I've explicitly explained to various spoken language agencies that I'm available only for the CDI type of work, I continue to receive these inquiries. Where is the accountability and transparency among the agencies that are supposed to do their best to assign interpreters that are appropriate for each request?

Bucky's Story

One day, I woke up thinking about all those complaints coming from the Deaf community on how interpreters are randomly assigned by interpreting agencies. These frustrations stem from mismatches between the interpreter and the Deaf consumer, mismatches in personality, gender, age, race, signing style, educational background, and many other variables. Many horror stories in such assignments, including mine, have swarmed across the community. That same morning, I took all those stories to heart, realizing something needed to be done. Determined to make a difference and thinking that a Deaf-run organization would be the answer, I started a local interpreting agency. Even then, as a Deaf owner of an interpreting agency, I struggled with the task of assigning interpreters, as I knew I was not the best person to make such decisions. After a few years, it dawned on me: there are no better people to choose the interpreters for their appointments or assignments than the Deaf individuals themselves.

We live in a society in which convenience is everything and money often becomes the bottom line. We want productive results in the quickest and easiest way. We see this through the prevalence of fast food restaurants, big box stores, and news briefs. The experience of enjoying a leisurely meal at a locally owned restaurant, getting personalized attention at a family-operated boutique, and reading a detailed article is disappearing in favor of fast and impersonal experiences of eating, shopping, and learning. Time is money and we are chasing more efficient and cheaper ways of living.

This shift in consumerism also comes with the demand for additional transparency and accountability from businesses and service providers to allow consumers to make quick decisions. Crowd-sourced reviews such as Yelp and Angie's List are becoming increasingly popular methods to vet providers and share personal recommendations. People are seeking both convenience and quality by posting their experiences publicly and using that as a tool to hold providers to a higher standard.[1] Deaf people deserve the same opportunity to vet and review their interpreters to promote accountability and transparency.

For much of the last century, the Deaf community vetted their own interpreters.[2] Although the number of interpreters was rather small and the scope of interpreting extremely limited, Deaf people made the point of finding out who was available to interpret and made personal requests for assistance.[3] These hearing individuals were those who interacted with them frequently. Typically, these were hearing people who had learned the language of the Deaf directly from Deaf people and consequently knew how to communicate effectively with both hearing and Deaf people.[4] Their process of sign language acquisition was therefore natural, and the experiences of being an interpreter began only after trust was developed.[5] In this unique way, Deaf consumers were ensured quality. And when things did not go well, Deaf people could consult, or even warn, others within the community about problem interpreters. Clearly, in order to be a trusted interpreter in the Deaf community, one would have to develop a genuine relationship with Deaf individuals first.[6]

In the last several decades, however, there has been a major shift in this process, with more and more interpreters being trained through formal interpreter education programs.[7] Because of the passage of the Americans with Disabilities Act (ADA) and the Individuals with Disabilities Education Act (IDEA), the demand for sign language interpreters has skyrocketed and with that has come the creation of numerous agencies and educational programs to meet that demand.[8] To the Deaf community, it may have seemed like change came overnight. The interpreting experience for Deaf people shifted from one that was nurtured and encouraged by personal relationships to one that is a professional-client relationship.[9] This shift has both positive and negative outcomes. The positive is that Deaf people are finally entitled to communication access and qualified interpreters are now entitled to fair compensation. In this sense, the relationship between Deaf people and interpreters has become more professional rather than coming out of charity or goodwill.[10] Unfortunately, during this process of the professionalization of the interpreting field, the accountability and transparency of the work the interpreters do has been removed from the Deaf community. Now, "Deaf individuals are being asked to give their trust to someone they have not met before, who has no prior or even current connection to their community, and who might not understand their values and culture."[11]As a result, Deaf people have largely been shut out of decision-making when it comes to ethics, best practices, and quality control. Interpreting agencies and professional entities such as the Registry of Interpreters for the Deaf (RID) have assumed the primary role of shaping the field.[12] Another negative outcome of this shift is that it is much more common nowadays to find new interpreters working within Deaf communities who have no personal ties to a Deaf person whatsoever.[13] This removal of accountability and transparency would have been impossible only a few decades ago.

Indeed, in today's interpreting world, many agencies are contracting with interpreters whom they have never met or seen work. Spoken language agencies are taking contracts with large entities, such as government or health care corporations, and then casting out a net in an effort to locate freelance interpreters. We have all had those emails from an unknown agency looking to fill a job near you, or asking you to drive 200 miles for a job that begins in two hours. Often, because many interpreters recognize the need to respect ASL-only agencies as the preferred providers,[14] they do not accept the work offered. As a result, the spoken language agency searches for smaller agency and subcontracts services for ASL interpreting. It would be exceptional and rare for an agency in this situation to actually be familiar with their sub-contractors.

The current practices used for assigning interpreters to jobs are so far removed from the Deaf consumer that it is nearly impossible for transparency or accountability to happen between the two parties. The default is for agencies to coordinate jobs from start to finish, leaving the Deaf person out of the equation.[15] Interpreters answer to the agencies they are contracted with and agencies answer to the paying parties. As Deaf persons, we have shown up to doctor's appointments, job interviews, and business meetings having no idea who our interpreters would be. We have left those situations unable to share feedback with those interpreters. Oftentimes, even if we would like to request the same interpreter for future appointments, it is never guaranteed. The underlying message has been: You are lucky to have access. Leave it to us. However, in our experience, leaving it up to the powers that be negates the importance of building actual relationships for effective communication access. Deaf consumers have often felt disconnected from the interpreters we are supposed to trust and depend on. This experience is not unique to us, and the limited literature on Deaf perspectives have pointed to similar concerns.[16]

So how does an interpreter get assigned to a job through an agency? To help us understand why this system operates the way it does, let us take a look at it as a whole. Each individual agency or freelance interpreter may handle the process differently, but the basic principles are similar. A request is made within the agency—possibly because of a long-standing contract or because it was the top Google hit, but the agency is then responsible for assigning an interpreter to the job. The price, stipulations, and interpreter will be predetermined by the agency and the billing party—information that the Deaf consumer is often not privy to. This process is almost like a twisted version of the dating game. The agency may have had the opportunity to match the best suited candidate for the job, or they may have chosen the interpreter who has been emailing and texting at least once or twice a week begging for more work, or they may have needed to look up interpreters in the area via the RID portal because no one was available for the job. The reputation and importance of the Deaf consumer may play into the agency's decision-making process. Either way, to the Deaf consumer it is a roll of the dice. The average Deaf person has absolutely no knowledge of the process of obtaining the interpreter, nor how much it costs, nor how to determine the best fit. Should the assignment go reasonably well, or if it was not a high-stakes situation, all stakeholders involved likely will have nothing to be concerned about. If it didn't go well, the results can be disastrous, and it is usually the Deaf person who bears the brunt. Now, what can the Deaf person to do to improve the situation for the future? Frankly, as it stands today, there is not much to do except discuss it within the Deaf community or post a disgruntled comment on social media. As has been shared with us, that often puts that Deaf individual on agencies' "black list," which limits their access even more. There has to be a better way to go about this.

Indeed, many considerations should go into matching the correct interpreter with the Deaf consumer. Agencies need to take into consideration numerous factors such as skill level and personality type and assign interpreters accordingly.[17] Yet, interpreters vary so greatly, which means expectations and experiences vary, too. There are certified interpreters and experienced interpreters, interpreters who may be comfortable and efficient with almost any consumer, interpreters who have highly specialized skills, interpreters who practice with little to no formal training but are beloved by the community, interpreters who have very limited proficiency.

Understand also that the attitudes of interpreters also vary dramatically, from those who are heavily involved with the community, sometimes called "having a deaf heart," to those who are detached and uninvolved, sometimes dubbed machines.[18] In addition, the situation itself may determine qualifications. An interpreter with extensive medical knowledge may not be the best fit for an educational individualized education meeting (IEP) meeting. The interpreter who nailed the interview for the female applicant at Macy's may not be the best fit for the young man attempting to land the contract with the federal government at the local military base. The phenomenal and extremely experienced interpreter with forty-five years of experience may not be the best match for the vibrant mainstreamed Deaf teen who is today giving a speech in front of the entire school as he or she runs for a position with the student council. And we expect schedulers at agencies to comb through all those factors to determine the best fit. In truth, unless you are the Deaf consumer, it is difficult to actually determine what a "good fit" is as each Deaf individual has their own preferences and needs for optimal language and communication access.[19]

We also must examine the disparity in language fluency among interpreters in a way that is constructive.[20] If we are to have a frank discourse regarding transparency in interpreting, we must include in this discussion those practitioners who are often far too self-conscious to be honest with all stakeholders. A novice interpreter may have a difficult time voicing for a Deaf consumer who utilizes ASL with a focus on classifiers, while using few English-influenced signs and few to no vocal cues. Too often have we been made aware of moments when the interpreter voiced something completely off topic but which perhaps seemed to him or her to be close enough. More critically, how many times have we NOT been made aware of that happening? Furthermore, we have slogged through once too often an exchange with an interpreter who forced us to reduce our ASL to a rudimentary register barely above home signs? And to add insult to injury, we walk away from those moments only to read off the lips of the inexperienced, uneducated hearing person, "You are amazing! Great job! Thank you!" as they thank the inept interpreter and toss our job application in the "circular file." The signing style, voicing style, and general demeanor of an interpreter can determine the outcome of a critical communication transaction with inexperienced hearing stakeholders in a way that only a member of an oppressed subcultural group would understand.[21] Given the tremendous disparity among interpreters, the need to involve the consumer in the process of matching the interpreter to the assignment becomes paramount. Yet, Deaf people frequently have no idea which agency will even be involved in setting up the assignment, let alone have a good understanding of the experience and qualifications of the interpreters who might be available, and thus are not able to participate in the process of choosing the best interpreter for each assignment.[22]

As all of the pieces of the puzzle fall into place, the interpreting assignment takes place. Given the complexity of the process for assigning interpreters, there is little doubt that each appointment, each formal interaction, may be met with apprehension by the Deaf person. Whether the interaction went well or not, upon completion of the appointment, it is not unusual for Deaf people to be left with a feeling of powerlessness, as we ourselves have felt.[23] Even when Deaf consumers are thrilled with the way the interpretation was done, they have a difficult time in making that known. Our world is fast paced. Interpreters book back-to-back jobs and often have to fight traffic to arrive on time for their next assignment. Consumers are busy as well. Once the appointment is finished, it is, in essence, checked off everyone's calendar and we are on to the next item. Is it any surprise that after an assignment, an interpreter would rush off before the Deaf consumer even learns their full name? A Deaf person may wish to work with that interpreter again, or hope to not work with that person again. But how do you find "Sarah" from somewhere in the Bay Area? Perhaps, the Deaf consumer wants to provide valuable feedback after a hurried appointment. Interpreters can certainly benefit from feedback after a job is completed. Where do they take their feedback? If the Deaf person is not the one handling the booking and funding of the assignment, then that Deaf person typically has no opportunity to provide feedback on the quality of work that was done. This approach is not working and it is not acceptable.

It is not only a Deaf consumer who is impacted by this impersonal process. Interpreters do not receive any feedback unless they check in with the Deaf consumer at the end of the assignment, which we have already established can be difficult to do given the busyness in everyone's lives. Another thought, which should be considered, is that often the most valuable feedback is only realized after people have had sufficient time to process an interaction. Most people do not end an interaction only to simply forget about it. We mull over things throughout the course of our day. While driving to our next destination, while talking things over with our family, we are digesting the interaction with all of its nuances and subtleties. At the moment one has fully digested the situation, they are ready to provide feedback. That is when the feedback is likely to be most valuable. Yet, where can consumers turn for that opportunity? For several reasons, many agencies do not facilitate feedback directly between the consumer and the interpreter. They may take note of preferences for future assignments, but as Deaf consumers, we are rarely guaranteed anything. Furthermore, in cases where it is more than a mismatch and also an ethical violation, the RID complaint process is lengthy and complicated. As a result, there is often no accountability or transparency in the work the interpreters do. Whether they do a good job or a bad job, they get new assignments and move on, leaving Deaf people to reap the rewards or suffer the consequences.

Deaf people deserve better. While seemingly antiquated, the original method of bringing our own preferred interpreter with us was the only way we as a community could ensure we would be operating with the level of trust which is so often necessary.[24] Therefore, as times are changing, and antiquated methods cannot function cohesively with a modern society, a new protocol needs to be instituted to increase accountability and transparency in the work of the interpreters.

This is why we created Linguabee, an interpreting agency with its roots in the San Francisco Bay Area and Colorado with the goals of recementing the Deaf community's relationship with the interpreting community, recentering the control of the interpreting requesting and evaluating process back to Deaf people, and restoring accountability and transparency of the work done by interpreters. All of these are made possible by the use of innovative technology such as providing a platform for selecting the most suitable interpreters and for creating crowd-sourced reviews.

Indeed, this is the new normal. In most other situations where professional services are rendered, people are able to turn to YELP, Angie's List, RateMyProfessor .com, or other crowd-sourced reviews to determine the reputation of a service provider. For example, in a modern marketplace, such as Uber, Lyft, and TaskRabbit, potential consumers will find ratings for all providers available for viewing. Consequently, the quality of the work is often enhanced as the service providers work harder to earn the trust of their consumers. In the past, prior to the availability of crowd-sourced review platforms, people were often in the dark when attempting to hire a plumber or seek a new dentist or such. Likewise, Deaf people usually do not have any information on the work history of the interpreter and are essentially operating in the dark when there is a need for interpreting services. The same mechanism of providing a crowd-sourced platform must be in place whereby Deaf people can select interpreters based on information made available by past consumers. In the end, the quality and reputation of the entire interpreting field will be elevated, as it is for most other service-oriented professions due to the availability of crowd-sourced reviews.

The ultimate goal is to create a mechanism that would result in a win–win situation for both Deaf consumers and interpreters with accountability and transparency as the basis of providing interpreting services. A description of how this is accomplished is provided here. Based on our experiences as Deaf consumers of interpreting services, we created a platform that addresses many of the critical issues facing the Deaf community and its interpreters as discussed earlier in this chapter. With this platform, requesters log into their account and post a description of the job that needs to be covered. The job is posted and sent out to interpreters via email with a request for bids. As bids come in, the Deaf consumer has the ability to view the profiles of those who are available to do the job and select the preferred interpreter.

In order to assist the Deaf consumer in choosing the most appropriately matched interpreter, this platform provides a space for each interpreter to have a profile page. This page includes both personal and professional information as appropriate. As such, background information such as where they grew up, how they began signing, and their personal interests and hobbies is provided. In addition, professional information such as certifications held, educational background, and social media links is also available for public perusal. Another prominent feature of the profile page is a video narrative that accompanies the text. This allows Deaf people to determine whether the signing presentation of the interpreter matches their needs and preferences for interpreting. One of the most important features of this platform is the "score" that the interpreter has earned based on the last twelve months' feedback as provided by the consumers. The ratings are based on categories such as: Accuracy, Professionalism, Delivery, Cultural Sensitivity, Punctuality, and the generic category "Other." The use of these specific categories allows for a positive learning opportunity for an interpreter and, just as important, allows Deaf consumers the option to choose an interpreter with strengths that match their needs and preferences. Each category is rated one through five, with one being the lowest possible rating. It is important to note that in the time since the implementation of the rating system, this platform has seen over a 99 percent rate of satisfaction among its Deaf consumers. One may ask how this is possible. The answer is simple, and all you need to do is look back at the way things used to be. When Deaf consumers are allowed to select their interpreters, they will likely have a better experience.[25] Napier and Rohan found that ". . . deaf people's reported comprehension and satisfaction are influenced by their prior experience with the interpreter, the interpreter's accreditation level, and whether they had chosen the interpreter."[26] Nothing is better than being wholly prepared for a situation prior to walking into it. Choosing our own interpreter truly allows for that symbiotic relationship to thrive.

We cannot and should not expect the Deaf community to be left behind as the world moves forward with elevated expectations of accountability and transparency in almost every aspect of the market place. Service providers including professionals are now routinely vetted by their consumers and they know it. Consequently, professionals work harder to provide superior service to their consumers, realizing that their work might be evaluated and posted on the web for public perusal.[27] In the end, consumers are protected from unknowingly being subjected to poor service or bad experience. At the same time, well-deserving professionals get additional business while the unqualified, poorly prepared, or unethical service providers are weeded out. Deaf people deserve the same when it comes to interpreting services. It's time to move forward and make it a win–win situation for Deaf people and interpreters alike. Let's reduce the amount of frustration and elevate the interpreting experience for everyone involved. This can be accomplished only through clear accountability and transparency, which is the missing link in ensuring quality in interpreting.

Notes

1. Lotte M. Willemsen, Peter C. Neijens, Fred Bronner, and Jan A. De Ridder, "Highly Recommended! The Content Characteristics and Perceived Usefulness of Online Consumer Reviews," *Journal of Computer–Mediated Communication* 17, no. 1 (2011): 19–38.

2. Robert Adam, Breda Carty, and Christopher Stone, "Ghostwriting: Deaf Translators within the Deaf Community," *Babel* 57, no. 4 (2011): 375–393; Stephanie Jo Kent, "Deaf Voice and the Invention of Community Interpreting," *Journal of Interpretation* 22, no. 1 (2013): 3; Sherry Shaw, *Service-learning in Interpreter Education: Strategies for Extending Student Involvement in the Deaf Community* (Washington, DC: Gallaudet University Press, 2013).

3. Janice Humphrey and Bob J. Alcorn, *So You Want to Be an Interpreter? An Introduction to Sign Language Interpreting* (Renton, WA: H & H Publishing Co., Inc., 2007).

4. Dennis Cokely, "Shifting Positionality: A Critical Examination of the Turning Point in the Relationship of Interpreters and the Deaf Community," *Sign Language Interpreting and Interpreter Education: Directions for Research and Practice* (New York: Oxford University Press, 2005): 3–28; Shaw, *Service-learning in Interpreter Education.*

5. Kent, "Deaf Voice and the Invention of Community Interpreting."

6. Cokely, "Shifting Positionality"; Shaw, *Service-learning in Interpreter Education.*

7. Charlotte Baker-Shenk, "The Interpreter: Machine, Advocate, or Ally?" *Expanding Horizons*, ed. Jean Plant-Moeller (Silver Spring, MD: RID Press, 1992): 120–40; Dennis Cokely,

"Curriculum Revision in the Twenty First Century: Northeastern's Experience," *Advances in Teaching Sign Language Interpreters*, ed. Cynthia Roy (Washington, DC: Gallaudet University Press, 2005a): 1–21; Campbell McDermid, "Social Construction of American Sign Language-English Interpreters," *Journal of Deaf Studies and Deaf Education* 14, no. 1 (2009): 111; Anna Witter-Merithew and Leilani Johnson, *Toward Competent Practice: Conversations with Stakeholders* (Alexandria, VA: Registry of Interpreters for the Deaf, Inc., 2005).

8. Cokely, "Shifting Positionality"; Bernhardt E. Jones, Gary M. Clark, and Donald F. Soltz, "Characteristics and Practices of Sign Language Interpreters in Inclusive Education Programs," *Exceptional Children* 63, no. 2 (1997): 257–68.

9. Witter-Merithew and Johnson, *Toward Competent Practice.*

10. Anna Witter-Merithew, "From Benevolent Care-taker to Ally: The Evolving Role of Sign Language Interpreters in the United States of America," *Gebärdensprachdolmetschen: Dokumentation der Magdeburger Fachtagung: Theorie und Praxis 4* (Hamburg: Verl hörgeschädigte kinder, 1999): 55–64; Cokely, "Shifting Positionality."

11. McDermid, "Social Construction of American Sign Language-English Interpreters."

12. Anna Witter-Merithew and Leilani Johnson, "Market Disorder Within the Field of Sign Language Interpreting: Professionalization Implications," *Journal of Interpretation*, 14, (2004): 19–55.

13. Cokely, "Curriculum Revision in the Twenty First Century: Northeastern's Experience"; Kent, "Deaf Voice and the Invention of Community Interpreting"; Witter-Merithew and Johnson, *Toward Competent Practice.*

14. Northern California Registry of Interpreters for the Deaf, "Recommendations for Agencies Providing ASL Interpreting Services," accessed June 5, 2017, https://www.norcrid.org/resources/Documents/Recommendations_for_Agencies_providing_ASL_services.pdf.

15. Eileen Forestal, "Deaf Perspectives in Interpretation Research: A Critical Element Long Overdue," *Signed Language Interpretation and Translation Research*, eds. Brenda Nicodemus and Keith Cagle (Washington, DC: Gallaudet University Press, 2015): 1–23.

16. Cokely, "Shifting Positionality"; Kent, "Deaf Voice and the Invention of Community Interpreting"; McDermid, "Social Construction of American Sign Language-English Interpreters"; Jemina Napier and Meg J. Rohan, "An Invitation to Dance: Deaf Consumers' Perceptions of Signed Language Interpreters and Interpreting," *Translation, Sociloinguistic, and Consumer Issues in Interpreting,* eds. Melanie Metzger and Earl Fleetwood (Washington, DC: Gallaudet University Press, 2007): 159–203.

17. Registry of Interpreters for the Deaf Standard Practice Paper, "Professional Sign Language Interpreting Agencies," accessed June 5, 2017, https://drive.google.com/file/d/0B3DKvZMflFLdb1Q1Ym1vZ3BrWEk/view; Northern California Registry of Interpreters for the Deaf, "Recommendations for Agencies Providing ASL Interpreting Services," accessed June 5, 2017, https://www.norcrid.org/resources/Documents/Recommendations_for_Agencies_providing_ASL_services.pdf.

18. Baker-Shenk, "The Interpreter: Machine, Advocate, or Ally?"; Kent, "Deaf Voice and the Invention of Community Interpreting."

19. Kent, "Deaf Voice and the Invention of Community Interpreting"; Napier and Rohan, "An Invitation to Dance."

20. Kent, "Deaf Voice and the Invention of Community Interpreting."

21. Kent, "Deaf Voice and the Invention of Community Interpreting."

22. Cokely, "Shifting Positionality."

23. Witter-Merithew and Johnson, *Toward Competent Practice.*

24. Kent, "Deaf Voice and the Invention of Community Interpreting"; Napier and Rohan, "An Invitation to Dance."

25. Bill Moody, "What Is a Faithful Interpretation?" *Journal of Interpretation*, 21, no. 1, Article 1 (2011).

26. Napier and Rohan, "An Invitation to Dance."

27. Lotte M. Willemsen, Peter C. Neijens, Fred Bronner, and Jan A. De Ridder, "Highly Recommended! The Content Characteristics and Perceived Usefulness of Online Consumer Reviews," *Journal of Computer–Mediated Communication* 17, no. 1 (2011): 19–33.

2

Understanding the Issues through Deaf Eyes

4

American Sign Language Interpreting in a Mainstreamed College Setting

Performance Quality and Its Impact on Classroom Participation Equity

John S. Pirone, Jonathan Henner, and Wyatte C. Hall

For the ASL summary of this chapter, go to https://youtu.be/YxWWtEOkP0c

John Pirone

In my public speaking class, I had to give a 15-minute presentation as part of the course requirements. I chose to talk about the importance of exposing Deaf children to American Sign Language. I was very excited because it was an important topic for me. I spent a few weeks on putting together my PowerPoint presentation and practiced several times. A day before class, I shared the slides along with my notes with the assigned interpreters. As I began presenting in front of 25 hearing students and the hearing professor, the first interpreter struggled to convey my message. The second interpreter looked uncertain as to what she should do. I saw puzzlement on students' faces. Some whispered to each other and others chuckled. The teacher wrote notes on a piece of paper. I became self-conscious and felt so humiliated. As a result of this interpreter glitch, my presentation was poorly delivered.

THERE CERTAINLY are challenges with American Sign Language (ASL) interpreting services, challenges that can adversely affect deaf college students' academic participation and success. This concern is especially critical because the Americans with Disabilities Act (ADA) requires colleges and universities to provide support services to ensure full and equal participation of disabled students in academic and social systems.[1] Accordingly, the demands on mainstreamed postsecondary institutions to provide appropriate support for deaf students have risen due to a dramatic increase in the enrollment of deaf college students since the passing of the ADA.[2]

Despite increased accessibility for students with disabilities, many deaf students still struggle to complete their college education.[3] Compared to hearing students, the withdrawal rate among deaf students is approximately 140% higher.[4] About 70 percent of all deaf students in higher education fail to graduate.[5]

Even when language interpreters are provided, many deaf students still experience academic and social challenges due to cultural and linguistic barriers.

Interpreters often struggle to facilitate college-level material because of their limited language and interpreting skills.[6]

Several studies have highlighted how poor signed language interpreting can be a barrier for deaf college students. Students may struggle during classroom lectures when their interpreters are unable to interpret effectively, potentially due to limited signing and interpreting skills, and limited knowledge of academic content. In spite of the need for more information on improving ASL competency and social skills in interpreters, limited research exists.

This study aimed to analyze the lived experiences of five Deaf students who struggled in mainstreamed undergraduate classrooms largely because of ineffective interpreting. The data for the study were collected using the Interpretative Phenomenological Analysis (IPA) method.[7] Based on the findings, potential solutions are offered for enhanced collegiate experiences for Deaf students whose learning processes are mediated through interpreters.

Five participants were recruited (Sara, Scott, Sam, Mary, and Adam [names have been changed for confidentiality purposes]) through email, a Yahoo! group mailing list, and Facebook. All participants were profoundly Deaf, self-identified as culturally Deaf, and used ASL as their primary language. Background information on their educational, communicative, and familial upbringing was not collected. Each participant attended an academic institution with 10 or fewer deaf students enrolled. For each participant, ASL interpreters were their primary means of accessing academic and social interactions. No data were available on these interpreters regarding their credentials or academic preparation. Data were compiled via video-recorded interviews, and the results were analyzed for emergent themes using the IPA analysis strategy.[8]

Three primary themes emerged from the data analysis: (1) ASL competency, (2) professionalism, and (3) intercultural competency. It is important to note here that the participants reported far more obstacles than positive aspects when asked about their experiences with interpreters.

American Sign Language Competency

Limited signing proficiency among interpreters was identified as a significant factor for all five participants' classroom involvement. They identified four specific areas of weaknesses that needed attention: vocabulary, syntax, information filtering, and overall signed language processing skills.

Vocabulary

Participants felt that interpreters with a limited vocabulary base often compensated by using signs with incorrect conceptual meanings than what was intended. Furthermore, the interpreters often made up signs. Scott said, "When my teacher used the words, 'basketball court,' my interpreter used the incorrect sign for 'court'—meaning the courtroom—not a playing field. That kind of mistake occurred many times."

Adam shared a similar situation, "For example, history, historicism, and historicity. Each word has a different meaning, but most interpreters used the same sign for all three words. So, I missed the nuances that gave each word a different meaning." These vignettes demonstrate how limited vocabulary can disrupt the learning process for Deaf students. Going back to the word *court,* interpreters with limited ASL vocabulary would use the sign COURT (as in judicial) to represent all instances of *court*, including athletic courts, wooing someone, and the other many meanings this word holds. The interpreter in Adam's story used the same sign for three words (history, historicism, and historicity) without recognizing the distinction in the meanings of each version. The participants reported that they had to mentally re-translate their interpreters' incorrect signs in order to understand the material.

Syntax Structure

Participants reported that interpreters often did not have a workable command of ASL syntax. Instead, they relied on English syntax in their interpretation work. Sam explained the effects of this, "I became tired and it took so much energy and effort to process information in English. Without any learning gained in class, I had to spend more time on reading books trying to understand what my teacher shared with the class."

Mary pointed out that watching an interpreter use English syntax affected her "thought processing and how I conceptualized information I received. English-based signs are like black and white and no color." Mary felt that she could have understood important concepts better if the information were presented in genuine ASL syntax. Her use of the phrase "black and white and no color" may be a useful metaphor to explain why Sam required so much energy and effort to process information in English; he had to "colorize" the English-structured information presented to him.

Processing information in a different syntactical system can increase cognitive load and prevent effective learning. It also presents language-anxiety challenges that often come with second-language structures.[9] Second-language information processing (including a different syntactical system) has been found to impact critical thinking skills[10] such as increased working memory demands.[11] This cognitive load requires more work for Deaf students, creating frustration, reducing motivation, and preventing effective engagement in the classroom.

In addition to over-reliance on English grammar, interpreters' poor use and limited understanding of ASL's use of spatial morphology had an impact on participants' learning experiences. More specifically, ASL uses spatial morphology to establish verb agreement, visualize temporality, direct placement of nominals relative to each other, and indicate verb directionality and path, all of which make signed messages clear. Sara explained:

> For example, [the interpreter] pointed to one location, "That [was] 1965" and provided information about that time, and then pointed to a different location to indicate "before 1965" and provided information about what happened before 1965. This helped me see a clearer picture. The interpreters who did

> not use space would interpret, "In 1965, before that, we only had 50 years of oppression. . ." without using space to indicate time.

Using space effectively allowed Sara to decode information more quickly and effectively. Other participants in the study reported similar frustrations with interpreters who had a limited understanding of spatial morphology. Without this spatial usage, the participants struggled to make sense of who did what to whom, what direction one's action took, the location of people and things, and time—all which had a profound impact on the mastery of the content presented in the classroom. Their discontent suggested that the use of space played a crucial role in their learning process.

Information Filtering

The participants recounted how their interpreters often filtered and/or simplified the information being discussed in the classroom. Mary had an interpreter who often filtered her professors' and classmates' comments. She explained:

> Sometimes I could tell the interpreter did not interpret everything that was said. I could sense that my interpreter skipped a lot of information because I noticed that my teacher gave a long lecture while my interpreter gave me a couple of sentences. Sometimes my interpreter told me, "They're talking about nothing. . ." and I asked him to tell me more. He said, "Well, it was a silly rumor." I felt frustrated because he filtered what information was to be shared.

Sara shared an experience in which her signed message was filtered by the interpreter. "The interpreter should have interpreted it even if she did not understand what it meant. She should not filter what can be interpreted and what cannot be interpreted. It is not fair to me because hearing students could say whatever they want while my comments had to be screened by my interpreter."

Based on these accounts, the interpreters disempowered their clients by determining what information to share.[12] Disempowerment via information filtering was identified as a serious barrier to the participants' education as it created unequal access to classroom information.[13]

Similar issues exist with interpreters who simplified information in their interpretation work. It was only when Adam read his class materials and teachers' emails that he realized that his interpreter had skipped some critical information. He explained:

> I realized that the concepts I read were not the same as what my interpreters shared with me. Also, I received emails from my teacher and they contained specific words and concepts that my interpreters did not mention during their interpreting work. I got a sense that my interpreters simplified what they conveyed to me. I felt like they treated their work like they would treat a middle school interpreting assignment and their language competency was inappropriate for the college level.

Scott had the same experience. He stated, "I noticed that they always summarized information and some important information was missing. I felt like I did not learn much because they summarized information." He recalled how one interpreter would repeatedly summarize information to the point that the team interpreter had to intervene to fill in the gaps.

Information filtering can cause Deaf students to feel less confident after becoming conscious of the fact that they are not getting full information. One recurring theme among these participants was the need for trust.[14]

Language Processing Skills

Poor signed language processing skills can lead to ongoing frustrations with students' efforts to participate in classroom discussions. Sara recalled an interpreter who struggled to understand her, limiting her ability to contribute:

> I get everyone else's words to me via interpreters, but I could not get my words out to them because the interpreter's receptive skills weren't great. And the result is that people had this misguided idea or assumption of who I was as a Deaf person, who appeared to be a less capable person to carry on a conversation. This obstacle bled into my ability to ask questions during lectures because my questions in ASL could not be understood by interpreters and therefore I became reluctant to raise my hand for class participation.

Both Adam, who also was hesitant to involve himself in classes, and Sara felt that they would have participated more had they trusted that their messages would be reliably and accurately represented.[15] Sara explained, "If an interpreter said something wrong, then my teacher or students would think that it was me saying something wrong, not the interpreter. Then they get a bad idea of who I am."

The participants sometimes had to help their interpreters. Sara explained, "I had to raise my hand to let the teacher know that the interpreter didn't understand and that we needed to go back to a point I missed. I felt like I had to do all the work for the interpreter." She cited an incident in her photography class when she was discussing a title with her teacher. The title of her artwork, which had a theme of imperfection, was *Pus Pocket*; however, the interpreter could not understand Sara. Sara frustratingly felt obligated to clarify for herself:

> I fingerspelled, "Pus Pocket," but my interpreter did not understand what I fingerspelled. I repeated myself, but the interpreter stubbornly refused to voice and said to me, "Do you understand what you just said?" I said, "Yes," and fingerspelled the words again. The interpreter fingerspelled back, "Pus???" I responded, "PUS, YES!" The interpreter said, "What does that mean?" I explained the meaning, and the interpreter responded, "Are you sure?" I felt so frustrated and my teacher saw my back-and-forth conversation with the interpreter. I wrote to my teacher explaining that my interpreter did not understand the words I fingerspelled. The teacher said, "Oh, *that* infection," and the interpreter was silent. I felt like I did his work by helping him understand what I meant. I wonder why the interpreter had to challenge me, and his asking me questions made me wonder if I used the word incorrectly.

This was not an isolated incident for Sara. She recalled the same problem when she tried to make a comment in her History of Sexuality class but the interpreter could not understand her. Sara felt "foolish and [I] had to use English grammar in order to help [my] interpreter understand what [I] tried to say." This situation made Sara feel disengaged and discouraged:

> Every time my teacher asked if we had any questions, my interpreter looked at me with full attention and was ready to interpret, but I did not bother to ask again because of that experience. I would ask questions via email but never through an interpreter. I was afraid that my teacher might not understand me again. I worked hard to come up with a good question and then would find out that my question was not understood by my interpreter. It was not worth my time and effort.

All participants in this study reported similar experiences of the need to change their language register to accommodate their interpreters' lack of ASL competency. Their narratives make it clear that ASL competency was a significant factor in their ability to participate in the classroom. The participants struggled with conceptually incorrect or made-up signs. ASL competency is clearly an important consideration when it comes to Deaf students' quality of participation in the classroom.

Professionalism

Professionalism refers to how interpreters conduct their work based on ideas, values, and norms practiced by their own profession. The Registry of Interpreters for the Deaf (RID), a national organization of certified signed language interpreters, has a Code of Professional Conduct (CPC) to which all RID-certified interpreters are expected to conform.

Four themes emerged when analyzing participant vignettes about professionalism: (1) incorporating *personal opinions* into translations, (2) distracting clients with *obtrusive behaviors* when not interpreting, (3) discussing work logistics in front of clients via *public negotiations*, and (4) engaging in *informal conversations* off to the side during work.

Personal Opinions

Interpreters must "refrain from providing counsel, advice, or personal opinions."[16] Sara shared one of her experiences in which an interpreter did not follow this tenet:

> I remember one class, Natural Disasters or something like that, and the interpreter signed, "BB." I was puzzled and asked what BB meant. The interpreter said Big Bear and that it was a mountain in California. I responded, "Oh, I see. Okay." However, the team interpreter, whom I disliked after what she did, said to me, "Oh, that is not Bragg or something." I said, "What did you say?" The team interpreter said, "Not Bernard Bragg." At that time, I did not know who Bernard Bragg was and responded, "I don't know." The team interpreter responded, "Oh, very typical for someone like you who went to a mainstream school." I was so angry and I said to myself, "Fuck her."

Typically, mainstreamed students are not afforded the same opportunity to learn about Deaf cultural figures and Deaf history as students in interpreter education programs. Interpreters therefore are privileged in ways that many Deaf students are not. The interpreter's conduct was extremely unprofessional and demeaning toward Sarah.

Obtrusive Behaviors

Interpreters have the professional obligation to "conduct and present themselves in an unobtrusive manner. . . .[17] Adam and Scott had interpreters who partook in leisurely activities such as playing games, sending texts on their phones, and even falling asleep while the team interpreter worked. The interpreter should have continued to monitor and assist as needed. Scott recalled one specific incident:

> Sometimes interpreters who were on break would read a newspaper and did not offer any help to their team interpreters. I also noticed that my interpreter [who was working] tried to get his team interpreter's attention but could not. The interpreter ended up telling me that he missed information and asked me to interrupt and ask my teacher for clarification. I felt frustrated that both interpreters did not use any teamwork.

In these cases, it was clear that the interpreters on "break" compromised the obligation to maintain professionalism. The CPC requires interpreters to provide "professional and courteous assistance when asked and [monitor] the accuracy of the message while functioning in the role of the support interpreter."[18]

Cooperative Teamwork

The CPC instructs interpreters to "work cooperatively with team members through consultation *before* (emphasis added) assignments regarding logistics. . ."[19] Sam recalled how one interpreter arrived late and interrupted the working team interpreter to say, "I have a doctor's appointment. Can you take over the whole morning assignment, then I take over the whole afternoon assignment?" The interpreter did not exercise professional responsibility in ensuring Sam's academic engagement in his classroom.

Informal Conversations

Informal conversations occur when interpreters talk to each other, or to people in the classrooms when they should be working. Adam shared a story:

> I worked in an environment where it was so casual and I had a lot of down time. It was easy for interpreters to have informal conversations with other people in the room. That did not bother me at first, but I realized that once it happened, it became a slippery slope. The interpreters did that again and again. That gave interpreters a voice that was inappropriate for them to assume, because this led students to converse with interpreters instead of me.

The interpreters' actions gave Adam's peers the impression that it was acceptable to converse with interpreters and, in the process, ignore Adam, making him invisible. One of the important professional duties for interpreters is to "facilitate communication access and equality, and support the full interaction and independence of consumers."[20]

Intercultural Competence

An interculturally competent person behaves appropriately and communicates effectively when interacting with people of different cultures and languages. Three elements (attitudes, knowledge, and skills) are crucial to attaining intercultural competence.[21] Two participants provided examples of how their interpreters' intercultural competence (or incompetence) affected their academic participation through two themes: cultural mediation and empathy.

Cultural Mediation

Sara reported that she was more engaged with her classes when she had interpreters who had cultural mediation skills and were children of Deaf parents (Coda).[22]

Codas often work with Deaf people to remove communication barriers to the dominant-English environment by utilizing cultural mediation tools. Some interpreters forget or do not consider cultural mediation so they approach interpreting as a "social change fighter" and assume that each interaction a Deaf person has with hearing people must be a *battle* in which hearing people need to be *educated* about Deaf people's rights, and needs. This may conflict with how Deaf people *want* to interact with the hearing world.

An analysis of Sara's description of cultural mediation informs us in several ways. First, Coda interpreters' ability to manage intercultural interactions reflects two elements of intercultural competence—knowledge and skills. More specifically, Coda interpreters have knowledge (sociolinguistic awareness and culture-specific knowledge) and skills (acquired knowledge from experience), likely owing to their bilingual-bicultural experiences growing up. Codas also have the luxury of watching their Deaf parents resolve cultural-linguistic conflicts within the dominant hearing society. Non-Coda interpreters may not have opportunities to observe similar cultural conflicts prior to their careers.

Empathy

Sam described Coda interpreters as being more empathetic about the Deaf experience. He said, ". . . she, the Coda interpreter, also checked in with me often to ensure I was following the classes, to solicit feedback, and inquire into my general well-being as a student." Sam added that empathy was important, especially when he was one of the few Deaf students at the university. The interpreter, through empathy, demonstrated the significance of quality interpreting on Sam's participation in the hearing world. The interpreter valued and respected Sam's expertise and experience as a Deaf student and was receptive to his feedback about her work.

Intercultural competence is a valuable skill for interpreters in facilitating Deaf students' classroom participation. The presence of at least two different cultures (hearing and Deaf), languages (English and ASL), and modalities (auditory and visual) demands effective mediation from skilled individuals. Deaf students engage more when their interpreters use effective intercultural mediation strategies.

Discussion and Recommendations

The study results show that Sara, Scott, Sam, Mary, and Adam generally did not feel that they had equitable access to the college classroom despite the presence of interpreters. This appeared to be a direct result of poorly prepared interpreters who may have lacked adequate training: in sign language mechanics, superior interpreting processes, and intercultural competency. Consequently, the participants felt they had diminished learning opportunities compared to their hearing peers.

The larger conclusion we can draw from this analysis is that interpreters' presence in the classroom does not automatically lead to equality. Rather, it is language skills, professionalism, and intercultural competencies that facilitate the "process of making [things] equal and fair."[23] Qualified interpreters need to have the language and intercultural competencies that best accommodate Deaf students' native languages and cultures. They also need to ensure, through appropriate language and cultural competency, that Deaf students have equitable experiences in the classroom. Equitable access allows Deaf students to learn new materials on their own terms, ask questions and offer input during class discussions, interact with classmates and professors, and listen in on conversations with other students or professors—just like their hearing peers.

To improve participation equity in the classroom for Deaf students, three parties—higher education administrators, interpreters, and Deaf students need to work closely together. Below are three recommendations to enhance Deaf college students' classroom equity via qualified interpreters.

1. Higher education institutions should develop and implement an institutional-level policy on quality control during the hiring and evaluations of interpreters.
2. To become fluent signers, skilled interpreters, and effective collaborators, interpreters must seek ways to immerse and integrate themselves within the Deaf community.
3. Quality interpreter mentoring—grounded in evidence-based practices—should be a higher priority in interpreter education programs and in the field.

Higher Education Institutions

Higher education institutions that provide interpreting services must have policies in place that include quality assurance mechanisms for their interpreting staff. This should include ASL competency, professionalism, and intercultural competency. The evaluation process must include Deaf students' input.

The quality assurance evaluation system should occur at two levels: pre-hiring and post-hiring. During the pre-hiring process, the interpreter coordinator should carefully evaluate candidates' ASL skills. This is necessary to ensure their ability to interpret effectively in a college setting, as RID certification is not always a good measure of a person's ASL competency. This is what makes such an evaluation necessary. Higher education institutions must additionally commit to ongoing evaluations of already-hired interpreters.

The five participants in this study reported that their interpreter coordinators, all of whom were hearing with limited understanding of Deaf culture, were not responsive to the poor performance of the interpreters at their universities. Quality control of interpreters' work performance cannot happen without active engagement by the coordinators. Who is more qualified than a Deaf person to perform this duty?

The evaluation process should include a certified ASL interpreter and an ASL-using Deaf individual with experience of using interpreting services. Interpreters who perform poorly must be provided with a remedial plan and support to improve their skills. Mentors can be a valuable tool in providing this kind of support (see below for details). During this period, these unqualified interpreters should not be working in the classroom because Deaf students should not be burdened with incompetent interpreters.

Cultural Immersion

For many expert interpreters, the key to their skilled work can be found in their dedication to cultural immersion. In order for novice interpreters to strengthen their language competency and cultural knowledge, they need to engage in regular and meaningful interactions with ASL-using Deaf individuals in a variety of settings in the Deaf community. These interactions will expose interpreters to diverse communication styles and registers, creating opportunities to develop linguistic and cultural intuition. Interpreters can, through immersion in the Deaf community, acquire a deeper understanding of the sociolinguistic dynamics between ASL and English, and the linguistic and cultural realities that shape deaf individuals' lives.[24] Being with diverse ASL users, they will see their ASL vocabulary expand, their command of ASL syntax improve, their receptive skills progress, and their understanding of Deaf experiences broaden. These outcomes are how interpreters build stronger competencies that can reduce, if not eliminate, the problems reported in this study.

Mentoring

Both novice and experienced interpreters should continuously seek mentorship support from more skilled interpreters and Deaf people. Mentorship has proven to be effective in addressing skill and performance gaps through a focus on refining language skills and increasing cultural understanding and sensitivity. Mentoring strategies should include evaluation/feedback, self-assessment, and dialogue. Although these strategies help interpreters elevate their competencies, optimizing the results of mentoring requires the involvement of Deaf mentors. Numerous studies have shown that the presence of a Deaf mentor produces positive results. For example, interpreting students reported that they learned more from Deaf mentors than non-deaf mentors because native ASL users offered rich insights on how and why ASL was used in certain contexts.[25] In addition, Deaf mentors are in a better position to build their confidence and comfort level in addressing culturally sensitive issues. While Deaf mentors are preferable, nondeaf mentors continue to provide value via their knowledge and experience of interpreter processes and working as interpreters.[26]

Conclusion

In summary, the results of this study lead to several important conclusions about the issues Deaf collegiate students experienced in the classroom. First, it is not the simple presence of interpreters alone, but the performance quality of those interpreters that determines participation equity. Second, creating equitable access requires an effective combination of strong ASL competency, intercultural competency, professionalism, and interpreting skills—a combination that appears to be more rare than it should be. In essence, participation equity will not be achievable until Deaf students are given the freedom to learn, communicate, and interact with their peers and professors and without being disempowered by their interpreters. Our recommendations discussed in this chapter can help support and increase the number of Deaf students being able to successfully pursue a college degree without having to also monitor and manage interpreter competency.

Notes

1. National Association of the Deaf, *Legal Rights: The Guide for Deaf and Hard of Hearing People* (Washington, DC: Gallaudet University Press, 2000).

2. Harry G. Lang, "Higher Education for Deaf Students: Research Priorities in the New Millennium," *Journal of Deaf Studies and Deaf Education* 7, no. 4 (2002): 267–80; Jennifer Lukomski, "Deaf College Students' Perceptions of Their Social–Emotional Adjustment," *Journal of Deaf Studies and Deaf Education* 12, no. 4 (2007): 486–94.

3. Daniel Boutin, "Persistence in Postsecondary Environments of Students with Hearing Impairments," *Journal of Rehabilitation* 74, no. 1 (2008): 25–31; Lang, *Higher Education*, 267–80; John T. E. Richardson, Marc Marschark, Thomastine Sarchet, and Patricia Sapere, "Deaf and Hard-of-hearing Students' Experiences in Mainstream and Separate Postsecondary Education," *Journal of Deaf Studies and Deaf Education* 15, no. 4 (2010): 358–382; J. Smith, "Deaf Students in Collegiate Mainstream Programs," *Proceedings of Deaf Studies Today: A Kaleidoscope of Knowledge, Learning and Understanding* (Orem, UT: Utah Valley University, 2004): 165–87; Michael Stinson and Gerard Walter, "Improving Retention for Deaf and Hard of Hearing Students: What the Research Tells Us," *JADARA–Rochester NY* 30 (1997): 14–23.

4. Mark J. Myers and E. M. Taylor, "Best Practices for Deaf and Hard-of-Hearing Student Success in Postsecondary Education," *JADARA–Rochester NY* 34, no. 1 (2001): 13–28.

5. Marc Marschark, Harry G. Lang, and John A. Albertini, *Educating Deaf Students: From Research to Practice* (New York: Oxford University Press, 2001).

6. Susan Foster, Gary Long, and Karen Snell, "Inclusive Instruction and Learning for Deaf Students in Postsecondary Education," *Journal of Deaf Studies and Deaf Education* 4, no. 3 (1999): 225–35; Smith, *Deaf Students in Collegiate Mainstream Programs*, 165–87; Marc Marschark, Patricia Sapere, Carol Convertino, and Rosemarie Seewagen, "Access to Postsecondary Education through Sign Language Interpreting," *Journal of Deaf Studies and Deaf Education* 10, no. 1 (2005): 38–50; Susan Foster, "Factors Influencing the Academic and Social Integration of Hearing Impaired College Students," *Journal of Postsecondary Education and Disability* 7 (1989): 226–35; Foster, Long, and Snell, *Inclusive Instruction*, 225–35; Smith, *Deaf Students*, 165–87; Gerard Walter, Susan Foster, and Lisa Elliot, "Attrition and Accommodation of Hearing-Impaired College Students in the U.S." Paper presented at the *Tenth National Conference of the Association on Handicapped Student Service Programs in Postsecondary Education*, Washington, DC (July 23, 1987).

7. Jonathan A. Smith, ed., "Interpretative Phenomenological Analysis," in *Qualitative Psychology: A Practical Guide to Research Methods*, 2nd ed. (Thousand Oaks, CA: Sage Publications, 2008): 53–80.

8. Jonathan A. Smith, Paul Flowers, and Michael Larkin, *Interpretative Phenomenological Analysis: Theory, Method and Research* (Thousand Oaks, CA: Sage, 2009).

9. Peter D. MacIntyre and Robert C. Gardner, "The Effects of Induced Anxiety on Three Stages of Cognitive Processing in Computerized Vocabulary Learning," *Studies in Second Language Acquisition* 16, no. 1 (1994): 1–17; Marlene Taube-Schiff and Norman Segalowitz, "Within-Language Attention Control in Second Language Processing," *Bilingualism: Language and Cognition* 8, no. 3 (2005): 195–206.

10. Carol Beth Floyd, "Critical Thinking in a Second Language," *Higher Education Research & Development* 30, no. 3 (2011): 289–302.

11. Jared A. Linck et al., "Working Memory and Second Language Comprehension and Production: A Meta-Analysis," *Psychonomic Bulletin & Review* 21, no. 4 (2014): 861–83.

12. Sofia Karina Trommlerová, Stephan Klasen, and Ortrud Leßmann, "Determinants of Empowerment in a Capability-Based Poverty Approach: Evidence from the Gambia," *World Development* 66 (2015): 1–15.

13. See Trudy Suggs for discussion on disempowerment, this volume.

14. See Thomas Holcomb for further discussion on trust, this volume.

15. See Leala Holcomb, this volume.

16. Registry of Interpreters for the Deaf, "NAD-RID Code of Professional Conduct," 3, accessed July 15, 2016, https://drive.google.com/file/d/0B-_HBAap35D1R1MwYk9hTUpuc3M/view

17. Registry of Interpreters for the Deaf, "NAD-RID Code of Professional Conduct," 3.

18. Registry of Interpreters for the Deaf, "NAD-RID Code of Professional Conduct," 4.

19. Registry of Interpreters for the Deaf, "NAD-RID Code of Professional Conduct," 4.

20. Registry of Interpreters for the Deaf, "NAD-RID Code of Professional Conduct," 5.

21. See reviews in Darla K. Deardorff, "Identification and Assessment of Intercultural Competence as a Student Outcome of Internationalization," *Journal of Studies in International Education* 10, no. 3 (2006): 241–66.

22. Harlan L. Lane, Robert Hoffmeister, and Benjamin J. Bahan, *A Journey into the Deaf-World* (San Diego, CA: DawnSignPress, 1996).

23. Elaine Unterhalter, "What Is Equity in Education? Reflections from the Capability Approach," *Studies in Philosophy and Education* 28, no. 5 (2009): 415–24.

24. Dennis Cokely, "Never Our Language, Never Our Culture: The Importance of Deaf Community Connectedness for Interpreters," in *English in International Deaf Communication*, eds. Cynthia J. Kellett Bidoli and Elana Ochse (Switzerland: Peter Lang AG, 2008): 57–73.

25. Witter-Merithew et al., "Deaf Language Mentors."

26. For more in-depth review of mentorship strategies, see Jeffrey Davis, Tan Fried, Cindy Herbst, Eileen McCaffrey, Charlotte Toothman, and Tracy S. Clark, "Mentorship: A True Course in Collaboration—the RITC Region IX Mentorship Program," *Mapping Our Course: A Collaborative Venture—Proceedings of the 10th National Convention of the Conference of Interpreter Trainers* (Charlotte, NC: CIT Publications, 1994): 129–43; Linda Delk, "Interpreter Mentoring: A Theory-Based Approach to Program Design and Evaluation," accessed February 2013, http://www.interpretereducation.org/wp-content/uploads/2013/03/Interpreter_Mentoring_Theory_of_Change_for_Program_Monitoring_and_Evaluation.pdf; Laurie Shaffer and Wendy Watson, "Peer Mentoring: What is THAT?" *New Designs in Interpreter Education—Proceedings of the 14th National Convention of the Conference of Interpreter Trainers*, (Minneapolis/St. Paul, MN: CIT Publications, October 9–12, 2002): 77–92; Lynne Wiesman and Eileen Forestal, "Effective Practices for Establishing Mentoring Programs," *A New Chapter in Interpreter Education: Accreditation, Research, and Technology—Proceedings of the 16th National Convention of the Conference of Interpreter Trainers* (San Diego, CA: CIT Publications, October 18–21, 2006): 183–92; Anna Witter-Merithew, Leilani Johnson, Betti Bonni, Rachel Naiman, and Marty Taylor, "Deaf Language Mentors: A Model of Mentorship via Distance Delivery," in *Proceedings of the 14th National Convention-Conference of Interpreter Trainers* (2002): 33–52.

5

The Heart of Interpreting from Deaf Perspectives

Kim B. Kurz and Joseph C. Hill

For the ASL summary of this chapter, go to https://youtu.be/I4wSbXprh_M

> At the 22nd International Congress on the Education of the Deaf (ICED) in Greece in July 2015, Kim Kurz was enjoying her stroll in the Syntagma Square in front of the Old Royal Palace when she encountered a group of Deaf colleagues who were also taking a break from the conference. At any other moment, this should be a happy occasion, but their faces told her otherwise. Their request to discuss an important matter conveyed the feeling of urgency. After sitting down at a nearby outdoor café, her colleagues began to vent their frustrations about the lack of highly qualified interpreters and accessibility at the conference. This discussion confirmed for Kim that this was not a unique situation. It was the moment she realized the importance of documenting and sharing Deaf individuals' perspectives on interpreting.

ALTHOUGH THERE have been countless discussions over the years among Deaf professionals about the qualities they want to see in sign language interpreters, the discussions remain largely anecdotal and not well-documented. This is the motivation that led Kim to recruit her co-author, Joseph Hill, to work on the project of documenting insights and expectations from a group of Deaf professionals about the language and interpreting qualities they consider "the heart of interpreting," hence the title of this chapter.

Background

Before sign language interpretation was established as a profession, Deaf people were naturally a big part of interpreters' development. Translation work was often done by individuals who were intimately familiar with the language and cultural practices of the Deaf community. They were teachers of Deaf children, educational administrators, religious workers, rehabilitation counselors or had Deaf parents.[1] These individuals often followed a helper model approach, whereby interpreting services were provided voluntarily, motivated by a desire to help Deaf individuals' conversational exchange with nonsigners.[2]

Over the years, there have been several changes to the conceptual paradigm of the interpreting model. The helper model was discarded in favor of a more professional delivery of work.[3] The professionalization of interpreting services began in the 1960s and initiated the shift from the helper model to the current bilingual-bicultural and allyship models. However, this shift resulted in a disconnect between interpreters and the Deaf community.[4] Further compounding the problem is the increasing number of interpreter education programs at academic institutions.

An unintended consequence of this shift to academic preparation for careers in interpreting was a reduction in budding interpreters' exposure to Deaf community members with their perspectives and insights on interpreting.[5] Under this new paradigm, individuals who desired to become interpreters often had minimal contact with Deaf people and were not vetted by the members of the Deaf community.

Given the wide access to academic offerings of ASL today, interpreting students are now less likely to be natural bilinguals, and their involvement in the Deaf community has become increasingly difficult to establish.[6] With this diminished exposure to the Deaf community, interpreters entering the profession today often lack a substantial knowledge of the capital of Deaf community cultural wealth.[7] To interpret as effectively as possible, they need to be aware of the linguistic and social capital through which linguistic resources, communication resources, and social networks are shared and maintained in the Deaf community.

More critically, the authors have noticed that interpreters and interpreting students today often lack sufficient linguistic and social capitals that could support their interpreting work. To identify exactly what the necessary capitals are to become effective interpreters, the authors undertook a qualitative study to document Deaf people's perspectives on critical linguistic and discourse features for effective interpretation or the "heart" of interpreting for Deaf people.

Methodology

A qualitative study involving personal interviews and focus groups was conducted to gather information from Deaf participants regarding their perspectives on effective interpreting. Qualitative inquiry is "primarily naturalistic, interpretive, and inductive . . . if you want to study context, analysis must be in-depth and focused on only a small sample or a few individuals' situations."[8] The authors chose this approach because personal interviews and focus groups have been demonstrated to be useful for collecting data on a subject that is still largely unexplored and not extensively researched. According to Wadsworth, "It is the interaction between people that generates a range of responses to only one or two key focus questions. . . . Groups are most valuable and exciting when you are utilizing the group dynamics to generate new ideas, collect a wider range of perceptions and experiences, or find innovative solutions to persistent problems."[9] Focus groups have been used successfully in interpreting research projects because they provide insights and experiences from which common themes may be drawn through content analysis using the grounded theory.[10]

Table 1. Demographic Information of the Participants

Age	*26-35*	*36-45*	*46-55*	*Over 66*
	5	1	3	1
Gender	*Female*	*Male*		
	4	6		
Race/Ethnicity	*Black*	*Latinx*	*White*	
	3	1	6	
Audiological Status	*Deaf*	*Hard of Hearing*		
	9	1		
Education	*Bachelor's*	*Master's*	*Ph.D.*	
	1	7	2	

Participants

The study involved a total of ten Deaf participants. Focus groups and one-to-one interviews were arranged based on the participants' availability. All participants lived in Rochester, New York, but they were not native to the region. Five of the participants were ages 26 to 35, whereas the remainder were older than 36. Six of ten participants identified as male. Of 10 participants, 6 identified themselves as white, three identified as black, and one as Latinx (this term is used as a gender-inclusive way to refer to people of Latin American origin). Nine of the participants identified themselves as Deaf and one self-identified as hard of hearing. All of the participants had higher education backgrounds, with the majority either holding or studying for master's or doctoral degrees (see table 1).

As for the language experience of the participants, six of them acquired ASL as their first language, whereas the others considered English as their first language. One participant viewed herself as bilingual since birth. Six participants were exposed to sign language immediately after birth and one learned the language when she was between the age of three and five years. These seven individuals had developed their native language during the critical age period of language development.[11] Three other participants learned sign language after the age of six. All participants use ASL on a daily basis and have been consumers of ASL interpreters for more than 16 years (see table 2).

A focus group of six Deaf participants, a group interview with two Deaf participants, and two one-to-one interviews were held over a period of several weeks. In the focus group session, a high-definition camera was used to record the conversation among the six Deaf participants. The data the participants provided in ASL was translated into written English. In the one-to-one interviews, the authors transcribed the data produced by the four participants and verified the transcrip-

Table 2. Language Data Provided by the Participants

First Language	*ASL*	*English*	*Both*	
	6	3	1	
Age of Acquisition	*Birth*	*3-5*	*6 and after*	
	6	1	3	
Interpreter Consumer	*16-20 years*	*21-25 years*	*26-30 years*	*30 years+*
	4	2	2	2

tion by reviewing the transcribed comments with the participants. In both cases, the transcription followed the standard English orthographic principle.[12] The participants were identified only by number, and their numbers were associated with their responses on the transcript.

Interview Questions

In the one-to-one and focus group interviews, the participants were asked ten open-ended questions regarding their preferences and expectations of ASL interpreters:

1. What skills would you like to see interpreters possess?
2. What skills are frequently missing in some interpreters?
3. Describe the "best" interpreter's skills.
4. What skills do the best interpreters have that other interpreters might not have?
5. What skills are considered "eye candy" from Deaf people's perspectives?
6. What do you wish interpreters would include in their interpretation?
7. What do you want to see less of from interpreters during their interpretation?
8. What would you suggest to interpreters as the best way to learn various registers?
9. What about language attitudes of interpreters?
10. Any additional comments?

Two of the questions included terms that prompted a number of participants to ask for clarification: "eye candy" in question #5 and "language attitudes" in question #9. "Eye candy" refers to aesthetically pleasing attributes in interpreting or signing that are attractive to Deaf consumers. "Language attitudes" was a new concept for the participants. The concept was explained to them as a psychological tendency involving affective, cognitive, and behavioral aspects that is expressed by evaluating language and language users with some degree of favor or disfavor.[13]

Content Analysis

The frequency of responses was computed for the open-ended questions and content analysis was performed on the responses collected during the focus group and one-to-one interviews. The summative content analysis approach was employed to identify and calculate the frequency of themes mentioned by Deaf participants.[14]A sample of quotes for each theme is provided in the results section below.

Results and Discussion

Finding a number of themes in the analysis, the authors classified them into two main categories: *linguistic competence* and *discourse*. The linguistic competence-related themes identified were bilingual skills, fingerspelling, and depiction. The discourse-related themes were identified as audience engagement, message equivalency, communication situations, and pragmatic enrichment. The results of the interviews may be beneficial to interpreter educators interested in pedagogy as they provide insights and directions for future curricula and research.

Linguistic Competence

Linguistic competence encompasses bilingual skills in both ASL and English, fingerspelling, and depiction. These features were frequent themes in the conversations among the participants in the focus group. The content analysis identified several sub-themes under depiction—surrogates, constructed action and dialogue, and signing space.

Bilingual Skills

Participants in the interviews generally agreed that interpreters need to be equally proficient in both ASL and English in order to provide effective interpretations. One participant commented,

> What is frequently missing from interpretation is the grammatical part. If interpreters do not have a strong foundation in either ASL or English, for me that is what makes their interpretation weak. A successful interpreter must be bilingual and have strong skills in both English and ASL. Being strong in just one language and weak in the other language is not enough. An interpreter cannot get by with just one strong language.

Another Deaf participant, an ASL tutor, made a similar remark regarding the importance of using his source and target languages effectively.

> When I tutor student interpreters, I frequently find that they do not even know what nouns and verbs are. It terrifies me because if they want to become future successful interpreters, they need to know what nouns and verbs are. They might make some good sign choices, but that doesn't help if they do not know their own grammar rules. Some of them go on to graduate without knowing grammar rules.

The two participants in the above examples echoed a similar concern raised in Witter-Merithew and Johnson's 2005 study. In that study, a Deaf professional discussed her interpreter's flaws in sign-to-voice interpreting, attributing them to a lack of self-monitoring and preparation.[15] By comparison, participants in the present study observed that too many interpreters do not have a solid meta-linguistic knowledge in their primary language, English. If they do not have a good linguistic foundation in English, it is likely to be true for ASL as well, especially given their limited exposure to ASL. One Deaf participant offered this observation regarding the difference between two groups of hearing signers—those who are Deaf-parented (i.e., children of Deaf adults [CODA]) and those who are not:

> I think that, like young Deaf children who grew up in Deaf families, those CODAs were given opportunities to play with their ASL skills and were raised in a safe environment where it was ok to make mistakes with their ASL skills and learn from them. They were able to learn from grammatical mistakes at a

> very young age. Now that they are older and working as interpreters, they have the ability to worry more about the content and make sure their information is accurate. Other interpreters who are not CODAs probably need to worry about making sure their grammatical features are correct in addition to the message content. Most interpreting students are not ready for that level of work. Most of them are still at the vocabulary and grammar level. I think there is a big difference between those two groups—interpreters who grew up with ASL being their first language and the other interpreters who grew up with English as their first language.

Another aspect of bilingual skills is knowledge of culturally specific form and meaning in both languages. Interpreters should recognize that not all English words have exact translation equivalents, as this Deaf participant pointed out:

> A fund of information and knowledge is the key. For example, I have an interpreting intern in my company who frequently signs SICK!; SICK! as if someone were ill. It took me a while to finally realize that she really meant "cool" or "awesome." I provided feedback to that intern related to the semantics of the sign and helped fix his/her signing error. Interpreters constantly need feedback.

It is evident that this young intern incorrectly assumed that the ASL sign SICK has a direct correspondence to the American slang use of "sick" to mean "cool" or "awesome" (see figure 1).

Slang is a nonstandard lexicon of popular words and phrases that are usually limited to a specific generation. So, while "this is sick" may be interpreted as "awesome" by her English-speaking peers in the same generation, this may not translate well in ASL in which the conventional sign SICK (an open handshape with the extended middle finger that touches the forehead) does not follow the similar trend. Her lack of understanding of semantic range in ASL contributed to an inaccurate and confusing translation, but this may be resolved by fingerspelling the English

Figure 1. SICK! SICK! (incorrect) COOL! or AWESOME! (correct).

word "sick" and expanding the meaning of awesomeness. Some would argue that fingerspelling is not part of ASL; nevertheless, it was one of the most frequent themes that the Deaf participants brought up during their focus group discussion. Many of them mentioned that they feel fingerspelling is part of bilingualism and thus important to overall discourse, which is discussed in the next section.

Fingerspelling

In addition to knowledge of grammar and semantics, effective interpreters understand that fingerspelling is an essential component of ASL; however, it is a difficult task for ASL learners to acquire.[16] While interpreters who exhibit linguistic competence incorporate effective use of fingerspelling in their interpretations, in general, Deaf participants in our study recognized that fingerspelling was often not a comfortable choice for interpreters. One of the Deaf participants made this point with the following comment:

> Oftentimes interpreters avoid fingerspelling and try to sign everything. I would prefer that my interpreters fingerspell so I can see the [English] vocabulary and connect it to the sign itself.

Another Deaf participant made a similar comment on the topic of fingerspelling about how she wishes she knew the English words for technical terms and becomes frustrated when the interpreter decides not to fingerspell them but uses technical signs instead:

> Sometimes I want to know the English word for the signs the interpreter used and I have to ask the interpreter for the words.

This indicates that fingerspelling is a necessary skill that interpreters should acquire and be comfortable using when they need to make a specific reference or provide clarification. Interpreters should also be familiar with the discourse structure in knowing when and how fingerspelling should be used; for example, discerning whether fingerspelling occurs before, after, or at the same time as depicting a person or an object. Depiction, which will be discussed in the next section, is another aspect that is difficult for some interpreters to acquire and use skillfully.

Depiction

Compared to the other topics in the interviews, participants in our study engaged in an extensive discussion regarding interpreters' use of depiction in ASL. Depiction is an expression of iconic mappings of mental and real spaces.[17] Mental spaces are imagined entities and events constructed by a narrator who then maps the mental spaces onto physical spaces, which include body and spatial locations. The narrator encodes the physical forms—handshapes (including classifiers), movement, location, and facial expressions—with the imagined entities and events in a grammatical manner. For example, a signer uses a classifier 3 handshape (with the thumb upright, the index and middle fingers extended, and the other fingers closed) to represent a car and moves the handshape 3 in a way that depicts the car's movement—in a straight line (see figure 2), in a zig-zag pattern (see figure 3),

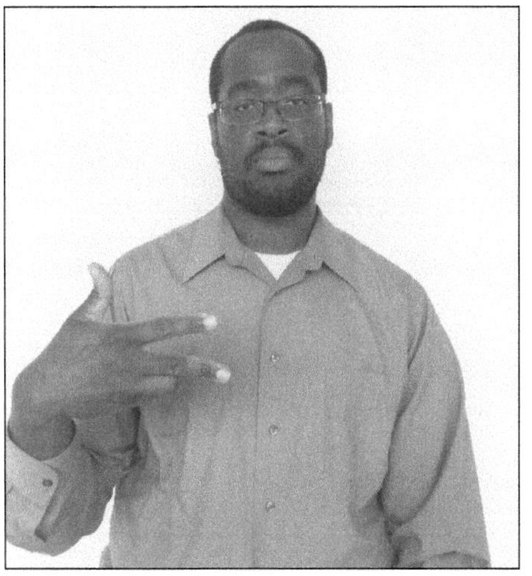

Figure 2. Depicting verb of a vehicle in a straight line.

Figure 3. Depicting verb of a vehicle in a zig-zag line.

Figure 4 Depicting verb of a vehicle on a bumpy road.

or in a shaky motion as if the car is moving across a rough road (see figure 4). The 3 handshape occupies the physical space, but the image of a moving car exists in the mind of the narrator, which is the mental space. The mapping is not visible to a listener so the narrator is able to encode the mental image by depicting the moving car with the 3 handshape. This handshape is a conventional classifier handshape for certain vehicles and the listener is able to decode it and produce the same mental image as the narrator's.

The keyword is "conventional" because if one does not use the handshape, movement, or location in a conventional way when describing an object, this may interfere with the listener's decoding process. The response below exemplifies thc expectation that one Deaf participant had about interpreters' ability to depict an object.

> The interpreter must know how to effectively use signing space, especially when establishing the setting. The organization of the information and cohesion of the message is as important as the delivery of the message. Excellent use of classifiers also makes a huge difference in the interpretation process. There are some interpreters who do not use correct forms of classifiers. I remember one time there was an interpreter who was at one of my medical appointments. The interpreter was trying to sign UTERUS but did not use the appropriate classifier for it. The interpreter used a classifier that looked more like an opened bent-5 with wrists touching each other (looks more like someone is holding a big bowl and carrying it carefully; see figure 5).

This participant valued effective use of classifiers, which are called "depicting verbs" in the research and practitioner literature on sign language. Deaf participants also discussed such complicated linguistic features as constructed action and constructed dialogue, which are types of depiction in a discourse. Constructed dialogue is also known as "role shifting," a form of character representation through the use of language in spoken or signed modality.[18] Constructed action is similar to constructed dialogue except that it involves the use of nonverbal gestures to represent a character. The Deaf participants agreed that constructed dialogue and action are linguistic features that are challenging for interpreters, especially when interpreting a storytelling session. A Deaf participant shared this perspective:

> Most interpreters play it "safe." They do not want to take risks with their interpretations. Frequently, I notice that interpreters use listing (on their fingers) instead of actually using the signing space in front of their bodies. I do not see enough use of role shifts or constructed action among interpreters. Those skills are probably one of the most important linguistic features that are frequently missing from interpretation work.

Figure 5. Incorrect classifier for UTERUS.

Constructed action and dialogue are pragmatic features that are typically used by skillful ASL signers when they want to re-create an impression or a message produced by a person. Like classifiers, the signers use their heads and bodies in the physical space but the impression or message exists in their minds, whether it is based on a real or imagined event, and they encode it by constructing a meaning with their body shifts and nonmanual signals. The instances of depiction can occur frequently,[19] and depictions must be constructed and used in a way that is conventional in an ASL discourse.

Discourse

The second thematic category that emerged from the data involved comments relating to discourse. Discourse is typically defined as a communication situation involving how language is used between people in a particular setting, how words or sentences are combined to make sense in this setting, and how people communicate in a way that engages or disengages one another. Discourse is not just about language itself; it goes beyond language and involves "ways of combining and integrating language, actions, interactions, ways of thinking, believing, valuing, and using various symbols, tools, and objects to enact a particular sort of socially recognizable identity."[20]

Interpreters create a different dynamic in a communication situation between two parties in which both parties, not just the Deaf participant, need an interpreter in order for the communication exchange to occur. In addition to language concerns, interpreters must also be cognizant of (1) how people engage one another and how they present themselves; (2) the use of language in order to make sense of the messages; (3) appropriate behaviors in communication situations; and (4) the appropriate amount of information to convey when expanding on a concept.[21] Next, audience engagement, message equivalence, communication situation, and pragmatic enrichment will be discussed as part of ASL/English discourse, which address the concerns raised by the study participants on interpreters' relationship with Deaf consumers.

Audience Engagement

Similar to depiction, audience engagement was another topic that was extensively discussed by the participants. Various comments were related to the concerns about the relationships between interpreters and hearing and Deaf consumers, environmental and discourse cues, sign-to-voice interpreting, expression of personality, and identities. In order for successful communication to occur, the relationship between two communication actors must be present and must include the elements that make the relationship work. Appropriate facial expression and use of space facilitate the establishment of connections between interpreters and Deaf audience members. A Deaf participant eloquently shared his perspective on these elements:

> It's important that the interpreter has a relationship with both the presenter and the Deaf consumer. It is not ideal when the interpreter chooses to maintain a relationship with only the presenter and excludes the Deaf consumers. This could

> lead to a feeling of disconnect between the interpreter and the Deaf audience. When the interpreter tries to connect with the Deaf audience, I feel that the interpreter is interested in providing clear information to us. When an interpreter puts extra effort into making sure the message is clear, I feel like that interpreter cares about the Deaf consumers and their ability to understand him/her. If the interpreter is disconnected from the Deaf audience by not showing much facial expression (in other words, stone-faced) and uses less space, I feel like I cannot connect with that interpreter. In other words, the interpretation can become really dry.

In connection with this point, another Deaf participant expressed appreciation for interpreters who take the time to get to know their Deaf consumers in order to make their relationship successful. I like it when my interpreters talk with me before the assignment to discuss my preferences. Everyone is different. Some Deaf people prefer their interpreters to fingerspell, while other Deaf people prefer their interpreters to use less fingerspelling. I've noticed that those interpreters who prepare in advance tend to do a better job of being able to adapt to the Deaf consumer's language skills.

Another Deaf participant discussed her experience as a behavioral health professional in a mental health setting where she had to consider the entire context, including her hearing client's physical and verbal behaviors and noises. She stressed that interpreters should not ignore those cues inaccessible to her, which might be important in her client evaluation:

> Interpret a person's behavioral sounds, such as foot tapping or clearing the throat. These sounds may be important for certain settings, such as mental health interpreting. Include environmental sounds in interpretation.

In addition to audience engagement and environmental sounds, another Deaf participant emphasized that interpreters should pay attention to the discourse cues relative to turn-taking provided by a hearing speaker's vocal inflection.

> I feel that it is the interpreter's job to get the attention of the presenter on behalf of the Deaf consumer. Hearing people in the audience usually know when it is a good time to interrupt the presenter, especially when the presenter's voice begins to lower or slow down. The hearing people in the audience can use their voice to interrupt the presenter. However, Deaf people in the audience usually do not use their voice to get the presenter's attention. Also, the Deaf consumers depend on interpreters to use their best judgment regarding when it is a good time to interrupt the presenters to let them know that the Deaf consumer has something to say.

Participants also discussed their experiences with interpreters who inaccurately portrayed personality through use of incongruous verbal or signing mannerisms. A Deaf participant shared the following story about an interpreter's representation of a hearing phone caller's personality:

> I made a phone call through video relay service (VRS) to a plumber whom I have never met before. The way the interpreter used facial expression and over-exaggerated her interpreting work indicated to me that this hearing plumber was an outgoing person who was maybe an Italian. However, when the plumber

> actually showed up, he was nowhere near the way the interpreter had portrayed him. It is very possible that the plumber's voice may be more animated when he is on the phone, but in person he was not as outgoing as I thought he would be.

A Deaf participant discussed how racial identity can influence the communication dynamic between the interpreter and Deaf consumer. The impact of racial identity has also been explored by Shambouger.[22] This participant expressed a preference for interpreters being racially compatible with presenters.

> I like it when my interpreters are clear in their messages and context. When the presenter is a black person and the interpreter is a white person, I would feel uncomfortable. If the presenter is a black person and the interpreter is a black person, I would have felt more comfortable.

Another Deaf participant shared a similar perspective regarding gender identity and its impact on the relationship between the interpreter and Deaf consumer (a relationship which is also discussed in Morgan's 2008 essay on the intersection of interpretation, conversation style, and gender).[23]

> If the presenter is a male and the interpreter is a male, that would be an ideal situation. It's important that both the presenter and interpreter are culturally compatible and a good fit for each other and the audience.

Both participants' comments highlight the importance of recognizing Deaf consumers' identities and their impact on the relationship between interpreters and Deaf consumers. In addition to relationships, interpreters must also be aware of how they appear to their Deaf consumers and how interpreters' judgments and evaluation of the Deaf consumers could impact the relationship. One Deaf participant expressed the view that interpreters should respect Deaf consumers' background and focus on mediating the message:

> In my opinion, interpreters should faithfully mediate the message without passing judgment. For example, suppose the Deaf person grew up as an oral student or used cued speech or some other communication system such as home signs or even a foreign sign language. In that case, the interpreter must accept the Deaf person's background and focus on making sure the message is being interpreted clearly. That is the primary job of an interpreter. However, if the interpreter has problems with the Deaf person's background or has an attitude about it, then that interpreter has no business being in the interpreting field.

As these comments have shown, participants appreciated interpreters who put forth the effort to get to know their Deaf consumers; employed linguistic features, discourse cues, and affect that foster social engagement; and demonstrated respect for Deaf consumers' communication preferences. Interpreters who do not successfully engage Deaf audience members run the risk of alienating their Deaf consumers and even skewing the message. In summary, Deaf professionals want to feel they are equally involved in communication with the hearing person and that the interpreters are representing them well as professionals. This leads to the next topic which Deaf professionals also felt is important—the importance of message equivalency.

Message Equivalence

When an interpreter focuses primarily on linguistic forms, he or she may lose sight of the message meaning. Interpretations should deliver equivalent meaning in a register (discussed next) that is appropriate to the situation. According to the study participants, interpreters can improve message equivalency by negotiating meaning, learning to think nonlinearly, and knowing how much additional information to convey. For example, a Deaf participant explained how interpreters and consumers can negotiate meaning.

> Sometimes interpreter(s) will ask me what is the sign for a word. Oftentimes, I tell the interpreter that it is not important. Most important is the meaning of the message you are trying to convey, rather than focusing on individual words and signs. The interpreter's definition of the word might be different from my definition. I would ask interpreters to tell me what the word means to them; then I can show the sign that fits the meaning of the word and is conceptually accurate. It's more important to be able to interpret the messages accurately in presentations/interpretations.

Another Deaf participant shared her opinion that linear thinking contributes to ineffective use of space:

> Based on my experience, most interpreters think linearly instead of fluidly. A good interpreter knows how to effectively use space to deliver the content and message. An interpreter who provides information in a linear fashion is more concerned with sign vocabulary than with conveying information by appropriate use of signing space.

Such linear thinking may lead interpreters to process at the lexical level rather than to conceptualize the overarching framework of the message. The resulting interpretation may not effectively communicate the intent of the message in a manner that is clear and appropriate.

Language Register

An additional problem noted by study participants relates to the use of register, which is the level of formality that is determined by different situations. Participants asserted that some interpreters demonstrate a limited range of registers and are, therefore, unable to convey the message in the manner most appropriate for a particular communication situation. During the focus group discussion, one participant remarked:

> Some interpreters are stuck with interpreting in academic settings and they do not do enough community interpreting to be exposed to a variety of signing registers and variations. An interpreter must become familiar with and accustomed

> to the setting he/she is interpreting in order to become a better interpreter. For example, talking with a doctor might be a little more formal compared to talking with a nurse. That type of interactive information is critical for interpreters. It's really important for the interpreters to study the setting and determine which register is appropriate for a specific setting.

Interpreters who are now attending or have gone through interpreter education programs are usually restricted to few discourse situations, especially with the reduced input from the Deaf community and the lack of opportunities to interact with the Deaf community on a regular basis. This suggests a need for additional training and practice with diverse Deaf consumers in a broad range of communication situations so that interpreters will be exposed to various registers and deepen their pragmatic skills. In addition, the interpreter should be able to use pragmatic enrichment as part of the discourse and by providing additional information related to concepts.

Pragmatic Enrichment

Pragmatic enrichment, as described by Sequeiros, is a "pragmatic process whose function is to develop the vagueness found in many natural language utterances in order to arrive at fully determinate thoughts . . . the development of a source text into its fully determinate conceptual representation by carrying out an enrichment and, secondly, the translation of this fully enriched thought into another language."[24] Another term that is similar to "enrichment" is "expansion"; that is, a contextualizing technique that provides additional information related to terms or concepts.[25] Even though *enrichment* and *expansion* can be used interchangeably, the latter term is one of the pragmatic processes of enrichment so the former term is used in the discussion of contextualizing techniques. However, the Deaf participants in this study explicitly mouthed the terms "expand" and "expansion" during their focus group discussion, so for this purpose the term is preserved in the quotes that follow. As Deaf study participants discussed their perspectives regarding the use of enrichment, it was evident that pragmatic enrichment requires skill on the part of interpreters to know how much, when, and with whom it should be used. For example, a Deaf participant explained that the contextualizing technique for information access may be different for hearing and Deaf people:

> Should interpreters give information that hearing people don't have—for example, the term photosynthesis, which is the energy from the sun. I would expand on the term photosynthesis and provide clarifying information to the Deaf students. The hearing students would not have access to that additional information. Is it fair to hearing students if the interpreters decide to expand on the vocabulary by providing Deaf students with additional information?

Access to additional information may be appreciated, but one Deaf participant cautioned against the overuse of enrichment technique:

> Overexpansion! I hate it when interpreters exaggerate during their interpretations. That includes overuse of classifiers. For example, describing a human

> heart by overuse of classifiers. Sometimes expansion is not necessary. Yes, appropriate expansion and use of classifiers are required in good interpreters—but they should not overuse them. For example, I already know that a heart beats. The interpreter doesn't need to describe how a heart beats. This is common knowledge that we all know.

Given the level of education of the study participants, it is possible that their perspectives on the use of enrichment do not reflect the wider views of the Deaf community. Just as interpreters need to thoroughly evaluate each communication situation to determine which register is most appropriate, they also need to take the initiative to know their Deaf consumers' preferences to determine whether enrichment is necessary in the interpretation.

Limitations of the Study

The results of this study may be limited in generalizability due to the fact that all participants were conveniently sampled and lived in the same region, which encompasses two universities with a large number of Deaf professors, researchers, and alumni. Because the participants were highly educated professionals, this sample did not reflect the characteristics of the general Deaf population in the United States. The bilingual Deaf participants were fluent in ASL and English and considered themselves to be active bicultural members of the Deaf community. Given this background, it is very possible that these Deaf participants' perceptions and issues may differ from the diverse experiences of the general Deaf population. Due to the presence of two local universities with a significant number of Deaf professionals, many interpreters in the area are more experienced with interpreting in academic and professional settings than most interpreters are. Naturally, expectations of interpreters may be higher than for interpreters in other regions with fewer educational opportunities.

Conclusion

Analysis of the testimonies from Deaf participants in this study reaffirms the importance of fluency in both English and ASL. Interpreters who desire to reflect the heart of interpreting should cultivate skills that enable them to ascertain the purpose of each interpreting assignment, assess their audience, and familiarize themselves with the content. Armed with this knowledge of the discourse situation and Deaf consumer preferences, they may be better able to make their work more accommodating for Deaf people by constructing their own nonlinear conceptualization that enables them to successfully encode the communication while matching the message intent. This is the heart of interpreting for Deaf people.

The "heart" of interpreting is often seen in the work of Deaf interpreters. The Deaf interpreters who are in high demand are the ones who possess the essential linguistic features as discussed in this chapter. With the natural incorporation of these features so valued by study participants, Deaf interpreters frequently render the "eye candy" that participants find comfortable and easy to watch and understand. When the heart of interpreting is well portrayed, Deaf consumers find it easier to cultivate relationships with other parties in the discourse situation and concentrate on the content of their messages rather than being distracted by the form in which messages are delivered. Thus, increased use of Deaf interpreters may be one strategy to enhance the delivery of effective interpretation. Furthermore, the incorporation of strategies used by Deaf interpreters among hearing interpreters can help them become more successful in their work.

It is for this reason that interpreter education programs play an important role in helping future interpreters understand better what the heart of interpreting is all about. A big part of this is self-analysis skills. The ability to self-analyze in evaluating assignment parameters and the appropriate use of register will go a long way in interpreting effectively and satisfactorily for Deaf people.

Clearly, there is a need for additional qualified interpreters, both Deaf and hearing, who have a good grasp of what the Deaf community wants in interpreted work. Developing specific skills that reflect the heart of interpreting requires self-analysis and healthy dialogue with the Deaf community.

Notes

1. Dennis Cokely, "Shifting Positionality: A Critical Examination of the Turning Point in the Relationship of Interpreters and the Deaf Community," in *Perspectives on Deafness: Sign Language Interpreting and Interpreter Education: Directions for Research and Practice*, eds. Marc Marschark, Rico Peterson, and Elizabeth A. Winston (New York: Oxford University Press, 2005): 3–28.

2. Sherman Wilcox and Barbara Shaffer, "Towards a Cognitive Model of Interpreting," in *Topics in Signed Language Interpreting: Theory and Practice*, ed. Terry Janzen (Amsterdam: John Benjamins Publishing Company, 2005): 27–50.

3. Wilcox and Shaffer, "Towards a Cognitive Model of Interpreting"; Charlotte Baker-Shenk, "The Interpreter: Machine, Advocate, or Ally?" in *Expanding Horizons: Proceedings of the 1991 RID Convention*, ed. Jean Plant-Moeller (Silver Spring, MD: RID Publications, 1991): 120–40.

4. Cokely, "Shifting Positionality."

5. Campbell McDermid, "Social Construction of American Sign Language—English Interpreters," *Journal of Deaf Studies and Deaf Education* 14, no. 1 (2008): 105–30; Anna Witter-Merithew and Leilani J. Johnson, *Toward Competent Practice: Conversations with Stakeholders* (Alexandria, VA: The Registry of the Interpreters for the Deaf, 2005).

6. Alessandro Zannirato, "Teaching Interpreting and Interpreting Teaching: A Conference Interpreter's Overview of Second Language Acquisition," in *Translator and Interpreter Training: Issues, Methods and Debates*, ed. John Kearns (London: Continuum, 2008): 19–38; McDermid, "Social Construction of American Sign Language."

7. Tara J. Yosso, "Whose Culture has Capital? A Critical Race Theory Discussion of Community Cultural Wealth," *Race Ethnicity and Education* 8, no. 1 (2005): 69–91.

8. Maria Mayan, *Essentials of Qualitative Inquiry* (Walnut Creek, CA: Left Coast Press, 2009).

9. Yoland Wadsworth, *Do It Yourself Social Research* (Walnut Creek, CA: Left Coast Press, 2011): 76.

10. Claudia V. Angelelli, "Validating Professional Standards and Codes: Challenges and Opportunities," *Interpreting* 8, no. 2 (2006): 175–193; Witter-Merithew and Johnson, *Toward*

Competent Practice; Jemina Napier, "'It's Not What They Say but the Way They Say It.' A Content Analysis of Interpreter and Consumer Perceptions of Signed Language Interpreting in Australia," *International Journal of the Sociology of Language* 2011, no. 207 (2011): 59–87; John Creswell, *Qualitative Inquiry & Research Design: Choosing Among Five Approaches* (London: SAGE Publications Ltd., 2013); Kathy Charmaz, *Constructing Grounded Theory: A Practical Guide Through Qualitative Analysis* (London: SAGE Publications Ltd., 2006); Barney G. Glaser and Anselm L. Strauss, "The Discovery of Grounded Theory: Strategies for Qualitative Theory," *Nursing Research* 17, no. 4 (1968): 364.

11. Rachel Mayberry and Elizabeth Lock, "Age Constraints on First Versus Second Language Acquisition: Evidence for Linguistic Plasticity and Epigenesis," *Brain and Language* 87, no. 3 (2003): 369–84; Rachel Mayberry and Ellen Eichen, "The Long-Lasting Advantage of Learning Sign Language in Childhood: Another Look at the Critical Period for Language Acquisition," *Journal of Memory and Language* 30, no. 4 (1991): 486–512.

12. Witter-Merithew and Johnson, *Toward Competent Practice;* Napier, "'It's Not What They Say."

13. Alice Eagly and Shelly Chaiken, "The Advantages of an Inclusive Definition of Attitude," *Social Cognition* 25, no. 5 (2007): 582–602; Peter Garrett, *Attitudes to Language* (Cambridge, UK: Cambridge University Press, 2010).

14. Hsiu-Fang Hsieh and Sarah E. Shannon, "Three Approaches to Qualitative Content Analysis," *Qualitative Health Research* 15, no. 9 (2005): 1277–88.

15. Witter-Merithew and Johnson, *Toward Competent Practice.*

16. Rhonda Jacobs, "Just How Hard Is It to Learn ASL? The Case for ASL as a Truly Foreign Language," in *Multicultural Aspects of Sociolinguistics in Deaf Communities*, ed. Ceil Lucas (Washington, DC: Gallaudet University Press, 1996): 83–226; Carol Patrie and Robert Johnson, *Fingerspelled Word Recognition through Rapid Serial Visual Presentation* (San Diego, CA: Dawn Sign Press, 2011); Campbell McDermid, Lynnette Finton, and Alexis Chasney, "Contextualized Recognition of Fingerspelled Words," *Journal of Interpretation* 25, no. 1 (2016): 1–23.

17. Scott K. Liddell, *Grammar, Gesture, and Meaning in American Sign Language* (Cambridge, UK: Cambridge University Press, 2003); Paul Dudis, "Body Partitioning and Real-Space Blends," *Cognitive Linguistics* 15, no. 2 (2004): 223–38; Mary Thumann, "Identifying Recurring Depiction in ASL Presentations," *Sign Language Studies* 13, no. 3 (2013): 316–49.

18. Deborah Tannen, *Talking Voices: Repetition, Dialogue, and Imagery in Conversational Discourse* (Cambridge, UK: Cambridge University Press, 2007); Melanie Metzger, "Constructed Dialogue and Constructed Action in American Sign Language," in *Sociolinguistics in Deaf Communities*, ed. Ceil Lucas (Washington, DC: Gallaudet University Press, 1995): 255–71.

19. Thumann, "Identifying Recurring Depiction in ASL Presentations."

20. James P. Gee, *An Introduction to Discourse Analysis: Theory and Method* (Abingdon, UK: Routledge, 2014).

21. Regarding the influence of interpreters on visual and tactile interpreted interaction, see Melanie Metzger, Earl Fleetwood, and Steven D. Collins, "Discourse Genre and Linguistic Mode: Interpreter Influences in Visual and Tactile Interpreted Interaction," *Sign Language Studies* 4, no. 2 (2004): 118–37.

22. Nicole Shambouger, "Navigating Language Variety: ASL/English Interpreters 'Giving Voice' to African American/Black Deaf Signed Language Users," Master's thesis (Monmouth, OR: Western Oregon University, 2015).

23. Elizabeth F. Morgan, "Interpreters, Conversational Style, and Gender at Work," in *Deaf Professionals and Designated Interpreters*, ed. Peter C. Hauser, Karen L. Finch, and Angela B. Hauser (Washington, DC: Gallaudet University Press, 2008): 66–80.

24. Sequeiros, Xose' Rosales, "Interlingual Pragmatic Enrichment in Translation," *Journal of Pragmatics* 34, no. 8 (2008): 1069–89.

25. Shelly Lawrence, "Interpreter Discourse: English to ASL Expansion," in *Mapping Our Course: A Collaborative Venture. Proceedings of the Tenth National Convention of the Conference of Interpreter Trainers*, ed. Elizabeth A. Winston, Conference of Interpreter Trainers; David Quinto-Pozos and Wanette Reynolds, "ASL Discourse Strategies: Chaining and Connecting—Explaining Across Audiences" *Sign Language Studies* 12, no. 2 (2012): 211–35.

ASL Head Movements

Critical Features in Interpretation

Keith M. Cagle, Sharon J. Lott, and Phyllis P. Wilcox

For the ASL summary of this chapter, go to https://youtu.be/Ws934pECZQA

> A Deaf man signed, "HEY, SEE BEAUTIFUL BIRD THERE" with a quick sideway head jerk as he signed BEAUTIFUL. The hearing signer asked if he meant that the bird wasn't beautiful. The Deaf signer quickly responded, "No, no, no, I said, 'very beautiful.' Didn't you see?" The hearing signer asked, "Why did you shake your head firmly? Isn't that negation?" The Deaf signer chuckled, understanding what had just happened. He explained, "In ASL, it can mean the adverb of 'very,' not a negation."

WHEN SIGNERS do not use the appropriate head movements as grammatical markers, it can be difficult to comprehend what is being said, especially when they are quoting speakers. Generally, ASL and interpreting students learn that head movements in ASL are associated primarily with yes/no questions, WH-questions, rhetorical (RH) questions, topic-comment statements, conditional statements, relative clauses, negations, and affirmations—but this is only the tip of how head movements are used. Furthermore, as we frequently see, some interpreters often do not use head movements appropriately for fingerspelling, numbers, specific words, grammatical markers, and/or discourse markers. This lack of appropriate head movements creates gaps in the intended message.

Detailed discussions on ASL linguistic features such as head movements are needed to assist interpreters in incorporating them more effectively and successfully in their work. This is the goal of this chapter: to present specific information on head movements and their functions in ASL. The authors share findings from their research and classroom observations. Critical head movements at all levels are examined, including fingerspelling and lexicalized fingerspelling, numbers, lexical signs, phrases, syntax, discourse, and listener's feedback.

LITERATURE ON NONMANUAL SIGNALS AND HEAD MOVEMENTS

There is abundant literature on body language, but the literature on ASL nonmanual signals is relatively new and scattered: *Faces of ASL* by MJ Bienvenu, *Deaf Tend Your* by Byron Bridges, *1000 ASL Faces* by Keith Cagle, *ASL Grammar and*

1. Head position: Tilt (Front and Back)	32%
2. Head position: Turn (Left and Right)	25%
3. Head movement: Nod	23%
4. Head position: Tilt (Left and Right)	16%
5. Head movement: Shake	3%
6. Head movement: Side to side	1%

Figure 1. Six sub-groups of head movement in Nicodemus's research.

Culture by Charlotte Baker and Dennis Cokely, *Basic Sign Communication: Student Materials* by Bill Newell et al., and *Mouth Morphemes in American Sign Language* by Kevin Struxness. There are also numerous research articles by linguists.[1] In the past two decades, researchers have attempted to understand the roles and functions of nonmanual signals (NMS) in ASL, including head movements. Numerous ASL instructional programs teach the importance of head movements for multiple syntactical functions including yes/no questions, WH-questions, RH-questions, conditionals, topic comments, relative clauses, negations, and affirmations.

It is helpful to note that the term NMS has increasingly been replaced with the concept of *prosody*. Nicodemus explains what prosody in sign language is:

> In signed languages, prosodic structure is expressed by changes in eye aperture, head movement, body leans, lengthening of signs, cheek puffing, nose wrinkling, and hand clasping, among other physical behaviors.[2]

Nicodemus also identified 21 prosodic markers in which the head movement is included, comparing them to spoken intonation, syllables, rhythm, tempo, stress, lengthening, volume, and pausing. She also identified that the head movements played significant roles in ASL as discourse boundary markers, categorizing them into six subgroups (see figure 1).[3]

To illustrate the importance of head movement in ASL, Thumann identified that body position was used 19 percent of the time, nonmanual signals 21 percent of the time, eye gaze 61 percent of the time, and head position 73 percent of the time (see figure 2).[4]

Overall, the literature shows that head movements is an area of research identifying crucial grammatical and discourse functions.

Functions of Head Movements

Head movements are similar to patterns of rhythm, patterns of stress, and intonation in spoken language.[5] They are like the spaces in written language such as paragraph breaks, and punctuation such as commas, semicolons, and periods. There are three major functions of head movements (see figure 3).

1. Lexical: Individual lexical signs, fingerspelling, lexicalized fingerspelling, numbers, and classifiers

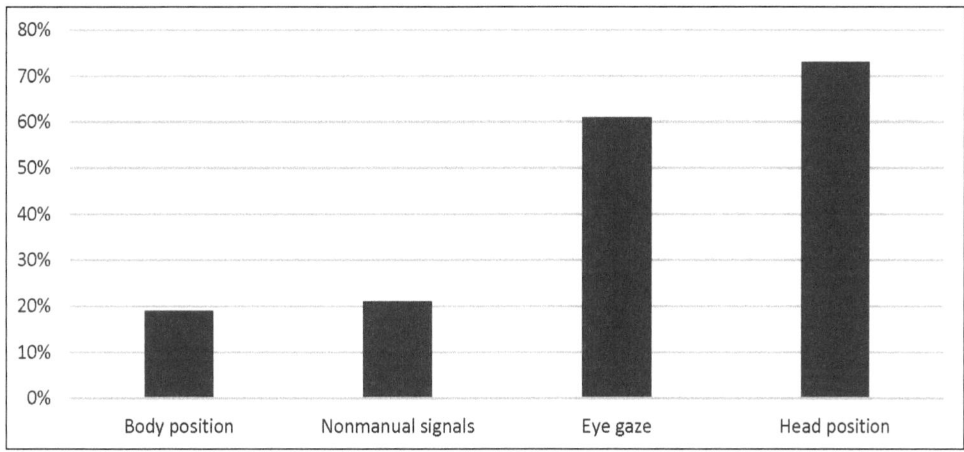

Figure 2. Thumann's research (2011).

2. Syntax: Grammatical features such as yes/no questions, WH- and RH-questions, conditional expressions, topic comments, and relative clauses
3. Discourse: Utterance boundaries (ending of a phrase, sentence, or paragraph) with accompanying head movement; listener's feedback also is important

To further explore head movements and their functions in conjunction with signs, Cagle analyzed four videotapes. The first was the SignStream CD-ROM, which contained eight sets of one-clause utterances by three signers. Four sets of utterances with 133 sentences signed by the three different signers were selected, and several patterns were detected.[6]

Continued Head Movements throughout Sentences

WH-questions, yes/no questions, and conditional expressions, with the head leaning forward, always superseded any other head movements such as head nod, head shake, or others (shown below in italics). The head movements also spread

Lexical level	Syntax level	Discourse level
Fingerspelling	Yes/no question	Phrase
Number	WH-question	Sentence
Abbreviation	Condition	Paragraph
Lexicalized FS	Topic comment	Listener's feedback
Classifiers	Relative clause	
	Adverbial clause	

Figure 3. Functions with head movements.

from the beginning to the ending of the sentence in 26 segments. See these selected examples:

Y/N Q

TEACHER *FINISH* ENTER HOUSE IX
Has the teacher gone into the house?

cond.

IX *FINISH* READ MAGAZINE, FUTURE READ BOOK
If you finish reading the magazine, will you read a book?

Some negation head movements always spread rightward and throughout the remainder of the sentence.

rapid head shake

STUDENT *NOT* LIKE CHOCOLATE
The student does not like eating chocolate.

rapid head shake

fs-JOHN *SHOULD NOT* BUY HOUSE
John should not buy a house.

Also, in the video, the negation of NOT, NONE, or NO in the ASL sentence was illustrated by a head movement:

rapid head shake

fs-JOHN SHOULD BUY HOUSE
John should *not* buy a house.

Yet, several negations such as NEVER, VOMIT, NO, NOT, DOESN'T MATTER, and NOT-YET triggered a head movement at the beginning of the sentence and continued through the rest of the sentence.

slow head shake

IX fs-JOHN CAR IX *NEVER* SEE IX
John never saw the car.

rapid head shake

IX TEACHER *THREW-UP* MOVIE
The teacher hates the movie.

regular head nod, head shake

TEACHER *ENJOY* READ++, BUT MOVIE *NOT*
The teacher enjoys reading, but not watching a movie.

rapid nod, head shake

IX STAND BETTER MORE CLEAR, BUT DOESN'T-MATTER
This place would give a better view, but it wouldn't matter.

rapid head shake

IX FS-JOHN READ++ *NOT-YET*
John hasn't read it.

rapid head shake

IX HOUSE BUY *NO* fs-JOHN MOTHER *NOT-WANT*
John's mother doesn't want to buy this house.

Spread Rightward

FUTURE and FINISH signs' head movements usually spread rightward.

Examples:

rapid nod

IX fs-JOHN *FUTURE* READ BOOK
John will read a book.

rapid nod

TEACHER *FINISH* READ MAGAZINE. NOW READ BOOK
The teacher just read the magazine. Now he is reading a book.

In only one utterance on the videotape did the head movement from the sign of FINISH start earlier.

rapid nod

AFTER CLASS, fs-JOHN *FINISH* READ BOOK
After the class, John was done with reading the book.

Spreading Leftward and Rightward

Some lexical signs such as PLAN, BUY, and LIKE also triggered head movements for the preceding sign and continued through the sentence.

rapid nod

IX MOTHER *PLAN* READ++ BOOK LATER
The mother plans to read the book later.

rapid nod y/q

IX MOTHER *BUY* CAR REALLY. WHY
The mother bought the car. Really? I wondered why she did?

Repeated Head Movement

The grammatical category of plurality in this example is associated with the sign READ++, which was signed repeatedly along with a repeated head nod (as indicated by ++).

+nod++

IX MOTHER BOOK *READ*++
The mother is reading the book.

nod++

TEACHER REQUIRE fs-JOHN FUTURE READ++ BOOK
The teacher requires John to read books.

Head Movement for Relative Clause

There was either a rapid nod or a single nod for the relative clause of WHO.

rapid nod++

fs-JOHN FATHER IX GIFT CAR fs-JOHN
John's father who gave him a car.

nod

IX MOTHER GIVE fs-JOHN CHOCOLATE YESTERDAY
His mother who gave John some chocolate candies yesterday.

The previous examples show that the head movements associated with grammatical NMS usually were more dominant than lexical signs' head movement for other purposes.

Other findings from the SignStream CD-ROM were the morphological patterns, which showed a certain head movement matching a particular sign's meaning, and the grammar of plurality co-occurring with the head nod for a plural sign, such as READ++, known as head movement agreement.

Next, three additional videotapes of signers telling stories and lecturing in formal register were used by Cagle to analyze the speakers' head movements and resting hands. The three native signers included:

1. Edward M. Gallaudet, the first Gallaudet University president and the hearing son of a Deaf mother, in "The Preservation of American Sign Language: The Complete Historical Collection." He shared a story about a woman, Lorraine, in England in 1910.

   The total signs of approximately half of his speech were 542.
2. MJ Bienvenu, a renowned ASL teacher and advocate, and the Deaf daughter of Deaf parents, discussed social rules in "Deaf Culture: Social Interaction Rules," filmed in 1985.

   The total signs in this video were 272.
3. Keith M. Cagle, the chairman of American Sign Language Teachers Association (ASLTA) Certification and Evaluation and the Deaf son of Deaf parents, presented an introduction and closing message in "The ASLTA Evaluation and Certification System," filmed in 1996.

   The total signs of his speech were 83.

Table 1. Tally of Head Movements in Three Videotapes

1. Edward Gallaudet Total: 542 signs	126 head nods 54 head shifts 13 rested hands 3 head shakes	1 per 4.3 signs 1 per 10 signs 1 per 34.8 signs 1 per 80.6 signs
2. MJ Bienvenu Total: 272 signs	77 head nods 22 head shakes 12 rested hands 10 head shifts	1 per 3.5 signs 1 per 12.4 signs 1 per 22.7 signs 1 per 27.2 signs
3. Keith M. Cagle Total: 83 signs	26 head nods 5 head shifts 5 rested hands 2 head shakes	1 per 3.2 signs 1 per 16.6 signs 1 per 16.6 signs 1 per 41.5 signs

The method of analyzing the head movements and rested hands began with identifying where they occurred and then continued with analyzing the data. A breakdown is in table 1.

After patterns among the different head movements (e.g., head nod, head shake, and head shift) and rested hands were identified, their functions were classified into categories as shown in table 2.

Discourse Markers

- A. Rested Hands
  1. To end a sentence and paragraph
- B. Head nod
  1. To end a sentence/phrase
  2. As a covert (hidden) conjunction sign (e.g., BUT, WHICH)
  3. To note a time phrase (e.g., once years ago, one day)
  4. As a referent (e.g., THAT, TWO-OF-THEM, THERE)
  5. After a fingerspelled word or phrase
  6. Co-occurring with an overt conjunction sign (e.g., AND, BUT, THAT)
  7. As the topic of a sentence
  8. As a special function of a certain sign for GROUP
- C. Head shift
  1. As a referent (e.g., THAT, GIRL, THEY)
  2. To set up a new topic, role, or referent (e.g., ANOTHER, CHARACTER, GIRL)

Table 2. Head Movements (HM)

General Head Movements (GHM)	X-Head Movements (XHM)
*Bow (bow)	* Bent-down
*Head nod (nod)	* Look-up
*Head nod++ (nod+)	* Z-hand movement
*Head shift (sft)	* Circular
*Head shake (shk)	* Bobbling (up-down++)
*Head tilt (tlt)	* Shift side to side
*Head-CS (hcs)	* Side to up to side (curve)
	* Wobble (move sideways)

Grammatical Markers

A. Head nod
   1. As an adverb to mean "very" and emphasis (e.g., very-beautiful)
   2. To indicate plural agreement (e.g., GROW++, PATH++)
   3. As agreement with a lexical sign (e.g., ENTER, VISITED, WENT)
   4. As affirmative agreement (e.g., CAN, HAVE, IS)

B. Head shift
   1. As agreement with location (e.g., PATH, UPHILL, HOUSE, FARM)
   2. As agreement with a preposition (e.g., IN, TO, BEYOND, THERE)

C. Head shake
   1. As agreement with an RH-question (e.g., WHAT)
   2. As a covert (hidden) RH-question signal (e.g., WHAT, WHY)
   3. As agreement with negation (e.g., DON'T, CAN'T)

The data from the three videos demonstrated the multitude of discourse and grammatical functions embedded in ASL. This type of data is useful for interpreters to understand so that they can strive to make their work more easily understood by Deaf people.

MODEL AND LEGEND FOR HEAD MOVEMENTS

After the analysis of the videotapes and findings, we propose a model and legend with new labels for two categories of head movement for head movement transcriptions (see table 2). These notations make it easier to identify General Head Movements (GHM), although X-Head Movements (XHM) are complicated and numerous.

LEXICAL-LEVEL FUNCTION

At the lexical level, head movements accompany numbers, fingerspelling, lexical signs, and classifiers.

Numbers

Lott's research and presentation identified key head movements for numbers such as phone numbers, social security numbers, addresses, ages, and birthdates. Her work demonstrated that head movements are to ASL as voice intonations are to spoken English. The following is an overview of her findings.[7]

A. Head nods between groupings of numbers: Head nods are typically used between groups of digits when stating telephone numbers. This is also true for social security numbers, where a head nod is seen after the first three digits, then the middle two digits, then the last four digits.
   1. ZIP codes
      28655 2 (nod) 86 (nod) 55 (nod)
      20002 2 (nod) 000 (nod) 2

2. Telephone numbers
   555-476-0214
   5 (nod) 55 (nod) 4 (nod) 76 (nod) 02 (nod) 14
   or
   555-343-0720
   (nod) 555 (nod) 343 (nod) 07 (nod) 20 (nod)

B. Age: The number sign begins at the chin and moves away, and the head moves down at the end of the sign.

C. Incorporation of number: For time combined with the day, week, month, or year, a head movement is usually made for the number incorporation.
   2-WEEK—nod
   2-WEEK-LATER—head tilts forward (hltf)
   2-WEEK-PAST—head tilts backward (hltb)
   2-EVERY-WEEK—nod++

Accompanying number signs with head nods helps make the number clearer and allows people to remember the numbers more easily. The authors' observations demonstrate that Deaf people often ask interpreters to repeat numbers if there are no accompanying head movements.

Fingerspelling

New ASL learners often find fingerspelling in a prosodic manner challenging. This is especially true with reading and producing fingerspelling fluently.

Fingerspelled Names

When fingerspelling names, Deaf people usually begin with the head up when giving the first name and then quickly bow before moving the head up again prior to starting the last name. After they finish spelling the last name, the head bows again. These nods are interspersed and help distinguish between the first and last names—which is why saying FIRST and LAST (such as saying MY FIRST NAME, last name) is unnecessary.[8]

MY (bow) NAME (nod) (head up) fs-TONY (bow) (head up) fs-SMITH (bow)

If the name has more than one syllable such as E-L-I-Z-A-B-E-T-H (E' liz' a' beth), it typically will have more than one head nod.

E-L-I-Z-A (quick nod) B-E-T-H (nod)

Abbreviations

There are many abbreviations in ASL, such as the names of buildings, organizations, clubs and stores, and technical terms. Head movements are typically included in these abbreviations.

Administration	ADM	- bow
National Association of the Deaf	NAD	- small Z-head movement
Overtime	OT	- bow

Lexicalized Fingerspelling

Lexicalized fingerspelling, or loan signs, are fingerspelled English words that take on unique characteristics. It is a combination of signing and fingerspelling that has endured evolution and assimilation. For example, if we spell W-H-A-T strictly, we see the letters W, H, A, and T; however, in lexicalized fingerspelling, we see 5, weak-A, and backward-T. Thus, to indicate lexicalization, #WHAT is used. Accompanying #WHAT typically is a strong Z-jerk head movement to show disbelief.

Other examples include:

#EARLY	head movement will be circular
#GROSS	head shake with disgusting look
#LAZY	Z-jerk head movement

Fingerspelled Adverbs and Adjectives

Fingerspelled adverbs and adjectives may easily be the most complicated category, given the many head movements matching different adverb and adjective semantics.

English	ASL	Head movement
very mad	MAD!-	Z-jerk head movement
very sexism	SEXISM-	head tilt from side and to side repeatedly
very slowly	slow-	head tilt far back

Lexical Signs

Lexical signs are individual signs that often have head movement agreements, such as the following examples.

A. Bow (move head down)
Verb signs: VISIT, GO, SIT
Affirmative signs (modals): CAN, HAVE, MAY

Example

(bow over GO)

ASL: ME GO RESTAURANT
English: I go to the restaurant.

B. Head nod (move head down and back)
Referent signs: THAT, TWO-OF-THEM, THERE
Overt (shown) conjunction signs: AND, BUT, THAT

Example

(nod over AND)

ASL: ME WANT MILK AND SUGAR WITH MY COFFEE
English: I want milk and sugar for my coffee.

Note: This sign of AND is a signal of emphasis, since some signers normally do not include the sign for AND; some of us would use the nondominant index and middle fingers to indicate milk and sugar while signing MILK and SUGAR.

C. Head Shift

A head shift head movement often agrees with a new referent word such as *that,* pronouns such as *she, he, they,* and *it,* or a new character or role in a message.

sftsft (over HE) sftsft (over SHE)

ASL: ME WANT VISIT MY FRIEND BUT HE TELL-me SHE very-SICK
English: I want to visit my friend, but he told me she is very sick.

D. Head Tilt

A head movement must agree with prepositions such as UNDER, OVER-THERE, ON-TOP, and BEHIND, which creates the head tilt.

tilt (over CL:3-there)

ASL: SEE BLUE CAR CL:3-there
English: See the blue car parked over there.

E. X-Head Movement

There are many different, yet specific, head movements in the X-Head movement category. For example, to say "veryshocked" or "verybig," a Z-head movement could be used. Or if talking about a car going too fast on a curved road, or slipping on an icy road, the head movement will follow the deep curve or pull of gravity while showing the car with CL:3.

Another interesting finding emerged from the analysis with the three videos: a clear co-occurrence between certain signs and their head movements.[9] The authors, in observing the videos, determined that the head movement functions are at the lexical level.

Nod (rapid, single, or normal)	FINISH
Nod (rapid or single)	FUTURE, LIKE, YESTERDAY
Nod (single)	GIFT (GIVE), MUST, NOW, SURE
	REQUIRE, LIKE, BUY, PLAN
Nod++	REALLY, SHOULD, ENJOY, KNOW
Head shake (rapid)	HOW-MANY, WHEN, WHICH
	WHY-all WH-Q
	WHAT'S-MORE
Head shake (single)	VOMIT
Head shake (slow)	NEVER, NOT, SHOULD NOT
Head shake (regular)	NOT, NOT-LIKE, NOT-YET

Classifiers

A classifier, which is within the category of depiction (the visual representation of semantic components), is a symbol for a particular handshape representing a noun with specific characteristic(s) such as shape and size.[10] A head movement usually follows along with the classifier action. Below is an illustration of how classifiers are correlated with the nouns and appropriate head movements.

Noun	Classifier	Head movement
Car	CL:3-bumpy	head bobbing up and down
Car	CL:3-sliding	CS and head tilt far down to side
Ferris wheel	CL: bent V-riding	head moves in a circular following wheel

SYNTAX LEVEL FUNCTION

Note that there are some utterances with head movements, but there is no lexical sign corresponding with a head movement. Rather, the head movement functions such as the be verb, conditional, or negation. More often than not, the head shake for negation occurs with a verb or a phrase that itself is not a negation.

Function as To Be Verb (e.g., IS, AM, BE)

nod++

MY NAME fs-JOHN
My name is John.

Function as Conditional

head tilt, head shake

RAIN, ME NOT GO OUTSIDE
If there is rain, I will not go outside.

Function as Negation

head shake

POINT-at-she UNDERSTAND WHAT POINT-at-he SAY
She does not understand what he said.

We also identified that other head movements work in agreement with grammatical functions.

A. Head tilt backward (htb)

- Topic Comment

  htb, nod

  BOOK WE DISCUSS ABOUT
  It is the book we will discuss.

- Condition

  htb, shk

  RAIN, NOT GO CAMPING
  If it rains, I will not go camping.

B. Head lead forward (hlf)

- Yes/No Question

  hlf

  YOU HAVE CAR?
  Do you have a car?

- Timeline for future tense

  hlf, nod

  TWO-WEEK-FUTURE, ME WILL GO-THERE
  In two weeks, I will go there.

C. Head lead backward (hlb)

	hlb
• Timeline for past tense	TWO-WEEK-AGO, ME FELL HURT Two weeks ago, I fell and got hurt.

D. Head shake (shk)

	shk
• WH-Question with negation	YOU NOT COME WHY Why didn't you come?

E. Head-CS (hcs)

	hcs, nod
• Relative clause	SEE GIRL THAT, HAVE MY BOOK See that girl? She has my book.

F. Head-side-up-side (sus)

	sus
• So, then, therefore (hidden)	BAD HEADACHE (SO) TAKE MEDICATION I have a bad headache so I'll take medicine.

Discourse Level Function

The discourse level function in the following section discusses the utterance boundaries (ending of a phrase, sentence, or paragraph) with accompanying head movement; X-head movements in registers, and listener's feedback.

Phrase, Sentence, and Paragraph

In all languages, there are linguistic features that allow people to know when a phrase, sentence, or paragraph starts or ends. For example, in written English, we use different punctuation—semicolons, commas, periods, and even paragraph breaks—to create clauses, phrases, and sentences. Similarly, in spoken English, speakers manipulate their pauses and voices to indicate similar functions. For example, their voice may rise at the end of a sentence to indicate a question and/or to indicate the other person's turn.

Comparable features can be found in ASL. As we have discussed, the head bow, head nod, and head tilt are heavily used to mark boundaries in phrases, sentences, and paragraphs. Signers usually do a head nod at the beginning of their discourse and often use a head nod as a semicolon to break the text into phrases. Signers also often use a head nod for each finger when ticking off a list on the nondominant hand (functioning as a semicolon). A slightly longer head nod and pause indicate the beginning of a new sentence, and then again to move to the next sentence. A bow and rested hand with a longer pause is typically used to show a major new topic (new paragraph).

Effective use of these head movements are critical in making any signed presentation clear and easy to follow. For this reason, skillful use of such head movements during interpretations can greatly assist Deaf people in following hearing speakers.

X-Head Movements in Different Registers

In sociolinguistics, register means the level of formality we use when we speak. It varies depending on whom we speak with, where we speak, and for what purpose. Joos categorized five register levels: frozen, formal, consultative, casual, and intimate.[11]

Signers change their choices of grammar, signs, and nonmanual signals, including head movements, in different registers. Two of the more common registers are formal and casual. In a formal register such as on a stage, the interpreter usually produces a longer bow, head shift, and head nod so the audience can see the interpretation better, yet there may not be much use of XHM commonly found in less formal settings.

In a formal register, a longer bow indicates the ending of text, whereas a longer head nod may inform the end of a sentence. A longer head shift serves as a referent to character or point of time (e.g., moving from left to right). This can be helpful in following a speaker's outline.

In a less formal register, there typically is more unrestricted use of GHM and XHM. In a continuum, as one moves from frozen register toward intimate register, there will be more unrestricted use of both GHM and XHM head movements.

Listener's Feedback

There is a Deaf cultural and linguistic story about a courtroom judge who misinterpreted a Deaf defendant's head nod as an admission of guilt. The Deaf defendant actually was nodding to signal understanding of the interpreter's message, as part of listener feedback.A listener's feedback in ASL conversation is crucial and also involves the use of head movements. If this feedback, or backchanneling, does not occur, a conversation breakdown likely will take place. For example, when this breakdown occurs as a result of a lack of head movements by the listener, the speaker may repeat information based on the interference that the listener did not understand or missed.

Clearly, backchanneling is a very important function in discourse for any language. It shows that the listener is paying attention, understanding, and staying involved in the conversation. Such feedback also shows agreement or disagreement and can serve as powerful turn-taking and conversational maintenance tools.

The four categories for listener feedback are:

1. Nonmanual signals (e.g., nodding, head shake, ugh!)
2. Opinion signs (e.g., NEAT!, AWFUL, AWESOME) with nonmanual signals, including various head movements

3. Question signs (e.g., HOW??, REALLY??, REASON?) with nonmanual signals, including various head movements
4. Response signs (e.g., YES, KNOW-THAT, NEVER KNOW THAT) with nonmanual signals, including various head movements

Nodding is perhaps the single most powerful head movement for feedback. This basic head movement is used to show interest and understanding in the message. The next most common head movement among listeners is the head shake to show disagreement or lack of understanding. However, it is imperative to understand that head movements should not be confused (remember the judge example at the start of this chapter), nor should fake understanding be demonstrated with nods and smiling all the time. It is most ideal to show a mixture of head movements that accurately reflect the listener's comprehension and reactions.

Conclusion

As discussed in this book, students and interpreters must recognize the importance of using appropriate grammatical and discourse markers with head movements and nonmanual signals. By including these movements in interpreting work for speeches, lectures, presentations, instructions, storytelling, and other contexts in formal, consultative, informal, and intimate registers, comprehension by consumers will greatly improve. This can also help Deaf listeners follow the organization of thoughts and understand the speakers' points and messages more successfully.

To ensure greater interpreting quality, ASL and interpretation teachers should include information about head movements and their functions along with nonmanual signals in curriculum materials, including structured and sequential lessons and exercises, modeling head movements, and more. The students and current interpreters could do some things on their own to continue learning and incorporating more head movements in their ASL discourse and interpreting. They can watch and study Deaf people in their conversations, discussions, presentations, and classroom instruction either live or through a variety of ASL videos and vlogs on the Internet; they also can videotape themselves and ask their trusted Deaf/veteran interpreters to mentor them. By incorporating appropriate head movements beyond the basics in interpreting work, interpreters will notice greater comprehension among Deaf consumers and minimize the gaps often found in achieving fluency.

The Deaf man signed, "HEY!!! SEE ANOTHER BEAUTIFUL BIRD THERE," jerking his head quickly in the direction of the bird. The listener looked but couldn't find the bird and asked where the bird was. The Deaf man pointed. The listener found the bird, leaned his head in the direction of the bird, opened his mouth slowly and signed AWESOME as he shook his head slowly.

Notes

1. MJ Bienvenu and Betty Colomonos, *The Face of ASL* (Burtonsville, MD: SIGN Media, Inc., 1991), DVD; Byron Bridges and Melanie Metzer, *Deaf Tend Your: Nonmanual Signs in*

ASL (Pittsburgh, PA: Calliope Press, 1996); Keith Cagle, *1000 ASL Faces* (Austin, TX: Signs of Development, LLC, 2000), CD-ROM; Dennis Cokely and Charlotte Baker, *American Sign Language: Grammar and Culture* (Burtonsville, MD: SIGN Media, Inc., 1980); William Newell, *Basic Sign Communication: Student Workbook* (Silver Spring, MD: National Association of the Deaf, 1983); Kevin Struxness, *Mouth Morphemes in American Sign Language* (Los Angeles, CA: DeBee Communications, 1996), video.

2. Brenda Nicodemus, *Prosodic Markers and Utterance Boundaries in American Sign Language Interpretation* (Washington, DC: Gallaudet University Press, 2009); Wendy Sandler, "Civilization and Prosodic Words in a Sign Language" in *Studies on the Phonological Word*, eds. T. Allan Hall & Ursula Kleinhenz (Amsterdam: John Benjamins, 1999): 223–54.

3. Nicodemus, *Prosodic Markers and Utterance Boundaries in American Sign Language Interpretation*, 67.

4. Mary Thumann, *Identifying Depiction in American Sign Language Presentations*, Diss., Gallaudet University, 2010: 155–57.

5. Nicodemus, *Prosodic Markers and Utterance Boundaries in American Sign Language Interpretation.*

6. Dawn Maclaughlin, Carol Neidle, and David Greenfield, *SignStream TM User's Guide. Version 2.0* (American Sign Language Linguistic Research Project, 2000).

7. Sharon Lott, "Get a Grip on Fingerspelling" (Land O' Sky NCRID Workshop, Asheville, North Carolina, 2010).

8. Sharon Lott, "Get a Grip on Fingerspelling," presentation at Land O' Sky NCRID Workshop, Asheville, NC, 2013.

9. Edward Gallaudet, *The Preservation of American Sign Language: The Complete Historical Collection* (Burtonsville, MD: Sign Media, 1997).

10. Cokely and Baker, *American Sign Language.*

11. Martin Joos, *The Five Clocks* (New York: Harcourt, Brace & World, 1961).

7

Whose Professional Reputation Is at Stake? A Case Study

Tara K. Holcomb and Aracelia Aguilar

For the ASL summary of this chapter, go to https://youtu.be/aZJLip3cHrs

It's not easy being a Deaf professional. One thing we've learned as we navigate through this world is how important reputations can be in determining our relationships: our personal reputations, our organizations' reputations, and clearly our professional reputations. We've also learned that as Deaf professionals, we already come across as an anomaly to many with whom we work. We have to work twice as hard to prove ourselves as capable human beings and to ensure our messages get across. Moreover, to live and work in a small community comes with the fact that the personal is professional and the professional is personal. We run an organization, DeafHope, which provides advocacy, education, and services for Deaf survivors of domestic or sexual violence and their children. It can be a constant juggling act to ensure we build trustworthy relationships with the survivors who seek our help, the communities we serve, the organizations we collaborate with, the systems we navigate, the funders we are tied to, and the interpreters we count on.

We not only advocate for individuals but also for the rights of Deaf communities as a whole. Interpreting costs are often astronomical, especially for smaller nonprofits and those in private practice. Even well-established systems such as police departments and large women's shelters are often still ignorant about the importance of qualified and accurate ASL interpreters and are reluctant to pay for interpreting services. Our personal and professional reputations straddle a delicate balance between building trust with hearing-based systems and building trust with our Deaf communities. Through years of experience, experiments, and successes, we have learned how to tread carefully and form successful relationships. It is disheartening when we discover time and time again that the interpreters we count on to carry our messages accurately and to act as our allies instead focus on their needs and their own reputations. It is frustrating when Deaf professionals get together and find ourselves sharing similar stories of being undermined by interpreters working with us.

> In the spirit of transparency, we want to share that it was difficult to write this chapter. We considered the possibility that by sharing our story, we would be burning bridges with the interpreting community. We were warned about potential backlashes for claiming to know better than professional interpreters. We were advised to add citations and current research to validate our points. With all that in mind, we have decided to share our story and our thoughts as they are. We invite you on this journey with hope for a greater conversation to take place about who makes decisions and whose reputation is at stake.

OUR PURPOSE

Thus, the aim of this paper is to explore the dynamics between sign language interpreters and Deaf professionals. As we share our story about/of working with ASL interpreters at a national advocacy training program for domestic violence advocates, we ask you to consider questions such as: When it comes to the interpreting process, who knows best?; who do ASL interpreters work for?; who is the "professional" in settings where Deaf people aim to network and interact as equals with their hearing colleagues?; who should make decisions about how the interpreting process is carried out?; when communication breakdowns happen, whose reputation ends up being at stake?

Those very questions came up when we participated in an 18-month advocacy training program that included other (hearing) organizations across the country. The two of us were the only Deaf participants in a group of 40 people. We had such widely contrastive experiences working with different interpreters during the months of the training program that it became imperative for us to take the time to reflect and process what had transpired. We are sharing those thoughts, feelings, and conclusions with the hopes of furthering the dialogue on what "best practices" for interpreting means in professional settings.

Ultimately, we want to send home this message: no Deaf person is exactly the same and no situation is alike; therefore, true access for Deaf people cannot be neatly packaged into something that is "one size fits all." Best practices should certainly exist as a guideline for the interpreting profession as a whole, but they should never be used to silence Deaf people or even worse, harm their reputations. This only serves to disempower Deaf professionals who are the experts in both their respective fields and their communication needs.

WHO WE ARE

First, let us share some things about our backgrounds and the work we do. We are Aracelia Aguilar and Tara Holcomb, empowerment directors at DeafHope, a nonprofit agency serving Deaf survivors of domestic and/or sexual violence and their families in California. We work within a collective leadership structure with a third empowerment director, who is a CODA (child of Deaf adults) and a certified ASL interpreter. When we attend trainings or present together, we use ASL and request interpreters to voice for all of us. We made the conscious decision to have our hearing co-director use ASL at all times with us, even when she is around other hearing people. This is to show that we are all on equal footing at DeafHope and that language access is an important issue. Often when hearing people find out she is hearing, they defer to her rather than talk with us, or ask her to interpret for free for Deaf survivors so they don't have to hire legal interpreters. We use ASL interpreters frequently in our work as legal advocates, community educators, and trainers. Like most Deaf professionals, we are intimately familiar with how the interpreting process works.

It is important to note that we are aware that we are in privileged positions as professional advocates. We have more resources and tools to self-advocate than the vast majority of Deaf people, including many Deaf professionals. In this particular situation we are discussing, our hearing, non-signing colleagues at the anti-violence organization and the faculty at the training program supported our requests for access throughout the entire 18-month program. We were allowed to make changes we deemed necessary and determine what worked best for us without sacrificing valuable professional relationships or losing communication access. Other Deaf people are often not so lucky and we hope that by sharing our story and analysis, we will contribute to the growing shift that Deaf people are indeed the experts in their own communication needs and they are capable of participating fully in the interpreting process.

Arranging for Access

When we were first accepted to an 18-month advocacy training program hosted by a well-known agency dedicated to ending violence against women, we were thrilled. This was an opportunity for the three of us at DeafHope to polish our advocacy efforts while connecting with other advocates across the United States. The trainers had worked with other Deaf organizations in the past, they told us, and interpreters would be provided without any problems.

We were to participate in monthly webinars and attend three in-person training events. We tapped into our preferred local interpreters for the webinars and eagerly prepared for the first in-person event. It was out of state and we admittedly didn't give the interpreting process much thought. We checked in with our peers from another Deaf agency who had previously gone through the same advocacy program. The feedback we got was that during their time, some interpreters were great and others were okay. Apparently, the training organization had a contract with a local interpreting agency for the on-site sessions. As per current best practices for Deaf participants at conferences, we were told we would each get two interpreters (four in total), which was great.

Before we arrived, we agreed to meet first thing in the morning on our first day with the organizers and the interpreters to make introductions and get on the same page. All good so far.

THE FIRST TRAINING

Our hearing co-director's plane was delayed due to severe storms and wouldn't arrive until late that day, so we prepared to go through the first day of training without her. As soon as we arrived, we immediately noticed the interpreters. They were impeccably dressed and came across as professional, polite, and friendly. There were four of them, as promised, and we reviewed the room set-up and the day's agenda. The trainers shared that the format would be a mix of lecturing, small-group discussions, and occasionally a larger group discussion with all of the participants. There were approximately 40 of us, from domestic violence and sexual violence programs all over the country. We agreed that two interpreters would team up for the main speaker and the other two would be responsible for the group discussions. One would sit at the table with us to do ASL to Spoken English interpreting, while the other one would stand around the table for Spoken English to ASL interpretation. The four interpreters would rotate throughout the day. We were happy with this set-up because it allowed us to see different interpreters for different speakers, lessening the chance of experiencing the fatigue or monotony that so often comes with staring at the same interpreter for eight hours.

Keeping in mind that we had never met those interpreters before, we likened the meeting to an arranged date. We had no idea what to expect, but we did not really expect to bond with the interpreters immediately. We were prepared for them to need some time to get to know us and get into a good rhythm. We would be working together for four days. However, we understood that they had interpreted for this same training in the past and had a good sense of the materials that were being presented. As part of this initial meeting, we told the interpreters we were comfortable with them stopping us if we signed too fast or if something was unclear to them. We emphasized that we wanted to know if things weren't going well rather than them covering it up and making it unknown to us that there were problems or issues with interpretation.

During the first small-group discussion, our table facilitator happened to be someone who was familiar to us as she had worked closely with us on several other projects. She had conversational ASL abilities and was very knowledgeable of our work at DeafHope. Two interpreters were there at the table with us to facilitate communication. Our group engaged in sensitive discussions about gender roles and how our beliefs were influenced by our parents, particularly our fathers. One of us shared that growing up, her identity as a "girl" came along with strong messages of "Don't be a slut" and "Be nice and sweet. Be passive. Be a good girl." and things of that nature. The discussion was intense, and at several points we noticed the other hearing women at our table appeared uncomfortable. The facilitator interrupted us often for clarification. The situation didn't feel good, but we didn't know exactly why.

After the day was done, the table facilitator asked if she could talk with us in private. She shared that our messages did not come across well and there were some communication breakdowns. She knew our work and it was clear to her that something was off with the interpreting process. We were disappointed that the interpreters at the table did not once interrupt us to ask for clarification or let us know that there may be some misunderstandings. After all, we had made this explicit request of them earlier that day, and yet, they didn't say one word. Did they not understand us? Were we unclear? What exactly came across to our colleagues? We then asked the table facilitator for her opinion, from her observations throughout the day, as to which interpreter did the best job voicing and which struggled the most at the table. She shared that two interpreters were clearly more skilled and comfortable at voicing for us than the other two. That observation fit with what we experienced that day. She urged us to make changes for the next day.

Fortunately, our third team member from DeafHope arrived in time for the evening session. We asked her to please fill us in whenever there were errors in the interpreting process so we could correct them on the spot. The evening session included many small-group discussions that often turned lively and intense. We wanted the opportunity to make corrections if our message didn't come across accurately. In addition, we asked our co-director to voice for us as needed if the topic was context-heavy and required specific vocabulary from our field. We figured this was a difficult situation for all of us, including the interpreters, and thought this would be a good solution after the day's struggles. Our co-director agreed and said she would support us in this aspect.

The next morning, we shared our observations and concerns with the four interpreters and made our specific requests:

1. The two stronger interpreters were to interpret for all the main presenters during the training.
2. The other two would interpret for the audience and small group discussions.
3. Our hearing co-director at DeafHope would support the interpreting process by alerting us if significant errors were made by the interpreters in their ASL to spoken English interpretation. We also wanted her to jump in and interpret for us immediately any time we requested her to do so.

The meeting with our interpreters didn't go very smoothly. It was extremely awkward and the four interpreters were visibly uncomfortable with our requests. It was difficult for us to point out the two interpreters who were more skilled, as identified by the facilitator the previous day. We attempted our best to be cheerful and positive but it didn't seem to matter much. In retrospect, it wasn't a pleasant meeting for any one of us.

They agreed to our requests, though, and our experience was much better during the rest of the training. It was still awkward every time our hearing co-director made a correction or when we asked her to interpret from ASL to spoken English for us. It felt like a huge elephant was in the room and we just didn't know what else to do except to make the best of the days. We found ourselves participating less and less, and sticking together for support, encouragement, and conversation.

On the last day, one of the interpreters that we asked not to do the majority of the work came up to us. She shared that she was surprised at the changes we had requested and wanted to know how she could improve. We had a great conversation about how it's hard to interpret for someone "cold" without any prior knowledge of the Deaf person and his or her work. We shared that it wasn't personal for us and that we found the other two simply a better fit for us at the time.

Before we left for the airport, we went up to the main interpreter, who also happened to own the agency that was contracted to support the training sessions. We thanked her for her flexibility and willingness to work with us despite all of us clearly being uncomfortable. She told us it wasn't a problem and that it was her job. She was there for effective communication. We closed with a "see you next time!" We had two more trainings to come and assumed we'd be sticking with the same agency.

Aftermath

A few weeks later, we learned the owner of the interpreting agency, the one who we asked to become one of the main interpreters and who told us "no problem and see you next time," had contacted the organizers of this training. She expressed that we were being unprofessional and unreasonable in our requests. She said that her agency worked with highly qualified interpreters and that they adhered to the field's best practices. She explained that we had no business making arbitrary requests as to who would interpret from ASL to spoken English for us and where they should stand while interpreting. She felt we were inappropriate in telling them how to do their jobs. They were willing to accommodate us—but wanted to make it clear to the organizers that *they* weren't the problem. *We* were.

Again, thanks to the hearing table facilitator, this information made its way to us. We learned that our interpreters were describing us as being "unreasonable and unprofessional" to the trainers, who were also our professional colleagues and leaders in our field. We were immediately put in a position of having to do some damage control by both explaining and advocating for ourselves.

What Next?

After the initial awkward conversation with the trainers where we learned that we were labeled "unprofessional and unreasonable," we regrouped to figure out where to go from there. Those terms stung badly and we were genuinely concerned about the possibility of our relationships with those domestic violence/sexual violence advocacy organizations and their leaders being somewhat fractured.

It is fortunate that we have strong relationships with those in our field and that our work was well known by the organizers of the training and especially the table facilitator, who acted in allyship with us. The table facilitator was the one who first alerted us to the struggle those interpreters had in voicing for us and encouraged us to make creative changes so we could be better represented. It is ironic that those interpreters went to her first to complain about us. Fortunately, we were able to get that information and had the option to decide our next steps.

After debating whether we would be willing to work with that particular interpreting agency again and if we wanted to address those comments with them, we decided not to. For one, we were not from the area and frankly, we were still in a state of shock.

As we didn't see this coming, this experience brought out deep-set fears that are often present in Deaf people. If we make special requests, we are seen as difficult and risk losing access. It is almost as if we must be in a constant state of gratitude and appreciation if we are to receive support from the interpreters with whom we work. Any criticism may be taken personally and put our access immediately at risk. This mindset is so deeply ingrained in both of us that we struggled to make changes in the set-up when we first saw the problem.

The comments made it clear to us that those interpreters did not view us as part of their team; fortunately the trainers at the anti-violence organization that arranged the training did. Therefore, our energy was better spent in finding different solutions for our communication access and focus on maintaining and building those professional relationships.

We decided we didn't want to waste time attempting to reconcile with those interpreters and the local interpreting agency. They had made their feelings about us clear and we were clearly not a good fit for each other. We needed interpreters who were willing to adapt to each situation and do whatever was necessary in order to provide us with optimal access. Our professional reputations were at stake here and we did not want to expend our time or energy dealing with those individuals from the local interpreting agency.

We decided to ask the trainers to allow us to choose our own interpreters for the next two gatherings, even if they had to be flown in. Mindful of the extra costs associated with travel and lodging, we agreed to settle for two interpreters (rather than four). They said sure without any questions. Later, we did learn that there was some debate within their organization and the table facilitator had to advocate for us and our requests. Nevertheless, we were able to choose our own interpreters and arrange for them to come to the next two trainings with us.

The Second and Third Trainings

For the second of the three training sessions, we tried a new approach. We flew in an interpreter who was from the San Francisco Bay Area and had worked with us many times. She suggested a freelance interpreter who was local to the training with whom she had worked in the past. They were skilled in both platform interpreting and interpreting from ASL to spoken English. And best of all, they had no problem when our hearing co-director interjected with specific vocabulary or phrases as needed for clarification. In fact, they thanked her when she did so. It affected our experience and ability to participate in discussions in a positive way.

For the last training session, we opted to fly in two interpreters from the Bay Area that had worked with us on many occasions. They had been doing the majority of interpreting for us while we participated in this program's monthly webinars at our home office, which meant they were familiar with the content, faculty, and our progress throughout this program. Our hearing co-director also signed for herself and those interpreters were very comfortable voicing for her.

This allowed us to participate, really participate. And participate we did!

This is not to claim that those two interpreters were absolutely perfect, because no one is. The art of interpreting between two languages will always include some missteps. The difference was that they were comfortable enough to tell us when they weren't sure what the hearing trainer meant or when the context was lost to them. They communicated with us constantly throughout the interpreting process, asking for clarification or specific signs. They accepted feedback with ease during the interpreting process. We could tell them where to move, to stand, to sit, so we could be comfortable and engaged in the discussions. This resulted in us working together as a team to ensure our needs were being met and to make changes when we encountered difficulties. It was an engaging process on both sides.

We were there as professionals, students, advocates, activists—working alongside colleagues across the United States in this movement to end violence against women. We were there to learn, to discuss, to share, to cry, to laugh, and to connect with each other. For once, the interpreting process was a part of this, enhancing our experience rather than being a barrier to it.

Analysis

We wondered how it could be acceptable in the first four interpreters' minds to completely bypass Deaf people by complaining about us to the hearing organizers, knowing full well that it could have hurt us professionally and make Deaf people overall look bad.

After the training was over, we started to process this situation and talk with others in our community about this experience. We discovered that the experience we had was not unique. Deaf people shared stories of having to choose between accepting subpar communication access and being blacklisted by agencies if they dared to complain about any aspect of the interpreting process. Our initial fears were validated again and again—and we wondered how our experience at the second and third trainings would have been different if the trainers chose to listen to the interpreting agency instead of responding to our needs as Deaf participants.

It was fortunate for us, again, that we had a strong relationship with the table facilitator and for the organization's commitment to ensure we got optimal communication access. She shared with us the interpreter's comments about us and allowed us to decide our next steps for future trainings. Otherwise, we would still have been in the dark about our reputations being at stake with the conversations taking place between the interpreters and the training agency that works closely with us.

The issue here wasn't whether those interpreters at the first training were qualified or not. They were qualified. They were as good as many interpreters with whom we've worked. Yet, two were clearly not able to voice-interpret effectively for us. It was a highly complicated setting with multiple speakers and multiple formats. We were participating in some high level, sensitive dialog with other professionals in our field. Nuance mattered, context mattered. The fact that our interpreters took offense to corrections and clarifications by our co-director demonstrated where their focus was—on their own professional reputations rather than on providing the best possible interpreting services for us. This in turn had a negative impact on our professional reputations as Deaf women in a predominantly hearing field.

Who's Working for Whom?

In the first training, an interpreting agency was contracted by the training organization. Their point of contact was with the hearing training organization. The hired interpreters met with us for the first time on the first day. When issues arose, they went to their point of contact, the training agency that hired them. They did not view themselves as working with or for us.

This brings up an interesting question. Often, it seems logical to coordinate things without involving the Deaf person(s) so as to not burden them with the details of coordinating interpreters. In theory, true equality may seem assured when we can just show up at the conference and have our interpreters there, ready to go. However, in practice it becomes startlingly clear that effective interpreting practices rely on relationship building and trust between the Deaf consumer and their interpreters. This cannot happen without direct contact before assignments and ongoing check-ins during assignments. If hearing conference organizers hire and pay for ASL interpreters without consulting with the Deaf clients, then this results in Deaf people being left out of the picture. This may carry over into other areas such as offering feedback, making decisions during the interpreting process, and determining who comes across as the expert to hearing conference organizers and trainers.

In the second training situation, we personally hired our interpreters, and then referred them to the organizers to coordinate the contract. The initial contact was made by us, Deaf professionals. We became their points of contact. During the assignment, they checked with us frequently to ensure we were satisfied with the process. Within this context, it seemed more natural for the interpreters to work with us to ensure the best access possible for us.

In the short run, coordinating and selecting interpreters may be more work for Deaf professionals, but in our experience it usually results in more successful outcomes of the interpreting process. When Deaf professionals aren't given the opportunity to select their own interpreters, the onus is then on the interpreters to include Deaf people as part of the team and defer to their unique communication and access needs for optimal results.

Decision Making

Many Deaf people do not have access to "ideal" conference interpreting situations because of lack of information, lack of opportunity, lack of resources, or lack of support from organizers. This results in Deaf people, including professionals, who are accustomed to accepting the bare minimum when it comes to their communication access and diminished opportunities to participate easily and freely. This also results in interpreters who are accustomed to setting the stage and making all of the decisions without the real involvement of the Deaf individuals present.

Adhering strictly to standards set by the interpreting field—standards that were developed by and for ASL interpreters—disempowers Deaf people who have unique needs and preferences. If one interpreter voices better than another, why not be creative with options for teaming so the work is balanced out? If it's a small group with a lot of overlapping dialogue, have both interpreters sign at the same time. Having one interpreter on for 20 minutes then switching to another doesn't always work for every single situation. Often, Deaf people can share those preferences with interpreters and organizers when prompted, and we will share more if we learn we won't face retaliation for expressing our preferences.

Signing Versus Speaking

We have a strong preference for hearing allies and colleagues to sign for themselves even in the presence of hearing non-signers, when in small-group discussions, when co-presenting, when in meetings, whenever possible! Having direct access to communication is rare for Deaf people in many situations and therefore is precious to many of us. At DeafHope, we make it clear that all presentations and workshops we give will be in ASL. This means ASL interpreters must be hired, even though we have a hearing co-director, which is often surprising to paying entities who assume that hearing co-workers can also perform as interpreters. This has shown to be incredibly helpful in putting us on equal footing (as much as possible) when interacting with other professionals in our field. In the same vein, when we attend conferences as a team, it is equally as important for our hearing co-director to sign for herself.

This doesn't always happen, because we have encountered interpreters who are not willing to voice for a hearing person. In the training we discussed previously, the interpreters we worked with were willing to voice for our co-director, but they were clearly uncomfortable. It shifted the dynamics between us in a way that was difficult to get past.

Why is having our hearing co-director sign for herself such a big deal to us? And why does this seem to make so many interpreters uncomfortable? The dynamics around this are complicated and could fill another chapter, so we won't delve into all of it. What we want to do here is express why it is so important and meaningful for us to have hearing allies sign for themselves, why we believe our access to direct communication matters more than interpreters' personal comfort.

In situations where we are in constant contact with non-signers (such as four-day trainings), and communicate primarily through a third-party, it becomes exhausting to access information solely through interpreters, especially during long meetings. We are essentially listening (watching) the same handful of interpreters convey messages from a wide variety of people. When someone, such as a hearing colleague, can offer us direct communication in ASL, it becomes even more meaningful and a powerful act of allyship. Yes, that means those hearing allies take on some risk of having their comments misinterpreted, but that is the risk we live with on a daily basis as Deaf individuals. Allowing the space for ASL to be used freely between Deaf and hearing colleagues within a largely non-signing environment sends a powerful message and relieves some of the stress on the Deaf person. Interpreters can support this by freely voicing for whoever signs, regardless of hearing level, and accepting corrections as needed.

The Concept of Access

Is providing access simply working toward the best English/ASL interpretation possible, or is there something more to it? If we take the view that the role of the interpreter is to simply interpret, and optimal access means the translation between the two languages is near perfect, then it would be logical for the interpreter to control the process. Interpreters know how to do their job and how to best do it. However, we would like to support a different view as to what optimal access means. It means much more than superb translation work. Optimal access is to take the Deaf person's needs as a whole and includes access to the environment, not just spoken words.

Lessons Learned

We learned several lessons during this period about the dynamics of interpreting and our roles in this process.

The biggest lesson for us here, and one that we want to share with you, is the difference in quality and access that Deaf people experience when they are embraced as a part of the interpreting team. They should be regarded as experts in their own access needs, and allowed to give feedback as needed. Navigating through hearing-centric environments as signing Deaf people can be complicated. But when given the opportunity to work *with* our interpreters, we should be allowed to experiment and become creative to make situations work *for* us. What a great opportunity for growth there is for everyone involved when this happens.

Thus, it doesn't serve anyone well when we show up to important events with no idea who our interpreters will be, are given only a few minutes to meet and brief them, and then expect things to go smoothly. We realized that in order to be full participants in the interpreting team, we have to take it upon ourselves as Deaf professionals to be involved from the beginning. This means we screen, hire, and work with our interpreters. This is not always possible, especially when traveling, but it's something we need to be much more proactive about.

Another thing we have learned to do is to make it crystal clear before any event what our preferences and expectations are for our interpreters. This allows for the best possible hiring decisions to be made, and for agencies and interpreters to have the opportunity to opt out.

Finally, we learned that the term *professional* is fraught with complications in itself. Of course, we want *professional* interpreters who are highly qualified, not just anyone who claims to know sign language. But then, what if the idea of "professionalism" itself allows interpreters to claim that they know better than us about what we need and what is appropriate in interpreted settings? As Deaf professionals in our own field, we found ourselves feeling as if we were dealing with dueling hierarchies between Deaf professionals and professional interpreters. Whose needs matter most? Who makes the decisions? At the first training, we found ourselves having to fight our way up. Do we honor our interpreters' claim to best practices in their profession and defer to them and their needs, or assert ourselves and our communication needs in order to forge the best professional reputations for ourselves? At the following (second and third/subsequent) trainings, we learned that it didn't have to be one or the other.

Final Thoughts

We have found ourselves relaying this story again and again as we engage in personal conversations and professional discussions about ASL interpreters. The more we talked about this experience, the more we realized how profoundly it impacted us as Deaf professionals.

The blatant disregard of Deaf individuals' communication needs in favor of some theoretical "professional standards" needs to stop. As Deaf individuals who are often marginalized within our respective fields, we are forced to fight for our own access, for equal recognition within our field, and to prove our worth as human beings. We ask the interpreting community to not add to the challenges Deaf people already face in the workplace. We ask interpreters to recognize that we are indeed the experts in our fields and of our communication needs. By sharing our story, we are inviting the interpreting community to pay close attention to the issues that are raised in this book and work with Deaf people in creating optimal solutions for communication access and interpreting standards.

8

Harnessing Social Media as a Tool of Empowerment and Change

Leala Holcomb

For the ASL summary of this chapter, go to https://youtu.be/NaH4SlkN4cQ

> I had full access to communication and education through American Sign Language (ASL) and English all my life—until I enrolled in a predominantly hearing university as a doctoral student. I was initially ecstatic about exploring the world of inclusivity in a hearing-dominant environment and went in with a mindset of doing whatever it took to benefit from my doctoral studies to its fullest. I believed if I had the same level of access as my hearing peers, not only would I benefit from full participation in university life but also that hearing people coming into contact with me would be rewarded with new ways of perceiving the world.
>
> After the first week, my good-natured optimism was extinguished. I felt like a fish out of water, gasping for air. I was hyperaware of how much I was missing, how differently I behaved, how disempowering my interactions with people were, and how restrictive the environment was even with interpreters present. I turned to social media to lean on the Deaf and interpreting communities for their collective wisdom, allyship, and support.

Trying to transform an academic environment to become truly inclusive of signing Deaf students is a daunting task. Fortunately, social media can serve as a powerful tool to combat audism, particularly in identifying systemic oppression within university settings and encouraging Deaf students and their allies to create positive changes. Put simply, media can and does serve as a modern-day Deaf club or a virtual Deaf club that can help bring about much-needed changes to oppressive environments such as academic settings.

An Overview of Systemic Oppression

While systemic oppression may be different for every population, its effects on oppressed members are very similar.[1] Often, when a society is largely governed by the majority's dominant narrative, an internalized sense of inferiority becomes part of oppressed people's reality. Those oppressed people then come to see themselves as their oppressors see them: unworthy of having the same dignity and rights as privileged people because they are supposedly not as capable, intelligent, beautiful, or productive. This sense of inferiority runs deep and becomes embedded in their consciousness, leading to acts of withdrawal, passivity, and docility.[2]

The negative messages oppressed people receive from the majority society, both covert and overt, make rising above internalized oppression and challenging the majority view a formidable feat. However, privileged people, more often than not, carry a superficial, feel-good understanding of inclusion and perceive the token presence of a few diverse people in the room as a major accomplishment. If oppressed people become aware of the injustice, assert their place in this world, and/or expect to be treated as true equals, privileged people often perceive them as disruptive, unreasonable, and a burden.[3] This is an example of how well-intentioned institutions and individuals trying to be "inclusive" can still place system-wide constraints on disenfranchised people and limit their choices and access. For these reasons, it is crucial for oppressed people to rise above internalized negative messages about who they are and their worth, be critically reflexive of practices entrenched in the system, and challenge status quo in equity and inclusion.

How do we put an end to false promises and hollow goals when talking about diversity and inclusion? How do we make systemic oppression visible and gain tools to transform our realities of true inclusion? How can the Deaf, interpreting, and mainstream communities be engaged in creating a more equitable society that empowers Deaf individuals to be fully included? One way is to harness the power of social media.

Systemic Oppression and Social Media

Social media has helped change the way revolutions take place. Opportunities for people from all walks of life to participate in dialogues about their disempowering experiences and harsh realities skyrocketed once social media became widespread.[4] In the past 10 years, spotlighting injustices through the aggressive use of social media has sparked protests all over the world: the Unity for Gallaudet protest in 2006, the Occupy Wall Street movement in 2011, the Arab Spring in 2011, Hong Kong's Umbrella revolution in 2014, and the Black Lives Matter movement in 2016. Through social media, people now can share information, tap into community resources, and take immediate action, all with just a few keystrokes. Disenfranchised people now have a platform to share their voices, exhort the system to be accountable, and demand greater public scrutiny against injustice.

Social media has been a valuable asset in providing Deaf people with safe spaces to share their experiences with oppression and to find solutions for injustice that has been imposed on them. Although turning to social media platforms to create much-needed spaces of affirmation, resources, and accountability is a common practice for many oppressed groups[5], social media also provides much-needed opportunities for Deaf people and interpreters to come together to address access issues. Social media makes the re-humanization of Deaf people possible by opening up dialogues and highlighting their life experiences in a medium where interpreters can become active listeners and supporters. For example, when a Deaf person was hospitalized and became frustrated with an interpreter who was behaving unethically, he posted on Twitter: "Is it acceptable for interpreters to do this?" This question sparked discussions on interpreting standards, ethics, and Deaf perspectives. Because of the support he received on Twitter, the Deaf person asserted himself enough to request a different interpreter and had positive experiences thereafter. This example demonstrates how the Deaf and interpreting communities were able to alleviate this individual's negative experience by providing encouragement, support, and resources, all without necessarily knowing this Deaf person personally. Sharing personal testimony is a powerful vehicle in prompting instant solidarity nationally, or even internationally.[6]

Another example of social media operating as a space of support and solidarity, much like Deaf clubs did in their heyday, is the case of a Deaf employee at Auntie Anne's getting fired by new owners simply because she was Deaf. Her (hearing) supervisor came to her defense and shared the story on Facebook.

> The new owners came in to interview my crew and have them fill out their paperwork. . . . They told every one of my employees that they will have a job when they take over the store except for Keri. They said she is incapable of doing the job. The same job she has done for 1 year and 9 months. Steve, one of the new owners, said that she will need to get an interpreter, have the surgery to get the implant "thing," or take classes to learn how to read lips. . . . Keri has been 100% Deaf her whole life! She has NEVER had an issue working. She is completely capable of doing every position in that store and she has! Including helping customers! I just got off the phone with the new owners and they are also firing me.

The post about the firing went viral, outraging the masses. This enabled Deaf people and interpreters to lead meaningful dialogues with hearing laypeople about the prevalence of discrimination, prejudice, and audism. The outcome saw the Deaf employee and her supervisor rehired and the employers stripped of ownership by the corporate headquarters. All of this happened within a week, demonstrating how social media can pack a powerful punch in addressing injustice.

While social media enables activism, it also provides space for emotional support.[7] Learning to recognize and talk about oppression can help create a sense of connection and empowerment among those who experience injustice. For example, Deaf students who are "alone"[8] at universities have created a private Facebook group with the goal of sharing experiences, strategies, and tools to fight for better and increased access. They exchange information about accessibility laws, talking points that worked or did not work for them, and names of disability rights lawyers or organizations. While these resources are important, the emotional support Deaf students receive by having their experiences validated and affirmed by other Deaf students is invaluable. Simply being in the company of other Deaf students on social media can improve emotional and mental health as they struggle to survive in a typical overwhelming, non-deaf friendly academic environment.[9]

Not only can Deaf people benefit from the intentional use of social media, interpreters have much to gain, too. Some interpreters have joined Deaf-focused or interpreting-focused Facebook groups to learn from other people's firsthand experiences and perspectives, including how specific behaviors can function either as an instrument of oppression or of liberation. Ironically, since there is leverage in social media to discuss the status quo and illuminate oppressed people's experiences, many people in positions of power now view this power as a threat.[10] This will be discussed later in this chapter.

Alone in the Mainstream but Not So Alone in Social Media: Personal Anecdotes

Before social media came to fruition, Deaf clubs provided invaluable space for Deaf people and hearing allies to converge and come up with ways to address access issues.[11] However, the closing of many Deaf clubs has meant the physical spaces that served as breeding grounds for support and resistance are being lost.[12] As a result, many Deaf people feel alone in the mainstream as they struggle to articulate their needs for access.[13]

I felt this isolation and separation as the only Deaf doctoral student at a predominantly hearing university trying to negotiate for fuller access and inclusion. The determination to make myself more included in my academic environment found me running to social media for support. After all, I was committed to being the best doctoral student I could be and to grasp all the university had to offer. Through Facebook and Twitter, I was immediately plugged into the collective wisdom and support from Deaf and interpreting communities nationwide.

After sharing my experiences on social media, the intricate factors related to power, privilege, oppression, and my suppressed voice became clearer to me. Instead of looking at the struggle for fuller participation in my university life as a problem that was inherent in me, I began seeing the problem as something deeply entrenched in U.S. society, one that has enabled ignorance and an imbalance of power to continue for so many years. I also saw how the system was malleable, and that people had the capacity to steer it into one direction or the other. The discussions online were not only beneficial for me as a Deaf person but also for interpreters who could enlighten themselves by following and participating in the conversations. They understood better the stifling burdens Deaf students carried, and learned more about their role in helping remove such burdens rather than contributing to them. The interactions I had with Deaf people and interpreters on social media carried me through challenging times and helped me survive and thrive.

I also relied on social media as a medium to document my experiences and thoughts. Sharing my stories became a form of catharsis and stress reduction. Other Deaf people also relied on my stories to improve their own situations. Interpreters learned to relate my experiences to their lives and worked to bring solutions to their work places. The excerpts from my posts that are shared below illustrate how the Deaf and interpreting communities responded to the sweat, tears, and triumphs involved in my sincere effort to meet the standards and requirements that are expected of all doctoral students at my university. There were some victories and setbacks in my effort to work with the university to create a barrier-free learning environment for myself. Fortunately, the Deaf and interpreting communities were behind every step of the process, helping me feel less isolated and more empowered to advocate for my needs as a doctoral student. The most important takeaway for me is that even though we Deaf people may be alone in our respective spaces, social media can be a meeting ground for mobilization, and interpreters are valued allies. My experiences demonstrate how social media can have a similar impact to Deaf clubs in supporting Deaf people and how it can become an even more powerful driving force for accountability and change. Selected posts related to my experiences are shown below along with responses from the community, starting with the initial post I wrote on inclusion.

Social Media Post #1

Many hearing people value inclusion under the premise that Deaf people accept not having full access to their environment. When Deaf people make requests for change so we can participate fully in hearing-centric environments, we often receive a "no" for an answer.

If hearing people support inclusion on the condition that Deaf people must accept having less access than their hearing peers then that is not inclusion. That is exclusion. That is marginalization.

I completely understand if hearing people feel they can't provide what Deaf people need in their environment . . . then at least say it. They can advocate for Deaf-centered spaces, Deaf-centered education, Deaf-centered organizations, and Deaf-centered programs. OR they can advocate Deaf people's desire to have full access, and support the existence of these environments for us.

If they really believe in inclusion, then please put their words to action. Don't say "INCLUSION! Oh, you are too expensive. Oh, we don't have the services. Oh, what you are asking is too much."

Community Responses to Post #1*

Their idea of inclusion is to have deaf people in the mix, and they expect deaf people to survive and "make do." Inclusion is like a "feel good word". . . It is all about looks.

Deaf people did not create segregation. The society created it.

When I wrote the first post, I was wrestling with internalized oppression. I questioned if I was asking too much from the institution. The affirmative responses I received assured me that the university needed to be more intentional in removing barriers preventing me from functioning like the capable student I was. This assurance led me to take a deeper look at the ubiquitous "two-week advance interpreting request" policies found at many universities.

---

*These community comments are from actual social media posts. All names have been removed to protect the privacy of the responders.

Social Media Post #2

> Office of Disability Services told me for any events, organization meetings, special guest lecturers, meetings with teacher, or study group with peers . . . I must make the request two weeks in advance. Two weeks in advance . . . is this reasonable? Is this considered equal access?
>
> I am having a hard time understanding how the 2-week policy is acceptable or how it enables Deaf people to have access to their professors and classmates. When I brought this up, they made me feel like I was ungrateful for the access they were working so hard to give me. They said they only can work with what they have, and that a two-week policy was the norm.

Community Responses to Post #2

> Very normal. More ways for your hearing peers to have advantages that you don't have.
>
> Two weeks is way too long. You should talk with the disability office, especially that you're a Ph.D. student. Unexpected group meetings will happen. It'd be wise to find one designated interpreter to support you throughout your doctoral studies with a list of preferred interpreters to team up with your DI.
>
> I had an interpreter with me all the time even in between classes so I could schedule meetings with my professors.

Feeling empowered after reading the posts, I met with the Office of Disability Services (ODS) to express my concerns about this two-week policy. Unfortunately, the response was a vehement "no" to the change in this policy. However, they said they would try their best to accommodate special requests that were less than the two-week minimum. While I was grateful for the "special" treatment, I still felt stuck, as there were many last-minute meetings and requirements. Being able to compare policy and strategies with other Deaf people and interpreters working in different universities on social media was insightful and beneficial. There were other issues that made it difficult for me to function fully as a doctoral student. I was dissatisfied with accessing academic information through English only or ASL only; I felt I needed to have access to both in order to obtain advanced information required of doctoral students.

Social Media Post #3

> If having both transcribers and interpreters is the only way I can have clear access to classroom lectures and discussions, why deny that to me? Their answer is no because of cost. Now, I have to figure out which accommodation I am getting the most from: transcribers (closer to direct access, exact information in English) or interpreters (interpretation of languages but capture the nuances and tones of the speakers). I have to think long and hard on this and weigh which would benefit me the most.

Community Response to Post #3

> I formerly thought that CART would be more tolerable in the hard sciences when there could be very little nuance (such as math) but found that assumption incorrect when interpreters were able to translate using spatial information that isn't as readily available in printed English. Mind blown!

In an ideal world, we should have both. One fringe benefit of having an ASL interpreter in class for me back in college was feeling a lot less lonely in a hearing-dominated environment, being able to flex my hands in a flurry of ASL than being surrounded by English-only for hours.

Actually you (or anyone else) are entitled to have any accommodations, but not limited to one choice after another. You can have text-based accommodation *AND* sign language interpreter at the same time.

Prompted by this online support, I met with ODS officials to communicate my concern that the existing policy of choosing only one service did not allow me to get the academic information I needed to succeed in my studies. I requested dual accommodations so that I could access lectures and discussions more fully and participate more effectively in my learning environment. ODS rejected my requests as unreasonable, which unfortunately resulted in my relatively poor performance in the program. By that time, I was exhausted from always swimming against the tide by advocating for opportunities to participate fully in my learning environment. I began to wonder if it would be a whole lot easier if I simply settled for less and had a subpar educational experience as compared to my hearing peers. However, the input via social media energized me to keep pressing on for my desire to participate as fully possible in my doctoral studies. After all, I did not move across the country only to settle for a less than optimal learning environment at a reputable university.

Thankfully, with the involvement of my dean and department chair, ODS eventually acquiesced and provided the necessary services (designated interpreters, transcribers, and such) which allowed me to shine as a doctoral student. That was a huge victory, one that I celebrated on social media.

Social Media Post #4

After a long semester of educating and advocating for my access needs (with support from colleagues, professors, family, and most importantly, the Deaf and interpreting communities), I finally had a wonderful, empowering meeting today with the Office of Disability Services.

They understood the value of seeing Deaf people as experts on their individualized access needs. They understood the importance of empowering Deaf people to pick interpreters that fit them the best, taking into consideration their diverse signing and voicing styles. They understood why I had anxiety throughout the semester not knowing whether interpreters voiced for me accurately. The climate completely changed!

It has been a long and emotional process. I often felt like I was a troublemaker and that it would have been easier if I just put up with what I had than trying to fight an uphill battle. But in the end . . . it was win–win for both of us. We both, ODS and I, learned and grew so much from this process in positive ways.

Things changed because the entire community came together from different levels to educate and advocate for me. It really takes a village to raise awareness and create social change. I hope we all can do the same for many others who are struggling in the education system with their access services. Things CAN improve but not when the Deaf person fights alone.

Community Response to Post #4

I'm so happy to see this result! Kudos to you and everyone who was part of this successful campaign!

Because of you fighting for us the community, we thank you! We all should do the same, fight for our rights. The fewer speak up, the less rights we will get.

Well said, nobody should ever have to fight alone.

Way to go! We all advocate for ourselves and others throughout our lives as Deaf people!

The response from the community was affirming and inspiring. Instead of having interpreters assigned to me without my input, I now was able to participate in the process of selecting interpreters, ones that would represent me as accurately as I'd hoped for. To commence the process, I asked each staff interpreter to watch a video of my presentation and record themselves voicing for me. The ODS officials provided a transcript of each interpreter so I could read how they translated my words. While reading seven transcripts of the same presentation, the ODS officials and I were astonished at how it seemed like there were seven different presentations. The quality of the interpretation varied dramatically among the interpreters, with some making me appear like an elementary-school student with poor choice of words and awkward grammar while others were able to represent me more appropriately as a doctoral student. This process was influential because the ODS officials understood for the first time why I struggled all semester long in trying to work with different interpreters assigned to me. Clearly, being consistent in how I was represented to my professors and colleagues was important for networking and relationship-building functions critical to the world of academia.

Going into my second semester, with dual accommodations and designated interpreters, I finally gained some semblance of control over my accessibility needs. Despite the resources and support I had, being the only Deaf person going into meetings and speaking up was *still* nerve-racking and intimidating. I often think about what it is like for Deaf students in K–12 mainstream settings dealing with similar situations as mine, and the unjust burden on Deaf children and youth to speak up about their access. I wonder if Deaf students finding support and empowerment through social media would alleviate the prevalence of learned passivity. I cannot say this enough, but the support I had received on social media was lifesaving. It transformed my reality into something better and re-humanized me as a Deaf person. For this reason, I exhort Deaf and interpreting communities to provide support through this channel. Even though I was successful in improving the accessibility of the environment for the most part, disempowering situations continued to emerge.

Social Media Post #5

Two of my hearing classmates know ASL. The professor split the class into small groups for discussions. I ended up being grouped with two signing classmates and one nonsigning classmate. Since 3 out of 4 people in the group could sign, and of course, I was desperate for direct access to communication, we agreed to have our discussion in ASL. To our shock, my interpreters refused to voice for the hearing signers and would only voice for me when I signed. The situation became awkward fast, and the hearing nonsigning classmate was left out of the discussion.

When I asked them why, they responded that when we voice for hearing people, they always criticize us. Tell us we interpreted what they signed incorrectly.

I responded, "I understand and I wish I had that privilege too."

"Well . . . we are here to provide services for you, not them."

I'm going to pay the Office of Disability Services a visit again. I would like to know if this policy is normal or not? Did anyone experience this before?

Community Response to Post #5

This happened in my university, too. We had many silly interpreting rules created by a coordinator of the interpreting service at Office of Disability Services. No matter how much we tried to change the policy, she wouldn't give in. Fortunately, she left her position and a new person was hired. All silly interpreting rules disappeared overnight.

The field is changing. It used to be that the interpreter was for the deaf student but it's shifting to the perception that the interpreter is there because the situation requires it.

The terp is interpreting for everyone. If Leala's signing classmates spoke English instead, the terp would *still* be interpreting for them, English-ASL. If they sign, the interpretation would be ASL-English. Either way, it's interpreting, and the terp doesn't get to choose which language who decides to use.

The interpreters working with you are not following the Code of Conduct . . . they are putting their own fears above providing full, complete, and accurate services. The interpreters behaved unethically here because the consequence of their decision direct affects you, not them, in a negative and likely permanent way. And it hinders the class's ability to function as it might were they not present. Now the level of trust and comfort has been altered, sadly. If you have the energy, I recommend approaching Disability Services about their lack of professionalism. You deserve the best!

After gathering community feedback, I called a meeting with the interpreters. It was not okay that their discomfort and preferences were prioritized over my need for direct communication with my peers. My goal was to work with the interpreters as a team so that my ability to participate fully in my environment was not at their mercy. Surely, there were creative solutions available to turn this situation into a liberating experience for me. This experience demonstrates how interpreters can be trapped in the mechanics of systemic oppression. Turning to social media for ideas can help interpreters learn more about supporting Deaf people more effectively in their quest to be fully included in their learning environments.

All five of the aforementioned situations had positive outcomes for the most part. I participated more in classes, learned more effectively, and had a closer working relationship with my designated interpreters. However, it was not all smooth sailing.

BACKLASH FROM USING SOCIAL MEDIA AS A TOOL FOR ACCOUNTABILITY AND LIBERATION

There is power in Deaf people and interpreters tapping into the Deaf community's wealth of resources and knowledge through social media. Unfortunately, when people try to address systemic oppression on public platforms such as social media, there can be backlash from institutions attempting to conceal the realities of such injustices.[14] The silencing of oppressed voices is a common practice to help institutions retain their power and maintain the status quo. Ward and Winstanley said, "Discourses authorize who can speak, what can be spoken about, how it is spoken about and what should be taken seriously; whilst simultaneously marginalizing and disqualifying other voices whose speech remains forbidden or derided."[15]

"Professionalism" is a construct that institutions commonly use to suppress and silence People of Color, women, LGBT, working-class people, Disabled people, and Deaf people, especially their efforts to voice their struggles and experiences. Professionalism is often an obstruction to social progress in that people are expected to conform to hierarchical norms. Open discussions about equity issues that lead to controversy could be justification for termination or punishment. Even asking for help on social media could be interpreted as a sign of unprofessional conduct, leading people to feel less comfortable speaking up or asking for support for fear of retribution. A phrase to describe this phenomenon is *respectability politics,*[16] which means disenfranchised individuals are to go out of their way to assimilate into the dominant culture or risk being perceived as disruptive or unprofessional. Backlash can be covert and insidious in the way people in positions of power describe oppressed people who attempt to change the system as troublemakers, extremists, immature, disruptive, irrational, or rabble-rousers. It can also be as overt and explicit as threatening to punish them for talking about their struggles openly.[17]

In my case, ODS warned me that my posts on social media were reflecting poorly on the university and that my actions were unprofessional. They alluded to the fact that my conduct could lead to trouble for me. This form of backlash was a way to silence me for sharing my journey as a Deaf person navigating access in hearing-dominated academia. While my case shows a small example of the institutional policing of Deaf people and interpreters working to improve their conditions and hold the system accountable, there are parallels with structural disciplines under the premise of "respectability" and "professionalism" toward oppressed people in general in present-day U.S. America.[18]

How can Deaf people and interpreters be safe from backlash for utilizing social media to gain support, participate in activism, and heal? There are multiple ways, but all still involve risk. Some people turn on the privacy setting on their social media platforms and filter who can access their contents. Others form private groups on social media and invite people, like the Facebook group for Deaf students alone at their universities. Some interpreters provided support to me discreetly through private messages, which I found to be very encouraging and helpful. Currently, as social media usage continues to evolve, there seems to be no clear answer to remedying potential backlash yet.

Space for Solidarity and Healing: Looking Ahead

When the establishment lacks understanding and resists change, social media provides a significant meeting space for interpreters to show up and act in solidarity with Deaf people to end systemic oppression. With the shift from Deaf clubs to social media for support and healing, deaf students do not need to endure isolation and disempowerment any more. Through platforms such as Facebook and Twitter, Deaf people have the autonomy to express their frustrations, pain, and traumas. When we do, we receive support and validation that is not always available to us in our immediate environment. It is my hope that people reading this chapter will grasp how social networks can be a powerful channel in giving Deaf people the support they desperately need in order to not only survive in but also transform the society at large. Amna and Ekman said that people could be "standby citizens" who "stay alert, keep themselves informed about politics by bringing up political issues in everyday life contexts, and are willing and able to participate if needed."[19]

Interpreters who function and work with Deaf people in ending oppression by taking Deaf people's needs into account will help strengthen the relationship between Deaf and interpreting communities. Since interpreters can function either as instruments of oppression or liberation for Deaf people, making this relationship a complicated dance, there are many opportunities on social media to incite collective action and solidarity, which could lead to relationship building and restoration of trust between Deaf and interpreting communities. Social media is a virtual Deaf club and a dynamic domain for Deaf people and interpreters to work together towards full equality.

Notes

1. Leslie McCall, "*The Complexity of Intersectionality,*" in *Signs: Journal of Women in Culture and Society* 30, no. 3 (2005): 1771–1800.

2. Teeomm K. Williams,"*Understanding Internalized Oppression: A Theoretical Conceptualization of Internalized Subordination,*" PhD Diss., University of Massachusetts, 2012: 627.

3. Paulo Freire, *Pedagogy of the Oppressed* (New York: Herder and Herder, 1972).

4. Christian Christensen, "Twitter Revolutions? Addressing Social Media and Dissent" in *The Communication Review* 14, no. 3 (2011): 155–57; Nahed Eltantawy and Julie B. Wiest, "The Arab Spring: Social Media in the Egyptian Revolution: Reconsidering Resource Mobilization Theory" *International Journal of Communication* 5 (2011): 1207–24; Nathan Jurgenson, "When Atoms Meet Bits: Social Media, the Mobile Web and Augmented Revolution" in *Future Internet* 4, no. 1 (2012): 83–91; Clay Shirky, "The Political Power of Social Media: Technology, the Public Sphere, and Political Change," *Foreign Affairs* (2011): 28–41.

5. Lazaro M. Bacallao-Pino, "Social Media Mobilisations: Articulating Participatory Processes or Visibilizing Dissent?" *Cyberpsychology: Journal of Psychosocial Research on Cyberspace* 8, no. 3 (2014): article 1.

6. Tina Askanius and Nils Gustafsson, "Mainstreaming the Alternative: The Changing Media Practices of Protest Movements," *Interface: A Journal for and About Social Movements* 2, no. 2 (2010): 23–41; Manuel Castells, Mireia Fernandez-Ardevol, Jack Linchuan Qui, and Araba Sey, *Mobile Communication and Society: A Global Perspective* (Cambridge, MA: MIT Press, 2006).

7. Ting-Peng Liang, Yi-Ting Ho, Yu-Wen Li, and Efraim Turban, "What Drives Social Commerce: The Role of Social Support and Relationship Quality," *International Journal of Electronic Commerce* 16, no. 2 (2011): 69–90.

8. Gina A. Oliva, *Alone in the Mainstream: A Deaf Woman Remembers Public School* (Washington, DC: Gallaudet University Press, 2004).

9. Rachel Grieve, Michaelle Indian, Kate Witteveen, Anne G. Tolan, and Jessica Marrington, "Face-to-Face or Facebook: Can Social Connectedness Be Derived Online?" *Computers in Human Behavior* 29, no. 3 (2013): 604–9.

10. Shirky, "The Political Power of Social Media."

11. Carol Padden and Tom Humphries, *Deaf in America: Voices from a Culture* (Cambridge, MA: Harvard University Press, 1988).

12. Carol Padden, "The Decline of Deaf Clubs in the U.S.: A Treatise on the Problem of Place," in ed. D. Bauman, *Open Your Eyes: Deaf Studies Talking* (Minneapolis: University of Minnesota Press, 2007).

13. Mark Drolsbaugh, *Madness in the Mainstream* (Spring House, PA: Handwave Publications, 2013).

14. Shirky, "The Political Power of Social Media."

15. James Ward and Diana Winstanley, "The Absent Presence: Negative Space Within Discourse and the Construction of Minority Sexual Identity in the Workplace," *Human Relations* 56 (2003): 1255–80.

16. Evelyn Brooks Higginbotham, *Righteous Discontent: The Women's Movement in the Black Baptist Church 1880–1920* (Cambridge, MA: Harvard University Press, 1993); Jes L. Matsick and Terri D. Conley, "Maybe 'I Do,' Maybe I Don't: Respectability Politics in the Same-Sex Marriage Ruling," *Analyses of Social Issues and Public Policy* 15, no. 1 (2015): 409–13; Leilani Riahi, "Respectability Politics: How 'Activism' Hurts 'Professionalism,'" *Daily Nexus, University of California Santa Barbara* (September 15, 2015), accessed at http://dailynexus.com/2015-09-17/respectability-politics-how-activism-hurts-professionalism/; Brandon Andrew Robinson, "Is This What Equality Looks Like?: How Assimilation Marginalizes the Dutch LGBT Community," *Sexuality Research and Social Policy* 9, no. 4 (2012): 327–336; Woodruff D. Smith, *Consumption and the Making of Respectability, 1600–1800* (New York: Routledge, 2002).

17. Nadera Shalhoub-Kevorkian, "E-resistance Among Palestinian Women: Coping in Conflict-Ridden Areas," *The Social Service Review* 85, no. 2 (2011): 179–204.

18. Evelyn Brooks Higginbotham, "Righteous Discontent"; Jes L. Matsick and Terri D. Conley, "Maybe 'I Do,' Maybe I Don't"; Leilani Riahi, "Respectability Politics"; Brandon Andrew Robinson, "Is This What Equality Looks Like?"; Woodruff D. Smith, "Consumption and the Making of Respectability."

19. Erik Amnå and Joakim Ekman, "Standby Citizens: Diverse Faces of Political Passivity," *European Political Science Review* 6, no. 2 (Cambridge, UK: Cambridge University Press, 2014): 261–81.

3

Exploring the Specialized Areas of Interpreting through Deaf Eyes

9

Higher Education

Higher Expectations and More Complex Roles for Interpreters

Tawny Holmes

For the ASL summary of this chapter, go to https://youtu.be/xkAQANLuzLY

> As I sat in the classroom with 149 other first-year law students, I thought to myself, "This is it. I'm in law school." I smiled at my accomplishment. I then looked up to the interpreter sitting on the stage near the professor and shifted my gaze to the second interpreter sitting nearby. She looked nervous. I immediately became anxious because I realized that not only did I have to steel myself for the first-year barrage of Socratic dialogue, the foreign language of law, and prepare for the unusual approach that my grades would be decided almost entirely by my performance on the final exam, but I also had to make sure the interpreters hired by the law school would not hinder me from surviving the program. Fortunately, I did successfully graduate in few years, but not before I had to replace several interpreters along the way. In fact, I had to spend one year fighting the Disability Services Office to get the kind of access I needed to succeed in school.

Legal Mandates for Educational Settings: What You Should Know

After my experience fighting the Disability Services Office in law school followed by several years serving as an education policy counsel for the National Association of the Deaf (NAD), I have accumulated a sizable amount of legal information about the services that deaf students are entitled to under the law. I am sharing my knowledge here for the benefit of deaf individuals and those who provide them with access, especially interpreters, so they will understand the legal mandates for the provision of access in educational settings.* In the United States, by law, students with disabilities must be provided with the same opportunities as their peers without disabilities to participate in all activities and functions at

*Note: Please see the Resources section at the end of the chapter for more detailed legal citations.

institutions of higher education. For deaf students, communication access is the key. In 1973, the first Federal law, Section 504 of the Rehabilitation Act, was enacted to address the exclusion of students with disabilities in educational settings. However, it applies only to institutions receiving federal funding. More specifically, Section 504 mandated that all federally funded organizations provide for participation and benefits to individuals with disabilities.[1] However, it was not until the U.S. Department of Justice drafted its own regulations in 1977 that the words, "effective communication" first appeared, with a direct application of the law to deaf people.[2]

In 1990, when the Americans with Disabilities Act (ADA) was passed and signed by President George W. Bush, people with disabilities everywhere rejoiced because it expanded the intent and application of Section 504 to private institutions along with all publicly funded (state/local) institutions. Justin Dart, Jr., a well-known disability rights leader, excitedly proclaimed, "This law will open doors for us!" However, twenty-five years later, we know the doors haven't been flung entirely open. Rather, the ADA merely cracked the doors open and it's up to us, deaf and people with disabilities, to open them wider through self-advocacy and public awareness. To maximize the effects of the law, deaf people and those with disabilities must be well-versed in the specifics of the ADA. For instance, when it comes to deaf people and interpreters, the ADA mandates that public entities shall ensure that communication with applicants, participants, members of the public, and companions with disabilities are as effective as communications with any other non-disabled person.[3]

What does that exactly mean? What are "reasonable accommodations"? What is "effective communication"? According to the ADA, the type of auxiliary aid or service necessary to ensure effective communication will vary and in determining what types are necessary, public entities need to give primary consideration to requests for access. In order to be effective, these aids and services must be accessible, timely, and protect the privacy and independence of deaf individuals.[4]

There has been some confusion among educational institutions regarding the scope of various federal laws such as Section 504, ADA, and IDEA (Individuals with Disabilities Education Act) as they relate to educational settings including higher education. Over the years, the U.S. Department of Justice and other courts have provided a deeper level of understanding and interpretation of these legal mandates. As an example, the U.S. 9th Circuit Court of Appeals determined in August 2013 that the lower court was wrong in automatically dismissing the ADA claims of two high school deaf students in Tustin, California, who requested CART (Communication Access Real-time Translation) services. In this specific case, it was determined that although the access via CART was not legally required under a different law—IDEA—the request was appropriate under the ADA law.[5] The two words, "effective communication" found in the text of the ADA in fact set a higher bar than IDEA for accommodations. Accordingly, it is appropriate to compare the issue of access for people with disabilities with non-disabled individuals. In contrast, IDEA does not allow such comparisons, but rather, access must be individualized to each person with a disability.

According to IDEA, the effectiveness of accommodations is based on services being "reasonably calculated to provide *meaningful access* [emphasis added]." This standard became the benchmark for accessibility after the first Supreme Court decision directly related to special education. In this case, *Board of Education v. Rowley,* the request by parents of a Deaf kindergartener for interpreting services to ensure full and equal access to classroom functions was denied. The court determined that services that provided a child with *some* educational benefit rather than achieving *full* potential were sufficient.[6] This standard was recently updated by another Supreme Court decision in 2017, *Endrew F. v. Douglas County School District,* which added a slight emphasis on including the student's annual progress in determining the appropriateness of the provision of access.[7]

These decisions illustrate the complexities associated with the concept of *meaningful access* in general and effective communication specifically for deaf people. Appropriateness has been determined by court cases as to include meaningful access.[8] However, meaningful access according to IDEA is different from how courts have defined "effective communication" as stipulated by the ADA. More specifically, the ADA provides the expectation that deaf people have the right to 100% access, equal to their non-disabled peers, whereas IDEA does not. The ADA concept of full access was reinforced by the Tustin case along with three other cases. These cases led to the release of guidelines by the U.S. Department of Justice and the U.S. Department of Education on the definition of effective communication for Deaf, hard of hearing, DeafBlind, Blind, and visually impaired students in K–12 educational settings.[9] These guidelines made it clear that those students need more than what IDEA currently provides to ensure effective communication in their educational environments.

Although IDEA does not apply to post-secondary settings, Titles II and III of the ADA do. These mandates require colleges and universities to provide auxiliary aids and services to ensure effective communication for deaf and hard of hearing students.[10] While Title II focuses on publicly funded institutions, Title III applies to private institutions that are "open to the public." In addition to the passage of the ADA, the U.S. Department of Education had determined that Section 504 of the Rehabilitation Act also applies to colleges and universities and that they are expected to provide necessary auxiliary aids and services for students with disabilities, including interpreting services for deaf students.[11] In addition, postsecondary institutions are expected to ensure that all services and programs within the college such as internships, clinical placement programs, student teaching assignments, or course work at other schools in a consortium do not discriminate against students with disabilities by denying necessary support services for them.[12]

In determining the kind of access service to be provided to deaf students, Title II made it clear that primary consideration be given to the deaf student in creating the service plan.[13] Unless the college can demonstrate that "another equally effective means of communication is available, or that the use of the means chosen would result in a fundamental alteration or in an undue burden," it must abide by the student's request. Even if the college found the requested service to be an undue burden or a fundamental alteration, it still has an obligation to provide an alternative aid or service that provides effective communication. Title III also requires private colleges/universities to consult with deaf students to determine appropriate aids or services to ensure that students' communication needs are met.[14]

Further reinforcing the concept that people with disabilities are the most knowledgeable about their access needs, the Committee on Education and Labor in the House of Representatives emphasized that "an individual with an impairment that substantially limits a major life activity should not be penalized when seeking protection under the ADA simply because he or she managed their own adaptive strategies or received informal or undocumented accommodations that have the effect of lessening the deleterious impacts of their disability."[15]

To settle this issue related to the expertise regarding the access needs of individuals with disabilities, the U.S. Department of Justice issued a reinforcement with this proclamation that "the individual with a disability is most familiar with his or her disability and is in the best position to determine what type of aid or service will be effective."[16] While this information may seem complicated and somewhat confusing, the bottom line is that deaf people have a right to the interpreting and/or captioning services they need for any class and for any university sanctioned activity, on or off campus. Achieving completely satisfactory access usually requires persistence in working with university administrators and disability services plus some creativity working with the interpreters themselves.

My Personal Journey: Applications Within the Classroom

At the initial meeting before the start of the first semester at my law school, the assistant dean and the director of Disability Services Office outlined a service plan consisting of only one interpreter per class. This was especially surprising to me because the average length of a law class is two or three hours long. I found it necessary to ask the interpreter at the meeting to step out of her role and explain the standard practice (note: standard practice, not the law) to have two interpreters assigned for assignments that last longer than one hour, with a 20-minute rotation schedule. This is an example of how a Deaf client and interpreter can work together here to educate others. I also had to explain in depth the complexity of interpreting and translating, especially in difficult areas of study such as law. Such work would be mentally exhausting for the interpreter, leading to ineffective communication. This exhaustion would result in insufficient access to information presented in the classroom for me. In the end, the assistant dean found it necessary to instruct the Disability Services Office to adhere to the standard practice and provide two interpreters for all my classes.

This demonstrates the importance of setting up an advance meeting with the school officials. In addition, the selection of interpreters for the semester (and often the entire program) is an important consideration. Each deaf person has different needs or preferences for interpreting support (e.g., such as interpreting from spoken English to ASL versus transliterating from spoken English to signed English; strong skills in interpreting from ASL to spoken English versus a deaf person who chooses to speak for him- or herself). Accordingly, it is important that the interpreters assigned are competent to meet each particular student's needs. Again, this attention to specific needs is reinforced by the ADA, where it states that the client's preference takes paramount priority in determining qualifications.[17] Interpreters themselves can facilitate this process by being selfless and ethical and helping identify others who may be better suited to the task at hand.

Although it is extremely important to meet with the Disability Services Office to discuss the selection of interpreters, it is often necessary to interview the interpreters to determine whether or not the person is capable of providing complete access. It is critical to note that the Disability Services Office personnel are not qualified nor are they in a position to determine the competence of service providers such as interpreters. Furthermore, holding a professional certification, such as those issued by the Registry for Interpreters for the Deaf, is no guarantee that the interpreter is capable of working in a highly specialized academic environment such as law. For this reason, I always insisted on personally interviewing potential interpreters for my classes. If I found the candidate to blink repeatedly and ask me to repeat my remarks at the initial meeting, I would immediately rule him or her out. I found this action necessary because interpreters often get away with being skilled only in the expressive part of interpreting as opposed to interpreting ASL to spoken English, which was equally important to me. Even with skilled interpreters, I found it necessary to make arrangements to meet with them outside the classroom so they could get extra practice in "reading me." This was especially necessary for courses where I was expected to present in class, such as my mock trial assignment.

In my interactions with professors to prepare for classes, I found an interesting range of reactions to my being Deaf. For example, after the introductory class of one course, the professor approached me (while looking at the interpreter) and said that I could be waived from doing the one required presentation and write a second paper instead. I quickly declined the offer and explained that I actually preferred to do the same work as my classmates. I also explained that I should not be given special treatment if I did not request such accommodations.

Another consideration related to the challenges of classroom interpreting is the specialized vocabulary found in fields such as aeronautics, medicine, and law. Because these fields do not commonly have large numbers of Deaf professionals, the corpus in ASL for specialized terms typically used in these areas is limited. Solutions vary from one Deaf student to the next. Some people prefer that the interpreters fingerspell every word that does not have a commonly known equivalent sign. One drawback of this approach is the difficulty of keeping up with the pace of the lecture if a lot of fingerspelling is involved. For this reason, I employed a system where I suggested a new (temporary) sign to meet the specific need of that particular situation, following the rules of ASL grammar. I also asked the second interpreter to sit by me and write the "new" word on a piece of paper on my desk. More often than not, the words would be in Latin, which is the traditional language of law. The second interpreter also took the responsibility to write down specific information, such as dates or page numbers. This was necessary as it was practically impossible for me to keep my eyes focused on the first interpreter while she furiously interpreted the rapid-fire lecture of the professor, write notes, and keep up with everything that was going on in class. Later, as the vocabulary of law school became more familiar to me and the interpreters, the interpreter would exaggerate mouth movements as she signed the familiar specialized vocabulary. This was also necessary when a certain ASL sign could be attributed to several English words (e.g., court, trial, judge). This arrangement with the interpreters resulted in effective communication for me, because we all worked closely together to create a workable system. This is an example of how other Deaf students can lead their interpreters and work together to find solutions to the problems of interpreting technical language.

My Personal Journey: Applications Outside the Classroom

Being a Deaf law student, I had to face the reality that I did not have easy access to any events or meetings outside the classroom. While interpreters were routinely scheduled for all of my classes every semester, I had to make multiple requests for interpreters for various meetings and events, many of which were required by my professors. The policy of a two-week advance notice by the Disability Services Office was not working for me. The law school would often announce events that would take place that very same week or even the same day. I also had study groups or group projects that would often be planned at a moment's notice. Even though I tried to explain my responsibilities as a law student, the Disability Services Office coordinator stood firm on their two-week requirement. This forced me to address the issue with the dean of the law school, who thankfully sided with me and forced the Disability Services Office to be flexible with the advance notice requirement. He also allowed me the latitude of using the interpreters after or between classes for impromptu meetings with professors or study groups, as long as I communicated with the Disability Services Office.

In analyzing this issue further, the two-week advance notice is a violation of the law for several reasons. Students with disabilities cannot be singled out and be expected to adhere to a different set of rules than non-disabled students. More specifically, deaf students should not be expected to wait two weeks for any meetings or appointments if their hearing peers are expected or able to be available at a moment's notice. There must be a consistent rule for both disabled and non-disabled students—either a two-week advance notice is required for all students, with or without disabilities, *or* all students should be allowed to schedule meetings as reasonably possible. For this reason, the requirement of a two-week advance notice by many Disability Services Offices is neither appropriate nor legal. This also applies to extracurricular events or academic events such as career fairs, job preparation workshops, and guest lectures. Many of these activities are announced with short notice through a daily digest email or on bulletin boards. Recognizing the fact that it can be difficult to secure an interpreter on such a short notice, it is reasonable for the Disability Services Office to request for advance notice from the faculty or administration as much as possible and to try their best to fill the request. Having a staff interpreter or arranging in advance to deal with last-minute requests would allow the Disability Services Office to respond better to such situations rather than requiring a blanket, restrictive, and illegal two-week advance notice. Knowledge of both the institution's contractual practices and the law is essential in developing strategies to work effectively with Disability Services offices to arrange for accommodations.

I faced another situation where I was not afforded the same opportunity to benefit from my law school education as my non-disabled peers. As part of the required coursework, I sought a summer internship with the Philadelphia School District. Initially, I was thrilled to make it through two rounds of interviews, including one with a table full of school district officials. They seemed eager to have me on board until the issue of interpreting came up. Based on my understanding of the law that students with disabilities were to be provided with accommodations for all aspects of their education, both within and outside the classroom, I naively assumed that my school would be taking care of the provision of interpreters. With this assumption, I assured them that it would not be a problem. I also assured them that we could also write notes back and forth or use email as much as possible, thus reducing the need for interpreting services. Everyone at the table seemed relieved and nodded with smiles.

Once the school district learned that the Disability Services Office at the law school declined my request for accommodation services for my internship, they sent an email to me stating that they regretfully did not have any space for a new intern and wished me all the best. Yet, less than two weeks later, there was a general email announcement informing law students at my school that there were internship opportunities within the Philadelphia School District.

My next experience turned out better when I applied for a different summer internship, this time with the Maryland Attorney General's office. After my experience with the fiasco in Philadelphia, I managed to secure approval from the Disability Services Office for a specific number of hours of interpreting in advance of my interview with the Attorney General. My future employer also agreed to provide additional hours of interpreting if needed. In the end, it turned out that I did not need as many hours of interpreting services as I had anticipated due to technology such as instant messaging, video relay service, email, and texting. Interpreters were only needed for public meetings/events, staff meetings, and periodical review meetings between my supervisor and me. This opportunity had a happy ending as I was able to have a rich internship experience.

The ADA makes it quite clear that "postsecondary institutions must also ensure that other programs in which students with disabilities participate do not discriminate."[18] Yet, confusion remains among institutions regarding their legal responsibilities for off-campus activities such as internships, clinical placement programs, student teaching assignments, or course work at other schools in a consortium.[19]

Strategies and Recommendations

The first piece of advice I give to any Deaf student preparing to go to college (other than Gallaudet, NTID, and CSUN) is to contact the Disability Services Office to become familiar with their services before making the final decision to apply for admission. I also encourage them to reach out to either current or former Deaf students at the school to learn about their experiences with the Disability Services Office. Once they decide on a particular college and have been accepted, my next piece of advice is to set up a meeting with the key administrators (usually an assistant dean or the chair of the department along with an administrator or coordinator from the Disability Services Office) a few weeks before the semester starts. This is critical to prevent any unwanted surprises. These steps are especially necessary because access services and policies vary a great deal from college to college. Some Disability Services offices have strict policies such as cancelling the service immediately if the student misses more than three classes regardless of reason, even if non-disabled students are allowed to decide whether to attend classes, without any penalty. On the opposite end of the spectrum, there are Disability Services offices that are so efficient that they are able to fill last-minute requests for any course-related event or meetings.

Once on campus, it is always helpful to meet the interpreters in advance. Better yet, insist on being able to interview and select the interpreters who will be able meet your unique interpreting needs. It's also becoming the standard practice for the Disability Services Office to serve as a resource for professors to ensure appropriate access for their deaf students and other students with disabilities. For instance, explaining in advance the protocol for working with deaf students in class (e.g., the presence of support staff such as interpreters or captioners in the room, the necessity of captioning all films/videos to show in class) is always helpful. It is also helpful for the professors to know that the Disability Services Office can be of assistance in such things as adding captions to movies.

Furthermore, it would be ideal for deaf students to approach the professor before the first class to discuss specifics such as where the interpreter will be sitting/standing. Be mindful that no matter how simple the requests might be, the reactions of professors to requests for accommodations will vary a great deal. The key to handling adverse reactions by professors is to be well prepared for such encounters. One idea is to have consistent interpreters, so that they become familiar to the professors (e.g., having the same interpreters for each class, or each semester/year). This ensures stability, not just for the student but for the interpreter as well. That way, they can become accustomed to the professor's style, the vocabulary used in class, and so on. Another way to be well prepared is for the student to "take charge" of the situation and work with the interpreter to deal with a problematic professor in a professional manner. Sometimes interpreters themselves are the problem, which necessitates that the student deal with the situation. For example, I had an interpreter who would interrupt the professor every time he couldn't hear well or missed something. This irritated the professor so much that he gave me a dirty look. To resolve this problem, I immediately raised my hands in mock surrender and pointed to the interpreter as if to say "It's all on her." After class, I sternly told the interpreter to not interrupt the professor again and to rely upon the second interpreter to assist her as needed.

If you are expected to give class presentations, working closely with interpreters is critical to ensure accurate representation of your work. Be sure to meet with them before giving a presentation to review the contents of your work including technical concepts, specifics and register of vocabulary, and intended emphasis and tone. Be sure that your interpreters are included in the email loop or are part of the online learning management system of your class. That way they will receive all of the handouts and announcements, just like you and your classmates, and be on top of things. The interpreters should also be supplied by the Disability Services Office with the textbook used in the course.

Even with all of these supports in place, if deaf students' access needs are not being adequately met by their interpreters resulting in less than optimal access to learning, Deaf students can reserve the right to make a request for a replacement. Students are entitled to pursue legal actions if their access to learning is denied by anyone on campus including the professors, disability services personnel, or even college administration.

If there is an issue, the first and often simplest step is to discuss concerns directly with the person preventing the student from having access, whether it is done purposely or not. This could be the professor who refuses to allow accommodations in the classroom, the interpreter who cannot interpret well enough for the student to understand the lecture or to represent the student when voice interpreting for him, or the Disability Services Office personnel who deny the student's request. If the student's concern is not resolved, follow up with an email to the Disability Services Office director outlining the complaint with a copy sent to appropriate administrators within the academic department. It is important to be specific with the complaint and include as much evidence possible. Evidence can include an audiogram, a log of dates/times that the interpreter did not show up, failing grades due to the lack or quality of the accommodations, or any emails that have relevant information. It is also helpful to cite the law that is relevant to the situation. Even better, include the website URL or citations outlining the federal mandates. If students continue having difficulty negotiating the sort of services they desire and need help advocating for themselves, they should contact a local deaf services agency or disability rights agency.

If the problem is still not solved to the student's satisfaction within the college, he or she can proceed and file a formal complaint. If the student is enrolled at a public institution such as a state university or community college, then he or she can file an ADA Title II complaint with the U.S. Department of Justice Civil Rights Division, Disability Rights Section within 180 days from the date of the discrimination. If the institution is private, then the complaint should be made under ADA Title III. There is no time limit for filing ADA Title III complaints; however, it is advisable to file sooner than later. An alternate or additional course of action is to file a complaint with the U.S. Department of Education Office of Civil Rights, which protects students attending institutions of higher education receiving federal funds such as student loans guaranteed by the federal government. Another place to file a complaint is through Section 504 of the Rehabilitation Act (applies to all colleges and universities that receive federal financial assistance) within 180 days of the discrimination. Websites and links to all of these federal agencies and filings can be found online.

Other than filing a complaint with the federal government, students also may seek legal representation and file a lawsuit in state or federal court. The National Association of the Deaf regularly provides resources to students in such situations by representing them, or educating them about their legal rights or referring them to an appropriate lawyer.

Conclusion

It's never easy to take formal action to address discrimination and oppression. In doing so, students can be seen as "troublemakers" by the college and can face years of struggle in getting their issues resolved, especially if the college administration is adamant about their position. The on-going struggle can also distract them from their studies and their goal of getting a college degree. However, persistence can pay off. It is important for the students to be clear and consistent when making accommodation requests. It is necessary to be pleasant but firm when discussing the issues and concerns with college personnel. It's always helpful to communicate in advance what the needs are. Ultimately, it is the college's responsibility to provide *all* students with opportunities to benefit from the college life.

Resources

Books

National Association of the Deaf. (2015). *Legal rights: The guide for deaf and hard of hearing people* (6th ed.). Washington, DC: Gallaudet University Press.

Legal citations

Section 504 of the Rehabilitation Act (Section 504, 29 U.S.C. Sec. 794 (a))

"No otherwise qualified individual with a disability . . . shall, solely by reason of her or his disability, be excluded from the participation in, be denied the benefits of, or be subjected to discrimination under any program or activity receiving Federal financial assistance or under any program or activity conducted by any Executive agency or by the United States Postal Service."

Effective Communication by Federal agencies under Section 504 (28 C.F.R. Part 39.160)

(a) The agency shall take appropriate steps to ensure effective communication with applicants, participants, personnel of other Federal entities, and members of the public.

(1) The agency shall furnish appropriate auxiliary aids where necessary to afford a handicapped person an equal opportunity to participate

in, and enjoy the benefits of, a program or activity conducted by the agency.

(i) In determining what type of auxiliary aid is necessary, the agency shall give primary consideration to the requests of the handicapped person.

(ii) The agency need not provide individually prescribed devices, readers for personal use or study, or other devices of a personal nature.

(2) Where the agency communicates with applicants and beneficiaries by telephone, telecommunication devices for deaf persons (TDD's) or equally effective telecommunication systems shall be used.

(b) The agency shall ensure that interested persons, including persons with impaired vision or hearing, can obtain information as to the existence and location of accessible services, activities, and facilities.

(c) The agency shall provide signage at a primary entrance to each of its inaccessible facilities, directing users to a location at which they can obtain information about accessible facilities. The international symbol for accessibility shall be used at each primary entrance of an accessible facility.

(d) This section does not require the agency to take any action that it can demonstrate would result in a fundamental alteration in the nature of a program or activity or in undue financial and administrative burdens. In those circumstances where agency personnel believe that the proposed action would fundamentally alter the program or activity or would result in undue financial and administrative burdens, the agency has the burden of proving that compliance with §39.160 would result in such alteration or burdens. The decision that compliance would result in such alteration or burdens must be made by the Attorney General or his or her designee after considering all agency resources available for use in the funding and operation of the conducted program or activity, and must be accompanied by a written statement of the reasons for reaching that conclusion. If an action required to comply with this section would result in such an alteration or such burdens, the agency shall take any other action that would not result in such an alteration or such burdens but would nevertheless ensure that, to the maximum extent possible, handicapped persons receive the benefits and services of the program or activity.

Effective Communication by Public Entities (28 C.F.R. § 36.303(c)(1))

A public accommodation shall furnish appropriate auxiliary aids and services where necessary to ensure effective communication with individuals with disabilities. This includes an obligation to provide effective communication to companions who are individuals with disabilities.

(28 C.F.R. §35.160(a)(1))

A public entity shall take appropriate steps to ensure that communications with applicants, participants, members of the public, and companions with disabilities are as effective as communications with others.

Types of Aids and Services for Effective Communication, Public (28 CFR § 36.303, (c)(ii))
The type of auxiliary aid or service necessary to ensure effective communication will vary in accordance with the method of communication used by the individual; the nature, length, and complexity of the communication involved; and the context in which the communication is taking place. A public accommodation should consult with individuals with disabilities whenever possible to determine what type of auxiliary aid is needed to ensure effective communication, but the ultimate decision as to what measures to take rests with the public accommodation, provided that the method chosen results in effective communication. In order to be effective, auxiliary aids and services must be provided in accessible formats, in a timely manner, and in such a way as to protect the privacy and independence of the individual with a disability.

Provision of Auxiliary Aids under Section 504 (34 C.F.R. §104.44(d))
(1) A recipient to which this subpart applies shall take such steps as are necessary to ensure that no handicapped student is denied the benefits of, excluded from participation in, or otherwise subjected to discrimination because of the absence of educational auxiliary aids for students with impaired sensory, manual, or speaking skills.
(2) Auxiliary aids may include taped texts, interpreters or other effective methods of making orally delivered materials available to students with hearing impairments, readers in libraries for students with visual impairments, classroom equipment adapted for use by students with manual impairments, and other similar services and actions. Recipients need not provide attendants, individually prescribed devices, readers for personal use or study, or other devices or services of a personal nature.

Participation in Activities Outside of Class s under Section 504 (34 C.F.R. § 104.43(b))
(b) A recipient to which this subpart applies that considers participation by students in education programs or activities not operated wholly by the recipient as part of, or equivalent to, and education program or activity operated by the recipient shall assure itself that the other education program or activity, as a whole, provides an equal opportunity for the participation of qualified handicapped persons.

Title II for State and Local Government Services (28 C.F.R. §35.160(b)(2))
The type of auxiliary aid or service necessary to ensure effective communication will vary in accordance with the method of communication used by the individual; the nature, length, and complexity of the communication involved; and the context in which the communication is taking place. In determining what types of auxiliary aids and services are necessary, a public entity shall give primary consideration to the requests of individuals with disabilities. In order to be effective, auxiliary aids and services must be provided in accessible formats, in a timely manner, and in such a way as to protect the privacy and independence of the individual with a disability.

Websites

ADA general website by U.S. Department of Justice: https://www.ada.gov/

Frequently Asked Questions for Effective Communication
https://www.ada.gov/doe_doj_eff_comm/doe_doj_eff_comm_faqs.htm

ADA National Network: Information, Guidance, and Training
What is the Americans with Disabilities Act (ADA)?
https://adata.org/learn-about-ada
Postsecondary Institutions and Students with Disabilities
https://adata.org/factsheet/postsecondary
Effective Communication
https://adata.org/factsheet/communication

Higher Education Compliance Alliance
http://www.higheredcompliance.org/resources/disabilities-accommodations.html

National Association of the Deaf: www.nad.org
Higher Education: Position Statements
https://www.nad.org/resources/education/higher-education/
https://www.nad.org/about-us/position-statements/position-statement-on-colleges-and-universities/
https://www.nad.org/resources/education/higher-education/private-colleges-and-other-post-secondary-institutions/
How to File a Complaint under Discrimination in Higher Education
https://www.nad.org/resources/how-to-file-a-complaint/
ADA Vlog Series
ADA25: #8 of 25—Higher Education
https://www.youtube.com/watch?v=cGWgGJPb9S0

National Deaf Center: https://www.nationaldeafcenter.org/
Americans with Disabilities Act (ADA) Video
https://www.nationaldeafcenter.org/get-resources/current-resources/americans-disabilities-act-ada-video
Disability Services Handbook Templates
https://www.nationaldeafcenter.org/get-resources/current-resources/disability-services-handbook-templates-revision
Hiring Qualified Sign Language Interpreters
https://www.nationaldeafcenter.org/get-resources/current-resources/hiring-qualified-sign-language-interpreters
Sign Language Interpreters in the Classroom
https://www.nationaldeafcenter.org/get-resources/current-resources/sign-language-interpreters-classroom
Dual Accommodations: Interpreters and Speech-to-Text Services
https://www.nationaldeafcenter.org/get-resources/current-resources/dual-accommodations-interpreters-and-speech-text-services

PACER Center: Q & A on ADA
http://www.pacer.org/publications/adaqa/504.asp
U.S. Department of Education Office of Civil Rights
Students with Disabilities Preparing for Postsecondary Education
https://www2.ed.gov/about/offices/list/ocr/transition.html
Auxiliary Aids and Services for Postsecondary Students with Disabilities
https://www2.ed.gov/about/offices/list/ocr/docs/auxaids.html

Notes

1. Section 504, 29 U.S.C. Sec. 794 (a).
2. 28 C.F.R. Part 39.160.
3. 28 C.F.R. § 36.303(c)(1), 28 C.F.R. §35.160(a)(1).
4. 28 CFR § 36.303, (c)(ii).
5. *K.M. v. Tustin Unified School District,* 725 F.3d 1088 (9th Cir. 2013), cert. denied 134 S.Ct. 1493 (2014), cert. denied 134 S.Ct. 1494 (2014).
6. *Board of Education of Hendrick Hudson Central School District, Westchester County v. Rowley*, 458 US 176 (1982).
7. *Endrew F. v. Douglas County School District,* 580 U.S. ____ (2017).
8. https://www2.ed.gov/parents/needs/speced/iepguide/index.html
9. USDOE and USDOJ, 2014, https://www2.ed.gov/policy/speced/guid/idea/memosdcltrs/doe-doj-eff-comm-faqs.pdf
10. 28 C.F.R. §§35.160, 36.303.
11. 34 C.F.R. §104.44(d).
12. 34 C.F.R. § 104.43(b).
13. 28 C.F.R. §35.160(b)(2).
14. https://www.ada.gov/doe_doj_eff_comm/doe_doj_eff_comm_faqs.htm
15. H.R. REP. NO. 110-730, pt. 1, at 15 (2008).
16. USDOJ, "Americans with Disabilities Act," Title II Technical Assistance Manual, http://www.ada.gov/taman2.html
17. https://www.ada.gov/doe_doj_eff_comm/doe_doj_eff_comm_faqs.htm
18. 34 C.F.R. § 104.43(b).
19. National Association of the Deaf, *Legal rights: The guide for deaf and hard of hearing people* (6th ed.) (Washington, DC: Gallaudet University Press, 2015),103.

Through the Eyes of Deaf Academics 10

Interpreting in the Context of Higher Education

David H. Smith and Paul W. Ogden

For the ASL summary of this chapter, go to https://youtu.be/YbFHq-15hb0

> This story is common to both authors: We are giving an important presentation in front of a number of prestigious faculty from other universities, most of whom are hearing and not that familiar with Deaf issues. We were assured by the organizers that the interpreters they provided were certified and qualified to do the job. They were provided our presentation materials well in advance and we met with them beforehand to go over the terminology and answer any questions they had. While presenting, we often watch our interpreters carefully and try to lip-read them. Whenever it appears that they are not voicing the correct terminology we repeat or rephrase ourselves. It seems like we do not have to correct them too often. In the audience are a few hearing people who know ASL fluently. After the presentation is over and everything seems fine, the ASL fluent individuals tell us the interpreters did a very poor job, voicing in such a way as to make our messages disjointed, confusing, and often substituting our academic terminology with common English words that sometimes were not even conceptually accurate. This is not the first time this has happened. This is actually a generic scenario that fairly describes more than a few specific incidences. The question that comes to us in these situations is this: Can we trust that the interpreter is voicing exactly what we want them to say? Why is it that we often have to watch them carefully when we should be free to focus on making eye contact with our audience?

Trust and *allyship*. These are two key words in any relationship between a Deaf professional and interpreters. The scenario we just described is one of the various situations, some quite disempowering, that we have faced as faculty members. Off-campus situations like this one provide both Deaf academics and interpreters less control than they would like to have due to lack of familiarity with each other. We have been able to empower ourselves as faculty through our long-term allyships and built up trust with the interpreters we work with frequently. How do we develop such a positive relationship? We do have some suggestions to share here.

Think of this chapter as sort of a guidebook that we never wrote in all our years of working with both interns and professional interpreters not yet familiar with higher education. We are writing this for both interpreters and Deaf academics. Although our focus is more geared toward working with higher education faculty, many situations here can also apply to roles such as adjunct faculty and graduate assistants. We will not discuss the administrative details frequently faced while accessing qualified interpreters.[1] First, we will focus more on the content knowledge, ethics, and socio-cultural issues that interpreters need to be aware of in higher education settings. Next, we will share some of the unwritten rules of academics in higher education and gaffes to avoid. Then, we will cover some of the more practical issues of interpreting in academic settings and work related social events. The more interpreters understand the unique challenges of Deaf faculty, the better they will be able to avoid actions that are inadvertently disempowering. Keep in mind we are not asking interpreters to empower us or act as interlocutors but to be allies to give us awareness of our situations so appropriate action can be taken as the need arises.

Role Reversal: We Are Not Students Any More

In higher education, and actually most educational settings, the Deaf person has traditionally been a somewhat passive student or client in a recipient role. In the past few decades, the number of Deaf faculty in higher education has increased tremendously.[2] Thus, we have more and more Deaf individuals shifting roles from a receiver of service as a student and client to that of the active provider upon becoming a faculty member, or before that as a graduate teaching assistant. This trend has caught a lot of institutions of higher education off guard as they try to accommodate the different needs of their new Deaf academics.[3] In a reversal of roles, new Deaf faculty are now the ones dealing with students and other faculty and staff in either an authoritative role or as a colleague and peer. Their needs are dramatically different from that of a student and the demands placed on interpreters also shift.

By different needs, we are talking in terms of a distinctive set of workplace demands. A basic example would be "problem students." We all have them: the ones who cheat or plagiarize, who complain about everything, beg us for better grades, or behave disruptively in class. And yes, there are those who will try to take advantage of our being deaf by such acts as whispering to each other under their breath during examinations. Obviously we need to address these situations in meetings with these students. We typically brief our interpreters before these meetings. Interpreters should be familiar with the written student code of conduct and know the course syllabus. They also need to be sure not to unintentionally change or "soften" the intent of our messages when we take disciplinary actions as can happen due to gender or cultural differences between Deaf people in positions of authority and interpreters.[4]

Another situation is working in department or college committees. Obviously politics comes into play here. These could be mutually respectful and friendly settings or could involve bitter factions and arguments. Thus far, we have been fortunate that most of our own meetings are the collegial sort, but yes, we have also been embroiled in some rather sticky situations. Having background knowledge and knowing written university policy is good for interpreters, of course, particularly related to promotion and tenure. Deaf academics should remember to brief their interpreters on the purpose of meetings and what sort of politics or hidden agendas they need to watch for. For interpreters, particular attention is needed toward the semantics of what other faculty are saying because the subtle nuances and implied assertions they may be hinting at need to be relayed so the Deaf academic can be aware of them. This sort of reciprocal informing is helpful to both academic and interpreter. We will explain more on the complexities of the promotion and tenure process later but we want our interpreters to keep us informed and vice versa so we can make good decisions to ensure our success and promotion as instructors and colleagues.

Working in higher education with a Deaf faculty member is different than in many other settings. It is imperative that both academics and interpreters new to the environment take the time to learn as much as they can about working together in academia.[5] Although many policies are in writing, there are also a whole lot of unwritten rules. We will try to describe some of these inside traditions of higher education in this chapter.

Demystifying the Promotion and Tenure Process

The tenure system in higher education is rather unique. Tenure is basically the awarding of a permanent job contract after an initial probationary period of six years. This tradition is supposedly necessary to protect the academic freedom of faculty to speak out on controversial topics without fear of retribution from the administration. Academics who are hired under this system are referred to as tenure-track faculty. Non-tenure-track faculty such as lecturers or visiting professors are given term-limited contracts of one or more years that may or may not be renewed. Adjunct faculty are hired on a semester-to-semester basis depending on course needs. Typically, a new tenure-track faculty member is hired just after completing their doctoral degree and is awarded the title of assistant professor. Granting of tenure and promotion after the probationary period to associate professor usually occur at the same time. After a period of several more years of satisfactory productivity, the associate professor can be promoted to full professor. When a tenured professor retires, they may be awarded the honorary title of professor emeritus by a vote of the department faculty.

The process of obtaining tenure or getting promoted in academic ranks is rarely clear-cut at most institutions; however, certain standard criteria need to be met. The number of publications in professional journals is usually the primary measuring stick. You may have heard of the phrase "publish or perish" in reference to this requirement. Exactly how many publications are required varies by the type of school. Top-tier research universities expect more publications than mid-level or small teaching-focused colleges. Other criteria include teacher ratings, and service to the university and profession. At some colleges, teacher ratings are valued more than the number of publications, with high ratings by students expected along with good peer reviews of teaching. Service to the university and profession generally includes serving on and chairing committees, being a board or committee member of a related professional organization, and being part of the editorial process of journals as an editor or reviewer. Tenure and promotion are usually decided by a vote of the already tenured faculty at department, college, and university levels. Deans and the provost (chief academic officer) can sometimes override faculty committee votes but rarely do so.

Although there are expectations as noted above, what exactly is needed for tenure can often be clear as mud and is fraught with politics. Collegiality, the ability to get along and work with colleagues within the department, the university, and the profession outside the university is critical to this process. There tend to be a number of unwritten rules surrounding collegiality but sometimes it even becomes a written tenure requirement. Becoming one of the "good ol' boys or girls" is certainly helpful but not absolutely necessary for promotion and tenure. Obviously, the more tenured faculty who know and like a new faculty member, the better the chance of getting the votes needed for tenure. Faculty, Deaf or not, do not need to be social butterflies, but they definitely need to make some attempt to interact with other faculty. This is probably where interpreting skill is most crucial outside of the classroom. The interpreters themselves can influence the interactions and any adverse behaviors can have negative impact.

Social events are not just "social"; they are also a form of networking. Getting to know and impress the right people can help not only with the tenure and promotion process, but also in gaining resources and funding for student programs and research projects. It is a good idea for an interpreter to find out exactly what sort of gathering they will be attending. They definitely do not want to show up in evening formal wear to the annual department pool party or vice versa. There is usually food available and may be alcoholic beverages involved. Interpreters need to resist the temptation to help themselves to the food. Sometimes other faculty and/or the host of the event might invite interpreters to eat. They need to use good judgment with this situation. Drinking alcohol at these events is a definite taboo even if invited to do so. If the Deaf academic drinks alcohol, that's an issue for their peers to judge, not the interpreter. If interpreters finds themselves uncomfortable with these social situations, they should decline to interpret and explain why. For example, one of us had an interpreter who was a recovering alcoholic and she preferred not to be asked to interpret at certain faculty receptions. Other interpreters might have religious or other personal objections to certain types of social events. Nonetheless, the Deaf academic and interpreter can work well together in the classroom, during presentations, and also enjoy networking with other faculty in the department or college.

Content Knowledge

Here's Rule #1 when it comes to voicing for us: "*Thou shalt not dumb down our message.*" This is easily our biggest frustration. When we sign something like "Our data analysis shows that the discourse practices of skilled Deaf teachers reflect the use of maintaining a moderate level of control in the classroom," then interpreters need to voice it *exactly* or as closely as possible. We realize this puts added demand on interpreters but as Dean and Pollard noted,[6] it definitely helps to be prepared and become familiar with the cues that a Deaf academic provides. One cue is when there is deliberate fingerspelling being used (with or without an associated sign). Another cue is to watch the mouth morphemes being used. It can cue interpreters as to which English version of the signed concept to voice. We normally tell interpreters that are new to us to watch our mouth movements. Of course, this approach does not work with all Deaf individuals. While some use very English-based signing and extensive mouthing, others follow a more traditional ASL structure, barely even using any mouth morphemes. Also, it does not hurt for interpreters to ask the Deaf academic to repeat a phrase or term. This can be done by backchanneling with a facial cue (e.g., raised eyebrows), simply signing AGAIN in a low-profile manner or other previously agreed upon cues. Most of us are more concerned with getting the right message out than worrying about occasional interruptions. Interpreters new to the Deaf academic should ask if they have any videos of themselves doing presentations to become familiar with their style of signing. Conversely, Deaf academics can help interpreters by using good presentation practices that promote clarity such as standing to the side of a podium instead of behind it, using a larger signing space, fingerspelling slowly and deliberately when specific vocabulary is desired. Pausing periodically is helpful for the interpreters as well so they can catch up and rest momentarily. Pausing when a new slide or written material is presented is one way to do this and is good practice particularly to give participants both Deaf and hearing time to read the material.

What we use in presenting material is typically some form of Academic ASL and tends to be in the upper range of registers.[7] These are common in all languages, including ASL, and come in five levels: frozen, formal, consultative, informal, and intimate.[8] We could use a frozen register if reading verbatim from print. Or we might use the formal level of register during monologue-type presentations that might make our signing *seem* English-like (e.g., more frequent use of subject-verb-object order).[9] There is also use of more signing space for a large audience and other features. Deaf academics can also be a bit more dynamic than formal in their approach and at times may lean toward consultative registers.[10] This latter register is typical for the type of exchange seen in classrooms and meetings when more audience participation is desired. Informal registers tend to be at the one-to-one level or in small group chats. Keep in mind that the use of register may vary depending on the Deaf academic's signing style, speaking skills, and experience. You'll see some who seem naturally comfortable as speakers and may use a less formal and more consultative style whereas others read text straight from their notes.

The vocabulary used in higher education is obviously more specialized. There is vocabulary that is common throughout academia, and there is even more highly specialized vocabulary used for particular disciplines. Interpreters will often pick up academic vocabulary as they spend time working with faculty. As for the specialized terminology, if you are not familiar with that discipline, ask questions and request reading materials. Ask for a copy of the textbook to keep during the semester and course presentation materials such as PowerPoint slides. In terms of sign vocabulary, although it is best to learn the content signs from the faculty you are working with, there are an increasing number of online sources.[11] The more terminology interpreters learn, the more likely they become an asset as a designated or preferred interpreter.

Conference and Professional Event Interpreting

As part of the promotion and tenure requirements for faculty, they are expected to present their work at academic conferences. The typical process for a faculty member to present at a conference involves responding to a "call for papers" from a host organization and sending an abstract or brief description for peer review and acceptance. This happens several months before the conference. Most Deaf-related conferences already provide interpreters for their main events such as opening and closing ceremonies and keynote speeches. They also usually provide a team for all of the smaller breakout sessions and workshops. However, this does not always occur and serious issues may arise.[12]

Some larger academic organizations that are not directly Deaf-related will also provide interpreters as part of their accessibility practices. One good example is the Modern Language Association (MLA). Several Deaf academics often attend their annual convention. They will even provide interpreters for the faculty job interviews that take place at their conventions, either for Deaf faculty conducting interviews or for Deaf candidates. They also have guidelines for providing access during the hiring process.[13] The MLA and other organizations such as the American Educational Research Association (AERA) will hire a coordinator who in turn hires a team of interpreters from around the country and even internationally if needed. These interpreters are highly professional and top-notch. However, the interpreters and Deaf academics still need to seek each other out before the presentation for preparation. Otherwise, our anecdotal scenario at the beginning of the chapter is surely bound to occur.

Aside from the major conferences, the smaller ones are either clueless as they have never used interpreters before and/or they balk at the high cost of providing interpreters. One good solution that we have used to help organizations save on the cost is to ask the conference to pay for the travel expenses of a team and our university pays for the interpreter's time. It should make no difference to the university whether the interpreters work on campus or at a conference. The cost to the university is the same. In fact, the only thing the university "sees" on the books is a time sheet or invoice for the interpreting. This is a good solution in some ways, but it can lead to inequities between the full-time faculty "haves" and the "have nots" like graduate students or adjuncts and part-time faculty. The best solution would be to have the conference take on the cost. But before doing that, we should consider the size of the organization. If it is large enough with thousands of conference attendees, then they cannot argue that the cost is an undue burden, which is one of the few exceptions allowed by ADA. If the organization is relatively small, then some creative solutions are possible as suggested above.

The nuts and bolts of actually interpreting at a conference are not much different than an everyday classroom lecture using academic ASL. The main difference is the audience: It will consist of the peers of the Deaf faculty, and they can and will evaluate the presentation much more critically than a roomful of students. The questions or comments will certainly be more philosophical or theoretical. There is little room for error here and we will repeat our first rule: *Do not dumb down our language*. This is why it is imperative that interpreters ask and even pester Deaf academics for a copy of their paper or even better a video of the presentation beforehand. It is only fair that if we expect a professional performance from interpreters that Deaf academics give them as much information beforehand as possible and meet with them to practice the presentation or at least chat long enough for the interpreter to get a good grasp of our signing style.

Interpreting in the Classroom

We would like to preface this section with a caveat: Although many institutions do a good job of training their doctoral students how to conduct and publish research, they may not be so great at training them how to teach. Just like any new faculty members, the young Deaf academic may have had little actual teaching experience. Interpreters need to be prepared to work with such neophytes to ensure clear communication is taking place. We have seen new faculty who just came into the classroom with only one interpreter and do a lecture nonstop for an hour and a half straight. This is not a good situation for either the interpreter, who will be exhausted, nor the students, who will not get a good translation. This type of practice could eventually produce poor teaching reviews that would hurt the Deaf academic. Our advice to new Deaf academics is to seek out the assistance of the university's faculty resources on teaching, learning, and curriculum development and bring their preferred interpreters along with them to their trainings. The traditional "stand and deliver" format in lecture halls is still widely used but is becoming less common. Some faculty are switching to "flipped classrooms" where they make videos of their lectures for students to watch before class with interpreter voice-over and/or captions and then during class focus on working on problems or having discussions. These are much more dynamic situations that can be more demanding for interpreters. Regardless of the instruction delivery format, we always recommend a close working relationship between interpreters and Deaf academics to determine the best possible arrangement.

It behooves the Deaf faculty member and interpreters to work as allies and strategize approaches on orienting students to appropriately participate in a classroom where interpreters are utilized. Some basics: Always remind students to direct questions and comments to the instructor, not the interpreter, and speak clearly and loudly enough for the interpreter, especially in large classrooms or noisy environments like laboratories. Warn students that any comments they make off-hand or toward other students can be interpreted. Explain the concept of lag time as interpreters process the messages. Ask the students to speak up and ask if anything the interpreter says does not make sense or if they want something repeated.

One thing that always should be discussed is the seating or standing arrangements for the interpreters in the classroom.[14] Obviously the type of classroom and delivery format have an impact. There are large lecture halls, small classrooms, computer labs, and science labs each with a different seating or standing arrangement. For a large lecture hall or room with rows of seats, having the interpreters sit in the front row will suffice. We sometimes have placed one interpreter in front to voice for us and another one in or near the middle to help field questions and monitor student comments or questions. However, this is not a preferred classroom setting. One seating arrangement we always like and use if possible is to have the students sit in a single U-shaped row around the classroom so that everyone can see each other. We will place the interpreters in the middle of the U-shape so they can hear every student better. For discussion groups, if the Deaf academic is able to get enough interpreters (this may be an issue of staffing availability at some campuses), they can seat or stand one near each group. However, if this is not the case, then interpreters can walk from group to group and sign what they can pick up from discussions before the students share their views with the class. Laboratories can be a bit difficult as they tend to have obstructions like computers on the desktops, or in science labs there may be racks and other equipment. This sort of situation may require placing interpreters on each side of the room.

Every Deaf faculty member will have their own preference for their mode of delivery. Some will use ASL, others may lean more toward signed English. There are even some who like to voice for themselves. In this case, the interpreter can sit or stand in the middle of the classroom and help monitor the faculty member's voice level and clarity for feedback and sign student responses. There are those Deaf faculty who might want to use simultaneous communication especially if they have a Deaf student, although we advise against doing this. We know this can be a sensitive topic, and if the Deaf faculty decides to try this, they should discuss this with any Deaf students in the class to ensure they are fully comprehending the lectures and discussion.

Having Deaf students and a Deaf faculty member in a classroom where the majority of students are hearing can create some logistical complications. One question that needs to be answered is whether Deaf students should request their own interpreters from the university's disability services if the Deaf faculty member already has their own assigned interpreter. The Deaf faculty, student(s), and disability offices should discuss this issue before the course starts. If the Deaf academic has a team of interpreters and the course is mostly lecture format it may not be necessary to have additional interpreters. However if the Deaf student will be required to interact extensively with classmates in discussion or laboratory situations, then they should have their own interpreter because the situation is already demanding enough for the Deaf faculty's own interpreting team. Debriefing together after these classes will help when unexpected situations arise. Of course, ultimately the decision on whether to retain their own interpreter(s) belongs to the Deaf students.

We have had some students who did not feel compatible with our interpreters and vice versa. Sometimes that even extends to sharing interpreters with fellow Deaf faculty as we will explain next.

Being a Preferred Interpreter and Ethics

Having a designated interpreter is still a rarity because most Deaf academics do not need one often enough on a daily basis. Instead, we keep a short list of preferred interpreters that we request as needed and we try to use the same few interpreters for the sake of consistency. For us, finding the right interpreters is like going through interviews and trial periods. We want to say that just because a Deaf faculty member decides someone is not a good fit does not mean the interpreter is mediocre. A lot of dynamics are at play besides interpreting skills. We have worked in the same university department for a number of years and had interpreters we both preferred. However, there were definitely a few that were not a good fit for one or the other of us. One reason could be that the interpreter would struggle with our style of signing while interpreting from ASL to spoken English. Another is that the interpreter's spoken English to ASL skill was not satisfactory. Of course, there were some whose personality or demeanor just did not connect with us. Even an interpreter's accent can make a difference. Interpreters become an extension of the faculty member and we are sensitive to the perception that other people have. We want to project a professional manner that is consistent with higher education and if an interpreter cannot do that, we do not ask them to work with us. Again, it is about the right fit, not just qualifications.

One major frustration can be interpreters who overstep their boundaries and disempower us. Being an ally and quietly letting us know is better than taking over the situation and acting on our behalf without our knowledge and consent.[15] Interpreters may become aware of situations where they feel the Deaf faculty member is being oppressed or being treated inequitably. The last thing we need are interpreters themselves confronting the offenders. The best thing to do is make the Deaf faculty member aware of the situation. We may already know, and we have our own ways of dealing with these situations. Sometimes we may decide silence is the best response. That might feel like we are being submissive, but interpreters need to be aware, like any workplace, that power and political dynamics are at play. Criticizing another senior faculty member or administrator over supposed inequities or infractions and making them defensive can lead to long-term negative consequences, especially when it comes time for faculty votes on promotion and tenure. Faculty might seem absent-minded at times, but they have memories like elephants; grudges can last a long time in academia.

There are a number of ways interpreters can be allies. We do recommend interpreters get to know the Deaf academic outside of interpreting assignments. The more you interact, the more you will understand each other, the better the message that will result when getting back to work together. Staff interpreters will learn and pick up a good amount of useful non-confidential information and "unwritten rules" and then relay this in a non-patronizing way to acclimate new faculty who may not be aware of some of them. Examples of other useful information to share might be location of meetings, names of other people present, pointing out the VIPs in the room, et cetera. Experienced Deaf academics like us will try to share this information with new staff interpreters. For both the neophyte and experienced faculty, it behooves interpreters to pay attention and keep an open ear about what others are discussing informally and quietly relay that information to us. It certainly is useful for us to know that someone is thinking of retiring next year, that some other faculty member is probably not going to get tenure, that a new rule is being pondered by the administration, or even more personal things. This is not just gossip but is useful incidental information that anyone would simply overhear in the hallways, restrooms, or public places. Conversely, if we share information with interpreters, it is always best to keep it confidential.

Something as simple as noting the nonverbal reactions of other faculty during discussions helps us. Our best interpreters are good at reflecting the vibes and tone of discussions. As an example, one of us recently participated in a meeting to consider a doctoral student for a fellowship. Although there was opposition and the committee vote went against the student, the interpreter did a great job using facial expressions and body language that reflected the tone of the fellowship directors, and hinting that they were still open to the idea of giving the fellowship. Based on that cue, we were able to successfully follow up with an appeal to the director and the student eventually got the fellowship. One of the caveats of Deaf culture is information sharing,[16] so the more the interpreter picks up on the workings of the department and college ecosystem and relays this information to the Deaf faculty, the better they can enable them to be productive members of their institutions.

As a nearly constant companion, preferred interpreters can cast either a positive or negative impression on those around the Deaf academic not just with their interpreting skills but also with their behavior and dress. Obviously, keeping good boundaries while being cordial with Deaf academics' peers is always the best thing to do. While higher education settings may seem somewhat informal in dress and much more liberal than a typical business environment, it is not a good idea for interpreters to let their guard down and get too casual. There are still standards of professionalism that need to be followed. It is always good to refer to faculty using the formal term "Dr. Smith" or "Professor Jones" and not by their first names. Academics may occasionally show up for work in jeans, flannel shirts, and an old comfortable pair of shoes, but that's usually when they are not expecting to interact with students or the public. When we request an interpreter, that often means we are in a meeting or teaching a class. Therefore, our dress code is going to be more business casual. There are some more highly formal situations requiring appropriate dress. Some examples would be ceremonies or interviews. If in doubt, interpreters should ask in advance about the protocol and any relevant materials (e.g., agendas).

Interpreters occasionally need to deal with other faculty who do not fully understand their role. Sometimes they will try to strike up a conversation with the interpreter, asking about their job, where they are from, and so forth while not even addressing the Deaf academic. The best response for the interpreter of course is to redirect the attention and questions to the Deaf academic so that person can respond. Interpreters have often told us that one of their pet peeves is when people address them directly instead of the Deaf person and say, "Can you tell or ask Dr. Ogden. . . ." It is an ongoing educational effort and a situation that needs to be handled with tact so the naïve faculty member does not become embarrassed or offended.

Most of the time, courteously redirecting the faculty member's attention toward the Deaf professional will work. Something like "Dr. Ogden will be happy to explain or talk to you about it." However, some still won't get it after being told several times. One of the more embarrassing types of situations we have had to deal with from time to time are the boorish behaviors or remarks from male faculty about our female interpreters. These and similar incidents can be sticky ethical situations, and on top of that is the need to be careful not to damage junior ranking Deaf faculty members' chances at tenure and promotion.

Conclusion

Interpreters and prospective Deaf academics have hopefully gained a good glimpse into what is involved in working together to develop trust and allyship for a good long-term relationship. There are other resources such as the noted chapters on working with Deaf academics.[17] Also, articles have been published related to some of the issues faced by Deaf academics in accessing interpreters and institutional resources needed to do their jobs.[18] Although we still have a long way to go, it is a huge improvement from the late 1970s when one of the authors, Dr. Paul Ogden, first started out in higher education. There were few Deaf academics working outside of Gallaudet College or the National Technical Institute for the Deaf (NTID). ASL was still in the process of becoming recognized as a bonafide language. Federal legislation such as Section 504 was still new and the Americans with Disabilities Act had yet to become law. The approach back then used by Paul, which we both still sometimes use now, was to seek out college students and train them as academic interpreters. They were mostly Interpreter or Deaf Education majors. Now there is the amenity in many metropolitan locations of having a pool of interpreters who have been trained in interpreting methodology but who still need the specific information and insight from chapters like this one. Just like any specialized profession, they will need to actually work with a Deaf academic to pick up the many nuances of the job. The demand is there, and it will grow over time as more and more Deaf individuals seek advanced degrees and work in higher education settings.

Notes

1. David H. Smith and Jean Andrews, "Deaf and Hard of Hearing Faculty in Higher Education: Enhancing Access, Equity, Policy, and Practice," *Disability & Society* 30, no. 10 (2015): 1521–36.
2. Smith and Andrews, "Deaf and Hard of Hearing Faculty."

3. See Leala Holcomb, this volume.

4. Elizabeth F. Morgan, "Interpreters, Conversational Style and Gender at Work," in *Deaf Professionals and Designated Interpreters: A New Paradigm*, eds. Peter Hauser, Karen Finch, and Angela Hauser (Washington DC: Gallaudet University Press, 2008): 66–80.

5. See Marika Kovacs-Houlihan, this volume.

6. Robin K. Dean and Robert Q Pollard, "The Application of Demand-Control Theory to Sign Language Interpreting: Implications for Stress and Interpreter Training," *Journal of Deaf Studies and Deaf Education* 6, no. 1 (2001): 1–14.

7. Maribel Garate, *A Case Study of an In-Service Professional Development Model on Bilingual Deaf Education: Changes in Teachers' Stated Beliefs and Classroom Practices*, PhD Diss., Gallaudet University, 2007; see Kurz, Kurz, and Harris, this volume; Raychelle Harris, "Sign Language as Academic Language," in *The Sage Deaf Studies Encyclopedia,* eds. Genie Gertz and Patrick Boudreault (Thousand Oaks, CA: SAGE Publications, 2016): 829–832; Linda L. Ross and Marla C. Berkowitz, "Academic ASL: It Looks Like English, but It Isn't," in *Putting the Pieces Together: Proceedings of the PEPNet Biennial Conference,* ed. Marcia Kolvitz (Knoxville, TN: University of Tennessee, 2008): 193–198.

8. Martin Joos, *The Five Clocks: A Linguistic Excursion into the Five Styles of English Usage* (New York: Harcourt, Brace & World, 1967).

9. Ross and Berkowitz, "Academic ASL: It Looks Like English But It Isn't."

10. See Thomas Holcomb's chapter on DEAM, this volume.

11. See Kurz, Kurz, and Harris, this volume.

12. See Bouldreault and Gertz, this volume.

13. MLA Committee on Disability Issues in the Profession, *Disability and Hiring: Guidelines for Departmental Search Committees*, Modern Language Association, 2006, retrieved on January 17, 2017 from http://mla.devtc.net/Resources/Career-Center/Career-Resources/The-Job-Search-Information-for-Job-Seekers-and-Hiring-Departments/Disability-and-Hiring-Guidelines-for-Departmental-Search-Committees.

14. See Thomas Holcomb's chapter on DEAM, this volume.

15. See Trudy Suggs, this volume.

16. Thomas K. Holcomb, *Introduction to American Deaf Culture* (New York: Oxford University Press, 2013).

17. Catherine Beaton and Angela Hauser, "Timeliness, Technology, Terminology, and Tact: Challenging Dynamics in Information Technology Environments," in *Deaf Professionals and Designated Interpreters: A New Paradigm*, eds. Peter Hauser, Karen Finch, and Angela Hauser (Washington, DC: Gallaudet University Press, 2008): 210–33; Linda Campbell, Meg J. Rohan, and Kathryn Woodcock, "Academic and Educational Interpreting From the Other Side of the Classroom: Working with Deaf Academics," in *Deaf Professionals and Designated Interpreters: A New Paradigm*, eds. Peter Hauser, Karen Finch, and Angela Hauser (Washington, DC: Gallaudet University Press, 2008): 81–105.

18. Smith and Andrews, "Deaf and Hard of Hearing Faculty"; Kathryn Woodcock, Meg Rohan, and Linda Campbell, "Equitable Representation of Deaf People in Mainstream Academia: Why Not?" *Higher Education* 53, no. 3 (2007): 359–79.

11

Case Studies of International Conferences

A Social Justice Framework for Interpreting

Patrick Boudreault and Genie Gertz

For the ASL summary of this chapter, go to https://youtu.be/XYDhIuYN8MY

> After a long day at a conference, filled with keynote presentations and poster sessions by well-respected scholars, we often find ourselves in conversation with other Deaf scholars, not about the quality of the content but rather the quality—or lack thereof—of interpreting access. Too often, these converations about inaccessibility overshadow the main purpose of attending a conference. Instead of engaging in intellectual discourse, we get caught up in discussion of the perennial problem of effective and accurate sign language interpretation, power dynamics, and lack of access to the conference proceedings. Not only this, but we come together to review the conference logistics ad nauseum in order to come up with new ways in which access can be improved for the future. This chapter is but one example of where ideas are shared and documented to support full participation of Deaf scholars in future academic conferences.

THE RESEARCH and work that came out of Gallaudet College's Sign Language Laboratory during the mid-twentieth century gave rise to the first wave of Deaf scholars. This linguistic shift in academia allowed for a multitude of Deaf scholars from various backgrounds to emerge from the shadows, producing a space wherein language use and knowledge production could be diversified. Deaf scholars have made significant advancements since that time, but there is always room for progress in ensuring equal multiparty access.

Sign language interpreters have played a role in this space, yet the best practices by which they should be guided have never been fully, formally documented, but merely passed along in the collective minds of Deaf scholars and interpreters over time. All too often, these best practices are forgotten with newer generations of interpreters. In this chapter, we, as third-generation Deaf-centric scholars, will discuss observations about specific cases wherein Deaf scholars were excluded from these academic spaces even with the mechanisms of inclusion in place.

We hope that our observations and analyses are impressed upon our audience in a way that they will be able to take on a productive, proactive role in multilingual spaces to either prevent or alleviate the inequities that we have witnessed and experienced at academic conferences. Rather than act as passive conduits of language exchange, we urge sign language interpreters to take on the role of becoming agents of change, working as primary collaborators alongside Deaf people and the event organizers, to ensure the rights of accessibility and inclusion of all parts of scholarly discourse are granted to Deaf people. We are extremely grateful to previous generations of Deaf scholars, interpreters, and legislators who have laid the groundwork to make our contributions to academic discourse around these issues possible.

In order to continue advancing the inclusion of Deaf scholars in academic settings, through a social justice lens, we will present our experiences and observations as a microcosm of what it means to be a Deaf scholar in today's world. We have deemed it to be part of our social responsibility to address issues that have long been part of, though not inherent to, the interplay of Deaf people and interpreters so that we can recognize and resolve the issues that arise as a consequence of larger, structural issues continually at work.

Social Justice: Equity, Agency, and Inclusion Defined

Within the last two decades, there has been a significant rise in the level of both popular and academic discourse surrounding the issues of individual and structural oppression. As such, social justice movements and their discourse have become increasingly common methods of addressing oppression. However, even with the increased attention being paid to issues such as racism and sexism, among many others, issues of audism have gone largely neglected by mainstream social justice activists. For this reason, we will specifically address issues related to academic interpreting from a social justice framework. Hopefully this will allow us to reimagine relationships between Deaf people and interpreters. This exploration should not be limited to contentious power struggles, but a collaborative relationship that works to resist the oppressive forces that emerge within these conference dynamics.

Before we continue, it is imperative to address what we mean by social justice, given that it has become entangled with the popular movement fueled by social media. In line with Lee Anne Bell's vision of social justice as both a goal and process, we propose to understand interpreting and access as a means to create "a world in which the distribution of resources is equitable and ecologically sustainable, and all members are physically and psychologically safe and secure, recognized, and treated with respect. We envision a world in which individuals are both self-determining and interdependent."[1] To this definition, we add equity and agency because the relationship between Deaf people and interpreters ought to be grounded in both. Interpreters serve a vital role in the equitable distribution of resources. It is essential that they work as agents of change toward leveling the playing field that is structured to put Deaf people at a disadvantage. In addition,

Deaf people need a space in which to act independently and in their best interests as they deem fit.

By *agency*, we mean "the subjective awareness that one is initiating, executing, and controlling one's own actions in the world. It reflects a sense of the interpreter being able to exhibit ownership and accountability as it pertains to his or her individual decisions and actions in the interpreted interaction."[2] Agency in this chapter is two-fold: Deaf people have the right to stipulate what it means to be included in spaces that are not necessarily originally designed with them in mind, whereas interpreters can work in conjunction with them to create an equitable space of discourse.

Underlying this movement toward reconceptualizing conference spaces in which equity and agency are possible is inclusion, one of the cornerstones of social justice movements. It is worth noting that inclusion, without specifically addressing access, maintains the imbalanced power structure that is often seen in academic conference settings. As such, inclusion is always ephemeral. In her discussion of deliberative democracy, Iris Marion Young stipulates two forms of exclusion—external and internal. The former refers to instances wherein people of diverse backgrounds are prohibited from entering the space of deliberation. The latter, which becomes pertinent here, refers to

> the way that some people's ideas and social perspectives are likely to dominate discussion and decision making even when a forum has diversity in the room [as] there are a whole set of practical norms about what "proper" speaking involves that are biased against people with accents, not to mention people who don't speak the dominant language—and biased against people who speak in a high voice or softly, biased against people who express themselves emotionally or haltingly, and so on.[3]

In other words, in order to provide a fully accessible space, one must consider that there is a multiplicity of power dynamics at play within a single space of discourse. Here, we would also add that there is a structural bias against sign language as a modality of language use. These biases that Young lays out do not account for a multimodal space. However, given the more complicated context in which hearing and Deaf people are placed, the issue of access becomes more pressing.

Legislation

In tandem with the rise of social justice discourse, there have been legislative movements to institute civil rights for those who have long been marginalized in society. With respect to civil rights legislation in the United States, we saw the implementation of Section 504 of the Rehabilitation Act of 1973 and the passage of the Americans with Disabilities Act (ADA) in 1990. We also witnessed the Deaf President Now protest at Gallaudet University in 1988.[4] These were all milestones in the journey toward full accessibility for Deaf Americans. During this period, the United States was a forerunner in the civil rights movement, and these legislative changes paved the way for emerging Deaf professionals and scholars during that time. These changes also coincided with the exponential growth of professional sign language interpreters, particularly with the advent of video relay services in the early 2000s.

Meanwhile, significant traction on the legislative front has also been made worldwide. The United Nations Convention on the Rights of Persons with Disabilities (CRPD), a legally-binding treaty that was established in 2006, has been ratified by 173 countries.[5] Countries that have ratified the treaty are required to submit a report in accordance with a specific time cycle to evaluate and monitor the government's implementation of the protocols in place. The responsibility of the CRPD committee is to review complaints or violations, and make general recommendations if these countries are not compliant. The burden falls to the aggrieved party to file a complaint in order for legal action to be taken. However, the CRPD has no significant impact, given that the mandate has no immediate effect and enforcement varies widely. In comparison, the ADA is considered more enforceable as allegations of violations can be brought to a court of law. Regardless, all of these have fundamentally shifted and ultimately improved the ways in which Deaf people can, and do, engage with society.

Conference Dynamics

These advancements cannot be discounted as they have radically transformed Deaf lives over the last few decades, and specifically their engagement with academic settings. However, these legislative actions, even when properly enforced, have been insufficient in creating equitable and accessible conditions that allow Deaf and hearing people to interact on a truly level playing field. Even with the establishment of these laws and policies, lack of access to and within conference spaces remains an unresolved issue. Examples illustrated later in this chapter will demonstrate that even with the presence of interpreters, true accessibility is not a given for Deaf conference participants. Consequently, the burden often rests on their shoulders to advocate for themselves for accessibility, which may include taking legal actions. The success of such legal action often depends on the complaining parties' ability to navigate a complex legal system.

Given the complicated dynamics of these academic conference settings where numerous players (conference organizers, interpreters, Deaf, and hearing scholars) are involved, it has become more important than ever to lay out a schema of how these players ought to interact with each other. Basically, there are two types of academic conferences: those that concern sign language and Deaf-related issues, and those that cover topics not directly related to Deaf people. For the purpose of this chapter, we have chosen to focus on the former setting, which tends to present fewer challenges to inclusion and access, yet these issues still remain. In order to eventually take on issues that emerge in predominantly hearing settings, we must first resolve the power imbalance that continues to take place in sign language and Deaf-related academic conferences.

Case Studies

The two examples presented below were international conferences that took place fifteen years apart outside of the United States. The focus of both conferences was on scholarly exchanges regarding signed languages and Deaf education. Given this topic, access for Deaf people should not have been an issue. Unfortunately it was, especially since many professionals were unable to or chose not to use sign language, even in the presence of their Deaf peers. The issue of interpreting became paramount but was poorly handled at both these conferences. This resulted in the feeling of exclusion among many Deaf conference participants, as they were unable to benefit from intellectual exchanges and rich networking opportunities among their peers. Devastated by this experience of exclusion, Deaf people found it necessary to draft official statements at the conclusion of both gatherings with the goal of avoiding repeat occurrences at future conferences. The following explanation provides a mere glimpse into what transpired in these multilingual and multimodal spaces and can serve as an example for the broader application of how interpreting can be handled effectively, as part of a larger social justice movement against audism.

The Amsterdam Manifesto

The Seventh Theoretical Issues of Sign Language Research (TISLR) conference in Amsterdam, Netherlands, took place during the summer of 2000. The TISLR conferences were and still remain a critical juncture for current and future Deaf scholars to become actively involved with the academic community that address the theoretical issues of sign language research. These conferences manifested in a convergence of both Deaf and hearing scholars, including students, research assistants, and Deaf community members. At the time, a significant number of international scholars were present at the conference who used a variety of sign languages. In principle, the spoken and written lingua franca of the Western academic community is English, as it was for this conference. In addition to English, given the location of the conference, the conference organizers opted to provide interpreting access to Deaf participants only in *Nederlandse Gabarentaal* (NGT) as opposed to International Sign (IS), which is often provided along with British Sign Language (BSL) or American Sign Language (ASL), depending on the region.* Because spoken and written English and NGT were the only languages provided for the platform for scholarly exchanges at this conference, many Deaf participants were left out.

In addition to challenges associated with only two languages (English and NGT) used at the conference, the overwhelming majority of hearing presenters chose to use spoken English as their method to communicate with their colleagues

*At the time, including Deaf interpreters trained in International Sign was not widespread among conferences of sign language and Deaf-related conferences. Since the early 2000s, it has become increasingly more common.

throughout the conference, both for their presentations and for networking. This created an additional layer of inaccessibility for Deaf conference participants as they could neither follow nor participate in the academic discourse with their hearing peers. For those hearing participants who knew sign language, the privilege of choosing to speak instead of using sign language in a Deaf-related conference space reinforced the significant power imbalance. This is emblematic of power and privilege of society at large, forcing interpreters into a difficult position of reconciling this inequality, which became problematic, for example, given the overwhelming majority of those who chose to use spoken language in comparison to the interpreters available.

Apart from the main presentations, the concurrent sessions were not uniformly accessible given the lack of interpreting support. In addition, the poster sessions, which are integral to academic conferences for intellectual exchanges, were dominated by people using spoken language. This prevented Deaf people from benefitting from the opportunity to network and learn from their peers. In a supposedly accessible space, this lack of linguistic access prevents and disempowers Deaf people.

Deaf people are often confronted with issues of access at a sign language or Deaf-related conference, including this one. At times, they arrive unprepared to face these issues and are consequently disempowered, experiencing the same kinds of linguistic barriers they face outside of these settings. Some of the more experienced Deaf scholars, familiar with the linguistic barriers that often emerge in conference settings, tried to come to the conference prepared to navigate the multilingual space by having a designated interpreter, developing a connection with the conference organizers, or debriefing with the interpreters.

For example, two Deaf graduate students from Canada and the United States respectively were able to receive funding from their own academic institutions to bring their own designated ASL/English interpreters to preempt this kind of exclusion. These Deaf students teamed up with their own designated interpreters to support the rest of the Deaf scholars present at the conference, alongside one volunteer interpreter from the United States who joined the effort to resolve the situation. This was merely an ad hoc solution to try and allow a significant number of the Deaf attendees from various parts of the world to better participate in the conference.

This is but one solution by Deaf scholars to approach inaccessible conference settings. If their institutions are able to support them with the necessary funding, they often feel a need to bring their own designated interpreters. This difficult situation resulted in an impromptu gathering at a nearby plaza at the end of the conference. Around 35 Deaf individuals, who held various positions within the academic community throughout the world, shared the concerns they experienced at the conference (see figure 1).

Outcomes

As a result of this assembly, the Amsterdam Manifesto was drafted to address the ongoing issue of exclusion of Deaf people in conferences that focus specifically on

Figure 1. Deaf attendees gathering for an impromptu meeting outside of the Singel Church in Amsterdam, Netherlands. Photographer Paul van Weel, July 20, 2000.

this population.[6] The ultimate goal of this document was to ensure full inclusion of and respect toward Deaf people for future conferences. The three main points of the manifesto are as follows (see Appendix 1 for the complete manifesto):

(1) That the official languages of the conference should include English, the local signed language, BSL, and ASL (in which case access through English should also be provided through computer-aided real-time captioning [CART] services)

(2) That the committee should ensure there are sufficient funds to provide sign language interpreters for all simultaneous sessions of the conference and for all social events during the conference

(3) That there should be at least one Deaf scientist on the organizing committee to ensure that necessary steps are taken to provide full access for the whole scientific community

With this manifesto in place, the subsequent TISLR conferences have evolved considerably and made the intellectual discourse more inclusive and accessible for everyone involved. For example, at TISLR 8 in Barcelona, Spain, in 2004, Dr. Richard Meir from the University of Texas made a point to secure adequate funding to provide six highly qualified ASL/English interpreters. In this case, the funding came from the National Science Foundation. Following this conference, an Access Advisory Committee was implemented to support the next conference, which was to be held in Florianopolis, Brazil, in 2006. Dr. Ted Supalla, a Deaf scholar and principal investigator of a National Institutes of Health grant for the ASL Access project, acted as a liaison with Ms. Sharon Neumann Solow who was the interpreter coordinator for the U.S. interpreters. They worked closely with a team of interpreters from England, Portugal, and Denmark to ensure access for everyone at the conference. This practice of collaborating with Deaf experts and interpreters has continued to this day and has been intensively and comprehensively documented.[7] This has become a point of reference for future TISLR conference organizers.

Another outcome of the Amsterdam Manifesto was the creation of the Deaf Academics in 2002, which hosted its first formal assembly in Austin, Texas. This inaugural gathering was limited to Deaf academics. The attendees ranged from graduate students to postdoctoral fellows, teachers, researchers, and professors instituting a tradition of biennial conferences with a barrier free, Deaf-centric, and supportive intellectual gathering. The organization's mission "is to foster interaction between Deaf and hard-of-hearing people in academic or research careers."[8] The Deaf Academics conference has been part of the Deaf scholarly landscape ever since and is serving as a critical platform to foster and support the work of emerging and established Deaf scholars.

The Athens Declaration

Fifteen years passed between the Amsterdam Manifesto and the 22nd International Congress on the Education of the Deaf (ICED) in Athens, Greece, in 2015. This conference was another unfortunate instance of inaccessibility in a Deaf-related conference. It is important to note that the CRPD, ratified by many countries, commits to provide full access and inclusion for all disabilities, including Deaf people through the use of sign language. Greece, the location of ICED 2015, is one of the countries that has ratified the CRPD, as of 2012, but its mechanism for enforcement is less apparent compared to the ADA.

Despite lessons learned from previous conferences and guidelines documented in the Amsterdam Manifesto and the article by Supalla and colleagues, the languages for the conference were limited to spoken English and Greek Sign Language. Eventually, before the conference began, the conference organizers acceded to revise the language policy to make it more accessible for all participants. The statement was as follows: "The official languages of ICED 2015 are English and Greek Sign Language. International Signing (IS) and Captioning will be offered in the plenary sessions. IS will also be offered in *some* [emphasis added] parallel and poster sessions."[9] No doubt, the congress faced budgetary restrictions, which led to their decisions that prevented a fully accessible conference space for all participating members at ICED. However, these kinds of restrictions ought not be an acceptable excuse for limited accessibility for Deaf people, especially when the conference is about them.

Even though attempts to provide additional interpreters were made by the conference organizers, due to limited availability, Deaf people were still denied access to many parts of the conference, including the breakout sessions. This prevented continued collaboration between Deaf and hearing scholars and professionals outside the main presentations. One of the international scientific committee members posted a demeaning response to a Deaf participant in Dutch on the Dutch website, Kentalis, which sparked vigorous debate among many conference participants about the issue of the multilingual space for Deaf scholars at the conference specifically and in professional settings in general.[10] Following this exchange, Drs. Annelies Kusters and Maartje De Meulder summarized the main issue in English in a blog entry, which emphasized the position of privilege held by the hearing conference organizers and participants without much regard for their Deaf peers.[11]

Upon the conclusion of the conference, it was clear that many non-signing participants were able to continue their academic activities among themselves, unburdened by the struggles experienced by Deaf people at the conference. By contrast, Deaf scholars were disturbed by the experience and had to deal with emotional distress, which they expressed in blog posts the following week. Interestingly, based on the discussions among participants and organizers in the social media sphere, there is little mention in those blogs of how interpreters could play a pivotal role in transforming inequity in these spaces.

Outcomes

As a result of the discussions among the Deaf attendees upon the conclusion of the conference, a document titled "Athens Declaration on Access for Deaf Participants at the International Congress on Education of the Deaf" was drafted to explicitly spotlight the barriers that were experienced by Deaf participants at the conference.[12] The following is an excerpt from the declaration (see Appendix 2 for the complete declaration):

> *(1) Therefore, be it resolved that members of ICED organizing committees henceforth will ensure the provision of universal language access for all participants in International Sign and English (printed, captioned, and spoken).*
>
> *(2) Therefore, be it further resolved that membership of ICED organizing committees henceforth will include Deaf individuals, representing Deaf communities.*
>
> *(3) Therefore, be it further resolved that members of the ICED Host Selection Committee will immediately develop guidelines for future conferences to ensure universal language access in International Sign and English (printed, captioned, and spoken), including guidelines for scheduling of, budgeting for, and recruitment of qualified interpreters.*
>
> *(4) Therefore, be it further resolved that such guidelines will be created in conformity with "Guidelines on Fees and Conditions for International Sign Interpreters Working for the World Federation of the Deaf," and "Perspectives on the Concept and Definition of International Sign."*[13]

ICED 2015 is yet another example of Deaf professionals and scholars having to take drastic action in order to get the attention of conference organizers regarding access issues and to prevent this problem from repeating itself. However, the responsibility to address these issues should not fall solely on the shoulders of Deaf individuals. Rather, conference planning should be a shared responsibility among organizers, scholars, professionals, and interpreters to ensure inclusion for all parties. This is important because often when inaccessibility issues arise, Deaf scholars who have the courage to speak out are branded with a scarlet letter for being problematic and difficult to work with. Consequently, this discourages their future involvement, resulting in a loss of agency. Regardless, a positive outcome of this experience is the productive movement currently underway for the next ICED conference in 2020 to be held in Brisbane, Australia, as well as all future ICED conferences. The organizing committee for this conference will include a selection of Deaf scholars and leaders to ensure the appropriateness of the multilingual discourse set-up.

Interpreters' Position Within a Social Justice Framework

Deaf scholars are often burdened by a sense of guilt that their participation in academic spaces causes financial hardship for the host organization, as discussed in Dr. Teresa Blankmeyer Burke's blog entry, "How (Not!) to Be Inclusive: Deaf Academic Version."[14] She lists real-world examples highlighting how Deaf scholars are often perceived as a financial liability rather than being seen as fellow contributors integral to intellectual exchange. In addition, only a few people usually have enough courage to speak out against injustice. When this happens, they are often criticized rather than supported. This ends up as a burden carried by only a few Deaf people when it should be shared by all affected by the overt or covert exclusion of Deaf people in the public space. More often than not, the issue revolves around the provision of interpreting services and the quality of the work.This issue is similarly addressed in another blog entry written by Dr. Maartje De Meulder titled, "'Are You Friends with the Deaf Person?': (Net)working with Sign Language Interpreters in Academic Settings."[15] In this entry, she muses over her experiences working with interpreters and lists advice that scholars should consider ahead of time. This reflects a daily reality that multilingual Deaf scholars must face and cope with to ensure their own access.

While we cannot dismiss the exorbitant costs of their professional services, interpreters are often the first to support the cause. They understand the issue of access and are often committed to working alongside Deaf people to address injustice experienced by Deaf people at conferences. The question then is how interpreters can be part of the equation of distributive justice.

More often than not, the power and privilege struggle between conference organizers and Deaf people occurs behind the scenes, leaving the interpreters out of the picture. Another challenge is the perception of an ulterior motive among interpreters when they advocate for more work for themselves. For these reasons, interpreters often find themselves treading a fine line between advocating for improved access and remaining silent to let others hash out the access issue.

Regardless, Deaf people must be granted an accessible and inclusive space to contribute to the intellectual diversity of an academic gathering; otherwise, all parties miss out on their contributions.[16] The cost of inclusion should not be a psychological, financial, and emotional burden on the part of Deaf people alone. Rather, true inclusion results only when all parties are involved, including interpreters.

Based on the two conferences presented above, it is clear that all players involved, including interpreters, need to reflect about ways we can improve the experience for everyone at professional conferences. Ultimately, these discussions must be viewed through a social justice lens so that we can engage in best practices. To this end, we are proposing five avenues in which interpreters can appropriately act as agents of change.

These five avenues have a life cycle of their own. For interpreters, reflection should be ongoing to determine the effectiveness of their work during different points in time. Eventually, this model may become part of the Sign Language Network of the International Association of Conference Interpreters (AIIC) to provide best practices and guidelines,[17] the World Association of Sign Language Interpreters (WASLI), and the World Federation of the Deaf (WFD).

1. *Community engagement and curriculum*: A reflective engagement between interpreters and the Deaf community is necessary to evaluate what it means to be an interpreter within the social justice framework in multilingual and multimodal spaces. It is essential to examine the position of power and privilege of an interpreter who can leverage this privilege as an agent of change to alleviate the communication disparities in academia. The implementation of a robust social justice curriculum in interpreting education programs is critical for students to examine what it means to be an interpreter in such a position. Most importantly, professional organizations must promote in-depth dialogue with the Deaf community. This first step allows interpreters to be equipped with social justice–based tools and strategies before working in the real world.
2. *Pre-conference*: Several steps in the process of requesting interpreters must be considered for an effective process to ensue. When a sign language interpreting service request has been made by the participants or the hosting conference organizers, in principle, an agency or the interpreters themselves are the first ones to be contacted for their services. Subsequently, interpreters can step in by connecting directly with the participants and inquiring about their needs, concerns, and proposed solutions. They can also provide wisdom and counsel to the conference organizers, preferably alongside Deaf participants to implement best practices and prevent any potential undesirable outcomes.
3. *During the conference*: The fluctuating schedule of events during the conference is a challenging factor in anticipating all possible barriers or inequities. Apart from careful considerations of logistics and content preparation by the interpreters or close collaboration with the organizers and the participants, there will always be a possibility of an oversight or unexpected situation to arise. Given the position of the interpreters in this space, they can check in regularly with the organizers, the coordinators, and the participants to evaluate the issues that may arise and broker the communication between parties toward a suitable solution.
4. *Post-conference*: A debrief should occur in conjunction with the interpreters and Deaf participants to evaluate the process and how it can be improved for future conferences. Inquiring with the conference organizers is a critical piece to gain insight into how things operated behind the scenes and ultimately to learn from the general audience, through various means of communication, about their perceptions and experience interacting with Deaf participants and interpreters.

5. *Documentation*: The transfer of knowledge is a critical component from which all parties can benefit. This can be done by documenting the best practices to be shared with all parties for future reference. Closing critical gaps will lead to an effective and accessible transfer of knowledge for future conferences. All of the knowledge from various organizations (e.g., AIIC, WASLI, WFD) must be made available and shared.

Concluding Thoughts

Given the complicated nature of academic conferences that involve a variety of participants, both Deaf and hearing, from a variety of language backgrounds, issues will likely arise concerning language access. However, by virtue of their role, interpreters are granted the inherent power to alleviate many of these serious issues. While an ideal conference anticipates and resolves access issues before they begin, the conference organizers should not be burdened by this responsibility alone. It is then the responsibility of the interpreters to work alongside Deaf participants as liaisons to broker instances of inaccessibility. To begin with, conference organizers ought to follow general guidelines in principle, such as the five-point model mentioned previously, to avoid these problems. However, the reality is such that problems will occur, and when they do, interpreters have the obligation to step in if the Deaf participants think intervention of some kind is warranted. In the end, the progression of intervention and evaluation inherent in every phase of the interpreting process assumes the premise that both Deaf people and interpreters have a sense of agency in preparation for and during conference proceedings. Without this, both parties are left disempowered. Interpreters can only function as agents of change in the world if they include Deaf people in the process of creating and navigating what it means to have access.

Discussing the concept of social justice and the redistribution of language power in multilingual spaces is a sort of intangible experience for many people. The act of providing the platform of language accessibility with sign language interpretation is a first step toward this inclusion but it does not address the deeper issues that Deaf scholars face. The act of inclusion is multifaceted and multidimensional; the deconstruction of the multilingual space around conferences is necessary to achieve a deeper understanding of how to support and ensure that the distribution of power and privilege takes place. The document drafted jointly by WFD and WASLI is a prelude to an in-depth discussion of social justice by the collaborative and critical examination of events in the context of inclusion, where both communities work in tandem.[18]

Appendix 1
Amsterdam Manifesto
(revised August 21, 2000)

SINCE THE TISLR 2000 conference, there has been general consensus among participants, Deaf and hearing alike, that the conference has not been Deaf-friendly due to various reasons. Over 35 of us gathered outside of the conference on Wednesday, July 26, 2000, to address the problems that have come up during the conference. The following manifesto summarizes the main points we have agreed on during the meeting.

One main problem is that there has been no full access to academic discourse for the Deaf participants. This has partly to do with the selection of official languages that were declared for the conference. We know that around the world, the lingua franca within the scientific community, if not in the broader community, is English.

It is just as important to agree on a "lingua franca" for the scientific Deaf community, since the advantages are many: (i) using a lingua franca that is widely understood by the international scientific Deaf community will provide access to as wide a Deaf audience as possible; (ii) it will be financially more efficient to pay for a few interpreters to translate into one language, i.e., the lingua franca, which is understood by most of the audience rather than pay for individual interpreters from each of the many countries which would perhaps benefit only one or two participants; (iii) if one provides interpreters in one sign language that all people know, and provides interpreters in that same language for all sessions, Deaf attendees will not be constrained by the availability of interpreters and will have full freedom in choosing which session to attend, like their hearing peers.

It seems that BSL and ASL are the two signed languages which fit the criteria for a "lingua franca" for the scientific Deaf community, since they are widely understood by Deaf scientists from around the world. Thus we have agreed at the meeting that the official signed languages to be used for linguistics conferences should gradually include, over a span of 10 years, both BSL and ASL. Since this is an international setting, one should show respect and cultural sensitivity to the international audience by reducing the American (and British) culture-specific aspects of these signed languages and by making heavy use of the universal aspects of the signed languages.

The signed languages named above are mainly for TISLR conferences, but for a smaller international conference, it may make better sense to use another sign language that is widely understood by the audience, e.g., Swedish Sign Language if the conference consists mostly of participants from the Scandinavia area.

Note that these languages are for the purpose of linguistics conferences only, since there is a need to discuss technical material in depth and therefore a need to use a full signed language. We are not discussing whether to select a "lingua franca" for other international Deaf-related events, like those focusing on sports, art, and/or culture (e.g., Deaf Way).

In addition to using the "lingua franca" at scientific gatherings, we fully support providing access in the local signed language, since this serves to recognize the signed language on an international level and empowers the local Deaf community, the kind of support which is always sorely needed everywhere.

Thus, we strongly encourage future TISLR (and other conference) organizing committees to follow these guidelines:

(1) That the official languages of the conference should include English, the local signed language, BSL, and ASL (in which case access through English should also be provided through computer-aided real-time captioning [CART] services);

(2) That the committee should ensure there are sufficient funds to provide sign language interpreters for all simultaneous sessions of the conference and for all social events during the conference.

(3) That there should be at least one Deaf scientist on the organizing committee to ensure that necessary steps are taken to provide full access for the whole scientific community.

One should keep in mind that most of sign language research is dependent on Deaf RA's (research assistants) and on data from native Deaf signers. If it were not for the hard work of these Deaf researchers, very little progress would have been made in sign language research!

One must never forget to acknowledge their contributions, and one way to acknowledge their work is by giving something back to the signing community. The sign language researchers can easily do this by following the above guidelines and thereby making the conferences more Deaf-friendly. Participants who bring their own interpreters can afford to do so only because they are receiving grants or have salaried jobs. This puts Deaf students especially at a great disadvantage, since they do not have either, a situation which is unfair since the conference is also for linguists-in-training. If the conference can be made Deaf-friendly through the above guidelines, it will provide a platform on which prospective Deaf linguists can learn about the state of art in sign language research. Attracting more Deaf linguists this way can only serve to raise the overall quality of sign language research.

In sum, the ultimate goal behind these guidelines is to promote academic discourse among the Deaf and hearing linguists so that they can learn and benefit from one another's knowledge. Of course, the ideal type of interaction would be direct, in which all hearing linguists can sign along with everybody else. We hope that everybody will become more sensitive and accord one another respect.

Appendix 2
Athens Declaration on Access for Deaf Participants at the International Congress on the Education of the Deaf (ICED)
July 8, 2015

Whereas, ICED is a valuable conference for researchers, academics, parents, administrators, and advocates;

Whereas, Deaf educators and academics make important contributions to the field of Deaf education;

Whereas, exchange within the scientific community at ICED between Deaf and hearing participants is the bedrock of a successful ICED;

Whereas, budget constrictions and conference planning have resulted in the lack of International Sign interpreters at a majority of breakout sessions at the 22nd ICED;

Whereas, this has resulted in limitations on Deaf participants' communication access and opportunities for professional and academic growth;

Whereas, both hearing and Deaf participants have been affected and grieved due to decreased collaboration between hearing and Deaf participants;

Therefore, be it resolved that members of ICED organizing committees henceforth will ensure the provision of universal language access for all participants in International Sign and English (printed, captioned, and spoken).

Therefore, be it further resolved that membership of ICED organizing committees henceforth will include Deaf individuals, representing Deaf communities.

Therefore, be it further resolved that members of the ICED Host Selection Committee will immediately develop guidelines for future conferences to ensure universal language access in International Sign and English (printed, captioned, and spoken), including guidelines for scheduling of, budgeting for, and recruitment of qualified interpreters.

Therefore, be it further resolved that such guidelines will be created in conformity with "Guidelines on Fees and Conditions for International Sign Interpreters Working for the World Federation of the Deaf," published by the World Federation of the Deaf and the World Association of Sign Language Interpreters, 13 March 2013, and "Perspectives on the Concept and Definition of International Sign," published by the World Federation of the Deaf, May 2010.

[Signed by 312 ICED delegates]

Notes

1. Lee Anne Bell, "Theoretical Foundations for Social Justice Education," in *Teaching for Diversity and Social Justice,* ed. Maurianne Adams et al. (New York: Routledge, 2016), 3.

2. Debra Russell and Risa Shaw, "Power and Privilege: An Exploration of Decision-Making of Interpreters," *Journal of Interpretation* 25, 1 (2016):15, http://digitalcommons.unf.edu/joi/vol25/iss1/7.

3. Archon Fung, "Deliberation's Darker Side: Six Questions for Iris Marion Young and Jane Mansbridge," *National Civic Review* 93 (2004): 49, doi:10.1002/ncr.70.

4. Rehabilitation Act of 1973, Pub. L. No. 93-112, 87 Stat. 355 (September 26, 1973); Katherine A. Jankowski, *Deaf Empowerment: Emergence, Struggle, and Rhetoric* (Washington, DC: Gallaudet University Press, 1997): 147; Americans with Disabilities Act of 1990, Pub. L. No. 101-336, 108th Congress, 2nd session (July 26, 1990).

5. "Convention on the Rights of Persons with Disabilities (CRPD)," https://www.un.org/development/desa/disabilities/convention-on-the-rights-of-persons-with-disabilities.html.

6. Deaf Academics, *Amsterdam Manifesto*, http://www.deafacademics.org/conferences/amsterdam_manifesto.pdf.; Christian Rathmann, Gaurav Mathur, and Patrick Boudreault, Amsterdamer Manifest *(*Amsterdam Manifesto), *Das Zeichen* 14, (2000); Ted Supalla, Patricia Clark, Sharon Neumann Solow, and Ronice Muller de Quadros, "Developing Protocols for Interpreting in Multilingual International Conferences," *Interpreting in Multilingual, Multicultural Context,* ed. Rachel McKee and Jeffrey Davis, (Washington, DC: Gallaudet University Press, 2010): 197–225.

7. Supalla et al., "Developing Protocols for Interpreting in Multilingual International Conferences."

8. "About Us," http://www.deafacademics.org/about_us/index.php.

9. "Congress Languages," http://www.iced2015.com/en/content.php?MG=2&Mid=74&sub1=1.

10. "Renske Daanje: ICED blog 5," *Kentalis,* July 10, 2015, http://www.kentalis.nl/Professionals/Academie/Professionals-vertellen/ICED-blog-5.

11. "Conversation with Harry Knoors," *Pigs Can Fly: A Weblog by Maartje De Meulder,* July 15, 2015, https://pigscanfly.blog/2015/07/15/conversation-with-harry-knoors/.

12. The 2015 Athens Declaration Working Group, "Athens Declaration on Access for Deaf Participants at the International Congress on the Education of the Deaf (ICED)," July 8, 2015, http://www.archipel.uqam.ca/9546/.

13. World Federation of the Deaf and World Association of Sign Language Interpreters, "International Sign Fee Guidelines for WFD Events," March 2015; https://wfdeaf.org/news/resources/international-sign-fee-guidelines-for-wfd-events-march-2015/; Johanna Mesch and World Federation of the Deaf, "Perspectives on the Concept and Definition of International Sign," May 2010, https://www.diva-portal.org/smash/get/diva2:683050 /FULLTEXT01.pdf.

14. "How (Not!) To Be Inclusive: Deaf Academic version," *Possibilities and Finger Snaps Blog,* October 14, 2016, https://possibilitiesandfingersnaps.wordpress.com/2016/10/14/how-not-to-be-inclusive-deaf-academic-version/.

15. Maartje De Meulder, "'Are You Friends with the Deaf Person?' (Net)working with Sign Language Interpreters in Academic Settings," *Pigs Can Fly: A Weblog by Maartje De Meulder*, July 12, 2017, https://pigscanfly.blog/2017/07/12/are-you-friends-with-the-deaf-person-networking-with-sign-language-interpreters-in-academic-settings/.

16. H-Dirksen L. Bauman and Joseph J. Murray, eds., *Deaf Gain: Raising the Stakes for Human Diversity* (Minneapolis and London: University of Minnesota Press, 2014).

17. "Guidelines for Positioning of Sign Language Interpreters in Conferences, Including Web-Streaming," last modified December 21, 2016, https://aiic.net/page/7821/guidelines-for-positioning-of-sign-language-interpreters-in-conferences-including-web-streaming/lang/1; "Guidelines for Spoken Language Interpreters Working in Mixed Teams," last modified February 7, 2014, https://aiic.net/page/6701/guidelines-for-spoken-language-interpreters-working-in-mixed-teams/lang/1.

18. WFD and WASLI, "International Sign Fee Guidelines for WFD Events," https://wfdeaf.org/news/resources/international-sign-fee-guidelines-for-wfd-events-march-2015/; World Federation of the Deaf and World Association of Sign Language Interpreters, "International Sign Interpreter Recognition Interim Policy and Guidelines," last modified March 13, 2015, https://wfdeaf.org/news/resources/international-sign-interpreter-recognition-interim-policy-and-guideline-march-2015/; World Federation of the Deaf and World Association of Sign Language Interpreters, "March 2017 Guidelines on Securing and Utilising the Services of Sign Language Interpreters for the UN," last modified March 21, 2017, https://wfdeaf.org/news/resources/march-2017-wfd-and-wasli-guidelines-on-securing-and-utilising-the-services-of-sign-language-interpreters-for-the-un/.

12

Going Beyond Trust

Protecting My Integrity as a Deaf Academic

Thomas K. Holcomb

For the ASL summary of this chapter, go to https://youtu.be/REv1FtYvy5s

> Trust . . . This is what Deaf professionals are often told when it comes to working with interpreters who translate their signed presentations into spoken English. In most cases, and like many of my Deaf colleagues, I am not able to monitor the work of my interpreters because their spoken words are inaccessible to me. When discussing this challenge with people in the interpreting community and my Deaf colleagues, the most frequent advice given to me was to have trust in the interpreters and let them do their work the best they can. For me, this is not acceptable as there is too much at stake.

As a Deaf academic who uses ASL, I have interpreters assigned to my classrooms to provide non-signers access to my signed lectures. Because of this, students' mastery of content and subsequently their test scores may depend on the quality of interpreters. On a different level, the effectiveness of my work, the results of my course evaluations, and my ability to move up in academic rank also depend on the effectiveness of the interpreters' work. Furthermore, my ability to participate effectively in college functions such as faculty meetings or college committees is affected by the quality of interpreters assigned to do each of these assignments.[1] And finally, as part of my professional obligations, I'm expected to make presentations at conferences. Again, my professional reputation depends on the ability of the interpreters to project my message as accurately as possible.[2]

Yet, however much my Deaf colleagues and I must trust, we also rely on various strategies to check on the interpreters' work.[3] Many of these strategies are passive and reactive. For example, we might rely on the reputation of the interpreters to determine the degree of trust we should have in the interpreters. We might seek input from hearing allies who are present to provide us with immediate feedback. We might resort to lipreading the interpreters while presenting. We might observe the interactions between the working interpreters and see how much support they needed from each other throughout the assignment. After the presentation, we might be able to check the English transcripts, if available. However, none of these strategies allow us to effectively monitor the work while we are presenting.[4]

This has always been unsatisfactory to me. I wanted to have more control of my interpreted situations. I wanted to know more about the work the interpreters do when they work with me. I wanted to know when I was being misinterpreted. I wanted to know when the interpreters were struggling. I wanted to know if the interpreters' word choices were inappropriate. I wanted to know instantly if the interpreters were making errors. Conversely, I wanted to know when they did well. I wanted to see the magic of their work when they provided superb interpretation. After the job, I wanted to be able to have a genuine discussion with the interpreters about the work they did with me. Basically, I wanted to work in tandem with the interpreters rather than being a bystander in my own classroom or in any other interpreted situation. I wanted to have a relationship that went beyond just trusting the interpreters without knowing the actual outcome of their work. To this end, I tried a new approach that went beyond simply trusting the interpreters and instead allowed us to work closely as a team to ensure the most accurate interpretation in order to strengthen my trust in their work.

In this chapter, I provide a brief overview of the literature associated with the issue of trust and interpreters. Then, I provide background information on the arrangement I made with the interpreters in my classroom along with the results from this change I made. In closing, I present my thoughts related to the implications for the field.

Review of the Literature

In this section, a review of the literature is presented on four different areas that are relevant to this experience. They include: (1) trust in interpreted situations, (2) team interpreting, (3) interplay between monitoring and trust behavior, and (4) transliteration. For each area, I will briefly provide a link between the information presented and the issue at hand.

Trust in Interpreted Situations

There are many components that make up trust, including interdependence and shared goals, which are made possible by qualities such as openness, authenticity, reliability, responsiveness, competence, vulnerability, benevolence, and honesty.[5] All of these are critical to the interrelationship between Deaf people and the interpreters with whom they work.[6] However, the trust issue associated with interpreters is not unique to Deaf people. Since interpreters have the responsibility of bridging the linguistic and cultural gaps between speakers who do not share the same language, the trust factor is a huge concern among many people who use interpreters, Deaf and hearing non-English speakers alike. Several authors discuss the importance of building trust between the interpreters and the individuals with whom they work. This includes the work of Edwards, Alexander, and Temple[7] who explained:

> Trust involves belief about the way that others are likely to behave. In the case of people who need interpreters, trusting someone to act as an interpreter for

> them involves the belief that the person will understand and correctly translate what they say to someone else and what that third party says back to them, and will keep the information involved in the interaction private. This entails the assumption that the person acting as interpreter is both technically competent to carry out the interpretation and that they are morally committed to the obligation to carry it out and treat it as confidential.

Because trust is a complicated, multidimensional concept that might be influenced both by social trust (e.g., trust in institutional regulations and normative expectations) and interpersonal trust (e.g., repeated interactions and existing identities)[8] trust is not easily achieved in interpreted situations. It is because, as Hoy and Tschannen-Moran[9] explained, trust is "an individual's or group's willingness to be vulnerable to another party based on the confidence that the latter party is benevolent, reliable, competent, honest, and open."

The issue of trust in the interpreters' work is paramount among professionals and government officials at the highest level. Klopprogge and Malkin reported on Deborah Welch Larson's keynote address at the Woodrow Wilson International Center for Scholars where she said, "A lack of trust does not mean distrust," but rather trust exists along a continuum.[10] Accordingly, there is a fine analytical line between confidence and trust. Here, the importance of the concept of "trust, but verify" emerged, where it is critical to establish some form of verification mechanism to ensure accuracy in the interpreted work.

Interplay between Verification and Trust Behavior

In business relationships, trust is often built upon the perception that quality work was done.[11] Several scholars investigated the interplay of verification and trust behavior in interdependent relationships. Three different ways trust is achieved in business relationships were identified including monitoring, assurance, and corroboration. Although these studies did not focus specifically on the connection between Deaf people and the interpreters with whom they work, their findings can be applied to this kind of "business" relationship.[12]

The first way trust is achieved is through monitoring, where an actual observation of the work being performed is done and serves as a basis for trust building. However, in many business relationships, people often have no way of actually monitoring the work that is being done. For example, it is difficult for customers to monitor the automotive work that is being done on their cars. Likewise, Deaf people have limited access to the interpreted work. Instead, Deaf people and automotive repair customers often rely on assurance and corroboration to build trust in their relationships with the service providers.

Assurance, as Gundlach and Cannon explained, "affirmatively provide(s) information in an effort to clarify their partner's expectations, reduce their uncertainty and/or elevate their confidence."[13] In this sense, service providers assure the consumers that quality work was done and that there was no reason for them to believe otherwise. Similarly, interpreters often find it necessary to assure Deaf presenters that their presentation went well and that there was no cause for concern.

Alternatively, consumers may resort to a third party to corroborate that the work was done well. Gundlach and Cannon defined corroboration as "a party's efforts to seek out information external to their relationship for evaluating and assessing the conduct and activity of an exchange partner."[14] Similarly, Deaf people depend on their hearing allies to corroborate on the work of their interpreters, which serves as a basis for their trust in the interpreters with whom they work.

Regardless of which avenue is used to build trust, transparency is the key in building trust. Del Vecchio, Thompson, and Galindo explained, "Whether you are trying to prevent a trust-eroding event or repair the damage after one has occurred, transparency is key."[15] Hence some form of monitoring or verification is a critical part of transparency and an important step in strengthening trust in the work the interpreters do on behalf of Deaf professionals.

The necessity of verifying the work of interpreters was reinforced by a blogger, Bug, in his post, "Should we trust interpreters?" He expressed his disgust of interpreters who violated his trust by claiming to be professional but were not able to do the job well. In his words, Bug explained:

> It's frustrating when you put much trust in the interpreter because they act like they know everything what you say until you notice something wrong or something else tell you that interpreter doesn't voice right and the information becomes lost and screwed up like they are unable to match the elevated register, vocabulary, or descriptive language used in a meeting because of limited sign language skills then the professional doesn't have full access to the flavor of the meeting. If in the interpreter skills, he or she is unable to produce English utterance that are complete, cohesive, using the jargon for the setting and at an appropriate register or style level, a power imbalance occurs. The interpreter is oppressing the Deaf client because of her lack of skill. I am sure there is a difference between a professional who is speaking vs. speaking professionally.[16]

Interestingly, just as in French and German, where the word for trust and confidence is the same, there is one single ASL sign for these two concepts. This seems to imply that trust cannot be built without having the confidence in the work the interpreters do. Hence, it is essential that Deaf academics be provided with increased access to the interpreted work and, in essence, be able to work as a team with the interpreters.

Team Interpreting

Most discussions in the literature associated with team interpreting revolve around two or more interpreters working together.[17] Furthermore, the Registry of Interpreters for the Deaf's (RID) standard practice paper describes team interpreting as "the utilization of two or more interpreters who support each other to meet the needs of a particular communication situation."[18] What is missing, however, is the need to support the Deaf professionals in situations in which interpreters are used.

In an attempt to shift the focus of the teamwork paradigm to include Deaf people in the team concept, Hauser, Finch, and Finch edited a book in 2008 titled *Deaf Professionals and Designated Interpreters*. Here, new ideas are presented whereby interpreters work closely with Deaf professionals to ensure the accuracy and success of the interpreted work. Unfortunately, this piece of literature is one of but a few that focus on the dynamics of the Deaf professional/interpreter team.[19]

Transliteration

One strategy to further trust-building relationships between interpreters and Deaf professionals is to add a transliteration service to the mix. Transliteration is typically described as a process by which spoken words are replicated in signs by the transliterators without any modifications in grammar or syntax.[20] For the purpose of providing Deaf professionals with immediate access to the way their signed presentation is being interpreted into Spoken English, transliterators can serve this function well. I expand on this next.

In summary, trust is a major issue for Deaf professionals who use interpreting services to render their message into Spoken English. Trust cannot be fully established without some form of access to the interpreted work. The use of a transliteration service is one possible strategy in which trust can be strengthened between Deaf professionals and their interpreters. This became the foundation for the arrangement I made for my class.

Adding a Transliterator to the Mix

Because I wanted to be able to trust my interpreters fully, I sought ways to gain immediate access to their work during my presentations. After discussing my concerns with various individuals and pondering this situation, I decided to try a novel approach in my classroom that would allow me instant and on-going access to the interpreters' interpretation while I teach. I made arrangements with my college to have another interpreter present in my classroom specifically to transliterate the Spoken English (of the interpreter's presentation of my ASL lectures) into Signed English. That way, I could see the exact English words the interpreters used in presenting my lectures to the non-signers in the audience. Details of this experience are outlined next.

This arrangement ran for several weeks, from the middle to the end of the semester. The college supplied me with not one, but two interpreters (transliterators) for this request, resulting in two teams of interpreters and transliterators in the classroom with me. This was made possible by the fact that some Deaf students at the college had dropped classes during the middle of the semester, freeing the full-time interpreting staff to do other tasks such as this one.

Each interpreter and transliterator was requested to share his or her thoughts, feelings, and reactions throughout the experience with me through email. To this end, I asked them to follow the demand and control schema in framing their reactions around the environmental, paralinguistics, intrapersonal and interpersonal framework.[21]

The course was Introduction to Deaf Education. The class met twice a week for 1½ hours each. There were twenty students in the class, four of whom were Deaf.

The in-person conversations and email communication from the interpreters and transliterators were then used to analyze the process and results of this experience.

Prior to the Start of the Arrangement

I discussed with the two interpreters who had been interpreting for my classes for several years about my need to have a clearer sense of their work. Even though I had an extremely comfortable relationship with these two interpreters, I recognized the delicate nature of this proposition. I didn't want them to think that I had doubts about their work. For this reason, I made sure to frame the discussion around my *need for access rather than the quality of their work*. I explained that I wanted to know exactly how they interpreted my presentations so that I could be a more involved team member in discussing their work. As always, the interpreters were receptive to any suggestions to make the environment better for everyone involved and were willing to participate in the experience.

Although the interpreters gave me the impression that they were willing participants in this experience, they later admitted at the final debriefing session that they felt somewhat threatened by the proposition. One interpreter explained how uncomfortable she was when learning about the arrangement, yet felt she had to conceal this feeling. She explained that her immediate reaction was that she felt as though she had to prove herself once again and that there was no end to the trust process between the two of us. The second interpreter also admitted that he was puzzled at my lack of confidence in his work, especially since we had a history of working well together. They also felt somewhat threatened by the presence of two other interpreters who would be privy to their work.

By contrast, the transliterators had no issue with this assignment because their reputation or my trust in them was not at stake. Prior to the start of the experience, I explained to them about my need to be more fully aware of what my non-signing students are getting from my lectures. I talked about the need for quality control on my part. I discussed how this process was entirely experimental in nature and that I needed to document people's reactions and feelings. They were honored to be part of this experience and looked forward to the challenge.

The First Week

None of us knew what to expect during the first week. I naïvely thought it was just going to be a simple task with the transliterators coming into the classroom to sign every word they heard from the interpreters for my benefit. It quickly became evident that it was not as simple as I thought. The interpreters struggled with the pressure of having their peers in the room and worried about how they would be represented by the transliterators, especially because they could not observe their work.

The transliterators sat right behind them and worked outside of the interpreters' sight line; the classroom interpreters had no idea how the transliterators were performing. They could not know if errors were being made on the transliterators' part. They worried that I might lose trust in them as interpreters if the transliterators had done a poor job in translating their spoken words into signs. Both interpreters shared their thoughts in their email entries:

> I really value my opportunity to work with you (Tom) and would not want anything to damage my relationship with you. I want you to trust completely that I am capable of doing the work. I must admit that I worry about the work the transliterators do as I have no way of ensuring the accuracy of their transliteration work. In case of errors being made, I don't want you to think their mistakes are mine. Because I don't want you to lose trust in me, this has become a distraction for me.

Similarly, the second interpreter commented:

> I did experience a bit of trepidation when it came to the actual transmission of the transliterated message. How would my interpretation be transliterated? Would words without signs be fingerspelled or would a signed equivalent be used? My concern was that synonyms that would possibly be utilized by the transliterators might not truly reflect the register of the vocabulary that we, as the interpreters, were using.

BINGO! This was the heart of the issue itself: the interpreters found it difficult to completely trust the transliterators without seeing their work and worried about how they were being represented. This is exactly what my Deaf colleagues and I worry about all the time. In my log, I wrote:

> I found it fascinating that the interpreters were concerned about how their work was being represented by the transliterators. Their concern is exactly the same as mine and the reason why I wanted the transliteration service in the first place. Not knowing how my work is being presented through a third party can be rather unsettling, especially when you want to make sure you appear intelligent, that the appropriate register is being used, that the best word choices are made, and so forth. It goes beyond the "trust" that is often called for by the Deaf professionals in these situations. It is my belief that the "quality control" should not be left to the interpreters alone and that creative ways need to be found to allow the Deaf party to monitor the work of the interpreters and to provide feedback. I wonder if this experience is helping the interpreters become even more sensitive and appreciative about the fact that this is not just about "trust" but more about working as a team.

This revelation by the interpreters provides strong evidence that it is unreasonable to expect Deaf professionals who use interpreters to develop a trusting relationship with their interpreters without having verification of or access to the interpreted work.

The Next Few Weeks

During the next few weeks, I was privy to several things that were lost to me all those years of working with interpreters. For instance, during one class where I shared several anecdotes, I saw for the first time how two interpreters could have different ideas of how to interpret my signed passages. One interpreter consistently used the first person while the second interpreter, during her turn, used the third person in representing my stories. It was the very first time I realized the scope of the decision-making process interpreters needed to partake in.[22] While I was thrilled at gaining insight into seeing how decisions need to be made on the spot by the interpreters, I was disappointed that I was never before consulted about the implications of such decisions. After this experience, I felt even more strongly that Deaf professionals should have more input as to how they are represented by the interpreters. The only way to have input is to provide them with increased access to the interpreted work.

For the interpreters, their biggest "demand" became the mere presence of the transliterators because now their peers were there listening to their work. However, they admitted that this pressure produced even more effective interpreting work on their part. In addition, their concern about not being represented sufficiently by the transliterators was mollified after a meeting with the transliterators:

> In the end, I needn't have worried. After discussing the process with the transliterators, they assured me that they were fingerspelling higher register words and turns of phrases. In this way, they could accurately convey the "flavor" of the interpreted message.

At the end of the semester, we had a debriefing session. There, it became clear that the trust factor was a dominant issue for everyone. Although the impetus behind the arrangement was to find ways to go beyond trust in the Deaf consumer–working interpreter dyads and help these two parties become a team in their working relationship, it was not intended that this arrangement itself focus on the trust issue. However, the issue of trust emerged as a major concern among the interpreters and transliterators right from the start. The interpreters needed to trust the transliterators. The transliterators needed to be assured that the interpreters trusted them, as otherwise it would become an additional demand for them. As for the arrangement itself, both the transliterators and interpreters needed to trust the process and understand that I would not use this experience against any of them in any way. Subsequently, I found it necessary to repeatedly reassure everyone to trust me and each other throughout the experience. The importance of teamwork was emphasized by a transliterator when she commented,

> It was difficult to work under the personal pressure of how our transliteration affected the perception of our colleagues' work product. You used the words "quality control." We think that the five of us need to have meetings where we can debrief and build trust. This would allow us to examine and understand the process as a whole, instead of just our individual parts.

I believe this direct experience with the trust factor resulted in the interpreters becoming more sensitive and aware about the unreasonable "expectation" that Deaf professionals can and should trust their interpreters fully and completely. One interpreter discussed how he realized the importance of providing the Deaf person with access to his work by stating:

> After bringing in the transliterators, it was like a breath of fresh air . . . making me even more alert and ready to work . . . knowing that Tom would finally have the access to what was being voiced by us. It generally "forced" us all to work closer together and provide more communication and feedback, and that is a good thing!

The interpreters also commented how much they appreciated having the opportunity to have an open discussion with each other about the work they all did. One of the transliterators expounded on this point by stating:

> I think that the dialogue that has been opened up between the transliterators and the Deaf consumer is a valuable exercise. Often as an interpreter I feel like I can't get adequate feedback to help me make decisions about how I work. The weight of decision-making was lessened because I knew what Tom was thinking about the work we did and what adjustments he would like to see happen. This guided me to be clear in making decisions about how to do my work. I wonder what would happen if these kind of decisions were happening in other assignments. I believe the satisfaction level for all stakeholders would increase.

She also discussed another benefit of this experience: "Personally this has allowed me to focus more on the process of analysis and interpretation and given me a new perspective from which to discuss my work."

For me, my trust in the interpreters with whom I work increased after I gained access to their work. For example, I was able to see for myself the work the interpreters had done in translating and delivering my presentation in spoken English, and more often than not I was impressed and pleased. As I noted in my log:

> I was inspired by the powerful words my interpreters used in their translation of my ASL. I was enthralled, inspired, and excited. My respect for and confidence in the interpreters increased exponentially.

Obviously, this explicit exposure to the work of the interpreters allowed me to gain a greater appreciation of the work the interpreters do. This illuminates the importance of providing Deaf presenters with some form of access to the interpreted work, especially at the beginning of their relationship with the interpreters. By seeing the actual words used by the interpreter, there is a genuine basis for trust that is expected of Deaf presenters.

Implications and Suggestions for the Field

I've come to believe that this experience has helped these four interpreters become even more sensitive to what Deaf people need to deal with in interpreted situations. This experience reinforced my belief that Deaf professionals need to invest more time and energy to participate in the quality control of the interpreted work. I believe interpreters should welcome the opportunity to have their work readily accessible to the Deaf presenters. The question is how.

Clearly, in most cases, it is not cost effective to have four support staff covering classes or meetings.[23] However, I do believe it is reasonable to arrange for transliterators to come in my classroom once or twice every semester just to give me a clearer sense of how my work is being projected by the interpreters. This would serve as a stronger basis for trust to continue between the interpreters and myself. In addition, this arrangement should be made for the first few sessions whenever a new interpreter is assigned to me or any Deaf professional.

Another situation where the transliteration service can be implemented is keynote or major presentations at conferences. During those times, interpreters assigned to cover the break-out sessions, but not the keynote address, are usually free as all conference participants are gathered in a room for the main presentation. Here, these interpreters can transliterate the work of the voice interpreters for the benefit of the Deaf keynoter. This can be especially beneficial for these conference presenters since they usually are expected to trust the interpreters without having much prior experience with them. I believe this arrangement would raise the bar for professionalism for both Deaf professionals and interpreters and create a new standard for the teamwork between Deaf presenters and interpreters.

For almost all other cases where the situation is limited to two interpreters, strategies could be employed to allow the second interpreter to transliterate the work of the first interpreter whenever possible and appropriate. One successful strategy that has worked well in the past is to use the second interpreter to transliterate when there is a long lag time during which the first interpreter is spending a few minutes catching up. Here, the Deaf presenter would pause to allow the "catch up" to occur. While the first interpreter is busy catching up (and not needing support from the second interpreter), the second interpreter is free to begin transliterating the spoken words of the first interpreter, allowing the presenter a glimpse of the work of the first interpreter. Short glimpses of such work go a long way in helping me get a sense of how I'm being represented by the interpreter. These rare opportunities to see the interpretation enabled me to continue building my trust in the interpreters who are assigned to me.

While I personally appreciate having access to the interpreted work of my presentations and having the ability to work directly with the interpreters during the course of my presentations, I realize not all Deaf people have the same desire. Perhaps it is because some Deaf professionals have been "conditioned" to trust and be removed from the process, however uncomfortable it may be for them. This conditioning comes in many forms. The "you do your work and I do mine" mentality is one. The dreaded advance paper request is another. Not knowing any other ways to deal with the situation is another reason.

Some presenters are not able to handle anything more than delivering their own presentations in ASL. The added burden of monitoring the interpreters is not feasible for them. Therefore, they have no interest in working with the interpreters and prefer to trust instead. Finally, many Deaf presenters are not aware of any alternatives and therefore do not realize they could and should be working closely with the interpreters to ensure precision in the interpreted work.

Conclusion

Clearly, trust cannot and should not be based on the unknown. Deaf professionals deserve more than being expected to just trust the interpreters to do the work that potentially has a huge impact on their professional career and reputation. Being in the dark or relying on less than optimal avenues to gain access to the interpreted work should no longer be tolerated by either Deaf professionals nor the interpreting community.

The next level of excellence and professionalism for the interpreter community calls for increased partnership with Deaf professionals in the interpreted work. Deaf professionals deserve no less. Interpreters deserve trust of the Deaf people based on concrete evidence of their work rather than just faith.

Instead of viewing this discussion as simply a trust issue, the focus should be on optimal working relationships between Deaf professionals and the interpreters who work with them. This experiment is but one effort in finding solutions to provide Deaf professionals and interpreters the support they need.

Notes

1. See Dave Smith and Paul Ogden, this volume.

2. Linda Campbell, Meg J. Rohan, and Kathryn Woodcock, "Academic and Educational Interpreting from the Other Side of the Classroom: Working with Deaf Academics," in *Deaf Professionals and Designated Interpreters: A New Paradigm,* ed. Peter C. Hauser, Karen L. Finch, and Angela B. Hauser (Washington, DC: Gallaudet University Press, 2008): 81–105.

3. Peter C. Hauser, Karen L. Finch, and Angela B. Hauser, eds., *Deaf Professionals and Designated Interpreters: A New Paradigm* (Washington, DC: Gallaudet University Press, 2008).

4. See Thomas Holcomb on DEAM, this volume.

5. Maureen E. Angell, Julia B. Stoner, and Debra L. Shelden,"Trust in Educational Professionals: Perspectives of Mothers of Children with Disabilities," *Remedial and Special Education* 30, no. 3 (2009): 160–76; Cristano Castelfranchi and Rino Falcone, *Trust Theory: A Socio-cognitive and Computational Model* (West Sussex, UK: John Wiley & Sons, 2010).

6. Jemina Napier, "'It's Not What They Say But the Way They Say It': A Content Analysis of Interpreter and Consumer Perceptions of Signed Language Interpreting in Australia," *International Journal of Society of Language* 207 (2011): 59–87.

7. Rosalind Edwards, Claire Alexander, and Bogusia Temple, "Interpreting Trust: Abstract and Personal Trust for People Who Need Interpreters to Access Services," *Sociological Research Online* 11, no. 1 (2006). Accessed April 8, 2017, http://www.socresonline.org.uk/11/1/edwards.html.

8. Steven D. Pearson and Lisa H. Reake, "Patient's Trust in Physicians: Many Theories, Few Measures, and Little Data," *Journal of General Internal Medicine* 15, no. 7 (2000): 509–13.

9. Wayne K. Hoy and Megan Tschannen-Moran, "Five Faces of Trust: An Empirical Confirmation in Urban Elementary Schools," *Journal of School Leadership* 9, no. 3 (1999): 184–208.

10. Nadia Klopprogge and Emily Malkin, "Trust But Verify: Confidence and Distrust from Détente to the End of the Cold War," in *Bulletin of the German Historical Institute* 50 (2012): 150–55.

11. Gregory T. Gundlach and Joseph P. Cannon, "Trust But Verify"? The Performance Implications of Verification Strategies in Trusting Relationships," *Journal of the Academy of Marketing Science* 38, no. 4 (2010): 399–417.

12. Kenneth W. Abbott, "Trust But Verify: The Production of Information in Arms Control Treaties and Other International Agreements," *Cornell International Law Journal* 26 (1993): 1–58; Maurice E. Schweitzer and Teck H. Ho, "Trust But Verify: Monitoring in Interdependent Relationships," *Experimental and Behavioral Economics* 13 (2005): 87–106; Duncan Snidal, "The Game Theory of International Politics," *World Politics* 38, no. 1 (1985): 25–57; Arthur A. Stein, "Coordination and Collaboration: Regimes in an Anarchic World," *International Organization* 36, no. 2 (1982): 299–324.

13. Gregory T. Gundlach and Joseph P. Cannon, "Trust But Verify: The Performance Implications of Verification Strategies in Trusting Relationships," *Journal of the Academy of Marketing Science* 38, no. 4 (2010): 399–417.

14. Gregory T. Gundlach and Joseph P. Cannon, "Trust But Verify."

15. Steve Del Vecchio, Chris Thompson, and George Galindo, accessed April 8, 2017, http://www.pwc.com/us/en/view/issue-13/trust-but-verify.jhtml.

16. Bug, "Should We Trust Interpreters?" *Fookem and Bug,* February 26, 2007, accessed on April 8, 2017, https://fookembug.wordpress.com/2007/02/26/should-we-trust-interpreters/.

17. Dennis Cokely and Jennifer Hawkins, "Interpreting in Teams: A Pilot Study on Requesting and Offering Support," *Journal of Interpretation* 16 (2003): 49–94; Paula L. Gajewski Mickelson, "Intentional Teaming: Experiences from the Second National Healthcare Symposium," *Journal of Interpretation* 24 (2015): 5; Jack Hoza, *Team Interpreting as Collaboration and Interdependence* (Alexandria, VA: RID Press, 2010).

18. Registry of Interpreters of the Deaf Professional Standards Team, "Team Interpreting," *Standard Practice,* Paper (Silver Springs, MD: Registry of Interpreters of the Deaf, 2007), accessed January 2, 2017, from http://rid.org/about-interpreting/standard-practice-papers/.

19. Hauser et al., *Deaf Professionals and Designated Interpreters.*

20. Jeff Davis, "Code Choices and Consequences: Implications for Educational Interpreting" in *Educational Interpreting: From Research to Practice*, eds. Marc Marschark, Rico Peterson, and Elizabeth Winston (New York: Oxford University Press, 2005): 112–41; Linda Siple, "Historical Development of the Definition of Transliteration," *Journal of Interpretation* 7, no. 1 (1997): 77–100; Elizabeth A. Winston, "Transliteration: What's the Message?" *Sociolinguistics of the Deaf Community*, ed. Cecil Lucas (San Diego, CA: Academic Press, 1989): 147–64.

21. Robyn K. Dean and Robert Q Pollard, "Application of Demand-Control Theory to Sign Language Interpreting: Implications for Stress and Interpreter Training," *Journal of Deaf Studies and Deaf Education* 6, no. 1 (2001): 1–14.

22. Bill Moody, "Literal vs. Liberal: What is a Faithful Interpretation?" *Journal of Interpretation* 21, no. 1 (2007): 179–220.

23. See Thomas Holcomb on DEAM, this volume.

13

Educational Interpreting from Deaf Eyes

Amy June Rowley

For the ASL summary of this chapter, go to https://youtu.be/Yb1jr87HbOY

> I want to bring light to the substandard communication access for Deaf children, especially those who use sign language interpreters in educational settings. Some may say that as a product of the mainstreamed education system, I am a success story because I am now a college professor. Yet, the irony is that I would never wish my experience upon any Deaf child, including my own Deaf children. I am appalled at the current educational situation and its role in language deprivation as you all should be. How can we be making strides in educational improvements when more deaf children than ever are continuing to experience language deprivation? Deaf history is deplorably repeating itself by courting public preference that deaf children be assimilated as much as possible. This also means mainstreaming has become the first placement consideration for deaf children, when it should be the very last option.

THERE ARE AN estimated 350,000 deaf and hard of hearing children nationwide. Of that number, an estimated 23 percent receive services under the Individuals with Disabilities Education Act (IDEA), and 86.4 percent are mainstreamed. Of this 86.4 percent, 53 percent are situated alone without any deaf peers.[1] These statistics raise two important questions:

1. How many of these students are provided with sign language interpreting services? Since only 23 percent of all deaf and hard of hearing children are receiving educational services under individualized education plans (IEPs) as required by IDEA, this leads us to question how many students actually receive education with appropriate support services such as access to a visual language.
2. For those without IEPs, are they receiving support services through alternative mandates such as a 504 plan under the Rehabilitation Act of 1973? If so, what kind of access services are they receiving? Furthermore, it is difficult to obtain accurate information on how deaf and hard of hearing students are accessing communication in the classroom. All these only serve to further

muddle the overall perception of the status of deaf education. Indeed, the landscape of deaf education requires some explaining.

Perhaps the most alarming statistics come from Holcomb where there is discussion of the 90 percent formula that is used to describe the situation of deaf children in the United States.[2] More than 90 percent of deaf children come from hearing parents who often cannot communicate fully and effectively with them.[3] The formula also applies to the number of deaf children who cannot speak intelligibly even after years of speech therapy along with Deaf people who were raised orally but ended up using sign language. At present, almost 90 percent of deaf children do not attend a deaf school, nor do they have equal educational access to both ASL and English at home or school. Consequently, many deaf children experience language deprivation despite technological advances such as cochlear implants.

Sign Language Usage in Schools With Deaf Children

Shaver, Marschark, Newman, and Marder analyzed a sample of Deaf students consisting of 870 students ages 13–16 and in the 7th grade or higher in various school settings. Regular school settings included students who were mainstreamed (i.e., in classes along with students who hear) where they were given support services, self-contained classrooms, and fully integrated (mainstreamed) but with no support. Special school settings would include programs such as schools for the Deaf and charter or magnet schools that were established specifically for Deaf students. From the sample, which included students in regular schools and special schools, 61.9 percent used sign language, including 51 percent of the Deaf children who were mainstreamed. For those who attended a special school, 98 percent used sign language.[4]

In an attempt to identify communication modes used in mainstreamed environments, Cawthon compiled a communication profile of deaf students in secondary environments, including mainstreamed students, representing 11,975 students. Her study showed spoken English was the primary mode of communication for 44 percent of mainstreamed participants. Simultaneous communication (signing and speaking at the same time) composed 15 percent of the overall communication profile, and regularly using speech and working with interpreters (not simultaneously) came to 22 percent. The remaining 20 percent used multiple forms of communication, including sign language as the preferred mode. This 20 percent included students who use Cued Speech as well.[5] Based on these numbers alone, it is safe to assume that just more than half of the students in this study could access some form of sign communication, aligning with the 51 percent figure used by Shaver and colleagues. Clearly, there is currently no homogenous approach to teaching deaf children, nor a consensus on language use in deaf education. Deaf students are being educated in any way possible—implying that there exists no consensus about how Deaf children should be educated. The plethora of philosophies in deaf education training programs indicates this lack of consensus as well.[6]

An area of concern is that many interpreters are not qualified to interpret in school settings.[7] Schick, Williams, and Kupermintz, based on their study about educational interpreters, concluded that many of them do not have the necessary skills to work in the classroom.[8] States that require educational interpreters to have credentials or certification typically use the Educational Interpreter Performance Assessment (EIPA). This assessment tool tests skills and abilities in Manually Coded English (MCE), Pidgin Signed English (PSE), and American Sign Language (ASL). On a five-point scale, a score of at least a 3.5 is typically required to work as a classroom interpreter, although some states only require a score of 3.0. Schick and colleagues noted that only 38 percent of their sample could achieve the 3.5 minimum as required by several states, even though most of the tested interpreters were currently working in educational settings. These researchers also noted that the interpreters who used ASL were more likely to score higher on the assessment while those using MCE were noted as weaker signers.

With this in mind, inclusion in schools that are primarily hearing should not be considered the first choice for Deaf children. Data show that successful mainstream learning environments exist only if the interpreters are phenomenal.[9]

My Personal Journey

When my Deaf parents discovered that I was Deaf at 18 months old, like most parents with a newly identified deaf infant, they began to explore educational options for me. There were few choices at the time, including the New York School for the Deaf (Fanwood) and my local elementary school, which would mean limited access due to a non-signing environment. That option was unthinkable to my mother, Nancy, who remembered clearly her own frustrations as a student in primary and secondary schools.

Shortly afterward in 1975, the Education for All Handicapped Children Act, also known as Public Law 94-142, was enacted. This law opened the door for children with disabilities to receive a free and appropriate public education (FAPE) in the least restrictive environment (LRE). My parents saw this new development as an opportunity for me to be mainstreamed and stay close to home. This was important to my mother, especially since I was progressing well in language development through sign language. I was not language-deprived like many other deaf children; rather, I was among the lucky 10 percent of the Deaf population to have had full access to language since birth. My mother felt that too many students at Fanwood were language-deprived because they arrived at the school with extremely limited language skills in English and sign language. In my mother's eyes, this made the local school option a better choice for me especially with appropriate accommodations available as mandated by PL 94-142.

However, being enrolled and receiving full access to the classroom was not going to be as simple as my parents thought. When I started kindergarten in 1977, the school refused to provide an interpreter for me. I had to rely on lipreading and my teacher's generosity. This included a lot of patience on her part in communicating with me, writing things down for me, and taking time to communicate with my mother on a regular basis. My mother, who was also a teacher, worked closely with me to make sure I kept up with my coursework.

At the same time, my parents initiated a lengthy mediation process, which eventually led to a lawsuit, *Rowley v. Hendrick Hudson Board of Education.*[10] At first, the court ruled in our favor and I was finally provided with an interpreter in the third grade. However, the decision was repeatedly appealed by the school district and ended up escalating all the way to the United States Supreme Court.

Having an interpreter in class was a huge improvement for me because I was able to enjoy school for the first time. I could follow along perfectly in classroom discussions. My interpreter in the third grade, who had Deaf parents and was fluent in ASL, made sure to interpret everything, including the side conversations and discussions among my classmates. My interpreter fully understood that she was a language mediator. At that time, there were no interpreter education programs, and interpreters often had to figure out their roles in various situations. She did just that, mediating language between the other students, the teacher, and myself. I was having conversations with my classmates as well as with the class as a whole for the first time. Since I was fluent in sign language, the interpreter opened up a new avenue of complete accessibility for me. I felt friendships blossoming with my hearing peers as I could communicate and follow group conversations. I even looked forward to recess because the interpreter would follow me out and interpret any interactions between my schoolmates and me. In the past, I would just follow other kids outside for recess and end up just playing by myself. The added bonus of having an interpreter in the classroom meant that when I got home from school, I did not have to relearn everything through my mother. I had a lot more time to play and "just be a kid." Indeed, third grade was a really good year for me. The experience that year was largely successful not only because of the interpreter but also because of the teacher. As a parent of a child with a disability herself, she knew to include me in class and not leave me alone in my interpreter's "care."

Things changed when I entered fourth grade, when the school refused to continue providing the interpreting services. Instead, a teacher of the deaf was assigned to work with me. Apparently, the school believed that this teacher could provide some one-to-one tutoring assistance as well as "interpret" in the classroom. So, instead of interpreting everything like the previous interpreter, she only summarized what the teacher lectured. I did not know what my classmates were saying inside and outside of the classroom. Thus, I dreaded recess and the entire school experience. This action, or lack thereof, further supported the notion that my school did not fully understand the role of the interpreter—and today, several decades later, the strict boundaries of the interpreter's role continues to be a common misconception.[11]

During the summer between fourth grade and fifth grade, the U.S. Supreme Court announced that the two previous decisions of the lower courts in my parents' favor had been overturned. The court sided with Hendrick Hudson School District in its claim that they did not need to provide me with an interpreter because I was already being provided with a free, appropriate, public education (FAPE) and I had performed well without interpreters. They did not make the connection that this success came because of my mother's support, not because I could learn easily without an interpreter.

Due to the decision by the Supreme Court, I did not have an interpreter or a teacher of the deaf in fifth grade. Because of this, my parents decided to move the following year to New Jersey, where there was a comprehensive day school program for deaf children. There, I was fully mainstreamed with an interpreter. Even better, there were other Deaf students at the school. This was a wonderful experience for me because not only was my interpreter fabulous but I could also talk freely with other students who were Deaf like me. This was a huge social milestone for me. There were no communication barriers and I really enjoyed going to school and having full access there. It was the first time I was able to "gossip" and just be myself with other students. Occasionally, I was pulled out of class to meet with a deaf education teacher for additional support. I did not like being pulled out because it made me different from my peers. In this sense, I felt like being mainstreamed made me feel like I would never fit in and would always be different from other people.

When I was ready for high school, the school district decided not to accept out-of-district students, which meant I stayed in the Deaf program alone since it was my local high school. That was really hard on me, and I was lonely most of the time even though there were interpreters. Even worse, I did not have the same interpreters for each class. That prevented me from becoming close to any one interpreter. Even though I was not able to become close to my interpreters, I still found myself depending on them for social satisfaction and stimulation. Generally speaking, schools do not encourage students to be close to their teachers, yet social dependency on adults is common among deaf students. In fact, some students become completely reliant on their interpreters for their social needs, especially those who have the same interpreter for the majority of their schooling years.

It is important that interpreters have the skills to interpret the content in which they are comfortable and knowledgeable. I took two years of Spanish in high school, and during the first year I had an interpreter who knew no Spanish. We had to "navigate" the course together, requiring some creativity on both of our parts. This included tons of fingerspelling, some signing, and creative ways of communicating with some degree of success. Unfortunately, she went on maternity leave the following year. That left us in a quandary over finding a new interpreter. Somehow it was decided that the new speech teacher, who was a staunch advocate of Cued Speech, would teach me that approach so that she could cue or "interpret" for me during Spanish class. I was very resistant to this because this seemed like more work for me, but I obliged. I learned Cued Speech and tried my best to follow along in Spanish class with the speech teacher "interpreting" by using Cued Speech. I had relied a lot on speech, lipreading, and cues to get me by during my earlier years, yet I struggled in my Spanish class. I had no idea what Spanish words were supposed to sound like, so I could not really follow her. Furthermore, the speech teacher did not know any Spanish herself so she could not interpret or translate anything. Later on, a trilingual interpreter replaced the speech teacher as my interpreter. Although he used ASL to sign everything, I still struggled because he would translate everything for me instead of letting me try to learn the language. Even though there were three different people who tried to "interpret" my Spanish class at different times, there was no good solution.

After a stint in Australia for a student-exchange program, I only had five months left of school before graduation. The district hired a new interpreter for me. The two of us became really good friends—close, in fact. I felt closer to her than any of the other people in high school and the two of us are still friends today. Although I appreciated that friendship at the time, I realize now that this prevented me from connecting with other students in my class.

I always struggled to fit in and continued to be a social outcast until I entered college. Many people told me when I entered college that I was "immature," "hyper," and socially awkward. This hurt a lot because I never felt I belonged at school and when I entered college, I felt I did not have much to show for all my years of being mainstreamed.

My Reflections

Looking back on this experience, I realize that educational interpreters often have to take on multiple roles and it might be a struggle for them to determine which roles are appropriate. I have always considered my interpreter to be someone with whom I can be engaged, have a conversation with during quiet time, and interact with as a real person. It was not until I was older and attending a class at the University of Wisconsin-Madison that I realized that the interpreter/student boundary can be very ambiguous. There, the interpreter in my microbiology lab inquired why I felt it was okay for us to converse while other students could not talk with each other after they completed their work out of respect for those still working. This interpreter, who went by the book, felt it was more appropriate to chat only outside of the classroom. I was stunned by her comment, but it really got me to think about my previous experiences with my interpreters.

If there is anything I feel strongly about, it is this: children should be allowed to be children. Too often, children are robbed of their right to grow up without the weight of the world on their shoulders. I know that weight squashed me down during my elementary school years. For this reason, I am very mindful of this, as a mother of three children, two of whom are Deaf, that they should never experience the same frustrations I did growing up in the mainstreamed environment.

The best educational experience of my life occurred during my college years. I went to Gallaudet University where everyone signed. There was no "third person" necessary to access information. I got everything I needed from my teachers and fellow students directly and effortlessly, which was a really refreshing experience for me. Similarly, I want my children to grow up feeling like they matter. For me, this means having a direct access to teachers and peers who use the same language they do. Additionally, if they cannot be in a class with all Deaf students, I would like their teachers to really want to teach them and not just have to barely tolerate having them in their classroom, which is a commonly reported feeling by many mainstreamed students.[12]

Based on my personal experiences, some of which I have shared here, I am making recommendations as to how the needs of mainstreamed Deaf students can be met the Deaf way.

Recommendations/Suggestions and The Deaf Way

Interpreter quality is the most important factor to make a mainstreamed situation successful. The younger the child, the more skilled the interpreters should be. Additionally, K–12 educational interpreters must have multiple skills, such as having the ability to be a language model, being an advocate, and exhibiting an outgoing personality.

Interpreter Quality

For deaf students to be academically successful, their interpreters must be highly qualified because every student's success relies heavily on the interpreter's ability to render all the information in the classroom as accurately, clearly, and fully as possible. Not only do interpreters need to completely understand all of the material being taught, but they also should work closely with the students to make sure that their translations are understandable.

Oliva and Lytle presented scenarios in their book in which the K–12 education interpreter is considered a "nemesis" of Deaf students. In their study, several Deaf adults who were mainstreamed disclosed that a major weakness of their interpreted experiences was that they only had access to communication in one direction. Often, the interpreter could not adequately voice interpret for Deaf students. When this is the case, it limits participation by the Deaf student. Also, these "weak" interpreters are more likely to be unable to interpret the academic content as well.[13]

Recent graduates of interpreter education programs are often encouraged to seek employment in an educational environment. In fact, some programs focus entirely on preparing students for educational interpreting.[14] This is not a pattern that should be encouraged. Educational environments should be reserved for more seasoned and skilled interpreters, and this principle must be supported in every interpreter education program. If interpreter educators, interpreters, and interpreting students are all on board with this, then it will prompt a reframing of the content and approach within the interpreting education curriculum. This will help ensure that interpreting students are not placed in educational environments during internships, or if they are, their mentors need to discuss with them very carefully why working in an educational environment should not be their first job upon graduation.

Stewart, Schein, and Cartwright detailed issues regarding interpreters seeking jobs in educational settings.The first is to look at the job description to make sure the school is aware of the accurate role of interpreters. If the job description is vague, then there will be more advocacy and education required by the interpreter for the Deaf student to create a successful relationship between the interpreter and the school. Second is the interpreter's role. It can be easily expanded by schools to include more tasks such as tutoring or taking notes. However, if the school sees interpreters as aides or paraprofessionals, then the teachers will likely view them similarly. This undermines the hierarchy of educational interpreting as a profession. Finally, because interpreters must adhere to ethics, working in an educational environment as part of a team can create an ambiguity of roles, especially for new interpreters who are still learning their roles.[15]

As a minimum standard of competency, all educational interpreters should strive for RID certification. Although this is not required in some states, Schick and colleagues found that educational interpreters who passed the EIPA assessment and who also had RID certification were more likely to have at least the minimum qualifications to interpret, more so than those who only had EIPA or no certifications at all. Since RID certification is a pass/fail system as opposed to the 5-point scale certification for EIPA, people who become RID-certified have attained the "minimum" standards needed to work as educational interpreters. The authors further noted that of 2,100 candidates who took the EIPA between 2002 and 2004, only 38 percent were qualified to interpret with a 3.5 point rating.[16] As reported by the DO-IT Center, 42 states require that the EIPA be used in some way. Twenty-four of these states require at least a 3.5 rating, whereas 11 require a 4.0 rating.[17] With these alarming statistics, we can see that 62 percent of these candidates were not qualified to interpret. Yet, despite the requirements, many of these interpreters are working in the classroom because they got waivers from their states. Clearly, this situation has serious ramifications for the quality of education for these Deaf students. At the very least, interpreters must meet the minimum qualifications. The state waivers must be stopped because unqualified interpreters should not be interpreting for children.

Interpreter as Language Model

More often that not, deaf students do not have full access to language at home.[18] More than 90 percent of deaf children come from hearing families, their communication strategies vary a great deal. Some may have "home signs," another form of signed communication, or use oral language only. Thus, often, the interpreter becomes the defacto language model for the deaf child.[19] This means that the student's ability to learn the language being used for instruction primarily comes from the interpreter. If the parents, school, or interpreter decide on a communication mode other than ASL, this leads to other ramifications than just academic communication. Choosing to use something other than a fully recognized human language constitutes a two-fold deprivation. First of all, not using American Sign Language as a natural language means that the brain is not being exposed to a natural language but only an artificial signed system. All artificial signed systems have been developed to mimic English grammatical structure, but when converted to signed form, the brain does not process it the same way as it does spoken English.[20] For instance, when using Signed English, the insect BUTTERFLY is denoted by two signs BUTTER and FLY. This can be extremely confusing because visually this conveys a stick of butter flying in the air, which is not a conceptually accurate representation of the winged insect. Additionally, many deaf students do not have access to sign language at home and when they arrive at school, often well past the natural language acquisition age, they are already language deprived and starting their education with little or no language base. Also, learning language in the educational environment is not the same as the natural acquisition environment that hearing students are exposed to at home.[21] Deaf education is already considered a dismal failure by many. The fact that there is no clear advocacy for ASL at all levels of deaf education shows that the value of teaching deaf students in a natural language seems not as strong as the value of forcing them to assimilate into an English-dominant society.[22] This makes it even more critical for interpreters to work with the Deaf community to improve this situation. When both communities work together, successful collaboration and allyship is possible.

Second, as a language model, when an interpreter uses a communication mode other than ASL, they are reinforcing a process of delayed development, which will result in difficulty being understood, which will then lead to alienation from others who use ASL. In my case, when I enrolled at Gallaudet, I was immersed in a Deaf social environment where everyone used ASL. It took me a long time to modify my language usage so I could communicate effectively. Even though I grew up in a Deaf family, my interpreters had used English word order and/or more English-based signs. Prior to Gallaudet, I struggled to fit in with my Deaf friends and never felt confident about my communication. Some people who had more experience with the syntactic order of Signed English understood me, but many did not. It was later after Gallaudet that I took formal linguistics courses and understood ASL rules and grammar. This finally enabled me to feel pride and confidence in my language and as a Deaf person. So it is important to allow deaf students opportunities to access ASL fully and not create more barriers hindering their language growth. If interpreters are not fluent in ASL, then they are modeling a type of communication that the deaf student will have a hard time using with other Deaf people in the future. This actually sets up more hurdles for the Deaf student to navigate in the Deaf community.

Interpreter as an Advocate

Since the interpreter is usually the only person in the classroom who has been trained in sign language, they are also most likely the only person in the school environment who has been educated about Deaf culture as well. As the person who knows the Deaf student the best, the interpreter will likely need to become an advocate for the student. In this process, it is important to remember that interpreters advocating for a student does not necessarily mean they are advocating for themselves or for their job. It might be necessary to advocate for something that may be better for the student in the long run, but not necessarily better for the interpreter.

I saw this happen with my own daughter. When she was three, she attended a private program with an excellent interpreter because the nearest Deaf school was almost 45 minutes away and she was too young to ride the bus for that long. When it was time for her IEP meeting, the interpreter could have advocated for herself by insisting that my daughter remain in the program so that she could keep her job. Instead she advocated for my daughter, saying that she was not thriving in her current environment. As a parent, I was impressed with the interpreter's ability to really see the bigger picture and admit that my daughter was not thriving in the mainstreamed program, so we decided to send her to the Deaf program all the way across town. She immediately thrived there where she was able to engage with many friends who signed. It turned out to be a great decision and I appreciated the advocacy of the interpreter and that her heart was truly in the right place.

Exhibiting an Outgoing Personality

My third grade experience with the child of a Deaf adult (CODA) interpreter who made sure I was included inside and outside the classroom is the reason for this particular recommendation. Interpreters should make an effort to step outside their comfort zones, if necessary, to help bridge communication between classmates, peers, teachers, and other people with whom Deaf students have contact throughout the day. Since it is hard enough being a deaf child in a predominantly hearing environment, it is easy for the deaf child to become isolated and experience stunted social growth.[23] Interpreters should try to be a bridge to communication with others rather than be the person who the Deaf student is communicating with all of the time.

Acceptable and Unacceptable Roles

To reiterate, the job of a K–12 sign language interpreter entails multiple roles, such as interpreting and advocating. However, there are many roles that the interpreter should *not* take on: tutor, friend, confidante, therapist, assistant teacher, or mentor/parent.[24] Oliva and Lytle shared concerns about one student they interviewed: "The deaf child has a friend who, as she said, was there eight hours a day and she was comfortable with, and while this fed some important socialization needs, we have to wonder if this was the kind of friendship we would ideally want for our children." They discussed further whether being so close to an interpreter cut off possibilities for this student to develop friendships with other students, or if the student would remain friendless if not for the interpreter.[25]

Such a relationship between a student and an interpreter can be difficult to navigate because interpreters are expected to "mediate" education. Since the keyword here is education, it is important to remember to question the role of the teacher in this process. For example, the teacher should teach and explain information and answer questions as needed. Interpreters should not be barriers to direct relationships between Deaf students and teachers or peers. Interpreters should not teach, explain information, or answer questions. Interpreters should be advocating for Deaf students to have the same relationship to the teacher that hearing students have. Basically, interpreters should advocate for Deaf students to build bridges and to ensure there is a transition to direct communication between them and their teachers or peers.[26] An example of this would be helping hearing students become comfortable with the Deaf student at lunch or recess and then leaving the environment so that direct communication can develop and continue. The same applies for developing direct communication between the student and the teacher. The interpreter can also make the teacher aware of ways to communicate directly with the student, and the student can be encouraged to explain how they communicate with other teachers. The interpreter can then leave them to develop direct communication independently. After all, Deaf people do not have interpreters attached to them 24 hours a day, so the same should be true for the school setting. Finally, the interpreter should be mindful of social opportunities for Deaf students and not be the source of the child's entire social opportunity themselves.

Interpreters need to respect the Deaf student's right to autonomy and privacy, which means that interpreters should not interpret at IEP meetings; rather, these meetings should be interpreted by a certified person out of the district so the classroom interpreter can attend as part of the team.[27] Additionally, students should have access to counselors at school with an external interpreter so that they can express thoughts without worrying about their regular interpreters' reactions.

CONCLUSION

In closing, deaf education needs to focus on truly educating deaf children by including all the key players: student, parent, interpreter, teacher, and administrator in a discussion of how mainstreamed deaf children can be better supported. Interpreters need to be involved in advocating for improvements and full accessibility in educational environments. Accordingly, they need to work with other key players from the Deaf community to improve the experience of deaf children in the mainstream setting. This is especially critical because of the high number of unqualified interpreters in classrooms, which results in a more restrictive communication environment for Deaf children.

I strongly believe being an educational interpreter is not for the faint of heart. Likewise, the experiences of being mainstreamed are not to be taken lightly. Only when ALL of us take this situation seriously, will the quality of educational experience for mainstreamed deaf children be elevated. This can only be accomplished when ALL school administrators hire only fully qualified educational interpreters, when ALL interpreter education programs stop encouraging their students to consider educational interpreting as the first step in their interpreting career, and when ALL educational interpreters commit to high standards of interpreting before accepting interpreting jobs within a school setting.

Regardless, as a mother of Deaf children, I will not subject them to an interpreter mediated education. Rather, my children are getting a quality education in a bilingual school where teachers communicate directly to Deaf children. More important, they are thriving in an environment where they are not burdened with the issues discussed in this chapter. I only wish I had had that kind of childhood myself, and that more deaf children today and in the future would have the same opportunity to access quality and effective education.

Notes

1. Thomas D. Snyder and Sally A. Dillow, *Digest of Education Statistics 2011* (Washington, DC: U.S. Department of Education; National Center for Education Statistics, 2012): 61.

2. Thomas K. Holcomb, *Introduction to American Deaf Culture* (New York, NY: Oxford University Press, 2013).

3. Jerome D. Schein, *At Home Among Strangers* (Washington, DC: Gallaudet University Press, 1989).

4. Debra M. Shaver, Marc Marschark, Lynn Newman, and Camille Marder, "Characteristics of Deaf and Hard-of-Hearing Students in Regular and Special Schools," *Journal of Deaf Studies and Deaf Education* 19 (2014): 203–19.

5. Stephanie W. Cawthon, "National Survey for Accommodations and Alternate Assessments for Students Who are Deaf or Hard of Hearing in the United States," *Journal of Deaf Studies and Deaf Education* 11, no. 3 (2006): 337–59.

6. Harry Lang, "Perspectives on the History of Deaf Education," in *Oxford Handbook of Deaf Studies, Language, and Education,* eds. Mark Marschark and Patricia Elizabeth Spencer (New York, NY: Oxford University Press, 2003): 9–20.

7. George A.Scott, "Deaf and Hard of Hearing Children: Federal Support for Developing Language and Literacy,"*Report to Congressional Requesters, GAO-11-357* (Washington, DC: U.S. Government Accountability Office 2011), retrieved from http://www.gao.gov/assets/320/318711.html; Marc Marschark, Rico Peterson, and Elizabeth A. Winston, *Sign Language Interpreting and Interpreter Education: Directions for Research and Practice* (New York, NY: Oxford University Press, 2005); Marc Marschark, Patricia Sapere, Carol Convertino, and Rosemarie Seewagen, "Educational Interpreting: Access and Outcomes," in *Sign Language Interpreting and Interpreter Education: Directions for Research and Practice*, eds. Marc Marschark, Rico Peterson, and Elizabeth A. Winston, (New York, NY: Oxford University Press, 2005): 57–83; Janice H. Humphrey and Bob J. Alcorn, *So You Want to Be an Interpreter?: An Introduction to Sign Language Interpreting* (Clearwater, FL: H & H Publishing Company, 2007).

8. Brenda Schick, Kevin Williams, and Haggai Kuppermintz, "Look Who is Being Left Behind: Educational Interpreters and Access to Education for Deaf and Hard-of-Hearing Students," *Journal of Deaf Studies and Deaf Education* 11, no. 1 (2006): 12.

9. Kim Brown Kurz and Elisabeth Caldwell Langer, "Student Perspectives on Educational Interpreting: Twenty Deaf and Hard of Hearing Students Offer Insights and Suggestions," in *Educational Interpreting: How It Can Succeed.* ed. Elizabeth Winston (Washington, DC: Gallaudet University Press, 2004): 9–47; Elizabeth Caldwell Langer, *Classroom Discourse and Interpreted Education: What is Conveyed to Deaf Elementary School Students,*" PhD Diss., University of Colorado at Boulder, 2007.

10. *Board of Education of the Hendrick Hudson* Central *School District v. Rowley*, 458 U.S. 176 (1982).

11. Gina A. Oliva and Linda Risser Lytle, *Turning the Tide: Making Life Better for Deaf and Hard of Hearing Schoolchildren* (Washington, DC: Gallaudet University Press, 2014).

12. Claire L. Ramsey, *Deaf Children in Public Schools* (Washington, DC: Gallaudet University Press, 1997); Oliva and Lytle, *Turning the Tide.*

13. Oliva and Lytle, *Turning the Tide.*

14. Oliva and Lytle, *Turning the Tide.*

15. David Stewart, Jerome Schein, and Brenda Cartwright, *Sign Language Interpreting: Exploring Its Art and Science* (Boston, MA: Allyn and Bacon, 1998).

16. Brenda Schick, Kevin Williams, and Haggai Kuppermintz, "Look Who is Being Left Behind: Educational Interpreters and Access to Education for Deaf and Hard-of-Hearing Students," *Journal of Deaf Studies and Deaf Education* 11, no. 1 (2006): 12.

17. Distance Opportunities for Interpreters and Teachers, "States that Require or Accept the EIPA: Summary," http://www.unco.edu/cebs/asl-interpreting/pdf/osep-project/eipa-data-summary.pdf, January, 2015.

18. Ramsey, *Deaf Children in Public Schools.*

19. Ross E. Mitchell and Michael A. Karchmer, "Chasing the Mythical Ten Percent: Parental Hearing Status of Deaf and Hard of Hearing Students in the United States," *Sign Language Studies* 4, no. 2 (2004): 138–63.

20. Colin Baker, "Sign Language and the Deaf Community," in *Handbook of Language and Ethnic Identity,* ed. Joshua Fishman (New York, NY: Oxford University Press, 1999): 122–139.

21. Ramsey, *Deaf Children in Public Schools.*

22. Commission of Education of the Deaf, *Toward Equality: Education of the Deaf* (Washington, DC: U.S. Government Printing Office, 1988); Scott, "Deaf and Hard of Hearing Children: Federal Support for Developing Language and Literacy"; Robert Johnson, Scott Liddell, and Carol Erting, *Unlocking the Curriculum: Principles for Achieving Access in Deaf Education,* Working paper 89-3. (Washington, DC: Gallaudet Research Institute, 1989); Oliva and Lytle, *Turning the Tide;* Ramsey, *Deaf Children in Public Schools.*

23. Oliva and Lytle, *Turning the Tide.*

24. Ramsey, *Deaf Children in Public Schools.*

25. Oliva and Lytle, *Turning the Tide.*

26. Oliva and Lytle, *Turning the Tide.*

27. Oliva and Lytle, *Turning the Tide.*

14 Hey Listen

Mainstreamed Deaf Children Deserve More!

Fallon Brizendine

For the ASL summary of this chapter, go to https://youtu.be/bPRfzblDqaE

> I grew up in the Deaf community. I have a Deaf family including Deaf grandparents, parents, and siblings. Sharing stories is one important hallmark of Deaf culture and my life has been enriched because of all the stories I've been told all my life. Many of these stories are related to real-life situations, told to share the harsh realities of the world. Wisdom is passed along with solutions provided for all kinds of challenges and problems. Continuing in this tradition, I will be sharing several true stories with deep implications for deaf children–stories that cannot be and should not be dismissed because they all are too real and common. Again, in following the rich tradition of Deaf culture, I will also be offering recommendations and solutions with the hope of supporting those who are basically left alone to survive in the mainstream.

ASL/interpreting students are often advised to start their career in educational interpreting and that working with young children is the best place to start as a professional interpreter.[1] It is easy to see why—young children generally have smaller vocabularies compared to adults, and interpreting for an elementary classroom is usually less intensive than perhaps a medical appointment. It also seems like a logical progression, just like any other field: start with a lower-paying job and work your way up. But we need to ask the following questions: At whose expense is this? Who is getting shortchanged here? The deaf children, of course.

I discovered quickly in my career in interpreter education that this low expectation for educational interpreters exists in so many ways and at so many points throughout a mainstreamed child's education.

A Scared Child

I began my career working with deaf children in a pre-kindergarten classroom. Interestingly, it was working at a Deaf school when I had a firsthand experience that demonstrated how critical it is to have access to quality interpreters, especially during a child's formative years. After college, I worked as a teacher at a Deaf school and fell in love with my young students. There was a new student, a four-year-old boy bursting with potential who came from a difficult home life and did not have much, if any, communication at home. Any language development he achieved had occurred at school. I remember how some co-workers perceived that boy as a "lot of work," "delayed," and "needing to work on his behavior." Fortunately, there were several of us who did not consider these issues to be problematic; what we saw in his eyes and behavior was motivation and a desire to do well. The only thing holding him back at school was his limited language skills.

Although I never really saw his home life, it was clear nobody in his family was making any attempts to communicate with him, teach him, or even bond with him. But this same boy who seemed lonely and dejected at home never wasted a single minute at school, grabbing every opportunity to communicate with his peers, teachers, and anyone who would spend time with him. In just one season, he showed a great deal of improvement in behavior and especially language.

One routine morning in a classroom filled with little flying hands, a group of dark suits from Child Protective Services (CPS) entered the room asking for that young boy to come with them. It was unsettling and a major disruption. The suits, accompanied by interpreters, were responding to a complaint about conditions at that student's home. The little boy looked at me with wide eyes, scared and clueless, begging to stay in the classroom with me. I assured him that he would be all right. Almost 20 minutes later, the interpreters returned and asked me to join the meeting.

It turned out that during the 20-minute interview with CPS, the boy had become completely unresponsive. The interpreters were having a difficult time communicating with him and were not sure why, so they asked for my help. I walked in the cold room and saw the boy sitting on a chair much too big for him, legs dangling with his head resting on one of the arms. I was able to break through his shell and communicate in an approach that he understood. It did not take long for his true colors to come out to CPS workers, and he was eventually released.

The CPS workers afterward told me that they initially thought the student was either being intentionally uncooperative or had no communication skills. The interpreters, although skilled in their own rights, had never experienced working with young deaf children, let alone a terrified four-year-old child with emerging language. Through little fault of their own, they had never met or been exposed to such a circumstance in their career. What would have come of that meeting had CPS relied solely on interpreters who were not in any way equipped to deal with the situation? Interpreters, who were likely to be by-products of an Interpreter Education Program, might never have found themselves in a circumstance where they would have had to communicate and connect with a terrified four-year-old child.

This meeting could have easily taken an entirely different direction had the interpreters not realized their limitations immediately and called me or another Deaf adult for assistance. Fortunately, this meeting took place at a Deaf school where there were many Deaf staff members who were linguistically and culturally competent to deal with this kind of situation. Imagine this scenario taking place in a public school, without Deaf teachers around or access to culturally and linguistically competent resources on hand.

As I walked back to my classroom relieved, I was also struck by a deep, unsettled feeling. How many cases are there in which deaf children are unable to express themselves because of unqualified, unprepared interpreters?

A Child Left Behind

Later, I worked as the internship coordinator for an Interpreter Education Program in a different state. Each semester, students were required to do their internship hours with interpreters (who were certified, if we were lucky) in educational settings at varying grade levels. Each intern was required to perform 240 hours of interpreting, with me observing them at the beginning and end of the semester. As a fourth-generation Deaf person who had full access to communication and language at home and in school, it was very painful to realize that most of these professional interpreters were the only links Deaf children have to their education and community. It was very difficult to ignore my internal screams to advocate for these children, given my role. This brings to mind another child I encountered in my work.

As I drove one hour south from the college to observe an intern's work, the area became quieter and more secluded. The school was only one hour from our interpreting education program. I pulled into the parking lot and did the usual security check to enter the school building. A school interpreter cheerfully greeted me and began talking about the school and the deaf student. I was struck by the interpreter's positive attitude. She shared with me that she was working toward her RID (Registry of Interpreters) certification. As we walked to the classroom, she informed me that I would be the first deaf person this four-year-old girl had ever met. I had a lump in my throat; I was not expecting that detail.

The first glimpse I had of the little deaf girl was her sitting at the far end of a large C-shaped circle. Everyone else in the room was hearing. The teacher was in the center, singing a song, with the interpreter signing in English word order without any attempt to present signs in a clear, conceptually accurate manner. Soon after, the deaf girl was rolling on the floor, restless. It became painfully obvious to me why she was not paying attention: there was no understandable language access. Even I—a college-educated professional—was lost. It felt like a train had just run over me. I realized with a jolt how privileged I had been to grow up in a fully accessible, Deaf environment at home and school. I watched the girl, and my heart broke seeing how the interpreter appeared unable to realize just how much she was contributing to the girl's language inaccessibility. No wonder mainstreamed education has such a huge risk of failure for so many deaf children.[2] In other words, because the interpreter was not providing appropriate language access, this little four-year-old girl was being set up for failure for the rest of her life.

I stood in the back as this little deaf girl turned and her big brown eyes landed on me. I saw that she had bilateral cochlear implants in both ears. Yet, I noticed how her sad eyes looked, hungry for information. A few minutes later, she was assigned to a group to identify and group colors and numbers. The other students easily spoke to each other, while this girl was completely left out because the interpreter did not sign the side conversations. The interpreter, separate from the group activity, sat down with the little girl to provide some one-to-one instruction. She held up a blue card and expressionlessly asked WHAT COLOR? repeatedly while pointing at an object. In sign language, there are several signs for WHAT depending on conceptual accuracy. This interpreter used the incorrect sign, moving her dominant index finger across her non-dominant open hand. Without the appropriate facial expression, it was difficult for me, and even more difficult for the little girl, to determine exactly what she was asking. As I looked on, I was battling inside because I wanted to correct her and sign COLOR WHAT? with the non-manual signals (lower eyebrows) appropriate of any visual language. The interpreter could even have used the contrast approach by signing, THIS PINK? NO NO. THIS RED? NO NO. COLOR WHAT? With this major gap in language access, it took the little girl seemingly forever with no response. It was clear she was not having fun like her hearing classmates in learning such exciting concepts. By this point, her enthusiastic classmates, who fidgeted in excitement as they threw out answers, had already moved on to two other activities. In contrast, the girl sat quietly as she worked with the interpreter. I wondered if it was like this daily for the girl and decided to try and communicate directly with her about the colors. When I took over, her eyes lit up, and her participation level immediately increased. She excitedly took more cards and communicated with me rapidly, with a solid interest and eye contact. In just a few minutes, I had achieved what the girl simply needed: full, organic, linguistically appropriate language access.

After class, I spoke with the teacher and suggested that the girl's family bring her to a nearby city, with its larger Deaf community and various Deaf literacy events (such as monthly read-aloud and ASL storytelling events). I also explained that the student would benefit from meeting similarly aged Deaf peers at such events. The teacher quietly explained that this was not possible because her parents did not have a car and do not speak English or ASL.

The next time I visited the school was several months later. The girl, a bit taller, still had gorgeous brown eyes that were alert and desperately seeking communication. She asked me to sit with her on the playground. By now, she was nearly five years old and still severely language-deprived. As I left that day, it dawned on me that educational interpreters are the ones who know exactly where those solitary mainstreamed deaf students are located. As Deaf people, we often say we wish we could find those children and provide resources to them, but interpreters are not allowed to share this information due to confidentiality and security reasons. So whereas the Deaf community does not know where all those solitary students are, educational interpreters do.

I tried to shake it off as I drove home, but I could not. "What-if" and "how" questions flooded my head. I kept returning to this little girl and the boy at the Deaf school, thinking about how many others were out there and the great impact educational interpreters have on those students and their families, teachers, and schools.

. . . But It Is Better Than Working in a Fast Food Restaurant

At one Interpreter Education Program where I worked there was this one interpreting student who had barely passed the required coursework required for graduation largely due to her weak skills and lack of commitment. Yet she was immediately hired as an educational interpreter upon graduation, even with her poor grades. My colleagues and I were disappointed to learn of this student's decision to take the job, especially after how heavily we stressed throughout the program that integrity was the greatest quality an interpreter could have. Her response was that interpreting was a better option than working in a fast food restaurant.

When checking with the employer about their low hiring standards for educational interpreters, they responded to our concerns by saying that as long as the interpreter could fingerspell and sign some, they were satisfied that the deaf child at the school was getting support. These low hiring standards seem to be prevalent throughout the United States. As noted by Humphrey and Alcorn, "In educational settings, standards vary dramatically from place to place. Some schools require that interpreters be certified; others hire anybody who can fingerspell or who has a great uncle who was Deaf."[3]

Why Is This Happening?

Why is it acceptable for such unqualified personnel to be deemed ready to interpret for deaf children in a classroom? Although this should not be acceptable, the issue lies with interpreting certifying bodies (or the lack of) and their varying requirements. The RID, for example, requires candidates to have a bachelor's degree in order to take the National Interpretation Certification test—or use RID's alternative pathway to certification, which is less demanding. The EIPA is yet another pathway, bypassing the bachelor's degree requirement of RID.

State assessments are frequently even less stringent. For example, in Texas, the Board for Evaluation of Interpreters (BEI) does not require a bachelor's degree to be certified and only requires interpreters to possess at least an associate degree from an accredited college or university.[4] It is difficult to understand how interpreter can express the concept fully when one holds a degree lower than teacher's credentials. Even as frustrating as this is, this requirement is better than in some states in which there are no requirements to work as an educational interpreter.[5]

Further compounding the problem is the fact that cash-strapped, desperate school districts are usually more than happy to bring on additional unpaid help in the form of interns, helping feed into the misconception that school districts are the best place to start an interpreting career, when it is in fact one of the worst places and extremely detrimental to the Deaf child. It is not uncommon to see a job posting for a school district interpreter paying as little as $70 a day, while interpreters in other settings can earn as much as $70 an hour. It is no wonder many skilled educational interpreters migrate out of school settings as fast as they can, leaving behind the less-skilled ones.

Why are Graduates So Ill-Prepared to Begin Work?

How is it even possible for any student to begin their studies to become a future interpreter when there are no prerequisite skills in ASL? In most spoken language interpreting education programs, the focus is on developing skills in interpreting between English and a student's native language or language used at home. Most students in these programs are already comfortably bilingual and culturally competent in dealing with the community where English is not used as the first language. The emphasis, then, in these programs is on effective interpretation techniques and cultural mediation.

By contrast, very few ASL/spoken English interpreters have ASL as their native language and often learn the language when they begin their college years. How, then, is it possible to expect a student to develop a reasonable level of fluency to begin interpretation studies within a four-year university program, let alone a two-year community college program?

Yet, a typical Interpreter Education Program begins with an entry-level ASL course such as ASL 101 and expects graduates to begin working as interpreters upon completion of the program. During the program, students are introduced to the Deaf community and the culture of Deaf people. Although the goal is often to encourage immersion in the culture while pursuing the interpreting degree, most students only have superficial contacts with Deaf people as most of the interactions do not occur naturally but rather in an observatory role. For example, interpreting students might visit a school for the deaf or attend a play that is put on by the Deaf community. They might have guest speakers coming in class to talk about their Deaf experience. They might watch movies featuring Deaf people. Very often, these students only have immersion opportunities during their internships in educational settings—which is hardly an "immersion" experience. Little wonder that graduates of an Interpreter Education Program are so woefully prepared to take on an enormous responsibility of providing mainstreamed deaf children with access to education they so desperately need.

Systematic Failure, Not Deaf Children's Failure

Why have these kinds of stories been shared repeatedly for decades? What is causing this stumble in the transition between graduating from an Interpreter Education Program and working as an educational interpreter? There are many possible reasons. First, a major failure in the Deaf education system is the lack of requirements in many states for educational interpreters to demonstrate their competencies. For example, there are states that do not require any certification to work as an educational interpreter. For others that do, their minimum requirements are so low that even novice signers will have an easy time passing the test. Yet other states with more stringent requirements routinely provide waivers in order to fill the positions in schools.[6]

Once on the job, there are few incentives for educational interpreters to continue their education or participate in professional development to advance their interpreting skills. Clearly, educational interpreters could benefit from observing bilingually taught Deaf classrooms, participating in workshops on bilingualism with Deaf or native ASL Deaf education teachers learning about language acquisition, and practicing signing and interpreting clearly. All of these would provide interpreters with the knowledge, skills, and confidence to deliver information in sign language clearly to benefit young Deaf children in the classroom, whether it be ASL. Like it or not, interpreters are frequently Deaf children's only language models.[7]

Furthermore, because educational interpreters work mainly around Deaf children, they usually do not interact with Deaf adults who possess advanced language proficiency. They are valuable language models for interpreters and can provide them with feedback, which in turn can help improve their interpretation skills. For this reason, novice interpreters need to be aggressive in maintaining their ties with the Deaf community and develop authentic relationships with the members of the community. Otherwise, deaf children will continue to suffer from weak interpreting competencies among educational interpreters. This goes the same for the interpreting faulty in Interpreting Education Program. How often do they involve the Deaf community or does the community even know the faculty members? In three different college-level interpreter education programs, when I proudly shared where and who I work with, most of the time people in the Deaf community do not recognize the interpreting faculty members' names. This also set an example for the interpreting students and educational interpreters.

Deaf Adults Are Affected, Too

Educational interpreters can certainly have a major impact on Deaf adults, as they often interpret for them as well. As the department chair at my college, I was part of a search interview committee with eight other individuals for a position that involved working closely with the college vice president. I requested my two preferred interpreters for the interview, but only one was available. The other interpreter was someone I had not met until that day. Immediately prior to the interview, the committee discussed the protocols for the interview and divided up the 12 interview questions; I was assigned Question 8. The interpreters and I discussed how we would manage the communication, and we agreed I would sign the question with one of the interpreters speaking, with a copy of questions in front of her. During the first interview, a committee member who was assigned a different question misspoke and read my question instead. I caught her mistake, and figured I would simply read her question instead. When it was my turn to ask the question, I signed the other person's question without pointing out her mistake, to avoid any embarrassment for her. The interpreter—who was not my preferred interpreter, but the one I had met just that morning—followed along, or so I thought. The candidate gave me a strange look, and the college vice president interrupted and said that Question 8 had already been asked, so I should ask a different question.

Mortified, I realized the interpreter had not followed the proceedings. Instead, she recited straight from the paper. The result was that I looked like an unprepared fool. I had worked hard to be in that position and prepared well, even saving face for the other person on the interview team. I had to swallow my pride and repeat what I had signed, and the interpreter ended up voicing based on what I signed instead of reading the other question. The previous interviewer passed me a note apologizing for her mistake, but I had to explain to her after the interview that her error was not as significant as the interpreter's.

On top of that, I had a difficult time understanding the interpreter, who was new to me. She clearly was not fluent in sign language. For example, "president and cabinets" was signed as NOW as in "present" instead of PRESIDENT and CABINETS as if referring to kitchen cabinets. I was mentally exhausted, and my eyes were as well, from constantly trying to make sense of her English-ordered, English-based signs instead of focusing on the interview itself. That interview made me think of that little four-year-old girl. If I could feel so incredibly unconfident because of an interpreter's lack of skills, how do children in their formative years feel?

SOLUTIONS

What can we do? Are there solutions? Are we at a crisis point in educational interpreting?

Yes, we are at a crisis point, and there are solutions—although complex and multifaceted.

Starting Point

The first step is that educational interpreting should not be considered as the ideal starting point for any new interpreter, certified or not. Rather, it should be the brass ring that interpreters aspire to; once they are qualified and experienced, they can then consider educational interpreting. Interpreter Education Programs should refrain from promoting educational interpreting as a launching point for interpreting careers and rather focus on career growth.

Students who enroll in Interpreter Education Programs need to seek out and pursue any and all language immersion opportunities. Note that this does not mean watching videos of sign language online; rather, these should be as organic as possible—for example, attending Deaf events and volunteering at Deaf schools. Better yet, curate a variety of sources and language models in the Deaf community and engage with them. Reach out to individuals, especially deaf children. Post comments, videos, or musings in the appropriate forums or discussion groups (that is, make sure they are open to having hearing people post in these groups). Get involved by sharing, donating, and serving as an ally. There are too many people who either believe that an Interpreter Education Program gives them all they need or that simply being a passive bystander online counts as immersion. Realize that exposing yourself to the nuances of ASL and our community will only strengthen your ability to do your job well and serve effectively in your chosen role as an interpreter.

Accepting Responsibility

Everyone, from the school administrators to parents to interpreters, needs to take responsibility for the horrendous learning conditions imposed on deaf students everywhere. Until then, deaf children will continue to struggle in their academic and social endeavors and graduate from schools with extremely limited skill sets. This needs to stop.

School Administrators

Do not view educational interpreters as paraprofessionals/teacher assistants but as professionals worthy of appropriate compensation commensurate with their education and training. Accept the responsibility to hire only qualified and licensed interpreters.

Policymakers

Do not equate Least Restrictive Environment (LRE) as the interpreted classroom environment with poorly equipped interpreters. Set the bar higher than the bare minimum of sign language requirements before you even consider individuals to work as educational interpreters. Accept the responsibility of recognizing the dismal failure of current practices.

Teachers of the Deaf

Do not accept the status quo (e.g., chronic poor performance of your students). Accept the responsibility of holding parents, administrators, and yourselves accountable for the poor academic performance of deaf children. Accept the responsibility to create a language-rich environment at school and encourage the parents to do the same at home.

Parents

Do not be blinded by the poor performance of your children. Do not put the blame for their poor performance on the fact that they are deaf. Realize that deaf children can and do reach language milestones just like their hearing peers, whether it be in English or ASL. Accept the responsibility to create a language-rich environment at home.

Deaf Community Members

Do not feel like your hands are tied and your role is limited to outside the school environment. Accept the responsibility to resist, complain, and take action for the sake of deaf children. Make yourselves available to serve as mentors to families with deaf children.

Interpreters

Do not fool yourselves into believing that you are doing no damage by working with a limited set of skills. Do not claim that "your presence is better than nothing." Accept the responsibility to build your skills to the level where deaf students can really understand and learn in the mainstreamed environment.

Conclusion

Basically, this is a plea for deaf children everywhere. If interpreter-mediated education is to be considered by schools as truly the LRE for deaf children, then everyone needs to do their part to make sure that these students are provided with appropriate support to succeed academically and socially. To address the ongoing injustices being done to deaf children everywhere, the stories and solutions offered by myself and other Deaf professionals need to be told far and wide. I'm doing my part and I hope you will, too.

Notes

1. David A. Stewart, Jerome D. Schein, and Brenda E. Cartwright, *Sign Language Interpreting: Exploring Its Art and Science* (New York: Allyn & Bacon, 2003): 171; Janice H. Humphrey and Bob J. Alcorn, *So You Want to Be an Interpreter?: An Introduction to Sign Language Interpreting* (Clearwater, FL: H & H Publishing Company, 2007): 325.

2. Debra Shaver, Lynn Newman, Tracy Huang, Jennifer Yu, and Anne-Marie Knokey, "The Secondary School Experiences and Academic Performance of Students with Hearing Impairments. Facts from NLTS2. NCSER 2011-3003," (Washington, DC: *National Center for Special Education Research*, 2011), 326.

3. Humphrey and Alcorn, *So You Want to Be an Interpreter?*

4. Texas Health and Human Services, "BEI Frequently Asked Questions" (Austin, TX; Texas Department of Health and Human Services), accessed on July 14, 2017, https://hhs.texas.gov/doing-business-hhs/provider-portals/assistive-services-providers/board-evaluation-interpreters-certification-program/bei-frequently-asked-questions.

5. "Regulations Governing Interpreter Requirements," accessed July 14, 2017, http://www.360translations.com/burnsat/stateregs.htm#Alabama.

6. Bernhardt Jones, "Competencies of K–12 Educational Interpreters: What We Need Versus What We Have," in *Educational Interpreting: How It Can Succeed,* ed. Elizabeth Winston (Washington, DC: Gallaudet University Press, 2005): 113–31.

7. Humphrey and Alcorn, *So You Want to Be an Interpreter?*; Christine Monikowski, "Language Myths in Interpreted Education: First Language, Second Language, What Language?" in *Educational Interpreting: How It Can Succeed,* ed. Elizabeth Winston (Washington, DC: Gallaudet University Press, 2005): 48–60.

15

It Takes Two to Tango

Crafting a Flawless Partnership in the Corporate World

Sam Sepah

For the ASL summary of this chapter, go to https://youtu.be/yH_4NvMvUK4

> As a global program manager at Google who is Deaf, I have a team of designated interpreters to work with me in concert with a multitude of predominantly hearing colleagues and senior leaders from around the world. Throughout my day, I attend group meetings with American, European, or Asian colleagues to drive strategic direction in delivering business solutions for a division of 1,200 employees. In the remaining time at work, I conduct regular one-on-one meetings with management to implement special projects. Designated interpreters serve a major role in my ability to perform up to Google corporate standards. Because of my expertise in human resources management, I am often invited to provide speeches at business conferences regarding leadership and best practices in diversity. My designated interpreters work with me throughout countless events so that I can empower and enrich lives.

My partnership with a designated interpreter is an example of a pivotal change in the American workplace, particularly with the proliferation of Deaf individuals achieving decidedly professional roles involving direct contact with non-signing clients. Clearly, sign language interpreters help solidify such opportunities for those who are Deaf—but having a designated interpreter is a recent trend that requires new thinking and practices regarding the critical and complex relationship between Deaf professionals and interpreters.

I employ the "it takes two to tango" approach in my day-to-day professional communications with others. The partnership between a Deaf professional and an interpreter is akin to dancing the tango. Both dancers must be willing to collaborate as equals, work together efficiently, respect each other's strengths, and learn from each other while sharing space and honoring boundaries. The tango does not allow for anyone to dance alone, yet creates a seamless performance together. Any dance requires movement that is *more* precise than everyday movement—just like the interpreting process.

Before we continue, I would like to elaborate on the definition of two specific terms: *client* and *consumer*. These two terms are often used interchangeably, but in the interpreting community, *consumer* is commonly used when it refers to a Deaf individual who uses an interpreting service. In the Oxford English dictionary, *consumer* is defined as a person who simply receives a service or good.[1] The term is appropriate for any situation in which a basic service is provided to an end-user (e.g., beverages from a coffee shop). It also does not require an in-depth relationship between the service provider and consumer (e.g., a Deaf patient who uses a freelance interpreter for a short medical appointment). In contrast, *client* should be used when an individual gets ongoing professional services.[2] This term is also commonly used in corporate America when clients have a dedicated relationship with a service provider for an ongoing period of time. In this chapter, I use the term *client* when referring to Deaf professionals who have a dedicated relationship with their designated interpreters.

Unique Challenges in the Corporate World

Before delving into the partnership between a Deaf professional and a designated interpreter, a quick overview of the corporate culture and its unique challenges is needed, especially as they apply to Deaf professionals.

Unconscious Bias

The workplace is fraught with unconscious biases that deeply affect Deaf people overtly and subtly. Unconscious bias is defined as "the hidden, reflexive preferences that shape most people's worldviews, and that can profoundly affect how welcoming and open a workplace is to different people and ideas," according to Manjoo.[3] Frequently, unconscious bias arises the first time a hearing person encounters a Deaf professional, or when a supervisor makes quick decisions that do not take a Deaf employee into consideration. For example, a manager is to send a team representative at an "all-hands meeting." The manager often will naturally assume that a Deaf employee is not a skilled public speaker because of the perceived communication challenges, so a hearing employee is selected as the representative instead.

Group Meetings

Participating in a group meeting with hearing peers is one of the biggest challenges for many Deaf professionals.[4] For example, in an all-Deaf meeting operated by Deaf cultural norms, each attendee has a role in the meeting and is given space and time to contribute to the discussion. In a predominantly hearing meeting, however, Deaf professionals have a whole host of challenges: working with interpreters who might not be familiar with the content and jargon, trying to stay on pace with everyone else due to the slight lag in interpreted information, and being adroit at finding the exact moment in which to interject.

Given the interpreting process and its timing, a Deaf professional may sometimes not fully articulate thoughts before being interrupted by a hearing participant. This is not a rare experience for Deaf people, who find this interruption anywhere: a hearing family dinner conversation, the store when trying to talk with employees, or a staff meeting. This "interruption syndrome," which I call "hearingerupting," often is exacerbated during short meetings because the goal of these meetings often is to be brief rather than inclusive. This term is tantamount to "manterrupting," where a man intentionally interrupts a woman while she is talking.[5]

High-Performance Culture

Most corporations create a high performance culture in which employees are expected to go the extra mile in their jobs to support business demands. This business model is critical for many organizations because it helps the company to stay ahead of its own competitive marketplace.[6] A fast-paced company culture often rewards employees who can do a speedy performance and create high-quality delivery.

Not all meetings are created equal. Even with all these extra factors from an accommodation standpoint, hearing and Deaf professionals are expected to participate in team meeting processes and decision-making at the same level and speed. When a group discussion goes faster than normal, people naturally talk over one another—and so a Deaf person often is unable to participate fully due to the interpreter's physical inability to sign everything that is said simultaneously. As a result, the Deaf person may be mistakenly perceived, due to hearingeruptings, as lacking confidence and/or being indifferent, shy, introverted, or even apathetic. This misperception may create an adverse impact on the Deaf professional's credibility and career, especially for one who works in a high-performance workplace.

The designated interpreter has a crucial role in navigating hearing cultural corporate norms to make participation possible and as seamless as possible. He or she has to be culturally savvy by knowing how to add the Deaf professional's message in a timely, appropriate flow with the conversation. Managing the timing and cultural navigation of participating in large, fast-paced corporate meetings is akin to mastering the special Argentine Tango: it takes nuanced skills, practice, confidence, and a mastery of the craft.

How Designated Interpreters Can Fit the Bill

In the dancing world, every dancer has to truly understand the partner's expectations and goals as well as personal boundaries *prior* to the performance. Before starting the interpreting assignment, both parties should discuss and agree on the definition of their partnership and any other expectations for the job. Both parties should also discuss what they perceive as the perfect interpreting performance that satisfies the Deaf clients' communication goals. Surely, a flawless interpreting performance can amaze the hearing audience, especially for hearing peers at work. A successful interpreting process also allows hearing co-workers to truly experience and understand the Deaf professional's capabilities, talents, and contributions.

Interpreters' ethical practices serve a critical role to ban interpreters from taking over or replacing clients in their job. The designated interpreter's expertise, commitment and professionalism can ensure that the Deaf professional grows and thrives in the workplace without communication barriers. This is only possible with a qualified designated interpreter. Without a qualified designated interpreter, promotion and growth in the workforce become much more difficult, sometimes impossible. Therefore, Deaf professionals require and deserve exceptional interpreting services.

What Is a Designated Interpreter?

According to Hauser, Finch, and Hauser, a designated interpreter is an interpreter who works with a Deaf client for a significant period of time and develops specific interpreting techniques within that Deaf person's discipline. They also stress that the designated interpreter is part of the Deaf person's professional interpreting team, as opposed to being in the traditional independent freelance interpreter role. "The Deaf professional and designated interpreter work together as a micro-team within the large macro-team of the Deaf professional's work environment" The authors also explain that "the Deaf professional's goals become the interpreter's goals."[7]

A designated interpreter differs from a staff interpreter, even though both may be hired by the company. While a staff interpreter usually works with a group of Deaf professionals who share one interpreter, a designated interpreter is specifically assigned to a single Deaf client for specific purposes.

Working with a designated interpreter requires a different level of commitment from both interpreter and client than a regular community interpreting job. Deaf persons typically prefer to have consistency in their interpreters to ensure appropriate and crucial knowledge about the job, the jargon, and the dynamics of the work environment. Both designated interpreters and staff interpreters should learn the ins and outs of the job, along with work environment jargon and dynamics. Designated interpreters and staff interpreters must be willing to commit to ongoing, consistent service in ways not typically found in community interpreting.

Some Deaf clients may have more than one designated interpreter. There are some circumstances in which it is necessary to have more than two designated interpreters. It depends on the client's service needs. Deaf professionals sometime prefer to work with two or more designated interpreters at a certain event. For example, I was invited to speak at a large diversity conference, and I preferred to work with a team of designated interpreters who can speak articulately by using human resources (HR) jargons in the front of HR professionals. Another example when I would not need more than two designated interpreters can be at a one-to-one meeting with a colleague.

Trust

Trust is the foundation of any relationship. For a client–interpreter relationship, trust is the ultimate backbone, especially since the Deaf client often puts blind faith in the interpreter at different points throughout the interpreting process.[8]

The Deaf professional is often not aware of the exact English words or phrases spoken before being translated into ASL. This means the Deaf professional must entrust the interpreter to convey any message accurately, with the intention, spirit, and meaning with which it was delivered. Word choice, phrasing, and the precision of information conveyed in interpreted exchanges can be crucial in making or breaking a deal for the Deaf professional. Certainly, there are some instances in which this is not as critical (e.g., casual conversations among friends, family conversations, scheduling appointments). However, there are many more instances in which the interpretation *is* significant and consequential. In such situations, an interpreter's poor word choice may create an adverse impact on others' lives in unimaginable ways. In the human resources field, for example, the misinterpretation of information such as compensation, retirement planning, legal liability, and employee rights can have dire consequences not only for the employee but also his or her family.

It is necessary to invest time and energy into building and maintaining trust with a designated interpreter. Tango dances are done slightly differently by each dancer because of physical build, comfort, flexibility, confidence, knowledge, and so forth. Similarly, each Deaf professional differs in the ways trust is built and maintained with designated interpreters. In my work, I find that communication is the basis for developing the rich and complex components of a successful working relationship. I also build trust and rapport with a designated interpreter by acknowledging each other's expertise, treating each other with integrity, providing feedback to each other, understanding ethics, being a good fit for the company, and serving as allies.

Integrity

Integrity is more than just making a deep commitment to do the right thing for the right purpose; it is about quality of character, intention, and action.

All interpreters have to skillfully, consciously, and respectfully navigate and manage their own powers and privileges when working with Deaf people. Designated interpreters who serve from a place of integrity will be aware of their personal power and hearing privilege. The tango always has one person who leads and one who follows. When the designated interpreter dances with integrity, they understand that the Deaf person leads, and because of trust that has been built, both can gracefully maneuver the missteps that may arise if the designated interpreter takes the lead or asserts privilege that disempowers the Deaf person. The designated interpreter must act with integrity as the guiding barometer for ethical choices and leave power in the Deaf person's hands. Reinforcing the client's desired goals should be the focus of any ethical interpreter's behaviors.

Given the embedded nature of a designated interpreter in a Deaf professional's workplace and quasi-team member role, instances will arise in which the designated interpreter must make communication choices that can be perceived in the freelance setting as stepping out of the interpreter role. For instance, a designated interpreter may need to add additional content or utter an additional sentence without letting the Deaf client know in that moment, whether because of the sensitive timing in the interpreting process or trying to meet a communication goal. If both parties have an established foundation of trust and integrity, the designated interpreter can inform the client later about the new information added and for what purpose. For example, the client conducts a video conference call with a hearing peer. When the client signs, JOHN IS AN EXPERIENCED INTERVIEWER, the designated interpreter voices, "John is a well-calibrated interviewer." When the video call ends, the designated interpreter immediately explains why she used the specific jargon (because "calibration" is a widely used term in the company, helping show the client that the designated interpreter utilizes the company's business language). This helps the Deaf professional be aware in case that information arises in later discussions. Being honest and transparent makes it easier for both parties to maintain trust and know that choices were made with integrity and in line with their communication goals.

Acknowledgment

Both the Deaf professional and the designated interpreter must respect and accept each other's expertise in their respective fields. Although the designated interpreter may feel he or she has gained some expertise in the Deaf client's field after working with the client over several years, acknowledgment is required that in-depth training and hard-earned education in the Deaf professional's field is much different than learning while interpreting on the job. In turn, the client must also respect the designated interpreter's expertise and judgment while on the job and that the designated interpreter is working in the best interest of all parties.[9]

As a deep and complex art form, the tango means different things to different people. Similarly, each Deaf client has their own individual definitions of what it means to trust an interpreter and the ways that confidence in designated interpreters is built and maintained. Both parties should discuss how to trust and empower each other during the interpreting process. When I call a hearing client with my designated interpreter, she is aware that I trust and empower her to make the best word choices for the words I sign that will make the most sense in English, or create more efficient communication.

In turn, when my designated interpreter speaks certain sentences or terms that might be different than what I signed, she voices the different word while signing it. This allows me to acknowledge what she chose to speak and to confirm we practice transparent communication during a phone call. This can also be a learning opportunity for me, showing me the way my coworkers discuss content, so that I can use similar language when I continue communication via emails or text messages. It also allows me to share feedback on the designated interpreter's word choices. Just like trusting a dance partner, trusting a designated interpreter creates a strong performance that can win the judges' vote of confidence.

Feedback

Sharing explicit feedback with an interpreter is one of the most important, and at times difficult, components of building trust and maintaining a healthy and effective relationship. It is also one of the most difficult because so few people know how to give effective and constructive feedback, as opposed to criticism, that will get them the results they desire. The ability to have open communication and to consider both parties' feedback is a key step in building and holding trust.[10] Like a dance rehearsal, giving and getting constant feedback is key to a smooth performance.

Two types of feedback events in the workplace should be held regularly: macro and micro.

Macro-Event

A macro-event usually occurs with three or more people in addition to the client. The ideal practice is always to reflect and share feedback with each other about a critical event, such as a group project or staff meeting. An ideal follow-up to a staff meeting starts with the designated interpreter asking the client how he or she felt about the meeting. This creates an open invitation for discussion on how the interpreting job was performed, such as the quality of the translation, or how a presentation or question-and-answer conversation was for the client.

Naturally, the more participants involved in the event, the more complicated interpreting needs can become. The size of the group has an impact on the client's understanding and on the amount of information sent and received. For every Deaf professional, being a respected and included member of the team is imperative. When the interpreting job is successful, the Deaf professional can have a stronger sense of belonging and acceptance by the larger workgroup—which in turn creates stronger trust in the interpreter. Take a look at this scenario:

> [Designated interpreter and Deaf professional walk out of the meeting room]
> Designated interpreter: Hey, what do you think about that meeting? *[follow-up]*
> Deaf professional: Well, I think it was fine, except there were some overlapping conversations when we discussed our budget planning. I could follow most of the conversation. It sounds like we agreed to settle for five thousand dollars less than the original number, right? *[reflection]*
> Designated interpreter: Yes, that is my understanding as well. *[confirmation]*
> Deaf professional: That's what I thought, but I will double-check with Ken about it. If this kind of situation occurs again, it would be great if you could just go ahead and speak up to remind them to talk one at a time. I trust your judgment when you make that call during our group meetings. Sound good? *[feedback]*
> Designated interpreter: Perfect. I'll do that next time.

Micro-Event

The micro-event typically involves two or fewer people, including the Deaf client. This could include a one-to-one meeting or a quick phone call. Informal and quick feedback typically can be shared in fewer than five minutes during or after the event, depending on the client's preference. For example, when a phone conversation is completed, the Deaf client can ask the interpreter about the hearing caller's tone, attitude, and other qualities implied during the call. Sometimes, the client will also inquire about the phone call content for clarification. The designated interpreter can then share, for example, that the hearing caller was not really upset about a situation; rather, the caller was disappointed. This feedback is valuable so that the client understands the kind of emotion the caller had. Alternatively, the client may provide quick feedback to the interpreter about how the call went:

[After the call is completed]
Deaf professional: I notice that this new customer sounds like a pleasant woman. Would you agree? *[follow-up]*
Designated interpreter: Yes, it appears that she is a friendly and calming person. She did become excited when you proposed your project idea to her. *[confirmation]*
Deaf professional: Great! I am also pleased that the call went well. *[feedback]*
Designated interpreter: Awesome. I am glad to hear that.

There certainly are some clients who are not interested in, or even resist, giving feedback to their interpreters. A common assumption among some clients is that feedback does not add any value to the interpreter's work. Some believe that every interpreter should perform proficiently on the spot. Theoretically, every sign language interpreter should indeed be a talented professional and be capable of interpreting effectively. To become a designated interpreter, the interpreter must be a well-qualified candidate with adequate professional experience. The designated interpreting job is a well-deserved position for highly talented professionals. Therefore, the expectations often are higher and there is less tolerance for mistakes, whether it is mispronunciation, making poor word choices, or "taking over" the lead. The more experienced a dancer is, the more efficient he or she should be at dancing.

Agreement

Creating an agreement, which can be done either verbally or in writing, helps create clear expectations and communication about an array of events at the client's workplace, including the interpreting process. Having an agreement can create less resistance and greater accountability for both parties. A Deaf professional may not want to provide any feedback. Even though this might not be in either party's best interest, the designated interpreter must abide by the professional's wishes.

The mutual understanding provided after making an agreement also clarifies what each party expects from each other and how they will work together effectively. This could include how much, if any, feedback the designated interpreter should expect from the Deaf client. For example, what happens if the Deaf client does not sign clearly in different situations, such as during a meeting as opposed to a phone call? Should the designated interpreter stop voicing and ask for clarification immediately, or give non-verbal cues if they "get lost" or are requesting clarity? Should feedback be given at all? If so, how much, how often, and when?

Both parties should consider such things before starting to work together. Making a long-term commitment is a big decision. For instance, I usually take about 30 minutes to review potential scenarios with a new interpreter, demonstrating my commitment to the process and ethical considerations. I also ask questions of the interpreters to learn about their competencies, styles, and other underlying concerns or skills. Additionally, throughout the process, the designated interpreter and I commit to have frequent, ongoing conversations about our collaborations and needs. This best practice also allows me, as a Deaf client, to determine whether or not the interpreter has the right qualifications to be one of my designated interpreters. It also helps the interpreter to decide whether to make an ongoing commitment to me as well as my work environment.

Allyship

Allyship with the Deaf professional is a major requirement. Interpreting is a significant tool for every Deaf professional who works in a predominantly hearing environment. The clients usually can identify if they do not have the access to some certain information, but not always. The designated interpreter's role is made to fill such gaps. Among the biggest concerns for many Deaf professionals is the lack of knowledge of missed information in the workplace. Knowledge is power, and gaps in knowledge can create adverse impacts for all involved. Just as a dancer must be knowledgeable of techniques, environmental information, timing, and what comes next before giving a performance, Deaf professionals need this knowledge to achieve optimal results.

Frequently, the designated interpreter plays a very large role in allyship. Being an honest person is a critical part of being an ally. The designated interpreter sometimes has to step outside of the interpreting role and share feedback with the client about the language, wording, or behavior to lighten the situation for everyone. One of my previous designated interpreters took the time to explain how to use a term of apology and how the definition of this term is different for a Deaf and hearing audience. Some other cultures have very different meanings for this term of apology as well as alternative belief systems about the role of apologizing. When I sign I AM SORRY in American Sign Language (ASL), it does not automatically mean I made an admission of guilt or fault to an incident. In ASL, I could mean to say that I am sympathetic with you. Understanding how to use the English term helped me to use a proper art of apologizing in the hearing world. The designated interpreter used his hearing privilege and experience to openly share with me, his client. The idea of allyship is greatly valued and is a big step toward challenging oppression.

How Designated Interpreters Can Help Level the Corporate Playing Field

A cold, hard fact in corporate culture is that nobody can rise through the ranks without being recognized as a valuable partner on the team—something that is achieved through assertive progress and participation. Thus, the Deaf professional must be an active participant in the group discussion in order to retain credibility and to be perceived as a worthy component of the company. One way to achieve this is to have a designated interpreter, rather than having an interpreter coming in from time to time. Although the definition and roles of designated interpreters have evolved as the American workforce evolves, the foundational philosophy of working with a designated interpreter remains the same.

Strategic Communicator

Many Deaf professionals are required to become masters in communication in their hearing workplaces. They must understand the importance of excellent business communication and relationships that are necessary to survive in the workplace. Working with a hearing audience through the designated interpreter's interpreting is a common tool for many Deaf clients.

The designated interpreter also possesses unique knowledge of the client's role and expertise that can help reduce barriers and bias for the clients. On television's *Dancing with the Stars*, during Season 22 in the spring of 2016, professional dancer Peta Murgatroyd taught her partner, Nyle DiMarco, who is Deaf, how to be an eloquent dancer. The fluidity of communication between them was an essential ingredient in making that process clear, smooth, and ultimately successful. DiMarco's designated interpreter, who stayed mostly out of the public eye, made a critical contribution to Peta and Nyle's communication and relationship building by strategically interpreting with confidence, clarity, and a bird's-eye perspective.

At Google, when participating in group meetings, I use a Double Dutch model when I need to communicate strategically in order to participate in group discussions. An ideal solution is akin to the skills needed for jumping into a Double Dutch jumping rope game. By allocating roles to each team interpreter (such as having one focus on ASL-to-English voicer, while the other focuses on English-to-ASL signer), the designated interpreters have more flexibility to jump in at the best time. When the Deaf professional indicates a desire to participate, the ASL-English voicing interpreter can engage in appropriate cultural norms and etiquette and take the floor accordingly.

The Double Dutch model is beneficial for all parties participating in workplace meetings because it allows for natural pacing and timely participation. It also increases the quality of interpreting because the interpreters are focusing on one task at a time. The ultimate goal is for the Deaf professional to fully participate and to exhibit full capacities and contributions while enhancing overall visibility and job performance.

Cultural Fit

Hiring the right interpreter in the right place at the right time will have a major impact on Deaf professionals and the corporation. The ultimate goal for every Deaf professional is to integrate into the professional and mostly hearing world effectively. A designated interpreter can help this happen; effective communication is the gateway to thriving in the workplace. The designated interpreter is responsible for helping eradicate all kinds of communication-related and cultural barriers and to pave a clear pathway for the client. Perfect communication is treated like winning a big grand prize and can greatly contribute to the success for Deaf professionals. Thus, the designated interpreter is a very valuable team member from the client's standpoint.

Learning Curve

The learning curve is challenging for every designated interpreter. Mastering knowledge in the Deaf professional's field may take time—even if the time given is short—and on-the-job experience. When a new competition arises, dancers typically adopt a new song (as well as a new dance format). To become efficient dancers, they must be willing to learn the Spanish tango's history and culture so they can eventually master its performance like locals. When a contest is scheduled, dancers often have to study and practice within a short timeframe to be able to perform well on the stage.

Similarly, designated interpreters have to understand the Deaf professional's specific work environment and culture, protocol, jargon, and many other components. An excellent designated interpreter should also have a strong understanding of how to appropriately mingle in the workplace. He or she also can speak articulately like the client's colleagues by using their jargon. Although the client may not necessarily or directly encourage the designated interpreter to become part of the larger team, the designated interpreter should be able to naturally acquire common word choices and jargon used within the corporation.

Most corporations are fast-paced work environments. Business strategies, trends, and decision-making processes are frequently changed, even from hour to hour. Making a commitment to constantly learn the business operation is essential and should be considered part of the designated interpreter's job responsibilities. The designated interpreter is usually expected to be self-driven, like any professional associate. The best dancers take time to study new movements and techniques, as well as new fad styles, in order to achieve the highest recognition. Designated interpreters must be open-minded learners. For instance, my designated interpreters constantly read news articles, review newly launched products, listen to the radio, and even watch presentations on the Internet (such as YouTube videos) to learn more about not only Google's, but also other companies' business strategies and announcements. Mastering the appropriate knowledge and techniques is extremely important to fitting into a corporate environment.

Conclusion

The ultimate goal for every Deaf professional is to integrate into the professional and predominantly hearing world successfully. The designated interpreter can serve a crucial role in satisfying the client's communication needs, since effective communication is the gateway to thriving in the workplace. One of the main considerations when hiring a designated interpreter is making sure that person will be an ideal fit for the corporate team. The designated interpreter is responsible for helping alleviate, if not removing, communication and cultural barriers for both Deaf and hearing professionals, creating clear pathways to them to communicate with each other.

Being a designated interpreter is a challenging and rewarding experience. Being a designated interpreter is a dedicated job for highly calibrated interpreters who carry the right expertise for service delivery.

Being a top-notch designated interpreter requires the talent of wearing many hats while facilitating everyone's positive experiences. Like the interpreting field, the tango is noble, honorable, and true gallantry for well-talented dancers. Whether dancing or interpreting, each individual creates a special and human connection to the world. Key to a successful Deaf professional and designated interpreter team are ongoing trust, respect, open communication, expertise, and allyship. If one team member has greater skill or expertise than the other, this skill and knowledge should be shared so that both achieve the same level of understanding for success.

NOTES

1. Oxford English Dictionary, "Oxford English Dictionary Online," accessed January 11, 2017, https://en.oxforddictionaries.com/definition/consumer.
2. Ibid., accessed January 11, 2017, https://www.merriam-webster.com/dictionary/client.
3. Farhad Manjoo, "Exposing Hidden Bias at Google," *New York Times,* September 24, 2014, accessed June 6, 2016, https://www.nytimes.com/2014/09/25/technology/exposing-hidden-biases-at-google-to-improve-diversity.html.
4. Jules Dickinson, *Signed Language Interpreting in the Workplace* (Washington, DC: Gallaudet University Press, 2017).
5. Jessica Bennett, "Hillary Clinton Will Not Be Manterrupted," *New York Times*, September 27, 2016, accessed August 08, 2016, https://www.nytimes.com/2016/09/28/opinion/campaign-stops/hillary-clinton-will-not-be-manterrupted.html.
6. Bain & Company, "Performance Culture," accessed January 15, 2017, http://www.bain.com/consulting-services/organization/performance-culture.aspx.
7. Peter Hauser, Karen Finch, and Angela Hauser, *Deaf Professionals and Designated Interpreters: A New Paradigm* (Washington, DC: Gallaudet University Press, 2008): 6.
8. See Thomas Holcomb on trust, this volume.
9. See Marika Kovacs-Houlihan, this volume; Thomas Holcomb on DEAM, this volume.
10. See Tara Holcomb, this volume.

Community Healthcare Interpreting 16

Susan Gonzalez, Lewis S. Lummer, Cynthia J. Plue, and Marta Ordaz

For the ASL summary of this chapter, go to https://youtu.be/L6cNIhVgDUM

As a local nonprofit agency, we get involved with various healthcare situations in which our Deaf clients are often poorly served by both healthcare providers and interpreters; this problem is heightened for foreign-born Deaf clients, as shown in the following example.

> A Deaf immigrant from Russia took her young daughter to see a physician. Throughout the appointment, the physician appeared rushed and spoke rapidly, extensively relying on medical jargon as he attempted to explain his diagnosis of the problem. Even though the interpreter worked hard to interpret everything the doctor had to say, the Deaf mother couldn't understand much of what the doctor shared. As communication was breaking down, the interpreter missed a critical opportunity to expand on the physician's explanation and instructions regarding the girl's illness. After prescribing medication and giving the mother a printed summary of the office visit, the physician hurried to his next appointment. The interpreter immediately followed him out of the office, leaving the Deaf mother feeling confused and uneasy.
>
> The mother visited our agency to request assistance with translating the physician's written instructions. It was only then that she understood the doctor's diagnosis of her daughter's condition, as well as the side effects and potential dangers of the medicine he prescribed. This example of ineffective interpreting resulting in a serious lack of understanding of critical medical information is unfortunately all too common in our community. Consequently, our agency is taking on more and more responsibilities to support deaf people in managing their healthcare.

Based on our decades of experience as Deaf community members working with interpreters in a host of roles, such as consumers, advocates, patients, caregivers, professionals, team interpreters, language facilitators, and cultural mediators, we are eager to provide insights on the issues related to community healthcare interpreting. Our firsthand experiences seeing loved ones struggling with healthcare professionals, although they had the services of interpreters, have shown us the severe consequences that result when their words and signs could not be interpreted and/or delivered with accuracy, compassion, and empathy. We have identified four key issues related to interpreters working in healthcare settings: effective communication, cross-cultural competence, language proficiency/fluency, and healthcare literacy.

Community healthcare interpreting is a mixed bag of experiences, both positive and negative, with multiple factors affecting interpreting quality. Subpar and ineffective interpreting services, due to the interpreters' lack of experience and/or awareness of differences in the lives of Deaf people, clearly can have adverse effects on communication and language access. Personal experiences from all subcultures of the Deaf community highlight both the successes and failures in an interpreted interaction, with individuals sharing many commonalities among/within their medical experiences. At the same time, each person's medical experience may be different due to the characteristics of their own individual cultures. Interpreters who demonstrate a conscious commitment in providing effective communication and ensuring the Deaf consumer's active participation in the healthcare process is sorely needed.

Healthcare services for deaf people are less than optimal. They also have relatively limited health literacy, resulting in poorer healthcare. This is likely due to the fact that numerous Deaf people share the characteristics of other limited English proficiency groups who typically have reduced access to public health information. It has also been stated that many deaf people have lower English literacy and healthcare knowledge, along with fewer opportunities for health education than their hearing peers.[1] Furthermore, and more recently, Napier and Sabolcec concluded that

> Deaf people encounter challenges in accessing healthcare and also in understanding healthcare information due to the lack of healthcare literacy and to communication barriers. Even when signed language interpreting services are provided, they may still experience challenges in understanding healthcare information if they do not have access to other forms of follow-up materials in the form of translated leaflets, and so on, presented in a signed language on video.[2]

Effective Communication in Healthcare

In community health arenas, effective communication between individuals, healthcare practitioners, and families is vital to achieving access to quality care and ensuring good health outcomes in clinical settings. This is nowhere more critical than in life-threatening situations in which lack of interpreted access to accurate, complete, and timely information can result in severe impediments to effective healthcare. The problems with meeting the Deaf population's communication needs in the essential area of healthcare are a cause for grave concern.[3] Therefore, it is imperative that the Deaf, interpreting, and healthcare communities work together toward the goal of meeting all parties' needs. Healthcare interpreters should have effective communication skills, cross-cultural competence, language proficiency and fluency, and healthcare literacy knowledge. This will then allow effective communication and foster positive relationships between patients and medical/healthcare practitioners. The ultimate goal is to ensure that the Deaf community's healthcare needs are successfully met.

Although effective communication is a protected right as mandated by the Americans with Disabilities Act (ADA), the interpretation of what constitutes "effective communication" varies widely among stakeholders, including deaf people, medical professionals, and healthcare management.[4] Clearly language proficiency and fluency as well as communication ability contribute heavily to healthcare literacy among deaf people. Healthcare professionals, as well as society at large—namely hearing people—often equate communication access with language access, which has caused confusion regarding providing effective communication services for deaf people.[5]

Communication Access and Language Access

> A Deaf Mexican immigrant made an appointment with a doctor for an allergy test. The medical facility arranged for a certified interpreter. During the appointment, the doctor outlined the testing procedure and proceeded with the test, using many medical terms. The interpreter relayed the information as best she could, situating herself closely to the doctor while he walked around the room. The doctor often stood in front of the interpreter, making it difficult for the patient to see the interpreter. The patient repeatedly asked the interpreter to stay in sight regardless of where the doctor was actually situated. The patient also asked the interpreter for clearer explanations because he couldn't understand much of what had been conveyed even though it had been given in sign language. And even though the patient had communication access in the form of an interpreter, he did not have language access.

In this situation, the interpreter was there with the goal of providing communication support and access—but this was not accomplished in an optimal manner. Just having an interpreter in the room rendering some message in sign language is no guarantee that the client with leave the office with a full understanding of what the doctor assumes was communicated. Language access was conspicuously absent as a result of the interpreter's inability to render the information in an understandable manner, one that fit the consumer's language needs. Clearly, language access is as critical as communication access in healthcare access, especially among deaf people.[6] The concept of language access has been noted within the Deaf community but is not yet a recognized concept nor a protected right understood by hearing people, especially medical professionals. By law, *effective communication* between the deaf consumer, healthcare practitioners, and families is required in healthcare situations. The key word here is "effective." In order to achieve this higher standard, attention needs to be given to what constitutes language access.[7]

It is imperative that Deaf consumers, interpreters, and healthcare professionals work together to ensure access to language *and* communication. Furthermore, interpreters must be able to adapt their interpreting styles and language use to meet the communicative needs of various groups, including those who are DeafBlind, DeafDisabled, hard of hearing, late-deafened, and foreign-born. Each subgroup possesses its own norms, cultural beliefs, traditions, and language foundations.

Diversity in the United States

Healthcare interpreting issues are not limited to the Deaf community; they also exist for other diverse communities and cultures in the United States.[8] The current demographics of the United States reflect a complex mix, with many different countries and cultures represented. The United States' 42.4 million immigrants represents the highest number of foreign-born residents ever in its history, and this number is expected to grow. In line with this migration trend, the U.S. Census Bureau data identified 64.7 million U.S. residents five years old or older who spoke a language other than English at home. More specifically, Spanish is, by far, the most spoken non-English language in the United States.[9]

Yet there seems to be one crucial difference between these groups when deaf patients and non-English speaking patients deal with healthcare providers. It seems that deaf people are more likely than hearing non-English speakers to be questioned by their doctors about their intelligence and by extension their ability to manage their healthcare needs. This may be due to the long history of linking deafness to low intelligence.[10] This perception of low intelligence is also reinforced by the fact that many deaf people struggle in learning English, which is often erroneously attributed as a direct outcome of their being deaf as opposed to having been linguistically deprived. Regardless of one's hearing status, healthcare interpreting is fraught with complications and legal implications and is a critical community issue.[11]

Diversity within the American Deaf Community

According to the World Federation of the Deaf (WFD), there are more than 70 million Deaf people worldwide. To support their communicative and linguistic needs, more than 128 different sign languages have been identified. The American deaf and hard of hearing population is estimated to comprise over 38 million people. Within this population are 45,000 to 50,000 individuals who have been identified as DeafBlind.[12]

Congregation within a specific group can occur either by virtue of personal characteristics or by choice. Deaf people of color often identify themselves as members of the Deaf community while also belonging to their own ethnic/racial communities. This intersectionality has led to incidents of culture clashes between communities as the norms of various ethnic/racial cultures may not always fit with those of American Deaf culture. This often places multicultural Deaf individuals in the position of having to balance or even choose between two cultures that are ingrained in their lives.[13] Similarly, DeafBlind individuals often need to straddle the DeafBlind community and the larger Deaf community.[14]

Sociolinguistic Accessibility

Even after emigrating to the United States, foreign-born Deaf people often rely on their native signed languages as their primary mode of communication. Further complicating the issue are the sign variations used by Deaf people born in the United States, such as Native Americans' tribal sign languages; Black signs; Filipino deaf signs; gay, lesbian, and bisexual signs; sexual and gender signs as well as regional variations.[15] Add to this mix the DeafBlind community along with deaf people with additional physical, cognitive, or/and other disabilities. This demonstrates the clear need for ASL interpreters to have the skills and flexibility to provide professional services for the diverse Deaf population. And, as is becoming more and more recognized, it is Deaf people, themselves, specifically CDIs, Certified Deaf Interpreters who possess the necessary experience communicating with a wide range of people in the Deaf community and should be utilized in any situation where "pure ASL" may not be effective.

Another issue to consider is multicultural Deaf persons' linguistic skills in written or oral form. Research has shown that some multicultural Deaf people also have various multilingual skills. For example, Asian Deaf immigrants often indicate that they learned their home language (mostly in written form and sometimes in spoken form), and then learned ASL later in life with many still struggling with English throughout their lives.[16] Cross-cultural education and competence are necessary for interpreters to work with various segments of the Deaf community. This is especially important for interpreters who live in metropolitan areas with large numbers of deaf immigrants. All deaf people, including those who immigrate to the United States, are entitled by law to effective communication in critical situations including healthcare.

Medical Care/Healthcare

Within the healthcare system, there are numerous stakeholders including patients, physicians, the government, hospital systems, pharmaceutical companies, pharmacies, pharmacy middlemen, and healthcare insurance companies. The primary stakeholders within the medical care system, however, are the patients, physicians, and individuals who provide direct care services such as nurses and physicians' assistants. The focus in medical care therefore is on providing immediate medical care, which can come in several forms including complementary, functional, holistic, homeopathic, and traditional medical care. It is worthy to note that without the primary stakeholders within the medical care system, there would be no need for a bigger healthcare enterprise.

There have been several studies on Deaf people's experiences with healthcare. Focus group discussions held in three cities showed that participants communicated best when medically experienced certified interpreters were provided, but they were available only infrequently. Also revealed were Deaf patients' skewed understandings of the healthcare provider's instructions and an overriding sense of fear in medical settings: a fear of the consequences of miscommunication and a fear of letting healthcare providers know that the communication was inadequate. The participants also reported their unwillingness to consider changing doctors out of fear that the new arrangement would result in the lack of interpreting services because of the new doctor's potential resistance to paying for interpreters. Results of this same study similarly concluded that Deaf people who use ASL had much in common with other linguistic minority groups: limited access to English communication, infrequent contact with healthcare providers who knew their language and culture, as well as the frequency of using family and friends as interpreters, and the preference for direct communication over interpreted encounters with non-deaf medical providers.[17]

Medical and Healthcare Interpreting in the Deaf Community

Clearly there is a critical need for interpreters throughout the healthcare system, beginning with admission and intake procedures that include the vital task of recording the patient's medical history. Additionally, there is a variety of other medical situations such as making appointments, getting laboratory tests, discussing upcoming medical procedures, obtaining consultations, getting physical checkups, making emergency visits, undergoing surgery, arranging for home healthcare visits, receiving nursing home care, and participating in physical or occupational therapy sessions.[18]

St. Catherine University in St. Paul, Minnesota hosted the first National Symposium on Healthcare Interpreting in 2010 with 110 people in attendance. Their report identified the need to create standards of practice for healthcare interpreting and a comprehensive curriculum to educate future medical interpreters as priorities in the advancement of the healthcare interpreting profession.[19]

In a published report, hospital quality and safety leaders, nursing staff, and interpreters shared their concerns about ongoing problems when medical care was provided to deaf patients without securing the services of an interpreter. The report also found that medication errors and lack of informed consent were more common among patients with language barriers, both deaf and hearing. Organizations such as the Registry of Interpreters for the Deaf and the National Association of the Deaf strongly advise against the use of a patient's family or friends as interpreters or language facilitators.[20]

In an article on an interpreting role in medical settings, Davidson suggested how doctors and patients often have different views of an interpreter's role in a medical encounter: "The doctor sees the interpreter as 'an instrument that keeps the patient on track,' and the patient considers the interpreter as a 'co-conversationalist.'" Also emphasized was the need for specialized training: "Given the obvious complexity of the medical interpreting task, it is clear that interpreters need preparation before working in this setting. Preparation includes both formal training and education, and knowledge needed for a specific medical encounter."[21]

Medical care interpreting is routinely provided by interpreters without much or any training in this area. Further compounding this problem is a massive shortage of specialized medical interpreters due to limited training opportunities—one factor contributing to the rampant use of video relay interpreting in healthcare settings.[22]

Video Relay Interpreting in Healthcare Settings

As previously stated, medical facilities, including hospitals, rehabilitation centers, hospice centers, and doctor offices, have turned to video relay interpreting (VRI) as a result of the shortage of local qualified interpreters who possess health care proficiency, and to offset the added expenses (e.g., travel, mileage) associated with hiring live interpreters. In recent years, the use of VRI has been expanded to settings such as the delivery room, the recovery room (post-operation), health education classes, and psychiatric appointments. While medical facilities typically assert that the use of VRI services meets the minimum standards as established by federal and state laws, this shift in the interpreting delivery model has been decried by Deaf consumers. Multiple lawsuits have been filed throughout the nation in protest of this trend, with Deaf people stating that medical facilities have failed to consider the effective communications criteria as outlined by the ADA. In addition, the U.S. Department of Justice has pursued multiple civil cases against more than a dozen medical facilities across the country under its 2012 Barrier-Free Health Initiative, However, legal results have been mixed, making it extremely difficult to maintain consistency in legal precedence. Clearly, medical facilities fail to realize that the mere provision of interpreting services (in-person or via video relay) does not ensure adequate language or even communication access.

To address the changing picture as a result of this VRI proliferation, the U.S. Department of Justice established four specific mandates for the use of VRI: (1) dedicated high-speed wide-bandwidth video connection or wireless connections; (2) sharp delineated images large enough to see faces, arms, hands, and fingers; (3) clear audible transmission of voices, and (4) adequate training for staff to quickly and efficiently set up and operate VRI.[23] Even with these minimal mandates, there are still many on-going concerns about the use of VRI in place of onsite interpreting services.

The National Association of the Deaf (NAD) issued a position statement on the use of VRI, emphasizing that VRI should be used only when it is not possible to secure the services of an onsite interpreter. The NAD cites the numerous limitations of VRI, such as the lack of access by people with vision impairments and/or who have psychiatric, cognitive, or linguistic impairments, are under sedation, or are seriously impaired in their ability to move, as well as the frequent occurrence of technical glitches or lack of adequate bandwidth and a number of other potential problems.[24]

Despite the prevalence of and access to technology, it is plain to see that VRI is not the solution for many Deaf people, especially those whose language and communication skills are not well developed. Another concern regarding the use of VRI is that it offers no benefits to the DeafBlind community.

DeafBlind Patients

The DeafBlind community is one of the most marginalized groups in both the Deaf community and the hearing world. Too frequently, DeafBlind patients are expected to use VRI or are provided with an interpreter who is unprepared, unqualified, or unskilled to do the job. For example, the communication needs of DeafBlind individuals may range from close-vision interpreting, tactile sign language, and/or protractile interpreting. Healthcare professionals and interpreting agencies are often clueless about these differences, with the burden consequently being placed on the interpreters to advocate on behalf of DeafBlind patients related to their communication access, even if they are not really well versed in working with this population.

Even with an interpreter present, family members sometimes take over the entire interaction and "take care" of the DeafBlind person's appointment. While this is often an issue with sighted Deaf people as well, this practice is even more prevalent among DeafBlind individuals. Furthermore, many hearing medical professionals find it easier to deal directly with the sighted hearing people in the room, leaving out the DeafBlind patient even more. This puts interpreters in an awkward position.

Unique Needs Among Foreign-Born Deaf People

Community health service resources have historically offered inadequate resources for the Deaf community, and as stated previously, especially so for foreign-born Deaf people whose communication and literacy skills are often even more limited. Additional challenges may include the fact that many of these immigrants are in the U.S. without family or friends, have limited or no income, have little or no formal education with minimal or no fluency in any language, and minimal knowledge of their native culture, Deaf culture, or American culture. On top of this, add that many foreign-born Deaf people utilize at least three or four languages (their native written language, their native signed language, English, and ASL) to communicate and function in their daily lives, even though none of these linguistic skills are well developed. Research on the needs of deaf immigrant adults demonstrates that very few have the functional ability to understand what was shared in a healthcare setting and, consequently, were dissatisfied with their experiences. The findings also reveal that in spite of their communicative and linguistic limitations, interpreting services were provided only 65% of the time.[25]

While the basics of interpreting are the same in most situations, the nuances of medical/healthcare interpreting are significantly different and unique in many regards, especially with foreign-born deaf individuals and DeafBlind people. Unfortunately, people in general and service providers specifically who are not intimately familiar with the Deaf community often assume that the mere presence of interpreters is sufficient to meet the needs of all Deaf people in any healthcare situation. They are often unaware of the role that CDIs could play in providing fuller language and communication access to Deaf people in healthcare situations.

Certified Deaf Interpreters

Deaf interpreters, certified and some non-certified (with caution), have shown to be successful in ensuring effective communication and fuller language access for all Deaf people, and especially for those who are DeafBlind, foreign-born, and have limited language development. Deaf interpreters are more skilled in the nuances of understanding and communicating information far beyond the mere linguistic levels typically associated with spoken-language-to-sign interpreting. Courts have incorporated Deaf interpreters in various legal settings with great success. In other settings, such as the Social Security Administration, Deaf interpreters have worked with Spoken English/ASL interpreters in facilitating communication between Deaf people including DeafBlind individuals and the hearing professionals.[26]

Randomly Assigned Interpreters

In addition to the complexities of information presented during medical appointments, an additional challenge is randomly assigned interpreters; that is, Deaf people come to appointments without knowing in advance who the interpreters are or what their qualifications are.[27] Usually, interpreters are hired by a medical office without consulting the Deaf patient, and/or the contracted interpreting agency may randomly assign an interpreter. Adding to the complexities already inherent in any interpreted event including medical situations is the lack of knowledge or awareness among medical/healthcare professionals about the necessary qualifications for interpreters to perform their duties successfully in a medical setting.[28] This lack of knowledge, preparation, and coordination can represent a double whammy on both sides when it comes to an appointment in a healthcare service setting. Clearly, strategies to improve the quality of healthcare and health outcomes for people, including minority Deaf citizens, are needed. This could involve educating clinicians and community members about health literacy, improving patient–provider communication, and implementing research-based practices as the new and improved standards.

The Problem of "9 to 5" Interpreters

Compassion is especially necessary for healthcare interpreting because emotions can run deep, especially with medical complications or the delivery of bad news. Deaf people do not need additional barriers presented by seemingly indifferent and inefficient interpreters such as what was portrayed and what was evident in this real-life scenario:

> Following a lengthy surgery, a Deaf patient was finally brought to the recovery room. Because the surgery went much longer than scheduled, the interpreter did not stay for the post-op recovery, stranding the Deaf patient and his Deaf family members. The interpreter also did not offer to contact the interpreting agency or work with the nurse in charge to arrange and ensure full communication access. During the recovery, complications ensued, creating additional chaos between

> the medical personnel and family members. After the ordeal, in a follow-up discussion with the interpreter, she claimed that it was not her responsibility to deal with the details, nor was it her fault the surgery went over time.

With the shift away from family members or friends to certified professionals doing the interpreting, there has been a corresponding attitudinal shift among some interpreters. Instead of being true allies of the Deaf community with a feeling of "Deaf-heart" for Deaf people, they view themselves as "9 to 5" or professional interpreters, working primarily to earn money and make a living. By contrast, an ally, or an interpreter with "Deaf-heart" is one "who listens to the concerns of the oppressed group and then advocates/speaks for them in the halls of power."[29] Often, interpreters are faced with conflicting emotions. They need to tread carefully and not take away the Deaf consumers' decision-making powers and rights, and at the same time follow/proceed with what feels like an ethically appropriate decision. Striking a balance between these opposing approaches/perspectives can present quite a challenge. The real-life scenario presented next exemplifies such a challenge.

> An interpreter arrived at the emergency room only to find the Deaf patient to be delirious, incoherent, and possibly psychotic. Realizing the complexities of the situation and her own language limitations, the interpreter asked for a CDI to ensure accuracy for the intake process. The emergency room personnel refused, claiming that the patient did not want one. The interpreter stood her ground and continued to insist that a CDI be summoned. She provided the hospital with RID's standard practice paper on the use of and rationale for CDIs, along with contact information for the interpreting agency who hired her. Finally, after the hospital personnel acquiesced, a CDI arrived who could decipher the Deaf patient's signs, resulting in an accurate diagnosis and appropriate intervention.

Conclusion: Steps to Create Improved Services

Clearly, there is always a fine line between being an advocate and someone who oversteps boundaries. In addition, the responsibility of educating medical professionals about appropriate approaches and behavior should fall on the Deaf community through agencies specializing in advocacy and awareness training. If there are no existing agencies in an area, then the interpreter might consider taking on the responsibility of educating medical personnel with the goal of improving the healthcare experience for deaf people—but with extreme caution and awareness of the potential conflicts of interest (if, for example, the hospital relies totally on the interpreter to advise them, instead of involving members of the Deaf community). An example that is considered acceptable would be when the interpreter quickly educates nurses and doctors prior to the appointment on communication, language, and literacy gaps between patients and medical professionals. More importantly, the interpreter could assist the medical facility in finding Deaf community members to assist in creating an overall accessibility plan. Such a plan would ideally include communication, cultural, linguistic, and literacy components. Here are some of the basic considerations:

Language accessibility: A communication plan should be established in advance as part of the accessibility plan to remove or minimize language barriers, such as offering language choices to the patient for visual, tactile, written, and/or signed language access.

Communication accessibility: The patient should be given options for communication accessibility, such as sign language via direct communication, on-site interpreting, video interpreting, and/or written language, and technology (e.g., email, texting, laptop use, online live chat). Determination should also collaboratively take place on what types of interpreting services are needed: ASL/Spoken English interpreter, translator (spoken English/Signed English) and/or deaf interpreter—all certified and qualified.

Cultural accessibility: Measures should be taken to ensure the Deaf patient feels comfortable linguistically *and* culturally. This includes the person's affinity to the Deaf community, religious orientation, and ethnic heritage.

Health literacy accessibility: Steps should be taken to ensure that health information and printed materials are accessible and understandable in the patient's language(s). Information about health issues should be accessible and provided at the patient's level of comprehension, communication, and comfort.

Healthcare advocate accessibility: When no interpreters or other communication accessibility tools are provided, procedures should be in place to ensure that patients know who to talk to or how to seek support to advocate for their rights.

Further exploration and studies are critically needed to address all of the issues in this chapter, especially to develop quality learning and training opportunities for medical interpreters, and to ensure more effective communication access for Deaf people within the healthcare system. Fortunately, the Collaborative for the Advancement of Teaching Interpreting Excellence (CATIE) Center at St. Catherine University in Minnesota, with the assistance of federal funds, has emerged as a national leader in this effort. In addition, Northeastern University's ASL program in Boston was awarded a federal grant to establish the center for Atypical Language Interpreting with the goal of improving interpreting services for Deaf and DeafBlind people whose language is atypical (e.g., those who were linguistically deprived, those who have delayed language development). Ultimately, these initiatives along with a sincere commitment by interpreters will result in improved healthcare communication and language access for all Deaf people.

Notes

1. Lisa Harmer, "Health Care Delivery and Deaf People: Practice, Problems, and Recommendations for Change," *Journal of Deaf Studies and Deaf Education* 4, no. 2 (1999): 73–110; Teri Hedding and Gary Kaufman, "Health Literacy and Deafness: Implications for Interpreter Education," in *In Our Hands: Educating Healthcare Interpreters*, eds. Laurie Swabey and Karen Malcolm (Washington, DC: Gallaudet University Press, 2012): 164–189; Anna Middleton, *Working with Deaf People: Handbook for Health Professionals* (Cambridge, UK: Cambridge University Press, 2010); Brenda Nicodemus and Melanie Metzger, *Investigations in Healthcare Interpreting,*

ed. (Washington, DC: Gallaudet University Press, 2014); Robert Q. Pollard and Steven Barnett, "Health-related Vocabulary Knowledge Among Deaf Adults," *Rehabilitation Psychology* 54, no. 2 (2009): 182–185; Laurie Swabey and Karen Malcolm, *In Our Hands: Educating Healthcare Interpreters* (Washington, DC: Gallaudet University Press, 2012).

2. Jemina Napier and Joseph Sabolcec, "Direct, Translated or Interpreter-mediated? A Qualitative Study of Access to Preventive and On-going Healthcare Information for Australian Deaf People" in *Investigations in Healthcare Interpreting,* eds. Brenda Nicodemus and Melanie Metzger (Washington, DC: Gallaudet University Press, 2014): 239.

3. The Joint Commission, *Advancing Effective Communication, Cultural Competence, and Patient- and Family-Centered Care: A Roadmap for Hospitals* (Oakbrook Terrace, IL: The Joint Commission, 2010); Nicodemus and Metzger, *Investigations in Healthcare Interpreting*; National Association of the Deaf, *Position Statement Supplement: Culturally Affirmative and Linguistically Accessible Mental Health Services* (Silver Spring, MD: National Association of the Deaf, 2008), https://www.nad.org/resources/health-care-and-mental-health-services/mental-health-services/culturally-affirmative-and-linguistically-accessible-services/; Lynn Nielsen-Bohlman, Allison M. Panzer, and David A. Kindig, *Health Literacy: A Prescription to End Confusion* (Washington, DC: National Academies, 2004); Laurie Swabey and Quincy C. Faber, "Domains and Competencies in Healthcare Interpreting: Applications and Implications for Educators" in *In Our Hands: Educating Healthcare Interpreters*, eds. Laurie Swabey and Karen Malcolm (Washington, DC: Gallaudet University Press, 2012): 1–26.

4. National Association of the Deaf, *Hospitals and Other Health Care Facilities* (Silver Spring, MD: National Association of the Deaf, n.d.), https://www.nad.org/resources/health-care-and-mental-health-services/health-care-providers/hospitals-and-other-health-care-facilities/

5. Hedding and Kaufman, "Health Literacy and Deafness."

6. National Association of the Deaf, "Position Statement on Health Care Access for Deaf Patients," Retrieved from https://www.nad.org/about-us/position-statements/position-statement-on-health-care-access-for-deaf-patients/ AD position statement.

7. Joint Commission, *Advancing Effective Communication, Cultural Competence, and Patient- and Family-Centered Care*; Elaine Hsieh, "Emerging Trends and the Corresponding Challenges in Bilingual Health Communication," in *Investigations in Healthcare Interpreting*, eds. Brenda Nicodemus and Melanie Metzger (Washington, DC: Gallaudet University Press, 2014): 70–103.

8. Claudia Angelelli, "Uh . . . I Am Not Understanding You at All": Constructing (Mis) Understanding in Provider/Patient Interpreted Medical Encounters," in *Investigations in Healthcare Interpreting*, eds. Brenda Nicodemus and Melanie Metzger (Washington, DC: Gallaudet University Press, 2014): 1–31; Bruce Downing and Karin Ruschke, "Professionalizing Healthcare Interpreting betweenSpoken Languages: Contributions of the National Council on Interpreting in Health Care" in *In Our Hands: Educating Healthcare Interpreters,* eds. Laurie Swabey and Karen Malcolm (Washington, DC: Gallaudet University Press, 2012): 209–28.

9. Steven A. Camarota and Karen Ziegler, *S. Immigrants in the United States: Profile of the Foreign-born Using 2014 and 2015 Census Bureau Data* (Washington, DC: Center for Immigration Studies, 2016), https://cis.org/Immigrants-United-States#frontpage.

10. Lisa Iezzoni, Bonnie L. O'Day, Mary Killeen, and Heather Harker, "Communicating about Health Care: Observations from Persons Who are Deaf or Hard of Hearing," *Annals of Internal Medicine* 140, no. 5 (2004): 356–62.

11. Hsieh, "Emerging Trends and the Corresponding Challenges in Bilingual Health Communication."

12. Carol J. Ertling, Robert C. Johnson, Dorothy L. Smith, and Bruce N. Sniders, *The Deaf Way: Perspectives from the International Conference on Deaf Culture* (Washington, DC:

Gallaudet University Press, 1996); Tom Harrington, *Deaf Statistics* (Washington, DC: Gallaudet University Library, 2014), http://libguides.gallaudet.edu/content.php?pid=119476&sid=1029190; Tonya M. Stremlau, *The Deaf Way II Anthology: A Literary Collection by Deaf and Hard of Hearing Writers* (Washington, DC: Gallaudet University Press, 2002); National Consortium of Deaf-Blindness, *The 2007 National Child Count of Children and Youth who are Deaf-Blind* (Sands Points, NY: *The National Consortium on Deaf-Blindness*, 2008), http://documents.nationaldb.org/products/2007-Census-Tables.pdf.

13. Glenn Anderson and Frank Bowe, "Racism Within the Deaf Community," *American Annals of the Deaf* 117, no. 6 (1972): 617–619; Anthony J. Aramburo, "Sociolinguistic Aspects of the Black Deaf Community," in *The Sociolinguistic of the Deaf Community*, ed. Ceil Lucas (Washington, DC: Gallaudet University, 1989); Cynthia Plue, "Multicultural Profiles in the Deaf Community." *Multicultural Review* 12, no. 3 (2003): 48–56.

14. Ina Mance, *Deafblind People and Self-Identity* (Herlev, Denmark: Information Center for Acquired Deafblindess, 2008), http://www.deafblindinternational.org/Docs/Review%20Archive/Deafblind%20People%20and%20self%20identity.pdf.

15. Jeff Davis and David Supalla, "A Sociolinguistic Description of Sign Language Use in a Navajo Family," in *Sociolinguistics in Deaf Communities,* ed. Ceil Lucas (Washington, DC: Gallaudet University, 1995); Aramburo, "Sociolinguistic Aspects of the Black Deaf Community"; Jackie Bruce, "A Comparative Study of Backchanneling Signals between an African American Deaf Speaker and African American and White Deaf Speakers," in *Communication Forum*, ed., Elizabeth A. Winston (Washington, DC: Gallaudet University School of Communication Press, 1993): 1–10; Susan D. Doughten, Marlyn B. Minkin, and Laurie E. Rosen, *Signs for Sexuality: A Resource Manual for Teachers, Counselors, Interpreters, Parents, and Hearing Impaired Persons Concerned with Deafness and Human Sexuality*. (Seattle, WA: Planned Parenthood, 1978); Mala S. Kleinfield and Noni Warner, "Variations in the Deaf Community: Gay, Lesbian, and Bisexual Signs" in *Multicultural Aspects of Sociolinguistics in Deaf Communities*, ed. Ceil Lucas (Washington, DC: Gallaudet University Press, 1996); Melanie McKay-Cody, "The 'Well-Hidden' People in Deaf and Native Communities" in *The Deaf American Monograph Series*, ed. Merv Garretson (Silver Spring, MD: NAD Publications, 1999); A. Thibeault, "Overlap in Filipino Sign Language Discourse" in *Communication Forum,* ed. Elizabeth A. Winston (Washington, DC: School of Communication Press, 1993): 207–218.

16. Lewis Lummer and Cynthia Plue, *Deaf Immigrants' Perspectives of Interpreter Services Panel Session*, Interpreter Workshop Series (Aurora, IL: Waubonsee Community College, 2000); Lewis Lummer, *Teachers' Perceptions of the Academic and Language Needs of Deaf Immigrant Students: An Exploratory Survey*, master's thesis (Beaumont, TX: Lamar University, 1999); Cynthia Plue, "Deaf Asian/Pacific Island Students: How Can We Enlarge Their Visions and Dreams" in *The Deaf American Monograph Series*, ed. Merv Garretson (Silver Spring, MD: National Association of the Deaf, 1998); Cynthia Plue, "A History of Deaf Asians/Pacific Islanders in America" in *Deaf Studies VI: Making the Connection* Conference Proceedings, April 8–11 (Washington, DC: College for Continuing Education, Gallaudet University, 1999).

17. Annie G. Steinberg, Steven Barnett, Helen E. Meador, Erin A. Wiggins, and Philip Zazove, Healthcare System Accessibility: Experiences and Perceptions of Deaf People, *Journal of General Internal Medicine* 21, no. 3 (2006 Mar): 260–266.

18. Janice H. Humphrey and Bob J. Alcorn, *So You Want to Be an Interpreter* (Clearwater, FL: H & H Publishing, 2001); Tamara Moxham, *Deaf Patients, Hearing Medical Personnel: Interpreting and Other Considerations* (Hillsboro, OR: Butte Publications, 2005); Jemina Napier, *Sign Language Interpreting: Theory and Practice in Australia and New Zealand* (Sydney, Australia: The Federation Press, 2006).

19. Swabey and Faber, "Domains and Competencies in Healthcare Interpreting."

20. Andrea Olson and Laurie Swabey, "Communication Access for Deaf People in Healthcare Settings: Understanding the Work of American Sign Language Interpreters," *Journal for Healthcare Quality* 39, no. 4 (2017): 191–199.

21. Interpreting in Healthcare Settings, "The Interpreting Role in Medical Settings," Healthcareinterpreting.org, http://healthcareinterpreting.org/faqs/lit-interpreting-role-in-medical-settings/.

22. George Major, "'Sorry Could You Explain That?' Clarification Requests in Interpreter Mediated Healthcare Interaction" in *Investigations in Healthcare Interpreting*, eds. Brenda Nicodemus and Melanie Metzger (Washington, DC: Gallaudet University Press, 2014): 32–69.

23. U.S. Department of Justice, Civil Rights Division, Disability Rights Division, "Effective Communication" (Washington, DC: U.S. Department of Justice, 2014), https://www.ada.gov/effective-comm.pdf.

24. National Association of the Deaf, "Advocacy Statement: Use of VRI in the Medical Setting" (Silver Spring, MD: National Association of the Deaf, 2008), https://www.nad.org/resources/technology/video-remote-interpreting/advocacy-statement-use-of-vri-in-the-medical-setting/.

25. Lummer, "Teachers' Perceptions of the Academic and Language Needs of Deaf Immigrant Students"; Lummer and Cynthia Plue, *Deaf Immigrants' Perspectives of Interpreter Services;* Nicodemus and Melanie Metzger, *Investigations in Healthcare Interpreting*; Plue, "A History of Deaf Asians/Pacific Islanders in America."

26. Patrick Boudreault, "Deaf Interpreters" in *Topics in Signed Language Interpreting: Theory and Practice*, Ed. Terry Janzen (Philadelphia: John Benjamins, 2005): 323–56; Eileen Forestal, *Deaf Interpreters: Exploring Their Processes of Interpreting*, Diss., Capella University, 2011.

27. See Taylor, Shephard, and Buckhold, this volume.

28. Hedding and Kaufman, "Health Literacy and Deafness"; Hsieh, "Emerging Trends and the Corresponding Challenges in Bilingual Health Communication."

29. Charlotte Baker-Shenk, "The Interpreter: Machine, Advocate, or Ally?" in *Expanding Horizons: Proceedings of the 1991 RID Convention* (Silver Springs, MD: Registry of Interpreters of the Deaf, 1991): 120–140.

4

Moving Forward with Deaf Eyes

17

On Resolving Cultural Conflicts and the Meaning of Deaf-Centered Interpreting

Wyatte C. Hall

To see the ASL summary of this chapter, go to https://youtu.be/toBKz5p_tss

> I have worked with sign language interpreters in some form for more than twenty-five years, since I was five years old. I grew up in a mainstreamed public school with a deaf program of approximately 20 to 30 students in a state that, in 2017, still does not have minimum standards or licensing requirements for sign language interpreters. It was not until my Ph.D. studies that I experienced working with, and continue to work with, an "empowering" interpreter who exemplifies the aspects of the Deaf-centered model proposed within this chapter. This empowerment via interpreters does not have to be rare or experienced so late–something that I hope this suggested model and way of thinking can help address.

THE ISSUE of cultural conflicts between sign language interpreters and Deaf people can be a polarizing one. A common generalization of opposing sides in these cultural conflicts might be summarized as interpreters who believe they are following the rules[1] versus Deaf individuals who feel some type of cultural norm has been violated.[2] In recent years, there is an increasing sense of empowerment for Deaf individuals to take more control of their own interpreting outcomes and having less patience for "good-enough" communication access while tolerating culturally insensitive behaviors. A truly Deaf-centered model of interpreting has not been a standard of interpreting practice to date.[3] Such a model is now becoming necessary to fulfill the increased expectations of Deaf people, expectations *rightfully* had for professionals who choose to use the Deaf birthright of sign language—a birthright denied to many deaf people, no less—as a means of personal employment.

Enculturation and acculturation can be distinguished as first- and second-culture learning respectively. Simply put, children of Deaf adults (CODAs) and

This work would not be possible without the numerous in-depth discussions, feedback, and collaborative work to date with Marlene Elliott, CI/CT.

Deaf interpreters are more likely to be *enculturated* interpreters, as opposed to non-CODAs as *acculturated* interpreters.[4] Cokely and Witter-Merithew's description of an organic, Deaf-led experience being their entrance into interpreting is a model of how Deaf leadership can develop an acculturative progression in which the members of the Deaf community and their allies are directly involved in the development of interpreters.[5] It is this acculturative process that appears to be missing in the academic focus of the interpreting field (i.e., interpreters learn *about* Deaf culture but are much less likely to *internalize* Deaf culture), an issue that may be one of the primary causes of ongoing cultural conflicts. Some examples of cultural conflicts are:

1. Interpreters using their position for personal attention and fame (e.g.. "Rock Star" interpreters[6]) rather than re-directing to deaf people with expert content knowledge
2. Assuming full control of the interpreting process and not sharing decision-making, such as when to voice and not voice or setting up seating arrangements[7]
3. Misunderstanding feedback as personal criticism when it is actually a gift[8]

There also appears to be fundamental differences in the expectations and perceptions of the interpreting process. The Deaf community, largely collectivist, expects an interpreter's duty to be toward the people whereas many academic training programs teach that an interpreter's duty is to the (spoken) word.[9] This is made evident in the concept of neutrality.

There is an inherent power imbalance in any hearing–Deaf interaction due to the majority–minority status of each group.[10] Although the conduit model has, in theory, been discarded, too many non-acculturated interpreters continue to follow "conduit neutrality" in which they simply relay the words back and forth between parties involved in the communication process with no personal responsibility for understanding.[11] As highlighted by Metzger,[12] this hearing-centered neutrality harms deaf people by allowing that power imbalance to continue. Rather than following "true" neutrality as examined by Metzger, however, *Deaf-centered* neutrality is suggested instead. Genuine Deaf-centered neutrality allows interpreters to use strategies, in collaboration with Deaf people, which equalizes the inherent power imbalance[13] between deaf and hearing people—a skill often seen in enculturated ally interpreters.[14]

Tensions and Historical Models

Prior to the professionalization of the interpreting field, the *helper* model was common, where CODAs and Deaf service professionals became interpreters as needed (often with patronizing attitudes).[15] The development of professional, ethics-based models of interpreting led to a natural shift focusing on translation, rather than working with people. This shift, in many ways useful, also created some tendencies that appear to still influence interpreters today. By moving away from people and toward words, some natural breakdowns occurred creating what could be labeled "tensions" between the participants of the interpreting process.

Discussions began in the late 1970s around the way the English language naturally embeds the concept of a conduit model in the forms it uses to talk about communication.[16] Language experts and philosophers, however, have long suggested that creating meaning is a shared activity among people—that meaning is created through interaction—and words simply represent agreements between people.[17] The conduit model focuses on meaning being encoded within words themselves by a sender—that one person creates meaning and gives it to another person to decode or "unpack" that same meaning. This English bias for conduit-style communication naturally creates tension when Deaf people expect to collaborate on creating shared meaning, yet interpreters expect to *give* meaning.

Another tension exists between form and meaning; essentially, the word-for-word style of interpreting in which English words are simply represented and relying on the Deaf person to find understanding in what was said versus producing ASL renditions of what the interpreter understood from English. Too many interpreters believe they can only give form (i.e., they have no right to make the shift to ASL for fear of depriving Deaf people of access to English words). This tension also exists the other way around, when interpreters are producing renditions into English from ASL and may use English glosses to represent more sophisticated and nuanced statements by Deaf people that are often perceived as less sophisticated. This tension exists largely because deaf people live, interact, and navigate in a spoken-language world. Interpreters have to weigh when form may be empowering to Deaf people (e.g., learning specific English words to use later) versus when to give a culturally accurate, visually understandable message—a skill that is easy to learn but difficult to master.

As the interpreting field grapples with tensions such as these—between "helping" versus providing access to spoken language, translating versus interacting, representing form versus meaning—various models have been suggested. As highlighted by Wilcox and Shaffer's[18] historical analyses of interpreting models, the initial move from the helper model to the *conduit* model was quickly seen as impractical. Interpreters who viewed themselves as a non-person in the room—acting as a machine, refusing to give their name—served to disrupt interactions, instead of facilitating them. Recognizing this, the *communication facilitator* model was proposed to allow more natural behaviors but still maintain a non-person status as much as was socially comfortable and acceptable.

Over time, the impact of cultural differences between the Deaf and hearing worlds on the communication process became more overt and recognized. This led to the *bilingual–bicultural* (bi–bi) model, essentially allowing interpreters to begin making cultural adjustments as needed. It is the bi–bi model that began to recognize and take more responsibility for addressing the tension between form and meaning, but many Deaf people were still unsatisfied with their interpreter experiences. The *ally* model sought to address not only cultural differences but also power imbalances. Interpreters still view themselves as translators but are more likely to exhibit specific behaviors around the interpreting process that may respond to clear power imbalances as they occur. The underlying tensions caused by the very *conduit*-nature of English, however, still remain unresolved by these models, except within the individual interpreter.*[19]

> Our contention is that despite our best efforts to rid the field of it, the conduit model remains, albeit driven underground as interpreting models have focused attention less on the cognitive act of communication and more on political and cultural behaviors of the interpreter. In moving away from conduit models of interpreting to those in which the interpreter takes a more active role, interpreter educators have gradually eliminated any discussion of the cognitive process of interpreting and, more importantly, any discussion of what it means to communicate.[20]

Wilcox and Shaffer addressed the conduit issue by proposing a cognitive model of interpreting—"an active process of constructing meaning based on evidence provided by speakers"[21]; however, this model is not widely used in the field. Despite the development of various models over time, Deaf people's complaints about interpreters (as highlighted in the introduction paragraph of this text) persists because they do not address the fundamental issue that plagues all models to date—the lack of Deaf-centeredness and a refusal or inability to recognize power imbalances as they occur.

Becoming Deaf-Centered

The inherent nature of sign language is dialogic,[22] and a Deaf-centered model of interpreting naturally develops from that dialogic nature. Being aware of the power inequalities, a Deaf-centered interpreter will perform more like a partner than a conduit. In contrast to many *voice-activated* interpreters (one who immediately signs when they hear the spoken word and feels internal pressure to follow an auditory pace) prioritizing auditory pace and representing auditory words visually,[23] a Deaf-centered interpreter will be cognizant of visual clarity above all else. A Deaf-centered interpreter will also have, with significant focus and practice, cognitive bandwidth that allows for effective multitasking and managing multiple points of focus simultaneously. This enables Deaf participants to be invited and incorporated in the shared construction of meaning as is seen in Open Process, an approach that allows for shared ownership of meaning.[24]

This book chapter details what are suggested to be critical aspects of a Deaf-centered model of interpreting. These aspects build upon Cecila Wadensjö's (a Swedish-Russian interpreter) theory of interpreting as interaction as opposed to interpreting as an act of translation,[25] an approach initially proposed to the ASL interpreting field by Cynthia Roy.[26] A Deaf-centered model includes feedback, pace, partnership, visual orientation, and cultural competence, among other things.

*Demand Control Schema—a model of occupational stress developed for medical students now applied to interpreters—has gained popularity in the interpreting field. Although it does not claim to be an interpreting model, it has become a primary framework for interpreters to view their work through the lens of their own stressful experiences.

Three common life experiences (formal auditory presentation, group discussion, and doctor's office) of Deaf individuals, where interpreters are used, illustrate the Pace, Partnership, and Visual Orientation sections to discuss the oft-overlapping dynamic skills used to ensure successful outcomes. The model aspects described here are by no means comprehensive nor are they set in stone. As the field of sign language interpreting continues to evolve, so should the concept of Deaf-centered interpreting beyond past and current models.

Feedback

To understand the context of feedback in the interpreting process, it must first be emphasized that the interpreting process is a type of relationship in itself. A productive relationship between interpreters and Deaf people must be able to survive healthy negotiation in which honest feedback, both positive and negative, can be given and received. Within this context, feedback is a *gift*, reflecting trust and intimacy in the other person, and a willingness to put work into strengthening that relationship and clarifying the message together. Feedback given to an interpreter means that the Deaf person cares enough to try improving or even validating that interpreter's work and professional skills for both that interpreter's personal benefit and for the whole Deaf community.

Feedback is such a common example of a cultural conflict that it borders on being a stereotypical expectation of interpreting interactions. This stereotype includes Deaf individuals being overly direct in their feedback to interpreters who they feel can improve in some way. This can offend interpreters who have internalized the hearing norm of giving feedback in a subtle and indirect way to avoid hurt feelings,[27] and can result in dismissing the feedback as simply a form of discharging emotions such as anger. This type of situation is a clash of collectivist and individualist values, which can see the Deaf person losing cultural trust in the interpreter.[28]

It is worth briefly unpacking the context in which a Deaf person may give what could be perceived as angry feedback. First, it must be emphasized that interpreters are tolerated guests—welcome or *unwelcome*—in the lives of Deaf people.[29] As such, Deaf people experience many different interpreters in a variety of situations. It is possible that feedback may be given to the last in a succession of different interpreters who exhibit similar behaviors. What that last interpreter might personally perceive as overbearing feedback may actually be built up from multiple experiences of that Deaf person. An interpreter aware of this potential context will be better equipped to "withstand" and separate the useful feedback from any unproductive comments, and make the formal apology often expected in return by the Deaf person.[30]

Indeed, the ability to recognize and internalize feedback is often tied with having a good attitude.[31] A study of Deaf professionals suggests that interpreters can be selected more for their ability to accept feedback than actual interpreting skills.[32] Interpreters who overtly reject or are unable to internalize feedback may get less and less feedback over time. This does not necessarily mean their work has improved beyond the point of needing feedback as they may like to believe, it more likely means their work is considered beyond saving by the community.

Feedback, however, is not always directly expressed. Sign language includes backchannel feedback during the translation process such as facial expressions[33] that would clearly indicate a need "to slow down, back up, find out what is not clear, and clarify."[34] As referenced above, cognitive bandwidth must be available for interpreters to perceive and process the sociolinguistic cues of backchannel feedback during the interpreting process. Repeated overlooking of these types of cues may lead to very direct feedback that, from the perspective of an interpreter who is unaware of these cues or too mentally involved in the translation process to notice them, can feel unwarranted.

Deaf-centered interpreters will be able to "listen" with their eyes and recognize the sociolinguistic cues that help guide the process of creating understanding, which should be the ultimate outcome of the interpreting relationship. They must be able to make adjustments on the fly, and incorporate direct and nondirect feedback immediately. This will continually build trust and elicit more feedback to create better understanding. Over time, interpreters who continually internalize and apply feedback to their work will become more skilled and specially requested by community members.

Pace

Auditory and visual pace are fundamentally different. Auditory pace is naturally linear and sequential whereas visual pace is naturally spatial and nonlinear; therefore, an interpreter is usually balancing two different pace requirements simultaneously.[35] Likely depending on their education, interpreters can have a stronger bias toward following auditory pace and being voice-activated—usually at the expense of the Deaf person's visual comprehension.

From my personal experiences, when the voice-activated interpreter's primary focus is on maintaining pace with the auditory speaker and processing at the linear word-by-word or phrase-by-phrase level (rather than conceptual level), then the risk of using incorrect conceptual signs and loss of opportunity to take advantage of spatial features and lacking general context of the material greatly increases. Additionally, signing at the auditory pace may not allow time for visual processing of the content. Spoken paces represented visually will generally create long strings of somewhat-related signs and fingerspelling that do not have clear conceptual meaning, leaving Deaf people solely responsible for understanding.

Skilled interpreters will be more comfortable allowing a speaker to be slightly ahead in terms of auditory pace and taking advantage of sign language spatial properties to hold relevant information. Indeed, longer processing times or "lag time" improves interpreter accuracy rather than compromising it.[36] It allows interpreters to better create *correct* meaning and balance both pace requirements. A visual pace allows for natural pauses at important points, discourse markers (e.g., folded hands, hands in lap, head movements) more likely to be absent in the auditory pace, which helps visual clarity and the utilization of spatial structures to create greater efficiency.

An English-speaking presenter will typically have a formal register (e.g., complex vocabulary usage, social distance, less interaction, less first-person narrative).[37] The pace of the presentation will be more akin to a quick reading style, especially if the presenter is reading from a prepared speech. This pace may be faster than a normal conversation, which heightens the pressure on the voice-activated interpreter not only to keep up but also continually represent the complex English vocabulary being used (often through finger-spelling). This type of common interpretation style can end up looking more like a long string of vaguely related words, primarily due to the lack of spatial structure and sign language grammar.

In contrast, a Deaf-centered interpreter will allow the presenter to be ahead in his or her content before beginning to produce the interpretation. The interpreter's head will be turned toward the presenter in a clear sociolinguistic cue that indicates to the Deaf person they are actively listening and not falling behind.[38] This phase of active listening will allow the interpreter to determine the major conceptual relationships and begin to spatially structure those relationships. The advantage of establishing the spatial relationships early will become evident as less and less time will be needed to represent those concepts throughout the presentation, even if they are very long spoken sentences. Utilizing spatial features of ASL to hold information can increase the efficiency of the translating process throughout the presentation, reducing pressure on both the interpreter and the Deaf person's available energy for developing understanding.

The goal of a Deaf person in the average spoken group discussion may be less about accessing information and more about participation. This means the interpreter must be very aware of timing and able to make space for a Deaf participant to be an active part of the discussion. Voice-activated interpreters will prioritize the spoken word, feeling internal pressure to keep up with the pace of the group discussion. When the Deaf person wants to participate, the opportunity might be lost because the interpreter has overlooked or ignored the pauses where the Deaf person's comments would have been most appropriate. This can result in the Deaf person being blocked from participating, or seeming to interrupt others who are beginning to comment themselves. The latter behavior can make the Deaf person appear antagonistic, annoying, or lacking respect for other group participants, which can have long-lasting effects for the relationships the Deaf participant may have with other group participants.

Even the best interpreter will be behind the auditory pace of the discussion, which can lead to the very brief pauses that represent opportunities for participation to become masked in the interpretation. An interpreter attuned to pace can recognize those brief pauses and prioritize them in the translation, visually signaling Deaf people when they can participate. Prioritizing the pauses does potentially mean falling behind pace-wise, or being unable to translate some comments made right before the pause. This is where partnership with the Deaf person is critical. If the interpreter is aware the Deaf person wants to participate, she can summarize the comments (i.e., "this person agrees" or "that person sympathizes" rather than provide literal translations) or abandon the translation midway while simultaneously signaling to the group with a verbal cue that the Deaf participant wants to say something. This allows the Deaf person to decide when and how to participate rather than being blocked by an interpreter's prioritization of auditory pace.

Of course, a Deaf person may not always be interested in actively contributing to the group discussion and would prefer to be a passive participant. An interpreter who recognizes this can "switch modes," prioritizing the translation process and ignoring the natural pauses at that point. The interpreter, however, should be ready to switch back any time she notices a cue from the Deaf person that indicates a desire to participate. The voice-activated interpreter may not even recognize these cues (as detailed in the Feedback section on page 229), prioritizing his or her own processing time needs to complete translations before potentially allowing the Deaf participant to contribute. Instead, a Deaf-centered interpreter will be skilled at dynamically adjusting processing time and pace prioritizations based on the back-channel feedback she receives from the Deaf participant.

A one-to-one encounter such as a doctor's appointment also sees pace playing a crucial role in interaction outcomes. Much like the formal presentation and group discussion, a voice-activated interpreter may experience pressure for immediacy—signing each word as it is spoken and keeping an auditory pace—which can result in a muddled message and confused interaction. In this scenario, the interpreter is ceding pace and participation control to the doctor, which can reduce the Deaf person to a passive, potentially confused participant.

In actuality, medical providers are usually willing to wait for an accurate interpretation in the service of clear understanding. The interpreter can reorient the pace if she is willing to take responsibility for ordering participation, such as a consecutive interpreting approach.[39] This requires advanced interaction skills that simultaneously put the doctor and Deaf patient at ease while also asking for time and space, and prompting for more information and clarification when necessary.

A common mistake by interpreters, especially newer ones, is to look at the Deaf person while they are listening to the speaker. Looking directly at a signer is a cue that one is about to say something.[40] The Deaf person may ask what is being said because the cue is being presented, and interpreters may feel they are not being given time to listen. Instead, looking at the doctor and giving affirmative head nods will clearly demonstrate to the Deaf patient that the interpreter is actively listening, creating time and space for understanding to occur. This also has the advantage of giving the Deaf patient space to look directly at and get a personal sense of the doctor directly. A Deaf-centered interpreter will not be afraid to take the necessary time to establish the consecutive ordering, which is greatly preferable in these type of interactions, allowing control of pace and ultimately saving time by reducing confusion. Interpreters who feel pressure to follow a busy doctor's pace may default to word-by-word simultaneous interpreting and unnecessarily make the interaction longer.

For too many academically trained interpreters, the ultimate goal of interpreting is to represent words, likely from a belief that this inherently creates access that then creates equality. For many Deaf people, the ultimate goal of the interpreting process is to ensure that understanding occurs. Understanding is when everyone is essentially on the same page. This can only happen when all involved parties have equal access to information; it is the responsibility of the interpreter to create time and space for understanding. From the three scenarios previously described, it is clear that auditory-paced interpreters can place the work of accomplishing understanding on the Deaf person. In this, an interpreter's belief of their "duty to the word" (e.g., merely relaying spoken words) prevents them from enabling the *shared* building of meaning and allowing understanding during the interpreting process. These types of interpreters may be called "language technicians" who are often academically trained and primarily view themselves as neutral conduits of words, much like a telephone line.[41]

Partnership

Too often, it seems that interpreting is not approached as a true partnership between the interpreter and Deaf individuals. A salient example of this can be the common sight of interpreters setting up seating for Deaf individuals before they arrive at the assignment. In fact, many academic programs teach interpreting students this is one of their responsibilities during an assignment.[42] This process can ignore the preferences of the Deaf person who may have a different idea of how to best position themselves. Instead, a simple acknowledgment of allowing a Deaf person to choose their own seating, perhaps negotiating based on where the interpreter may have to be, is more akin to a genuine partnership. This perspective can extend to many different events during the interpreting process.

Much like dancing always requires one partner to lead, an interpreter should be conscious of following the Deaf person's lead. After all, Deaf people are the experts on their own lives, experiences, and preferences. The common interpreting agency structure of first-come, first-serve for delegating assignments, rather than curating assignments for the best fit, means that a series of doctor's appointments for one Deaf individual will likely have a different interpreter each time. This heightens the need for interpreters to follow Deaf people's lead, as they will have already created their own strategies for successful outcomes of common life experiences where interpreters are often present.

During the formal presentation scenario, following a Deaf person's lead does not include solely determining seat placement but being vigilant about understanding. This includes closely watching backchannel feedback cues that may indicate how well the Deaf person is following the presentation and a need to clarify or rework the message before moving on. Background knowledge of the Deaf person can be helpful here as well; if the presentation is in the area of the Deaf person's expertise, the interpreter should be receptive to being fed field-specific terminology and signs during the presentation. Taking the time to elaborate field-specific concepts and fingerspell terminology may be requested here to help the Deaf person learn *how* others in their field may describe things, not solely what they meant.

Following the Deaf person's lead in the group discussion setting was hinted at in the Pace section on page 230, including dynamically adjusting the translation process to prioritize depending on the Deaf participant's desire for participation. While seemingly a simple statement, it requires the interpreter having enough cognitive bandwidth to perceive the backchannel feedback from the Deaf person, continue translating while waiting for the appropriate pause, and expressing a verbal cue to hold space for the Deaf person's comments. Vice-versa, being aware of backchannel feedback suggesting the Deaf person does not want to participate also gives information to the interpreter about how best to structure their process.

Likewise, in a doctor's office, partnership with the Deaf patient may not only be allowing for a Deaf-centered pace, but framing the Deaf patient's comments in a way that medical professionals expect to receive information. In the Deaf community, credible sources of information often include other Deaf people with similar experiences. That style of evidence in the hearing world can be considered anecdotal and not often considered credible.[43] A patient who says, "My friend has the same problem as me, and they take a red pill for it. I want to try that," will likely find their doctor dismissive, as compared to receiving a more sincere reaction with "I saw a story on 60 minutes about a newer medication being used to treat the condition I have. Can we try that?" Although both are culturally valid sources of information, the interpreter can try to bridge the doctor's expectations with the Deaf person's belief of credibility. When a Deaf person may express that their friend has a specific type of medication, the interpreter instead could frame it as "I have a friend with the same condition and his medication is very effective for him. I do not remember the name of it, but I do remember it is a red pill. Do you know what I am talking about?" Additionally, a Deaf patient who has seen the same provider for a long time will likely give cues on how they want to interact with their doctor. A Deaf-centered interpreter will be flexible on how much to, or not to, interject and clarify with the doctor if there is a clear preference indicated by the Deaf patient.

Naturally, these scenarios are not necessarily what every Deaf person might prefer for their own life experiences. This means that an interpreter who works constantly with various Deaf individuals will need to develop the "art" of reading Deaf people, being flexible, and having a willingness to "go with the flow." Negotiation and incorporating cues through backchannel feedback will allow the partnership and the interpreting dance to proceed smoothly with the Deaf person's lead, ultimately making the interpreter's job easier.

Visual Orientation

Interpreters are a natural demand for a Deaf person's attention. When an interpreter is signing, the Deaf person's full attention will be typically focused on the interpreter. This means the Deaf person is relying on the interpreter not just for access to auditory signals in the environment, but *visual* ones as well. An important person arriving in the room or two co-workers eye rolling at a presenter's comments are visual cues that might be overlooked by the interpreter-focused Deaf person. When interpreters do not relay this extra-linguistic information—subtle social cues that can be critical for building and maintaining relationships, and navigating political landscapes of work and education environments—they can become a barrier.[44] Therefore, an interpreter's work goes beyond strict "voice-activated" translating and includes relaying important visio-environmental cues. Essentially, an interpreter should provide *full* access to an environment; solely representing auditory words at the expense of visual access prevents this.

A formal presentation may include a need to give Deaf people time to look at slides, demonstrations, and connecting moments. A voice-activated interpreter, again, prioritizes spoken words and does not allow a Deaf person to break their attention lest content is missed. A Deaf-centered interpreter gives Deaf participants time to look at any visuals that are presented while mentally holding any important content to give when the Deaf person looks back. This type of behavior is commonly seen in Deaf-led presentations, viewed and also practiced by myself, where it is normal to put up a slide and allow time for the audience to look at it before proceeding with commentary. Any interpreter can easily allow for this with hearing presenters by simply directing their own eye gaze to the slide and sometimes pointing to the screen and then deliver any content *not already on the slide* (even if slide content was repeated by the speaker). In hearing culture, there is often a belief that there should be no silence or "dead air" in the jargon of the radio industry; thus, hearing presenters often read aloud exactly what is on the slides before adding their own commentary. This is a cultural behavior meant to put a hearing audience at ease. What puts Deaf people at ease is the opportunity to look at the visuals being presented and then receive any extra content not part of the visuals, instead of being forced to choose between missing the visuals or the signed content.

A visually oriented interpreter must also be competent in sociolinguistic cues and nuances a Deaf person might use. A simple nostril flare might express discontent or raised eyebrows a request for clarification. Such cues include eye gaze, mouth movements, head tilt, and torso movement, among others. Being aware of, and understanding, these cues provide an interpreter with greater context of how best to manage multiple cognitive demands.

Visual orientation skills center on backchannel feedback in a group discussion setting. A fast-paced and overlapping discussion may have a Deaf participant begin to indicate a clear lack of understanding. At this point, a prioritization of visual orientation may have the interpreter summarize the discussion from a third-person narrative, rather than the first-person content typically seen in the discussion. Presentation of content this way allows for slowing down and visual clarity, which can leave the Deaf person still feeling a part of the discussion.

One-to-one encounters such as at the doctor's office can actually be simpler for a visually oriented interpreter. Because of the "no dead air" rule in hearing culture, medical professionals will often narrate what they are doing. This type of narration does not require the interpreter to translate because the doctor is already *visually* demonstrating what he is saying. Instead, the interpreter can shift eye gaze toward the doctor, giving a cue to the Deaf person that they should look at the doctor as well. Simplifying the interaction through visual orientation also can apply to things beyond the demonstration such as the physical exam itself. "Squeeze my fingers," and "hold your arms like this and do not let me push them" can be simple gestural commands in sign language if the interpreter expresses them in a natural, visual manner rather than word for word.

Mastering visual orientation skills requires active development beyond the interpreting curriculum. The curriculum should make interpreting students aware of the importance and need to balance multiple visio-environmental demands for full access. Ongoing learning and practice beyond interpreting preparatory programs will be essential to having visual orientation skills become second nature.

Cultural Competence

Because the majority of interpreters experience sign language and the Deaf community as their secondary language and culture, cultural competence is especially important to consider. Deaf people may tolerate interpreters who are not culturally sensitive for the sake of access, but this is far from ideal. Academic programs need to take a more holistic approach of ensuring interpreting students become culturally competent as community *participants*. Some aspects of participating include "getting your passport stamped," being prepared to answer cultural questions, understanding your place as an interpreter, and avoiding Rock Star tendencies.[45]

Getting your passport stamped is a reference to becoming accepted by Deaf community members. Much like travelers must pass through a country's border control and get a stamp of approval to enter, new interpreters must show cultural attitudes and behaviors that demonstrate a willingness and desire to be part of the Deaf community before being accepted within its "borders." This process does not happen overnight and takes many interactions at public community events over time to become accepted by members. It is not surprising that acculturated community interpreters—those who have had their passports stamped—are generally more likely to be considered "champ" interpreters and the best signers, likely in part due to their everyday immersive social experiences of Deaf cultural norms and using sign language.

Part of that passport process includes being prepared to answer cultural questions such as why one became an interpreter. This type of question could be framed as testing what the interpreter's motivations are: Are they solely money and career driven, expressing a desire to "help" deaf people, or more akin to loving the community's language and wanting to participate? An interpreter should always be prepared with three versions (extra-short, short, and long) of the story behind why they became an interpreter. Not being aware of or being able to answer this type of question on the spot can be a red flag to Deaf community members that perhaps the interpreter is not aware of Deaf cultural norms.

Rock Star Interpreters

Cultural conflicts have been on the rise in recent years,[46] seemingly in part due to interpreters having individualistic attitudes and acting like "rock stars." Rather than understanding their place, where they are situated in Deaf-hearing interactions, they—at best, inadvertently—take the spotlight for themselves and exclude

Deaf people. The most visible examples of this are interpreters who become famous *because they are interpreters*. These are individuals using the Deaf community's language and individually benefitting from it without necessarily redirecting attention back to (or sharing the benefit with) the community.

> The individualistic cultural norms of interpreters often appear to be a primary cause of conflicts. These norms have most prominently been seen as what the community labels, "Rock Star" interpreters. The term "Rock Star" is meant to reflect when interpreters put themselves first, making their use of the community's language their own vehicle for personal attention.[47]

The event that prompted the formal creation of the rock star definition was the very public conflict between an interpreter and a Deaf professor of economics at Gallaudet University. In this situation, a reporter from the *Wall Street Journal* (WSJ)[48] approached the interpreter about economic ASL signs when he was working for the professor. Among other possible ethical violations, including using incorrect signs during his WSJ interview, the interpreter did not redirect the WSJ to the actual expert in economics, the Deaf professor. Eventually, the interpreter holds a managerial position of interpreting services within the U.S. government and the WSJ article is prominently featured in his LinkedIn profile as a reason for some of his career success. As highlighted by Solomon and Miller,[49] the common hearing view of interpreting being performance art frequently elevates interpreters at the expense of Deaf individuals.

Music festival interpreting is somewhat an intersection between interpreting and performance art; it is where literal rock star interpreters become known. News stories are published about them with minimal to no redirecting toward actual Deaf performance artists. One example of this was an interpreter's performance on a late night talk show leading to notable press attention centered around her. This same interpreter eventually attempted to leverage her fame into a fund-raising webpage for her own financial benefit.

Another subsequent interview with a news website angered many community members due to repeated feelings of cultural misappropriation and misinformation. This interview also contained other factual inaccuracies such as the interpreter describing ASL as a "fairly new language . . . approved in the early 1960s. . ." when it has been a natural evolving language for centuries and recently *recognized* by the hearing world *only* after a hearing person brought attention to its linguistic status in the 1960s. The regrettable word choices of "fairly new" and "approved" carry connotations that Deaf people can only achieve legitimacy through recognition by hearing people and that hearing legitimacy is more important than Deaf legitimacy.

The dangers of interpreters not having cultural and academic community knowledge or recognizing the power of word choices can create public cultural mistakes and perpetuate misinformation that hurts Deaf people. Another interpreter even went so far as to offer a general apology on her personal Facebook page for such behavior:

> To my Deaf, DeafBlind & Hard of Hearing friends: I'm sorry another video is gaining attention focusing on a hearing person getting fame and recognition for

> your language, your culture, and your history. If that wasn't bad enough, I'm sorry she's giving bad info and MISrepresenting what she is appropriating. To my hearing friends and colleagues who care about this community: It is our job as hearing people to hold each other accountable. It's not about one interpreter, even though there is some persistence in this case. We need to do better. . . .

From an individualistic cultural standpoint, these sort of interpreters are (from their own perspective, rightfully) seizing an opportunity to elevate their own careers and success. A truly acculturated interpreter could accept the same opportunity but with a mindset of "how can I connect this to the community?" After all, the opportunity arose from the use of the community's language, and the community should share in the benefits of that opportunity.

CONCLUSION

The concept of Deaf-centered interpreting still requires ongoing discussion by Deaf interpreting stakeholders. The model aspects discussed in this chapter are suggestions to encourage and shape that discussion. The discussion must be ongoing to keep pace with ever-increasing personal and professional participation of Deaf people in the larger hearing world and what that means for interpreters' roles. Deaf-centered interpreting should grow to become *the* expectation for all interpreters and education programs. As a minimum standard of competence for graduating from interpreting education programs, it will likely reduce cultural conflicts and greatly increase Deaf people's participation equity in interactions with hearing people.

Interpreter education programs that wish to be Deaf-centered must retool their course masks to reflect an understanding of *interaction* as the primary context for all interpreting processes. This necessitates the inclusion of Deaf people at every level of training. Instead of the currently common compartmentalized approach, programs can use a holistic approach (grounded in interpreting theory) in which every course includes Deaf people, language development, cultural practices, roles, ethics, partnership, and constant practicing of receiving feedback within various situational contexts. These contexts include all of the common life experiences of Deaf people (e.g., education, professional, medical, psychiatric, vocational, social, video relay services) becoming the foundation for interpreting courses, and the Deaf experiences as the starting point for exploration and learning.

Already-working interpreters will need to encourage this shift within their own communities. This includes becoming an active participant in the Deaf community (e.g., developing relationships), learning how to be present without taking over, watching and internalizing how feedback functions within Deaf interactions, and becoming aware of how visual orientation is used for effective understanding. A Deaf mentor, and likely at least one other interpreter also making this shift, is crucial as well. The goal should be to build into one's personal and work life natural opportunities to practice a Deaf-centered approach with Deaf and hearing people along with active, ongoing analysis of how the approach is working and where refinements can be made.

It should be emphasized that interpreters are not expected to be perfect, but they are expected to recognize when mistakes are made, acknowledge those mistakes, make transparent (culturally appropriate) repairs, and learn from them. Good interpreters will be forgiven for mistakes if there is a clear overall indication that they are culturally sensitive and committed to continually improving their work. Interpreters who make clear repairs to previous interpretations as more information becomes available receive more trust from Deaf people, not less.

The Deaf community demanding more accountability for what they perceive to be repeated bad behaviors naturally leads to greater involvement and leadership of Deaf people in the academic setting of interpreter development. This will grow an intuitive paradigm of Deaf-centered interpreting. This growth will never be finished, it will constantly evolve and become more inclusive just like the community it is grounded in. A new Deaf-centered model of interpreting comes back to a community understanding of interpreting in which sign language interpreters are no longer interpreting for the Deaf but *with* them.[50]

Notes

1. Elizabeth Williamson, "Interpreters for Deaf Cut Through D.C.'s Political Jargon," *Wall Street Journal,* July 22, 2017, https://www.wsj.com/articles/no-headline-available-1389655017; Andrea K. Smith, "Saving Lives," December 28, 2014, https://www.andreasmithinterpreting.com/saving-lives/.

2. Patrick Boudreault, *The Future of Interpreting: Owning the Process,* http://www.gallaudet.edu/tedx/presenters/boudreault.html; Byron Bridges, "How Can Interpreters Stay Invisible?" December 30, 2013, https://www.facebook.com/bridgesbyron/videos/10152110551654165/; Eileen Forestal, *Deaf Interpreters: Shaping the Future of the Profession,* paper presented at Street-Leverage–Live 2014 Conference, Austin TX, May, 4, 2014, http://www.streetleverage.com/2015/02/deaf-interpreters-shaping-the-future-of-the-sign-language-interpreting-profession/; Khadijat Rashid, "Dr. Rashid's Response to the Wall Street Journal Article on Signed Language Interpreting," February 16, 2014, http://www.deafread.com/go/115625; Caroline Solomon and Jeffrey A. Miller, "Sign Language is Not Performance Art," *The Baltimore Sun,* April 25, 2014, http://articles.baltimoresun.com/2014-04-25/news/bs-ed-media-and-sign-language-20140426_1_american-sign-language-deaf-americans-deaf-people; Trudy Suggs, "Deaf Disempowerment and Today's Interpreter," http://www.streetleverage.com/2012/12/deaf-disempowerment-andtodays-interpreter/.

3. See discussion in Wyatte C. Hall, Thomas K. Holcomb, and Marlene Elliott, "Using Popular Education with the Oppressor Class: Suggestions for Sign Language Interpreter Education," *Critical Education* 7, no. 13 (Oct. 31, 2016).

4. Nigel Howard, *Deaf & Hearing Worlds: Enculturation and Acculturation,* Plenary Presentation Conference of Interpreter Trainers, Portland, OR, November 1, 2014, http://www.streetleverage.com/cit-2014-plenary-deaf-hearing-worlds-enculturation-and-acculturation/.

5. Dennis Cokely and Anna Witter-Merithew, "Interpreter Education: History is a Relentless Master," January 21, 2015, http://www.streetleverage.com/2015/01/interpreter-education-history-is-a-relentless-master/.

6. Marlene Elliott and Wyatte C. Hall, "Creating Deaf Hearts: Using Popular Education with Interpreting Students," Paper presented at the *2014 Conference of Interpreter Trainers,* October 30, 2014.

7. See Tara Holcomb and Aracelia Aguilar, this volume.

8. Hall et al., "Using Popular Education with the Oppressor Class."

9. Hall et al., "Using Popular Education with the Oppressor Class."

10. Charlotte Baker-Shenk, "The Interpreter: Machine, Advocate, or Ally?" *Expanding Horizons*, ed. Jean Plant-Moeller (Silver Spring, MD: RID Press, 1992): 120–140.

11. Bill Moody, "What is a Faithful Interpretation?" *Journal of Interpretation* 21, no. 1 (2011): 37–51; see discussion in Sherman Wilcox and Barbara Shaffer, "Towards a Cognitive Model of Interpreting" in *Topics in Signed Language Interpreting: Theory and Practice,* ed. Terry Janzen (Philadelphia, PA: John Benjamins Publishing, 2005): 27–51.

12. Melanie Metzger, *Sign Language Interpreting: Deconstructing the Myth of Neutrality* (Washington, DC: Gallaudet University Press, 1999).

13. Charlotte Baker-Shenk, 1992.

14. Hall et al., "Using Popular Education with the Oppressor Class."

15. Marina L. McIntire and Gary R. Sanderson, "Who's in Charge Here? Perceptions of Empowerment and Role in the Interpreting Setting," *RID Journal of Interpretation* 7, no. 1 (1995): 99–109.

16. Michael Reddy, "The Conduit Metaphor—A Case of Frame Conflict in our Language about Language," in *Metaphor and Thoughts*, ed. Andrew Ortony (Cambridge, UK: Cambridge University Press, 1979): 164–201.

17. Mikhail M. Bakhtin, *Speech Genres and Other Late Essays* (Austin, TX: University of Texas at Austin, 1986).

18. Wilcox and Shaffer, "Towards a Cognitive Model of Interpreting."

19. Robyn K. Dean and Robert Q Pollard, Jr. "Application of Demand-control Theory to Sign Language Interpreting: Implications for Stress and Interpreter Training," *Journal of Deaf Studies and Deaf Education* 6, no. 1 (2001): 1–14.

20. Wilcox and Shaffer, "Towards a Cognitive Model of Interpreting," 1.

21. Wilcox and Shaffer, "Towards a Cognitive Model of Interpreting," 27–51.

22. Forestal, *Deaf Interpreters.*

23. Eileen Forestal and Stephanie Clark, "The Teaming Model and Transparency for Deaf and Hearing Team Interpreters: Who Owns the Interpretation?" Paper presented at the 2014 Conference of Interpreter Trainers, Portland, OR, October 31, 2014.

24. Molly Wilson, personal communication, November 22, 2014.

25. Cecilia Wadensjö, *Interpreting as Interaction* (New York, NY: Routledge, 2014).

26. Cynthia B. Roy, *Innovative Practices for Teaching Sign Language Interpreters* (Washington, DC: Gallaudet University Press, 2000).

27. Thomas K. Holcomb, *Introduction to American Deaf Culture* (New York, NY: Oxford University Press, 2013); Anna Mindess, Thomas K. Holcomb, Daniel Langhotz, and Priscilla Moyers, *Reading Between the Signs: Intercultural Communication for Sign Language Interpreters* (Boston, MA: Intercultural Press, 2014).

28. See discussion in Hall et al., "Using Popular Education with the Oppressor Class."

29. Elliott and Hall, "Creating Deaf Hearts."

30. Marlene Elliott, *Sign Language Interpreters and the Quest for Cultural Competence,* December 18, 2013, http://www.streetleverage.com/2013/12/sign-language-interpreters-and-the-quest-forculturalcompetence.

31. Elliott and Hall, "Creating Deaf Hearts."

32. Karen Bontempo, Tobias Haug, Lorraine Leeson, Jemina Napier, Brenda Nicodemus, Beppie van den Bogaerde, and Myrian Vermeerbergen, *Deaf Consumers' Perceptions of Signed to Spoken Language Interpretation in Eight Signed Languages,* Paper presented at the International Symposium on Sign Language Interpretation and Translation Research (Washington, DC: Gallaudet University, 2014).

33. Risa S. Shaw, *Meaning in Context: The Role of Context and Language in Narratives of Disclosure of Sibling Sexual Assault* (Cincinnati, OH: Union Institute & University, 2007); Sherman Wilcox and Barbara Shaffer, "Towards a Cognitive Model of Interpreting" in *Topics in Signed Language Interpreting: Theory and Practice,* ed. Terry Janzen (Philadelphia, PA: John Benjamins Publishing, 2005): 27–51.

34. Hall et al., "Using Popular Education with the Oppressor Class," 6.

35. See discussion in Hall et al., "Using Popular Education with the Oppressor Class."

36. Dennis Cokely, "The Effects of Lag Time on Interpreter Errors," *Sign Language Studies* 53 (1986): 341–76.

37. Martin Joos, *The Five Clocks,* Vol. 58 (New York, NY: Harcourt, Brace, & World, 1967).

38. See Cagle, Lott, and Wilcox, this volume.

39. See review in Debra Russell, "Consecutive and Simultaneous Interpreting," in Terry Janzen, ed., *Topics in Signed Language Interpreting: Theory and Practice* (Philadelphia, PA: John Benjamins Publishing Company, 2005): 135–64.

40. Susan A. Mather, "Eye Gaze & Communication in a Deaf Classroom," *Sign Language Studies, 54* (1987): 11–30, doi:10.1353/sls.1987.0008.

41. Wyatte C. Hall, Thomas K. Holcomb, and Marlene Elliott, "Using Popular Education with the Oppressor Class: Suggestions for Sign Language Interpreter Education," *Critical Education* 7, no. 13 (2016); Moody, "What is a Faithful Interpretation?"

42. David Stewart, Jerome D. Schein, and Brenda E. Cartwright, *Sign Language Interpreting: Exploring Its Art and Science* (Boston, MA: Allyn & Bacon, 2004).

43. Holcomb, *Introduction to American Deaf Culture*; Mindess et al., *Reading Between the Signs.*

44. See Smith and Ogden, this volume.

45. Elliott and Hall, "Creating Deaf Hearts."

46. Elliott and Hall, "Creating Deaf Hearts"; Hall et al., "Using Popular Education with the Oppressor Class."

47. Elliott and Hall, "Creating Deaf Hearts," 4.

48. Elizabeth Williamson, "Interpreters for Deaf Cut Through D.C.'s Political Jargon," *Wall Street Journal,* January 13, 2014, https://www.wsj.com/articles/no-headline-available-1389655017.

49. Solomon and Miller, "Sign Language is Not Performance Art."

50. Lillian Beard, *Lillian Beard at RID Opening Ceremonies*, Philadelphia, 2009, https://www.youtube.com/watch?v=Py-4B_PHlqQ.

18

The Ingredients Necessary to Become a Favorite Interpreter

Marika Kovacs-Houlihan

For the ASL summary of this chapter, go to https://youtu.be/Al6mtsY9SN4

> One day, when my staff interpreter was unavailable, a substitute certified interpreter was hired to interpret a meeting at the university where I am a full-time faculty member. I noticed that when the substitute wasn't familiar with the information, she fell back to signing in English word order instead of American Sign Language (ASL). This forced me to mentally translate the utterance back into ASL to understand what was being said. Each time this happened, by the time I understood the message, the meeting usually had progressed on to other topics, denying me a chance to participate, which frustrated me. Also, as someone who usually isn't afraid to speak up or make witty remarks, I noticed my hearing colleagues weren't responding appropriately to my comments. This substitute interpreter clearly wasn't voicing my words accurately, so I began to worry about what the others were thinking of me. I chose to stay quiet rather than continuing to participate and risking my reputation—all because of this poor interpreting work. After this disconcerting experience, I realized how much my credibility and professionalism could be jeopardized simply because of an interpreter's skill set (or lack of one). It took me a long time to earn my colleagues' respect and be recognized as a leader at the university, and I shouldn't have had to worry about that hard work being demolished within mere seconds by an interpreter. This situation helped me recognize how important it is to have a preferred interpreter throughout my journey toward accomplishments and success.

THINK ABOUT HOW you use the same ingredients each time you make your favorite cookies. The reason for this is simple: you know it's a successful recipe. This is akin to the way that Deaf people often have favorite or preferred interpreters; they know it's a successful recipe for communication and success. A favorite interpreter can emerge in many different ways, ranging from an interpreter frequently requested through an interpreter referral agency, a regularly contracted

This chapter would not be possible without Jen Hayes and our collaborative work.

freelance interpreter, or a staff interpreter who works closely with a Deaf person. Often, when an interpreter works repeatedly with a Deaf person, she or he ultimately becomes that person's favorite interpreter. As a result, this unique working relationship between the Deaf person and the interpreter frequently evolves into something more than what is typically expected of an interpreter.

For me as a professional, the concept of a designated interpreter emerged when a staff interpreter at the university worked closely and regularly with me.[1] The work of a favorite interpreter and a designated interpreter are similar in many ways. When an interpreter is assigned repeatedly to the same Deaf person for various assignments, the interpreter often evolves into the role of the designated interpreter for the Deaf person. The concept creates a unique working relationship between the interpreter and the Deaf person and requires more than what is typically expected of an interpreter. It is also important to note that the term "designated interpreter" is not commonly used within the Deaf community; rather; they sign FAVORITE INTERPRETER. The question then becomes: What are the necessary ingredients to become a favorite interpreter?

Ingredient #1: Acquiring a Taste for Building Genuine Relationships

The first ingredient is a genuine relationship, which takes time to develop. Just like acquiring a taste for certain foods, this acquired taste or preference for specific interpreters develops as the relationship between the Deaf person and the favorite interpreter solidifies over time. Indeed, developing a relationship with a favorite (and/or designated) interpreter is akin to an appreciation of food and its ingredients. This is often accomplished by experimenting with ingredients to perfect the recipe. For example, when searching the Internet for a recipe for lasagna, the search will bring up hundreds of recipes, all requiring different ingredients that result in different outcomes. Each cook has to consider which ingredients to choose to create five-star lasagna, and the end result can differ dramatically from one cook to the next. Similarly, Deaf individuals may try different interpreters and approaches to create the most genuine and successful relationships—like I did with my favorite interpreter.

In my current job of nearly a decade, I have worked closely with two interpreters at different times, with completely different outcomes. During the first four years of my job, the staff interpreter and I struggled to connect even though she was certified, skilled, and qualified. This affected my ability to perform my work at the highest level possible. After she left the university, the replacement interpreter and I immediately got off to a good start and have continued the momentum ever since. Since her hiring, my job has been extremely rewarding because there is open communication and respect between the interpreter and me. As a result, my understanding and thoughts about the role of interpreting have evolved. I now believe in the importance of a designated interpreter who understands fully my goals, motivations, and especially my personality. Another important factor to her becoming my favorite interpreter was that she allowed me to get to know her on both a personal and professional level. Our countless conversations on interpreting as well as learning about each other's values and beliefs have allowed us to excel professionally, and helped propel my status and leadership credibility at the university.

Food for Thought #1

It is unlikely that one will make a perfect meal on the very first try. Often, the food will be burned, become watery, or lack flavor. A perfect meal usually requires several tries in order to achieve perfection—and this is true for becoming a favorite interpreter. For many Deaf professionals, having their favorite interpreters become the designated interpreters in their work is a dream. The relationship between a Deaf individual and his or her favorite interpreter should always evolve without an end in sight. For example, the designated interpreter's job is to infuse the Deaf professional's role and responsibilities, leadership goals, and work environment with nothing but professionalism—according to the Deaf person's needs, preferences, and goals. Furthermore, designated interpreters need to work well with Deaf professionals and their hearing colleagues to develop an ease of communication among themselves. As explained in *Deaf Professionals and Designated Interpreters,*[2] the designated interpreter role is unique in that it requires specialized knowledge of the work place, systems, social roles, and jargon. At the same time, both the Deaf individual and designated interpreter must understand each other's strengths, limitations, and quirks, which requires a huge learning curve throughout the relationship development. Creating seamless transparency in interpreted interactions is also an important factor in the relationship to ease the dynamics between Deaf individual and work environment.[3]

With any designated interpreter situation, both the Deaf person and interpreter must continually learn about each other's values and beliefs. When values are openly shared, the likelihood of the relationship turning into a favorite interpreter situation increases. As is true for any relationship, it takes both individuals being honest about their likes and dislikes. Ultimately, they will need to determine if their differences are endearing or deal-breaking.

Ingredient #2: Savoring the Expertise of Deaf People

The second ingredient is trusting Deaf experts regarding professionalism in their fields and working with interpreters. Whenever anyone tries to re-create Grandma's favorite dish, it may be difficult because everything Grandma made came from her heart and from years of experience. Deaf individuals, too, must trust their hearts along with their expertise and knowledge in identifying their favorite interpreters. This is especially important because of the way that hearing people often disempower Deaf people.[4] Unfortunately, whether intentional or unintentional, an interpreter is involved in performing these disempowering acts.

One of the many acts of disempowerment I experienced took place during an all-day retreat. Throughout the morning, a faculty colleague curiously observed my designated interpreter's work. During lunch, he approached the interpreter to ask about her experiences working with Deaf people. I later learned that he had also invited her to meet with him after the meeting to discuss this further. This was unnerving to me given the fact that I had put a lot of energy into asserting myself as a competent and knowledgeable peer among my hearing colleagues. I decided to approach the interpreter to discuss my concerns. It was during this discussion that she realized that this was a missed opportunity for her to redirect the faculty member to me so that he could gain new knowledge through me as the expert instead of her. Our ongoing dialogue forced us to constantly realign the power imbalance between us, which was not necessarily an easy process for either of us.

Food for Thought #2

Many grandmothers are wonderful cooks from their years of experience, but that does not mean these grandmothers are less skilled or knowledgeable than those with degrees from culinary schools. Similarly, interpreters need to honor Deaf people for their years of experience in being Deaf. It is often necessary to deal with difficult situations like the one above by revisiting the decisions previously made by interpreters and exploring how such decisions can affect other people's perceptions of the roles of Deaf professionals and the interpreters involved. It is paramount that Deaf people be viewed as the experts in their professions and remain in control of their environment, whereas interpreters be seen as specialists in facilitating communication.

The terms *specialist* and *expert* are often used interchangeably because the distinction between the two roles is subtle. However, in discussions about interpreters and Deaf people, the distinction is significant. A specialist is a person who is dedicated to being skilled in a particular subject or pursuit, whereas an expert is a person who has special skills or knowledge because of what they have learned or experienced.[5] In this sense, professional interpreters should be considered specialists—yet they are often erroneously viewed as experts on all things Deaf or related to the Deaf person's profession and granted authority that rightfully belongs to a Deaf person.

This power imbalance occurs easily and often because hearing people commonly approach interpreters with questions, concerns, and comments instead of the Deaf person. This, then, leads to the mistaken impression among hearing colleagues that Deaf people lack the ability to effectively participate in academic discourse, resulting in disenfranchisement of these Deaf people.[6] Even worse, hearing people often view interpreters as spokespeople for the Deaf community or as having authority on topics associated with Deaf people. For this reason, it is imperative that both working interpreters and future interpreters fully recognize and understand the ramifications of their disempowering actions when they assume the roles that rightfully belong to the Deaf person with whom they work.

Moreover, the credibility of a professional title such as "professional interpreter" may lead to the perception that they have an authority status.[7] To avoid this potential abuse of power, interpreters must understand, accept, and acknowledge this confusion among hearing people and work hard to defer to Deaf people as experts in their field as well as in issues related to the Deaf community. This requires interpreters to acknowledge Deaf people's overall experiences with oppression and commit themselves to being allies for the Deaf community. This kind of commitment is necessary in order to achieve the "favorite interpreter" designation.

Ingredient #3: Embracing Humanity as Vital to Good Health

The third ingredient is humanity. A cook has full control of the ingredients, such as quality and freshness. More important, preparing a meal with carefully chosen ingredients allows people to enjoy the food and each other's company. This is a wonderful way to engage with each other, especially when talking about which ingredients or techniques worked and which did not. This connectedness also requires the cook to be vulnerable and open to feedback in order to improve. Basically, to be vulnerable is to deal with uncertainty, risk, and emotional exposure.[8] Despite the emotional risk, this connectedness with others is the essence of humanity. Such connectedness is also true for interpreting: the goal to acquire the necessary humanity skills to become a favorite interpreter is made possible through working diligently, becoming engaged, and being vulnerable in efforts to connect with Deaf people, something I have witnessed in working with interpreters who did those things.

My designated interpreter works hard to remain connected to me. We have agreed to meet prior to my presentations as well as afterward. By having discussions before each presentation, I can stay true to my personality, my work style, and my goals. This is necessary to prevent me from feeling the need to shift my communication style or worrying about her ability to represent me accurately. For example, I was asked to give a TEDx presentation, where we worked together preparing for many hours. I recorded my presentation on video, and my interpreter transcribed her spoken interpretation. This allowed me to verify that she understood the true intent of my message and ensured that she used appropriate words and phrases. She was open and vulnerable, with a willingness to hear my feedback. The outcome was a top-quality presentation on both our parts. This was possible only through ongoing dialogue and engagement from the start to the end of the process. While the process was long and laborious, the relationship we established and nurtured reminded us of the importance of human connection and vulnerability on both our parts.

Food for Thought #3

When people get creative with their food, they often want feedback from others. However, this makes them vulnerable to criticism, something many people become uncomfortable about. In actuality, this vulnerability is an opportunity for cooks to evolve and shine through their creations—which is also true for interpreters. When interpreters allow themselves to be vulnerable, they create an opportunity for an improved connection and stronger empathy with Deaf people. Otherwise, by allowing fear to be a controlling factor, it is easy for interpreters to stay within their comfort zones and focus only on their ASL skills development without having the added benefit of engaging with Deaf people.

To investigate the connection between humanity and language development, the research was conducted in collaboration with Prof. Vince DeGeorge (Joseph Weinberger Chair of Acting for the Lyric Stage, CCM) and Prof. Elizabeth Jean Baptiste (Signed Language Interpreting, UC) at the University of Cincinnati, College-Conservatory of Music (CCM). This research was supported by a CCM Special Project Grant awarded to Prof. DeGeorge. The project had two aims: finding the key to human connection among ASL/English interpreting students and discovering the common core of communication allowing for a human connection. The hope was that a curriculum or training materials could be developed to help interpreters, ASL students, and hearing people develop a greater awareness of humanity.

The experimental project began with the recruitment of three groups of people: hearing individuals with no exposure to the Deaf community or ASL, Deaf people, and sign language interpreters. The first task required the participants to describe a memorable incident in their lives using their preferred language. The hearing group used spoken English with each other, the Deaf group signed to each other, and the interpreter group went back and forth between speaking and signing among themselves. In a second activity, a participant from each group was pulled out and placed in a different group. These new group members were then asked to share the same story in their new group—but without instructions on how they should communicate. In the mixed groups, the interpreters automatically took over as communication liaisons between hearing non-signers and Deaf people. According to the personal reflections during the post-activity session, all participants in the mixed groups did not feel connected to each other during the second activity. For the third activity, with a new group of mixed participants, they were asked to retell their stories, but the interpreters were not allowed to function as communication liaisons. This forced the participants, both Deaf and hearing, to find ways to communicate effectively. In their self-reflection, the interpreters shared their difficulty in watching the Deaf participants and hearing participants struggling to share their stories and not assisting with communication. In contrast, the Deaf and hearing participants reported that they felt the most connected to each other during that third activity because they had to engage directly with each other and were willing to be vulnerable.

Later, after all the groups were provided with training on visual-gestural communication without the use of English or ASL, they were to share stories in mixed groups. This time, the playing field was leveled for all parties in communication. Each time a participant tried to share a story, he or she was deeply invested in making sure others understood his or her story, unlike their previous efforts.

This experiment showed how the mere presence of interpreters had unintentionally prevented humanity from flourishing between hearing non-signers and Deaf people. By assuming the role of communication facilitators, the interpreters had inadvertently prevented these two groups from sharing vulnerability and connecting with each other. This demonstrates the importance of shared humanity whether between hearing people, Deaf people, or interpreters. Cycling back to the concept of becoming a favorite interpreter, to do so one needs to understand the importance of humanity in promoting favorable connections between Deaf people and others.

PUTTING IT ALL IN THE MIX

Now it is time to put all the ingredients into the mix. Just like when you combine the right number of ingredients and in the correct amounts, chocolate chip cookies come out of the oven delicious and warm, with the gooey chips melting in your mouth. It takes guidance and years of practice to determine the exact amount of each ingredient in order to result in the most delicious cookies. This is true, too, for aspiring interpreters if they wish to achieve the role of FAVORITE INTERPRETER.

Clearly, aspiring interpreters cannot do it alone. Interpreter Education Programs are responsible for providing a hand to aspiring interpreters while fostering their efforts in developing a genuine relationship with Deaf people.[9] The interpreters, rookies, and experienced alike must have a journey that begins with an open mind before they can become a "favorite" interpreter. One must be cognizant of the fact that these ingredients are not like magic beans: they do not suddenly sprout and grow. This kind of journey requires ongoing self-analysis from the beginning stages of learning ASL to the completion of an Interpreter Education Program and for many years beyond. Furthermore, all these ingredients cannot be obtained or used properly without the involvement of Deaf people, with an emphasis on a recommendation made by Forestal: "the Deaf community, Deaf people, and Deaf interpreters must always be part of the power structure and decision-making."[10] When contemplating my years of working with interpreters and in the Interpreter Education Program, the latter part seems to be a foreign concept to many.

I participate in the screening process for students wanting to enroll in the Interpreter Education Program at my university. With the prerequisite of two years of ASL and relevant cultural courses, one question is always asked of all candidates: "What is your relationship with the Deaf community?" I have found some of their responses affected me like fingernails scratching on a blackboard. Responses often include, "Well, I have not really been involved with the Deaf community yet," or "I went to some Deaf events here and there," or "I hope that the Interpreter Education Program will help me to connect with the Deaf community." These answers always raise red flags for me because the students clearly do not really embrace the most important aspect of language and culture learning: connection with Deaf people. Consequently, reframing students' learning experiences has become the priority in the ASL Studies Program at my university. Students should not wait until entering the Interpreter Education Program to become connected to the Deaf community. Otherwise, they will perceive Deaf people only as their consumers instead of as equal partners.

By infusing key ingredients discussed earlier in this chapter in Interpreter Education Programs—acquiring a taste for building genuine relationships, savoring the expertise of Deaf people, and embracing humanity—the potential outcome is a totality of positive student experiences throughout the students' educational process. The ultimate goal is to achieve FAVORITE INTERPRETER status by Deaf people by mixing these ingredients together using the proper cooking tools. The tools are service learning within the Deaf community; reframing program contents to highlight Deaf people as community, cultural, and language experts; and creating an intergroup dialogue approach through a Deaf-centric lens.

Mixing in Ingredient #1: Genuine Relationships

The educational process for future interpreters should immediately include developing relationships, the first ingredient, with the Deaf community through a service learning model as part of the program curriculum.[11] The service learning approach must be introduced at the very beginning of the ASL Studies Program (which is usually when students discover the interpreting profession), rather than in the later stages of an interpreting program. From the very start of their language learning experience, students must learn about and be exposed to civic engagement and community responsibility within the Deaf community and understand that it is not about serving or helping Deaf people; rather, it is about being engaged with them. As Shaw wrote, "Service learning is a means of aligning students with the goals and values of the Deaf community through a reciprocal, respectful and mutually rewarding partnership, resulting in progress toward the Deaf community's goals and enhanced learning of the responsibilities associated with alliances between future practitioners and the communities in which they work."[12] In this sense, service learning should be about developing a meaningful relationship without interfering with the culture, boundaries, and norms in the Deaf community. The bottom line is that Deaf people are the gatekeepers of the community, and interpreting students need to understand that they must work hard to be accepted and welcomed by such gatekeepers.[13]

To do so, both interpreting students and interpreters must continuously reach out to the Deaf community. Too often, experienced interpreters feel they know, or understand, what the Deaf community needs and therefore keep their outreach efforts on the back burner. Equally important, interpreting students must understand that the Deaf community is not merely there to teach sign language and culture. For these reasons, service learning should not be limited to only one course; rather, it should be spread out throughout the ASL and interpreting program from beginning to end, and with Deaf people leading the service learning. Otherwise, one-time service learning requirements will send the wrong message and possibly create a skewed view, that of interpreting students as taking advantage of the Deaf community.[14] Clearly, future interpreters and even working interpreters must be taught to value building relationships with Deaf people and let the experts and gatekeepers (i.e., Deaf people) guide their development.

Mixing in Ingredient #2: Deaf People as Experts

To add the second ingredient in the mix, the curriculum of the Interpreter Education Program needs to be reframed to highlight Deaf people as community, cultural, and language experts.[15] Although the proliferation of Interpreter Education

Programs was intended to meet the growing needs for qualified interpreters, it has also caused a shift in social positions among interpreters and Deaf people. This shift has sent an implied message to students that interpreters (while functioning as specialists) are of a higher status, while minimizing Deaf people's role as the experts.[16] As Forestal wrote, "It further implied that they [Deaf people] had no role to play in instructing interpreting students, developing curriculum, or guiding students' involvement within the Deaf community as allies."[17] For this reason, Interpreter Education Programs must be consistent in their message that Deaf people, not interpreting programs, are the gatekeepers of the community and language.

This reframing can be accomplished in a multitude of ways. One is the creation and utilization of an advisory board predominantly composed of Deaf experts, which is empowered to dictate program planning and design. This will create a sense of trust in the Deaf community that the Interpreter Education Programs are capitalizing on Deaf people's talents and knowledge to strengthen interpreting work and development.

Interpreter education is predominately done by hearing people with very little involvement from the Deaf community.[18] Although it is true that Interpreter Education Programs often ask Deaf people to serve on screening panels or invite them to classrooms as guest speakers, this practice often presents Deaf people as mere tokens in the educational process.[19] Instead, Interpreter Education Programs should take an authentic approach and inject the Deaf community throughout the program while honoring Deaf people as gatekeepers. This calls for Deaf individuals to play major roles in Interpreter Education Program planning and be directly involved in training interpreters. Cokely reflected how in times gone by, the "[Deaf] community would determine when someone possessed sufficient communicative competence and had also demonstrated sufficient trustworthiness that they would be asked to interpret/transliterate."[20] Yet over time, as a result of the proliferation of Interpreter Education Programs, the Deaf community has played less of a role in determining interpreter qualifications. As a result, Deaf individuals no longer retain the power and control over evaluating an interpreter's competence. This changing dynamic has shifted the relationship between interpreters and the Deaf community as well as their status.[21] Moreover, when Deaf people are not involved with research or academia, that kind of deficit thinking mistakenly disqualifies them from being gatekeepers.[22] Interpreting programs need to eradicate this deficit thinking and reframe Deaf people as community, cultural, and language experts, regardless of their academic background.

Mixing in Ingredient #3: Humanity of Deafhood

The final mix is achieved by adding the third ingredient, humanity, by creating an intergroup dialogue approach through a Deaf-centric lens throughout the program. In order to incorporate the humanity lens, it is important for instructors to encourage students to participate in self-reflection about their own identities and privileges and how those may or may not contribute to the quality of their interactions with Deaf people. This can be accomplished through discussions revolving around the concept of Deafhood.[23]

The concept of Deafhood should be introduced to interpreting students and professional interpreters as well. As defined,"Deafhood is a concept that aims to disrupt medically oriented and oppressive discourses, by offering a deaf constructed model that grows out of deaf people's own ontologies (i.e., deaf ways of being in the world), emphasizing positive, experience-oriented views of deaf people."[24] It is important to note here that Deaf people need to process their Deafhood journeys at their own time and pace in their own space. Then, using the intergroup relations model developed at the University of Michigan,[25] both groups can come together to engage in healthy and constructive dialogue. This mindful approach helps facilitate learning about social group identity, social inequality, and intergroup relations. Through engaged intergroup relations, interpreting students are educated and prepared based on special interests in social diversity and social justice—or in this case, Deafhood. Experiential pedagogy is useful as it encourages students to understand the social conflict(s), intergroup relations, and issues of diversity and justice. This also encourages all parties to pay attention to their thoughts and feelings, be present in the moment, and allow Deaf individuals and both current and future interpreters to develop skills in communicating, relating, and connecting well.

Conclusion

Just like a cook aiming to create the perfect lasagna or cookie recipe, it takes years of learning, experience, and a willingness to be vulnerable to feedback before interpreters can be "perfect" enough to become a five-star interpreter. An even better recipe for success would be when they can demonstrate that they are cognizant of the necessary ingredients by starting very early in academics of learning ASL and Deaf culture, can combine them in the correct proportions, have sufficient experience in putting them all together, have accepted guidance from the experts (i.e., the Deaf community), and have been taught what the proper cooking tools are that produce a successful mixture of ingredients. Only then can they become Deaf people's favorite interpreters.

Notes

1. See David Smith and Paul Ogden, this volume.

2. Peter Hauser, Karen Finch, and Angela Hauser, *Deaf Professionals and Designated Interpreters: A New Paradigm* (Washington, DC: Gallaudet University Press, 2008).

3. Annette Miner, "Designated Interpreter: An Examination of Roles, Relationship, and Responsibilities," *Signed Language Interpretation and Translation Research,* eds. Brenda Nicodemus and Keith Cagle (Washington, DC: Gallaudet University Press, 2015): 196–211.

4. Anna Witter-Merithew and Leilani J. Johnson, *Toward Competent Practice: Conversations with Stakeholders* (Alexandria, VA: RID Press, 2005): 32.

5. Merriam-Webster, *Merriam-Webster's Collegiate Dictionary, 11th ed.* (Springfield, MA: Merriam-Webster, 2003).

6. Linda Campbell, Meg Rohan, and Kathryn Woodcock, "Academic and Educational Interpreting from the Other Side of the Classroom: Working with Deaf Academics," in *Deaf Professionals and Designated Interpreters: A New Paradigm*, eds. Peter Hauser, Karen Finch, and Angela Hauser (Washington, DC: Gallaudet University Press, 2008): 81–105; Sherry Shaw,

Service Learning in Interpreter Education: Strategies for Extending Student Involvement in the Deaf Community (Washington, DC: Gallaudet University Press, 2013).

7. Robert Cialdini, *Influence: The Psychology of Persuasion, Revised Edition* (New York: HarperCollins Publishers, 2007): 220–35.

8. Brene Brown, *Doing Greatly: How the Courage to Be Vulnerable Transforms the Way We Live, Love, Parent, and Lead* (New York: Penguin Random House, 2012): 33–56.

9. See Sherry Shaw, *Service Learning in Interpreter Education: Strategies for Extending Student Involvement in the Deaf Community* (Washington, DC: Gallaudet University Press, 2013).

10. Eileen Forestal, "Deaf Perspectives in Interpretation Research: A Critical Element Long Overdue," in *Signed Language Interpretation and Translation Research*, eds. Brenda Nicodemus and Keith Cagle (Washington, DC: Gallaudet University Press, 2015): 1–23.

11. Shaw, *Service Learning.*

12. Ibid., 8.

13. Forestal, "Deaf Perspectives."

14. Shaw, *Service Learning.*

15. Dennis Cokely, "Shifting Positionality: A Critical Examination of the Turning Point in the Relationship of Interpreters and the Deaf Community," in *Sign Language Interpreting and Interpreter Education: Directions for Research and Practice*, eds. Marc Marschark, Rico Peterson, & Elizabeth A. Winston (New York: Oxford University Press, 2005): 3–28; Christine Monikowski and Rico Peterson, "Service-learning Interpreting Education: Living and Learning," in *Sign Language Interpreting and Interpreter Education: Directions for Research and Practice*, eds. Marc Marschark, Rico Peterson, & Elizabeth A. Winston (New York: Oxford University Press, 2005): 188–207; Shaw, *Service Learning.*

16. Witter-Merithew and Johnson, *Toward Competent Practice*, 32.

17. Forestal, "Deaf Perspectives," 5.

18. Ibid., 1–23.

19. Shaw, *Service Learning.*

20. Dennis Cokely, "Shifting Positionality," 4.

21. Ibid., 3–25.

22. Forestal, "Deaf Perspectives," 1–23.

23. Thomas K. Holcomb, *Introduction to American Deaf Culture* (New York, NY: Oxford University Press, 2013).

24. Annlies Kusters and Maartje De Meulder, "Understanding Deafhood: In Search of its Meanings," *American Annals of the Deaf* 158, no. 5 (2013): 428.

25. The Program on Intergroup Relations (The Regents of the University of Michigan), January 1, 2017, from https://igr.umich.edu/about.

19

Effectively Interpreting Content Areas Utilizing Academic ASL Strategies

Christopher A.N. Kurz, Kim B. Kurz, and Raychelle Harris

For the ASL summary of this chapter, go to https://youtu.be/FCeZS2vmKaE

> Raychelle Harris, one of the three co-authors of this chapter, grew up attending a school for Deaf students and was always able to communicate directly in American Sign Language (ASL) with her teachers. In high school, she took two courses at a local private high school, learning academic content through a third party—interpreters—for the first time ever. In photography class, the interpreters followed her into the darkroom, struggling to interpret under a single red light at one end of the room. In biology, Raychelle had to crane her neck to watch the teacher demonstrate an experiment as well as watch the interpreter, all while completing complex hands-on tasks in a crowded lab. Eventually, she dropped out of both courses and returned to her Deaf high school where she learned directly from her teachers. Did the language skills of interpreters contribute to her decision to drop out? Or was it the environmental conditions in a mainstreamed classroom that made it difficult for her? Or was it a combination of both?

When it comes to working with educational interpreters in school, many Deaf people have stories to share. Their stories often involve situations dealing with content-specific classes (e.g., mathematics, science, language arts).

Language shapes our brains throughout our lives. Our brains are constantly seeking meaningful patterns to build relationships between entities.[1] As natural language scientists, we work and even play with our language(s) to categorize concepts in our minds and produce meanings, phonemes, words, phrases, and sentences.[2] Language development becomes limited when there are minimal opportunities or abilities to observe, analyze, and create parts of language both at home and in educational settings.[3]

Academic language is the language students need to see, learn, and create in order to complete learning tasks in schools.[4] Gee defined academic language as a specific social practice of certain academic (and school-based) domains that must be learned (not acquired).[5] Academic language derives from "expectations and norms for language use in an academic setting"[6] and "the extent to which an individual has access to and command of . . . the academic registers of schooling."[7] Access to and command of academic language is necessary for a successful scholastic career for everyone, deaf and hearing alike. Lange and colleagues found that Deaf students typically developed academic English skills at their grade level in five to seven years with consistent support in their native language (ASL) after primary school placement.[8] Thomas and Collier found that without support in a native language, academic language may take longer, as long as seven to ten years or even more, to develop skills in the second language.[9] Similarly, Cummins found that students from other countries quickly became comfortable with the social language used in their new environment; however, their acquisition of academic language required an additional five years or more to approximate that of native speakers.[10] In the past twenty years, there has been a tremendous growth in the literature dealing with English as an academic language and its role as the language vehicle for success in academia. One might ask what the role of ASL is as an academic language and educational vehicle for success.

Bahan stated, "There is no question that there are different sets of discourse principles, expectations, ways of talking, expressing one's views in ASL in academia" (personal communication, March 5, 2008). Baer first coined the term *Academic ASL* as an academic register for the delivery of information through ASL.[11] Gárate defines it as the use of linguistic features of ASL for language functions that are part of the classroom routine.[12] Academic ASL includes academic content areas, such as mathematics, science, social studies, and literature. To distinguish academic ASL from colloquial ASL, Kuntze suggested a careful examination of the different ways the features of the language are allocated for different illocutionary goals.[13] For both ASL and English, language functions serve as instructional tools for students to demonstrate knowledge and skills. What about Deaf students in mainstreamed academic settings where the classroom language is spoken English?

That is where educational interpreters come into the picture. While these interpreters may have specialized training in sign language interpretation, most of the existing ASL curricula for interpreting students is designed to teach social and conversational skills instead of academic ASL.[14] This is one reason why research interest in the effectiveness of education mediated through sign language interpreting has increased in recent years.[15] Questions such as whether interpreted instruction is equal and adequate (in the amount of information delivered and its comprehension) to direct instruction in sign language have been posed. The goal is an examination of the common assumption that language access through an interpreter is complete and that interpreters are adequate language models for Deaf children. However, research findings have disputed this claim.[16]

These findings lead us to ask how educational interpreters can effectively utilize linguistic features of academic ASL for information delivery in content areas. The key to unlocking this question should lie within the framework of language modality (ASL/English) and delivery, not merely the communication modality (spoken/signed). Deaf children who work with educational interpreters need to see information in both targeted languages (i.e., ASL and English). Specific ideas for utilizing linguistic features of academic ASL in interpretation are offered next.

First, it is critical for all educational interpreters to prepare effectively to work in elementary and content-specific classrooms. This requires time, commitment, and effort. In preparation for each class, educational interpreters should implement data-driven techniques by asking questions, reading extensively, and being familiar with the content before they begin interpreting.[17]

Ideally, consecutive interpreting should be the standard in educational settings as it allows for more accurate and clearer interpretation work.[18] However, in reality, simultaneous interpretation is typically used in schools. In order to prevent unintentional or deliberate omission of the intended message or emphasis, interpreters should allow for sufficient processing time to allow for conceptual understanding or intention of the message in their interpretation work.[19]

Furthermore, in following a typical ASL grammatical structure, educational interpreters should use appropriate pauses or transitions in their work. This should occur every time before and after new concepts are introduced, between related concepts, and when conveying complex information. These pauses allow Deaf students to assimilate the information more easily, follow the transition from one topic to another more clearly, and make connections between concepts more successfully.

When signs that are unfamiliar to Deaf students are introduced, effective interpreters will clearly fingerspell the word after introducing the sign. Once students make the sign-to-fingerspelling association, fingerspelling can be dropped unless the teacher stresses the word's spelling. In addition to these specific ASL-related strategies, it is always ideal to stand in close proximity to any visual information being presented, such as on the board, a map, or any form of print, in order to reduce eye fatigue. Research shows that the greater the distance between teacher, projected image, and interpreter, the more fatigued Deaf students become.[20] In addition, research also demonstrates that Deaf ASL speakers naturally sign in close proximity to the visual information on a board or in a book.[21]

Beyond these strategies, several other factors need to be taken into consideration for optimal academic language delivery in interpreting. They include register, cognitive, lexical and semantic, fingerspelling, ASL phonological pattern, assessment translation, and testing considerations, all of which will be discussed here.

Register Considerations

The Concise Oxford Dictionary of Linguistics defines *register* as a set of language characteristics used specifically for a situation or activity or by a specific group of people. An example of the differences in register usage is the language used in a church sermon as opposed to the language used to tell smutty stories.[22] Academic register is a type of register used specifically in school settings. Academic language is not superior to other sets of discourses; other registers, such as the conversational register, can be as complex and advanced.[23] Ladd asserted that "all sets of dialogue, whether taking place in a pub or at a medical conference, are of equal intrinsic merit."[24]

Cummins explained that mastery of the academic register "is directly linked to future educational and economic opportunities."[25] Like Ladd, Gilmore and Smith argued that academic genre/discourse is not "simply academic writing, but also knowledge of traditional rules for creating and disseminating knowledge."[26] Since linguists validated ASL as a language equal to spoken and written languages only forty years ago; people are still transitioning from rejection and devaluation of ASL to acceptance of ASL as a full-fledged language that is worthy of being used as an academic language.[27] To this day, people still debate the role of ASL in schools. Some promote a "diglossic continuum where sign language varie[s] from more like ASL to more like English."[28] Others endorse a pidgin situation "when speakers of one language [change] their vocabulary and grammar to accommodate speakers of a different language."[29] Others endorse language engineering, modifying the ASL lexicon and pronouns for the purpose of providing an optimal learning environment in the classroom.[30]

Harris found that academic ASL has a formal style that includes an authoritative delivery in a bigger signing space, usually in the upper-half area of normal signing space. This style is associated with the language used in one-way delivery by an expert on the topic. Delivery is crisper, more explicit, and larger. Harris also found that academic ASL has a consultative style associated with the language used in two-way discourse between subject area experts (teacher) and novice subject area speakers (students). This style includes a clear and explicit delivery of information where new signs are introduced with enriched explanations and questioning prompts are used to elicit responses. Because of the different styles of signing required of academic ASL, educational interpreters need to cultivate skills in each area and determine the most appropriate style to match the intended register of the message.[31]

Cognitive Considerations

Vygotsky believed that in order to study the cognitive development of a child, the external world of that child had to be examined.[32] The external world includes individuals who are more fluent users of language and thought, which in turn influence and guide new learners. When the more fluent users of the language interact with children, they subconsciously provide linguistic, cultural, and cognitive tools in support of cognitive development. Research supports the claim that there is a strong relationship between language acquisition and cognitive development. A strong language base is the most important tool for higher-order cognitive development, and the development of higher cognitive functions is the major development of early childhood.[33] Children's participation in cognitively demanding conversations with adults correlates positively with later literacy and academic achievement.[34] Cognitive development is not only associated with language development but also holds a significant relationship with bilingualism. Additionally, bilinguals perform better than monolinguals on cognitive tests.[35] These findings supply theoretical and empirical support for the development of cognitive and linguistic knowledge and skills among deaf children in ASL and their transfer to the second language, English. To stimulate academic cognition, teachers using the bilingual approach employ language functions for targeted learning tasks. This calls for educational interpreters to be skilled in ASL in order to support the cognitive development of Deaf children in the classroom.

Language functions "refer to how individuals use language to accomplish specific tasks."[36] In conversations, the most common language functions involve describing, giving information, or expressing feelings. Academic language functions are essential in schools, including functions such as comparing, debating, persuading, evaluating, ordering, classifying, inferring, justifying, and synthesizing.[37] By working with teachers, educational interpreters can learn more about language functions for upcoming instructional lessons. They would then be able to incorporate more academic ASL features in their interpretation, allowing Deaf students to use academic ASL to accomplish specific tasks as outlined in the lesson's language functions more successfully.

Chamberlain and Mayberry stated, "One of the oldest questions in the history of Deaf education is whether and how signed language knowledge will affect the learning of spoken and written language."[38] Research has shown that the degree of ASL proficiency in children correlates with the degree of English proficiency. In fact, Cummins concluded, "The degree of proficiency that children develop in ASL during the elementary school years is positively related to the development of English reading and writing skills."[39] For this reason, educational interpreters need to take this responsibility seriously by expanding their ASL and English repertoire. One way to accomplish this is to learn from Deaf heritage ASL speakers who are content area experts. Working with Certified Deaf Interpreters (CDIs) is another valuable resource in learning how to achieve optimal academic ASL delivery in the interpretation work.[40] Through ASL skill development, educational interpreters are in a better position to support students' ASL proficiency. This, in turn, can help promote students' mastery of English.[41]

Lexical and Semantic Considerations

Harris found that academic discourse in the classroom requires increased use of specialized vocabulary as students progress through the academic year and beyond. As the number of specialized vocabulary, phrases, and sentences increases over the years, educational interpreters may find it challenging to use appropriate signs that match the intended message.[42] To increase their own ASL proficiency, educational interpreters need to also consider lexical and semantic implications when interpreting concepts. The traditional—but not the best—method of learning ASL is lexical-based signing. The problem with this method is the lack of context in which the word is used, which often leads to rigidity in sign repertoire and inaccurate sign choice.

Contributing to this problem is the fact that online lexical databases are often maintained by people who are not heritage ASL speakers, leading to faulty sign production and loss of meaning. In particular, one website shows the inaccurate use of the E handshape for the mathematical sign EXPRESSION. Educational interpreters who look up signs online should check with Deaf heritage ASL speakers who are content area experts about the phonologically and semantically appropriateness of the sign choices.

Semantics should be considered when evaluating sign choice accuracy. As an example, in English, *run* has multiple meanings that derive from the context. The ASL lexicon includes distinct signs to express each of those meanings. Another example is the mathematical noun *expression*. Choosing the wrong sign would convey a verb meaning to "express from the heart" rather than a mathematical expression. For example, the mathematical sign EXPRESSION consists of both hands in the F handshape, similar to the sign SENTENCE. The sign EQUATION requires two combined signs—EXPRESSION + EQUAL—as the definition of the word is a statement with the values of two mathematical expressions being equal.

The word *root* has multiple meanings in different content areas: in science, it refers to the underground part of a plant; in mathematics, the x-intercept of a graph; in history and English, the causal origin. Each is expressed using a different ASL sign. Because semantics involves an element of a language or a combination of elements to create meaning, it is crucial that ASL-English translation takes into consideration the context. If and when there is no known sign for a concept, fingerspelling is often a replacement—but it should be done cautiously, lest this becomes a habit of interpretation and a shift in language delivery.

ASL–English Fingerspelling Considerations

There is increased dependence on fingerspelling among interpreters and Deaf education teachers in advanced academic courses. Such dependence skews the interpretation toward English-like signing.[43] It is true that ASL has some lexicalized fingerspelling, such as #BCK (back), #EARLY, #BNK (bank), #OWN, and #WY (why). Those examples show how ASL borrows some English words and transforms them into lexicalized or loan signs. However, caution is urged for resorting to fingerspelling when a sign is unknown because it promotes the use of English sentence structure instead of ASL structure. This is problematic as Humphries and MacDougall pointed out: English-influenced signing, "by design excludes or disrupts the normal phonological, morphological and syntactic structures of ASL in order to achieve the intended goal of linking fingerspelling or signing to English."[44] Yet, fingerspelling is employed surprisingly often in any content-specific classroom, especially in higher grades.

Literature shows that teachers of Deaf students and educational interpreters often use fingerspelling to reinforce English vocabulary development.[45] To support this activity, a widely used national educational interpreting assessment, the *Educational Interpreter Performance Assessment* (EIPA), evaluates a number of specific interpreting skills in four skill domains, including one that has a component on fingerspelling.[46] Ultimately, the role that fingerspelling plays in student learning needs to be examined by asking who is responsible for reinforcing English vocabulary development: the educational interpreter or the teacher. This is imperative because educational interpreters often feel responsible for both ASL and English vocabulary development among Deaf students. This burden can lead to cognitive overload or information gaps during interpreting. Our recommendation is for the teacher to be responsible for English vocabulary development, allowing the educational interpreter to concentrate on clear information delivery in ASL.

The two most frequent comments regarding fingerspelling in discussions conducted among educational interpreters are: (a) If there is no standard sign for the content-specific term, I fingerspell; and (b) Fingerspelling specialized words helps Deaf students learn content better.[47] Literature shows that fingerspelling helps English reading fluency.[48] However, there is insufficient empirical data supporting content understanding with the use of fingerspelling. Deaf people do not see fingerspelled words when reading English on paper. Therefore fingerspelling and reading English employ two different modalities, which require a special skill set to make the connection between these two functions. Not all Deaf students are able to master this task without targeted support. Although literature shows that Deaf toddlers are able to understand fingerspelled words at an early age, fingerspelling does not seem to be natural in ASL language development, requiring relearning later in school.[49] In a personal communication with John Lee Clark (August 29, 2016), a well-respected DeafBlind writer/poet, he explained that some members of the Deaf and DeafBlind community prefer to avoid fingerspelling as much as possible because fingerspelling represents a switch from ASL to English "on the hand," which can be jarring, almost akin to switching from ASL to the Cyrillic alphabet and back.

Regardless of these challenges, numerous studies show that fingerspelling can act as a bridge from ASL to English through sandwiching (signing + fingerspelling) and/or chaining (signing + fingerspelling + other modalities).[50] To reiterate the strategy mentioned earlier, when unfamiliar signs are introduced to Deaf students, interpreters should clearly fingerspell the word after introducing the sign. Once students make the sign–fingerspell association, the fingerspelling can be dropped.

However, if there is no standard sign for a certain word or concept, then it is not possible to use fingerspelling to bridge ASL to English. Instead of resorting to fingerspelling only when there is no known standard sign, educational interpreters could promote enrichment by providing additional information or pointing to the printed word on a board or book to assist with conceptual development, which will eventually lead to language transfer. This requires a shift in the delivery paradigm for educational interpreters who are accustomed to fingerspelling in the classroom to reinforce English language development. Through collaboration with teachers, Deaf students can effectively learn bilingually when teachers use academic English that interpreters interpret into academic ASL, with appropriate ASL linguistic features.

ASL Phonological Pattern Considerations

Part of the responsibility of working with deaf children in educational settings is, in essence, enabling them to become language scientists. As language scientists, Deaf children need to see ASL phonological patterns in specialized vocabulary and discourse. Czubek suggested that Deaf education professionals consider and examine ASL phonology when discussing academic words and texts.[51] An ASL phonological pattern occurs with a set of signs that share a similar handshape, location, movement, orientation, and/or nonmanual markers, and implies possible classifications of vocabulary and phrases. Additionally, patterns are used to build content knowledge relationships for recall and retrieval. One of the brain's functions is to seek language patterns in order to build relationships and organize knowledge for future retrieval.[52] For example, in English, we typically recognize any word starting with *anti-* as suggesting that the word is against or in opposition to something. That English prefix pattern helps clarify any word that starts with *anti-* and make connections to the word's meaning.

ASL phonological patterns often consist of one or more similar parameters (handshape, location, palm orientation, movement, and nonmanual markers) to portray a category of vocabulary or phrases that share similar characteristics, actions, or classifications. For example, in science, the sign WEATHER consists of both hands in the 5 handshape moving in a wavy, downward movement. The signs WIND, RAIN, DRIZZLE, POURING RAIN, SNOW, CLOUDY, SUNNY, FREEZING ICE, and HAZY all also consist of both hands in the 5 handshape in different locations using different movements. Additional adjectives and adverbs in ASL are used to describe the range of weather conditions. A science example includes the three states of matter: gas, liquid, and solid. The standard signs for these states have no phonological patterns, although the states are all related. However, on the molecular structure, they all have microscopic particles, that all behave differently. This requires different sets of handshapes to represent these distinct concepts appropriately. For example, the particles can be represented with the fingertips of two 5 handshapes. For the sign GAS, one would wiggle the fingers in the air (upper part of the signing space) as if the particles are moving around in the air (see figure 1a). For the sign LIQUID, one would intersect the fingers loosely to form the surface of liquid with arms moving as if the particles are moving along each other and up and down in the waves (see figure 1b). For the sign SOLID, one would intersect the fingers firmly with the palms facing each other to form an object (see figure 1c). Conversely, ASL phonological patterns can be detected to demonstrate phase changes between the states for EVAPORATION, CONDENSATION, FREEZING, MELTING, DEPOSITION, and SUBLIMATION.

In mathematics, FRACTION consists of the passive hand in the 1 handshape with palm orientation down and the active hand in a Bent L handshape with palm orientation toward the passive hand and a downward movement from above the passive hand to under the passive hand to represent a number in the numerator of a fraction and another number in the denominator of a fraction. This sign is preferable to the initialized F handshape for the active hand because the initialized sign could be misconstrued for the number or the expression ; the Bent L handshape sign represents a number. The signs NUMERATOR, DENOMINATOR, PROPER FRACTION, IMPROPER FRACTION, MIXED NUMBER, DIGIT, BASE, EXPONENT, SUBSCRIPT, SUPERSCRIPT, COEFFICIENT, VARIABLE, TERM, and PLACE VALUE all include the Bent L handshape (see figure 2 for examples). For

(a)

(b)

(c)

Figure 1. Gas (a), liquid (b), and solid (c).

a long time, the sign for improper fraction was made of three signs in sequence: NOT + PROPER + FRACTION. Another ASL phonological pattern can be found in the signs LINE, SLOPE, INTERCEPT, and any 2-D figures (e.g., RECTANGLE, TRIANGLE, CIRCLE, QUADRILATERAL, PARALLELOGRAM, TRAPEZOID), all of which are made with both hands in the 1 handshape. The signs for 3-D solids (e.g., SPHERE, CONE, CYLINDER, PRISM, PYRAMID) are made with both hands in the 5 handshape to represent the surface of the solid.

For advanced mathematics, the signs DERIVATE and INTEGRATE consist of two Bent 1 hands with the palms touching each other (similar to the sign CHANGE), with the movement reversed for INTEGRATE. DERIVATE is made with one movement, clockwise for the dominant right hand and counterclockwise for the dominant left hand (see figure 3). INTEGRATE is made with the counterclockwise movement for the dominant right hand and clockwise for the dominant left hand (see figure 3). These patterns follow the sign FUNCTION, made with two 1 hands with their palms touching each other in repeated twisting movements (see figure 3). All these support the importance of phonological patterns in ASL, especially for academic content.

Because ASL phonological patterns are likely to help Deaf students develop organizations and schemas of knowledge based on similar characteristics and relationships for recall and retrieval, educational interpreters need to be well versed in this area.[53]

Assessment Translation/Testing Considerations

The two most frequent comments from a pair of studies on the challenges of translating assessments and interpreting testing sessions were (a) "When I translate assessment items, I need to avoid any signs that may give clues, so it is best to fingerspell specialized words"; and (b) "When translating assessment items, I fingerspell specialized words because Deaf students should know the words in English."[54]

Fraction

Improper Fraction

Mixed Number

Place Value

Figure 2. Math sign examples with the Bent L handshape that represents a number.

Function

Derivate

Integrate

Figure 3. ASL for function, derivate, and integrate.

When interpreting for testing or assessment situations, educational interpreters often worry about either giving away answers through signs or causing misunderstandings with inaccurate signs. As a result, they frequently resort to fingerspelling to avoid using signs that may give clues. Educational interpreters who translate English assessment items into ASL should stay with ASL information delivery. If new signs are produced, they should follow the sandwiching approach (signing + fingerspelling).

Higgins and colleagues conducted research focusing on cognitive considerations of K–12 Deaf students in math assessments. The team examined the comprehension of information presented to the students in different formats, including ASL and English-based fingerspelling. The results showed that overall, students did better with the delivery mode in ASL, or signed and fingerspelled, as opposed to just fingerspelling. At the lower grade levels, fingerspelling with signing was preferred by the students. The fingerspelling-only modality was examined at the high school level and none of the fifteen participating students favored this approach. These findings provide evidence of some of the challenges Deaf students face when test items contain only fingerspelling of key terms. The findings also demonstrate that comprehension is increased when the delivery mode is in ASL rather than only fingerspelling, which is usually the mode interpreters choose when interpreting standardized tests.[55] This is consistent with Kurz and Hill's findings that Deaf consumers prefer that interpreters use fingerspelling with signing at the beginning of their interpretation before the fingerspelling is dropped later during the interpretation.[56]

Conclusion

To achieve optimal interpretation for Deaf students who receive education through interpreters, it is essential that educational interpreters utilize academic ASL strategies for information delivery in content areas. Although educational interpreters are language scientists, too, they rarely receive formal training in academic ASL and, therefore, cannot apply this knowledge to their interpretation work. To improve their academic ASL skills, educational interpreters should consult with Deaf heritage ASL speakers, preferably those who teach content areas, and those who are CDIs working in education settings. By becoming more aware of the conceptual, phonological, and semantic appropriateness of the signs they use, their work as educational interpreters becomes more effective. Although there may be a difference of opinion regarding specific signs[57] because each person has an individual style, accent, and values, Deaf heritage ASL speakers are invaluable resources. If Deaf heritage ASL speakers are not readily available for support in your community, technology can also be a valuable resource. For example, using videophones to connect with Deaf heritage ASL speakers, or computers to access academic ASL models, can provide support to interpreters who do not have direct access to Deaf heritage ASL speakers.

Deaf children should be encouraged to become language scientists and be provided with opportunities to explore ASL phonological patterns. Such patterns aid in recall and retrieval, which has been found to be valuable in building content knowledge relationships. Educational interpreters can support this development by becoming intimately familiar with linguistic features of ASL such as phonological patterns and semantically/conceptually accurate signs.

Notes

1. Jane Healy, *Your Child's Growing Mind: Brain Development and Learning from Birth to Adolescence* (New York, NY: Broadway Books, 2011).
2. George Lakoff, *Women, Fire, and Dangerous Things: What Categories Reveal about the Mind* (Chicago: University of Chicago Press, 1987).
3. Tom Humphries, Poorna Kushalnagar, Gaurav Mathur, Donna Jo Napoli, Carol Padden, Christian Rathmann, and Scott R. Smith, "Language Acquisition for Deaf Children: Reducing the Harms of Zero Tolerance to the Use of Alternative Approaches," *Harm Reduction Journal* 9, no. 1 (2012): 16.
4. Jim Cummins, *Language, Power and Pedagogy: Bilingual Children in the Crossfire* (Buffalo, NY: Multilingual Matters, Ltd., 2000); Courtney Cazden, *Classroom Discourse: The Language of Teaching and Learning* (Portsmouth, NH: Heinemann Educational Books, 2001).
5. James Gee, "What is Academic Language?" in *Teaching Science to English Language Learners: Building on Students' Strengths*, eds. Ann S. Roseberry and Beth Warren (Arlington, VA: NSTA Press, 2008): 57–70.
6. Cazden, *Classroom Discourse*, 172.
7. Cummins, *Language, Power and Pedagogy*, 67.
8. Cheryl M. Lange, Susan Lane-Outlaw, William E. Lange, and Dylan L. Sherwood, "American Sign Language/English Bilingual Model: A Longitudinal Study of Academic Growth," *Journal of Deaf Studies and Deaf Education* 18, no. 4 (2013): 532–44.
9. Wayne P. Thomas and Virginia P. Collier, "Language Minority Student Achievement and Program Effectiveness," *California Association for Bilingual Education Newsletter* 17 (1995): 19–24.
10. Jim Cummins, *Language, Power and Pedagogy: Bilingual Children in the Crossfire* (Buffalo, NY: Multilingual Matters, Ltd., 2000).
11. Anne M. Baer, *Academic ASL*, DVD (Maryland Heights, MO: Signs of Development, 2002).
12. Maribel Gárate, *A Case Study of an In-service Professional Development Model on Bilingual Deaf Education: Changes in Teachers' Stated Beliefs and Classroom Practices,* Diss., Gallaudet University, 2007.
13. Cheri Smith, Ella Mae Lentz, and Ken Mikos, *Signing Naturally: Unit 1–6 Student Workbook* (San Diego, CA: Dawn Sign Press, 2008).
14. Marlon Kuntze, "Turning Literacy Inside Out," in *Open Your Eyes: Deaf Studies Talking*, ed. H-Dirksen L Bauman (Minneapolis: University of Minnesota Press, 2008): 146–57.
15. Kim B. Kurz, Brenda Schick, and Peter C. Hauser, "Deaf Children's Science Content Learning in Direct Instruction Versus Interpreted Instruction," *Journal of Science Education for Students with Disabilities* 18, no. 1 (2015): Article 5; David A. Stewart and Thomas N. Kluwin, "The Gap Between Guidelines, Practice, and Knowledge in Interpreting Services for Deaf Students," *The Journal of Deaf Studies and Deaf Education* 1, no. 1 (1996): 29–39.
16. Mindy Hopper, "*Positioned as Bystanders: Deaf Students' Experiences and Perceptions of Informal Learning Phenomena*," Diss., University of Rochester, 2011; Brenda Schick, Kevin Williams, and Laurie Bolster, "Skill Levels of Educational Interpreters Working in Public Schools,"

Journal of Deaf Studies and Deaf Education 4, no. 4 (1999): 144–55; Ramsey, *Deaf Children in Public Schools* (Washington, DC: Gallaudet University Press, 1997).

17. Donovan Cresdee and Trevor Johnston, "Using Corpus-Based Research to Inform the Teaching of Auslan (Australian Sign language) as a Second Language," in *Teaching and Learning Signed Languages: International Perspectives and Practices*, eds. David McKee, Russell S. Rosen, and Rachel McKee (New York: Palgrave Macmillan, 2014): 85–110.

18. Debra Russell, "A Comparison of Simultaneous and Consecutive Interpretation in the Courtroom," *International Journal of Disability, Community & Rehabilitation* 2, no. 1 (2003), http://www.ijdcr.ca/VOL02_01_CAN/articles/russell.shtml; Bistra Alexieva, "The Optimum Text in Simultaneous Interpreting: A Cognitive Approach to Interpreters' Training," Paper presented at the annual meeting for the First Language International Conference, Elsinore, Denmark, May 31–June 2, 1991; Kevin Bruton, "Consecutive Interpreting—The Theoretical Approach," in *Interpreting as a Language Teaching Technique—Proceedings of a Conference*, eds. Noel Thomas and Richard Towell (University of Salford, England: Centre for Information Language Teaching and Research, 1985): 2–5.

19. Jon Shive and Brian Cerney, *Processing Time: Developing the Interpreter Muscle.* (Rochester, NY: Hand & Mind Publishing, 2014).

20. Raja Kushalnagar, "Distance Between Deaf Viewers and Interpreters," *Journal on Technology and Persons with Disabilities* 3 (2015): 246–56.

21. David H. Smith and Claire Ramsey, "Classroom Discourse Practices of a Deaf Teacher Using American Sign Language," *Sign Language Studies* 5, no. 1 (2004): 39–62; Susan Mather, "Eye Gaze and Communication in a Deaf Classroom," *Sign Language Studies* 54, no. 1 (1987): 11–30.

22. Matthews, Peter H., ed. *The Concise Oxford Dictionary of Linguistics, 3rd ed.* (New York, NY: Oxford University Press, 2014).

23. Cummins, *Language, Power and Pedagogy.*

24. Ladd, Paddy. *Understanding Deaf Culture: In Search of Deafhood* (Tonawanda, NY: Multilingual Matters, Ltd., 2003): 104.

25. Cummins, *Language, Power and Pedagogy,* 77.

26. Ladd, *Deafhood*; Perry Gilmore and David M. Smith, "Seizing Academic Power: Indigenous Subaltern Voices, Metaliteracy, and Counternarratives in Higher Education," in *Language, Literacy, and Power in Schooling*, ed. Teresa L. McCarty (Mahwah, NJ: Lawrence Erlbaum Associates, 2005): 71.

27. Richard Ruiz, "Orientations in Language Planning," *Journal of the National Association for Bilingual Education* 8, no. 2 (1984): 15–34; Tom Humphries and Carol Padden, *Inside Deaf Culture* (Cambridge, MA: Harvard University Press, 2005).

28. Humphries and Padden, *Inside Deaf Culture*, 128.

29. Humphries and Padden, *Inside Deaf Culture,* 128.

30. Humphries and Padden, *Inside Deaf Culture,* 128.

31. Raychelle Harris, "Sign Language as Academic Language" in *Deaf Studies Encyclopedia*, eds. Genie Gertz and Patrick Boudreault (Thousand Oaks, CA: The Sage Publication, 2016): 829–32.

32. Lev Vygotsky, *Foundations of Paedology* (Leningrad: Izdanie Instituta, 1935): 58–78.

33. Elena Bodrova and Deborah J. Leong, "Vygotskian Perspectives on Teaching and Learning Early Literacy," in *Handbook of Research in Early Literacy Research, Vol. 2*, eds. David Dickinson and Susan B. Neuman (New York, NY: Guildford Publications, Inc., 2006): 246.

34. Bodrova and Leong, "Vygotskian Perspectives." 245; David Dickinson and Patton Tabors, *Beginning Literacy with Language: Learning at Home and School* (Baltimore, MD: Paul H. Brookes Publishing Co., 2001); Betty Hart and Todd Risley, *The Social World of Children*

Learning to Talk (Baltimore, MD: Paul H. Brookes Publishing Co., 1999); Peter V. Paul and Ye Wang, "Literate Thought and Multiple Literacies," *Theory Into Practice* 45, no. 4 (2006): 304–10; Lev Vygotsky, *Thought and Language* (Cambridge, MA: MIT Press, 1986).

35. Robert T. Jiminez, Georgia E. Garcia, and P. David Pearson, "The Reading Strategies of Bilingual Latina/o Students Who Are Successful English Readers: Opportunities and Obstacles," *Reading Research Quarterly* 31, no. 1 (1996) 90–112; Kenji Hakuta, *Mirror of Language: The Debate on Bilingualism* (New York, NY: Basic Books, 1986); Rafael Diaz, "Bilingual Cognitive Development: Addressing Three Gaps in Current Research," *Child Development* 56, no 6 (1985): 1376–88; Kenji Hakuta and Rafael Diaz, "The Relationship Between Degree of Bilingualism and Cognitive Ability: A Critical Discussion and Some New Longitudinal Data," in *Children's Language, Vol. 5*, ed. Katherine Nelson (Hillsdale, NJ: Lawrence Erlbaum Associates, 1985): 319–44.

36. J. Michael O'Malley and Lorraine Pierce, *Authentic Assessment for English Language Learners: Practical Approaches for Teachers* (Reading, MA: Addison-Wesley): 31.

37. O'Mally and Pierce, *Authentic Assessment,* 31.

38. Charlene Chamberlain and Rachel I. Mayberry, "Theorizing About the Relation Between American Sign Language and Reading," in *Language Acquisition by Eye*, eds. Charlene Chamberlain, Rachel I. Mayberry, and Jill P. Morford (Mahwah, NJ: Lawrence Erlbaum Associates, 2000): 221.

39. Jim Cummins, "The Relationship Between American Sign Language Proficiency and English Academic Development: A Review of the Research" 母語・継承語・バイリンガル教育 (MHB) 研究 3 (2007): 75–94.

40. Sharon Baker and Jessica Scott, "Sociocultural and Academic Considerations for School-Aged/Deaf and Hard of Hearing Multilingual Learners: A Case Study of a Deaf Latina," *American Annals of the Deaf* 161, no. 1 (2016): 43–55.

41. Cummins, "The Relationship Between American Sign Language Proficiency and English Academic Development."

42. Raychelle Harris, *A Case Study of Extended Discourse in an ASL/English Bilingual Preschool Classroom*, Diss., Gallaudet University, 2011.

43. Harris, *Case Study of Extended Discourse.*

44. Tom Humphries and Francine MacDougall, "Chaining and Other Links: Making Connections Between American Sign Language and English in Two Types of School Settings," *Visual Anthropology Review* 15, no. 2 (1999): 85.

45. Rosalee Wolfe, John McDonald, Jorge Toro, Souad Baowidan, Robyn Moncrief, and Jerry Schnepp, "Promoting Better Deaf/hearing Communication Through an Improved Interaction Design for Fingerspelling Practice," in *International Conference on Universal Access in Human-Computer Interaction* (Cham, Switzerland: Springer International Publishing, 2015): 495–505.

46. Brenda Schick, Kevin Williams, and Laurie Bolster, "Skill Levels of Educational Interpreters Working in Public Schools," *Journal of Deaf Studies and Deaf Education* 4, no. 2 (1999): 144–55.

47. Christopher A. Kurz, *Academic Language—Mathematics in ASL: Educational Interpreters as Language Scientists,* Boys Town National Research Hospital, Omaha, Nebraska, 2016, DVD; Christopher A. Kurz and Jeanne Reis, "Science, Technology, and Math, Oh My!" Workshop presented at the State Department of Education, Vinton, Iowa, June 2014.

48. Adam Stone, Geo Kartheiser, Peter C. Hauser, Laura-Ann Petitto, and Thomas E. Allen, "Fingerspelling as a Novel Gateway into Reading Fluency in Deaf Bilinguals," *PLos ONE* 10, no 10 (2015): e0139610. doi:10.1371/journal.pone.0139610

49. Carol Padden, "Learning to Fingerspell Twice: Young Signing Children's Acquisition of Fingerspelling," in *Advances in the Sign Language Development of Deaf Children*, eds. Brenda Schick, Marc Marschark, and Patricia Spencer (New York, NY: Oxford University Press, 2006): 189–201.

50. Padden "Learning to Fingerspell Twice"; Tom Humphries and Francine MacDougall, "Chaining and Other Links," 84–94; Carol Padden and Claire Ramsey, "Reading Ability in Signing Deaf Children," *Topics in Language Disorders* 18, no. 4 (1998): 30–46; A. B. Kelly,"Fingerspelling Interaction: A Set of Deaf Parents and Their Deaf Daughter," in *Sociolinguistics in Deaf Communities*, ed. Cecil Lucas (Washington, DC: Gallaudet University Press, 1995): 62–73.

51. Todd A. Czubek, "Apprenticeships to Comprehension," presentation at Boston University, 2010. Todd A. Czubek, "Blue Listerine parochialism, and ASL literacy," *Journal of Deaf Studies and Deaf Education* 11, no. 3 (2006): 373–81.

52. Hakuta and Diaz, "The Relationship Between Degree of Bilingualism and Cognitive Ability."

53. Karen Emmorey, Barbara Tversky, and Holly Taylor, "Using Space to Describe Space: Perspective in Speech, Sign and Gesture," *Spatial Cognition and Computation* 2, no. 3 (2000): 157–180.

54. Kurz, *Academic Language—Mathematics in ASL*; Kurz and Reis, "Science, Technology, and Math, Oh My!"

55. Jennifer Higgins, Lisa Famularo, Stephanie W. Cawthon, Christopher A. Kurz, Jeanne Reis, and Lori Moers, "Development of American Sign Language Guidelines for K–12 Academic Assessments," *Journal of Deaf Studies and Deaf Education* 21, no. 4 (2016): 383–93.

56. See Kim Kurz and Joseph Hill, this volume,

57. Kurz, *Academic Language—Mathematics in ASL*; Harry G. Lang, Kim Kurz, and Christopher A. Kurz, "Vital Signs: Optimizing the Teaching of Science and Mathematics Through Research," *NTID Research Bulletin* 11 (2006): 1, 3–5.

20

YOUR NAME WHAT? YOU FROM WHERE?

Naomi Sheneman

For the ASL summary of this chapter, go to https://youtu.be/vEq4eESzdLA

It has been my experience that upon meeting a hearing interpreter for the first time during an appointment, I frequently find myself having to ask interpreters for their name and the organization that enlisted them. Rather, the interpreters introduce themselves in American Sign Language (ASL) as ME INTERPRETER without disclosing their names or additional details. Even with my prompt, I often get their first name only, compelling me to follow up with an additional prod: LAST NAME HAVE? Following Deaf cultural norms, I then ask the next question, FROM WHERE (who enlisted you)? When the hearing consumer is added to the mix after this initial interaction, the interpreter usually says, "I am the interpreter," to the hearing consumer(s) to communicate that the interaction between the hearing consumer and me should commence without further ado. This has been a puzzling phenomenon, considering Deaf cultural norms. There are three problems with this common, yet puzzling scenario. First, the lack of introduction violates Deaf cultural norms. Next, it promotes the conduit model, which should have been abandoned long ago. Finally, it does not promote a positive professional reputation or branding on the interpreter's part.

WITH THE professionalization of the sign language interpreting, different interpreter models or metaphors have been developed in an effort to describe what interpreters do; the conduit model is one example.[1] First, there was the helper model in which the interpreter was overly involved in trying to aid Deaf consumers, making them seem incapable.[2] Upon the collective realization that interpreters were not conducting themselves professionally using this approach, the conduit model emerged, supporting the idea that the interpreter is not a person but a "machine" that transmits information from one language to another. The interpreter acts as a conduit, relaying only the verbal information from one language to another without incorporating cultural mediation and managing turn-taking strategies. Only explicit ideas are interpreted, and not the implied meanings.[3] For example, if a Deaf person expressed confusion about something that was interpreted, the conduit interpreter would not pause the process to ensure clarification, but instead merely continue to interpret.

Professionalization of sign language interpreting began in 1964 with the establishment of the national Registry of Interpreters for the Deaf (RID) with a strong push by Deaf people and Deaf-parented interpreters. The organization's original purpose was to develop and maintain a registry of interpreters across the country as well as recruit and train sign language interpreters. However, RID quickly evolved to become much more by offering testing, certification, and professional development training of interpreters.[4] Professionalization typically dominated by those with privileges becomes a conflict of political and cultural values.[5] Thus, the professionalization of sign language interpreting in the United States eventually pushed out the Deaf community's involvement in the development and training of future interpreters.[6]

Academic institutionalization of interpreter education programs in higher education institutions made the exclusion of Deaf community even more apparent.[7] It is important to note that this problem is occurring on an international level as well.[8] As Kent indicated, the majority-group members typically make decisions while disregarding the input of the marginalized groups that they aim to serve. Additionally, she stated, "Professionalization is a raced, gendered, and classed endeavor."[9] The Deaf view, collectively and individually, was minimized in the latter phase of this process; although the Deaf community continues to push for its participation.[10] Instead of building a pool of interpreters from within the Deaf community, this organization assumed the primary role of increasing the number of professional interpreters that do not always meet expectations that are deemed important by the Deaf community.[11] Subsequently, this has brought criticism from the Deaf community for interpreters' increasingly audistic behaviors and practices.[12] One result of the shift from a community-based screening to a professional organization's screening protocols is the widening gap between interpreters and Deaf people in their respective view of what it means to be a professional interpreter.[13] Regardless of the varying perceptions on the severity of this divide between Deaf people and interpreters, the grassroots Deaf community are often in the dark when it comes to the interpreting profession based on my conversations with Deaf individuals across the country. They often do not know what the issues are with the current standards and practices as they are usually not involved with RID or any other professional entities of the field, largely due to being marginalized by RID.

This disconnect between the Deaf and interpreting communities is unfortunate. Van de Ven, in his book *Engaged Scholarship: A Guide for Organizational and Social Research,* discussed the importance of ongoing engagement between researchers, practitioners, consumers, and stakeholders in the applied areas of management and organization.[14] In this vein, it is crucial that interpreters remain involved with the Deaf community in order to understand the impact of their work on Deaf consumers, in addition to promoting trust in their work.[15] In support of Janzen and Korpiniski's position that trust should be earned by interpreters, I believe that one major misstep toward accomplishing this trust is when hearing interpreters do not properly introduce themselves to Deaf consumers at the start of interpreting assignments. Frequently, the interpreters focus on the actual interpreting task rather than the interactions with consumers before and after the interpreting event, thereby supporting the continued usage of the conduit model. This is a pedagogical problem as students often complete interpreter education programs without thorough understanding of the Deaf culture and experience.[16] Deaf culture "proper" introductions are an example of a positive interpreter behavior *before* the task. This issue will be the focus of this chapter.

Introductions in Deaf Culture

It is customary in the Deaf community to introduce yourself with your first and last name along with some relevant details.[17] As such, an introduction often includes a brief biographical sketch of where one lives, grew up, attended school, or has worked.[18] Their family's hearing status and identification of other Deaf relatives, if any, are often provided.[19] In addition, Deaf people often seek personal connections by exploring possible mutual acquaintances within the Deaf community, as well as any shared background and/or experiences. This cultural norm of making introductions in this fashion is one characteristic of a collectivist culture.

Various types of cultures have been described by different scholars. The two most relevant here are "individualist" and "collectivist." Hofstede explained that members of individualist cultures typically focus on themselves and their families, in which members of collectivistic cultures place high value on maintaining relationships among the members of the groups to which they belong.[20] Hall contrasted high-context cultures in which relationships are valued more than the task, with low-context cultures. Interpersonal contact is a priority in high-context cultures[21] such as Deaf culture, as opposed to mainstream American culture, a low-context culture.

Because Deaf culture is high-context and collectivistic, introductions play an important role in helping Deaf people find a common ground.[22] Holcomb described introductions in the Deaf community as being "detailed and extensive."[23] In contrast, especially in the United States, hearing people tend to be individualistic and private; thus, brief first-name introductions are considered acceptable. Conversely, Deaf people are likely to be more liberal about sharing personal information.[24]

By introducing themselves just with first name, interpreters are practicing the norms of their majority culture and superseding the practices of the Deaf minority culture. Clearly, language use by members of a majority culture can demonstrate power over minority culture members also involved in the interaction.[25] Baker-Shenk described power as the ability to act.[26] Interpreters make Deaf-centered decisions that could ensure a positive experience for Deaf consumers or they could be unconsciously partaking in the ongoing oppression against Deaf people. This further upholds the power imbalance that is apparent within an interpreting event because the interpreter stands between the "'empowered' and 'disempowered' communities."[27] Rather, the interpreter should gain social capital in the Deaf world by honoring the long-standing cultural practice of providing detailed introductions rather than resorting to the introductory norms of their mainstream American culture.

Hearing people who want to be involved with the Deaf community should be prepared to share relevant information about themselves. Details about how they acquired ASL and who their ASL teachers were should be part of their standard introduction. This kind of information makes it easier for the Deaf person to form connections with the hearing individual, which is critical in the Deaf culture.[28] Interpreters should follow this same practice. Rather than identifying themselves with just their name, interpreters should also quickly explain before the assignment, when time permits and if the situation is appropriate, how they began their interpreting career as well as their connections to the Deaf community. This is essential to reassure Deaf people of their alliance to the Deaf community and helps build trust. Indeed, trust was identified by Deaf people in Napier's study as an important ingredient in the interpreter–consumer relationship.[29] By performing culturally appropriate introductions, interpreters practice a form of cultural mediation and promote trust.

Cultural Mediation in Interpreting

Cultural mediation is an important component of good interpreting work.[30] Interpreting is not merely the act of transmitting information from one language to another (e.g., spoken English to ASL). Rather, interpreting also involves cross-cultural mediation, which requires understanding and sensitivity toward both cultures involved in the interaction. Yet, the traditional focus of the interpreter's work has been on mediating linguistic rather than cultural differences.[31]

Both aspects should be considered important in the work of an interpreter. In fact, the second tenet of the National Association of the Deaf (NAD)-RID Code of Professional Conduct emphasizes the importance of knowing American Deaf culture in order to make appropriate linguistic and cultural adjustments.[32] Cultural mediation is recognized as an essential component of a sign language interpreter's work. Deaf interpreters in Sheneman's study took this component seriously as they claim that they do more cultural mediation than hearing interpreters.[33] One reason for the difference is due to Deaf people's own experiences living in the Deaf community and navigating the hearing world on a daily basis.

Yet, interpretations without cultural mediation often do not clearly convey the intended meaning.[34] Clouet emphasized the importance of cultural mediation in the interpreting work by identifying that linguistic and cultural mediations are key ingredients in a successful intercultural communication.[35] For this reason, possession of intercultural competence is critical for successful interpreting work to transpire.[36] This includes interpreters familiarizing themselves with the introductory rituals of both cultures. Possessing this knowledge would enable interpreters to make the necessary adjustments in their introductions to make them culturally appropriate. Interpreters are often the only hearing individuals in an interpreting event that have knowledge about the Deaf culture.[37] Choosing not to apply their cultural knowledge in their interactions with Deaf consumers is the interpreters' way of taking the power and furthering the oppression of Deaf people. Llewellyn-Jones and Lee asserted that when interpreters try to maintain their invisibility status, essentially practicing the conduit model, their conduct is counterproductive as it "further de-normalizes and, hence, inhibits the interaction."[38] In the absence of a proper introduction, the interpreter disregards the long-held Deaf cultural behavior and instead perpetuates the outdated conduit model.

The Lingering Effects of the Conduit Model

The pattern of non-informative introductions is one consequence of the model of interpreters as conduits. The conduit model espouses the idea that the interpreter is invisible and has minimal bearing on the interpreting process and interactions between people involved in the interpreted situation.[39] The conduit model continues to be practiced by sign language interpreters despite receiving training on newer, alternative approaches.[40] The practice of the conduit model further promotes the misunderstanding of interpreters' function.[41] Wilcox and Shaffer recognized that the conduit model has been abandoned when it comes to the interpreter's professional behavior but that the conduit model continues to be used in the interpreting process thereby preventing needed adjustments to the message.[42] However, the conduit model continues to exist within the interpreter's conduct. Interpreters willingly utilize the conduit model because they falsely believe it is best that they are just doing their job and that it promotes equal power between Deaf and hearing consumers.[43] In reality, the interpreters are purposefully ignoring the fact that hearing and Deaf consumers are not on equal footing and they are empowering the hearing consumers while disempowering the Deaf consumers by practicing the conduit model.[44] Interpreters should be interacting with consumers to build relationships, which in turn makes Deaf consumers feel engaged because "'good interpreters' are those who interact with clients and are human rather than distant and cold."[45] In the absence of proper introductions, interpreters continue to sustain the idea of invisibility in their interactions with consumers making the Deaf consumers feel distant from interpreters.

This rigid and ineffective model was eventually replaced with the communication facilitation model. With this model, the interpreter is empowered to adjust the interpreting situation to ensure effective communication access.[46] Eventually, the bilingual-bicultural mediator model emerged, enabling the interpreter to practice cultural mediation and include cultural nuances in the interpreted work.[47] More recently, the ally model has become popular. Interpreters are encouraged to recognize and manage power imbalances within an interpreted situation. It has been suggested that ally interpreters are Deaf-centered by supporting the wants and needs of Deaf consumers.[48] By respecting the Deaf cultural norm of appropriate introductions, Deaf people will more likely perceive the interpreter as an ally.

Several studies have supported the idea that interpreters should be active participants in the interpreting process.[49] In contrast to the conduit model, the interpreter is now charged as the person who is the mediator for both cultural and communication exchange between the two parties.[50] With the interpreter acting as a communication mediator, some have challenged the existing belief that the interpreter is neutral, or rather invisible (as a conduit), in the communication process because the interpreter has to act as an active participant in the dialogue to ensure the turn-taking process is occurring smoothly.[51] This demonstrates the duality of the interpreter's function—the interpretation of the message and the coordination of the communication.[52] Thus, cultural mediation is a necessary skill for interpreters to develop.[53] In fact, it has been argued that the profession has moved away from the misconception that the interpreter's main function is to be a conduit. Still, many interpreters continue to follow the conduit model, however unintentional.[54]

The emergence of the Video Relay Service (VRS) has also contributed to the perpetuation of the conduit model. The policies set forth by the Federal Communications Commission (FCC) mandate that interpreters can only provide their interpreter identification number, which is a violation of Deaf cultural norms. However, the practices within the VRS industry should not carry over into community interpreting, where positive relationships with Deaf consumers are critical and valued.

For so long, the profession has been married to metaphors, including models that do not allow flexibility in the decision-making process to be dependent on the consumers and circumstances of the interpreting situation.[55] Additionally, Dean and Pollard proposed that the profession reject the use of models and the word *role*, which limits sign language interpreters to a certain set of behaviors that could be perceived as a one-size-fits-all approach.[56] Llewellyn-Jones and Lee suggested a role-space model that allows interpreters to have flexibility to ensure successful interactions for consumers involved in a particular situation.[57] If interpreters value culturally sensitive practices, they should abandon the conduit model and behave in a manner that embraces the values within the Deaf community. As such, culturally appropriate introductions are expected by Deaf people and allow for interpreters to simultaneously identify or brand themselves as professionals from the time they arrive until they leave, not just during interpreting. Supporting Llewellyn-Jones and Lee's premise, how introductions are conducted would be dependent on the consumers and the situation. For some consumers and situations, a longer introduction might be warranted whereas for some others, a brief introduction indicating name and affiliation would suffice.

Branding of Professional Interpreting Services

By practicing culturally appropriate introductions, interpreters are essentially branding themselves as professionals. Establishing a good reputation from the start of an interpreting career is essential.[58] If they were dispatched by an interpreter referral agency, a positive branding image is extended to the agency as well. Branding is an important part of providing professional services.[59] "Your brand is derived from who you are, who you want to be, and who people perceive you to be."[60] This is especially important for interpreters because Deaf people often exchange with each other their assessments of individual interpreters' work, communication competence, trustworthiness, and subsequently the level of involvement in the Deaf community.[61] In their discussions, they also identify interpreters who demonstrate acts of microaggression against Deaf people. Because of this, interpreters should work hard to maintain and value their professional brand, as it reflects positively on their own integrity and reputation as an ally of the Deaf community.

Ultimately, interpreters are in charge of managing their own professional reputation. This is accomplished through adoption of positive branding strategies that allow them to be viewed by the Deaf community as reputable interpreters. One way to do this is to incorporate culturally appropriate introductions on a regular basis, which in turn present a positive image of the interpreter as a professional service provider. The act of creating and maintaining one's own professional brand is an ongoing marketing strategy as professionals consider how they want to be perceived in the professional world.[62] The lack of a proper introduction does not lend credence to a positive professional reputation, nor does it promote trust. Thus, it is vital for professionals, in any profession, to properly introduce themselves. Augustine argued "it's best to introduce yourself to others using your full name. Not only will you sound more professional, but you're likely to be more memorable."[63] Therefore, it is important for professional interpreters to be aware of the Deaf culture, as well as consumers' needs, to ensure effective services.[64]

In following Deaf cultural norms, it is imperative for interpreters to introduce themselves using their full name and to indicate their enlisting entity, whether it be an interpreter referral agency or a direct contract with the organization. If the time permits and if the situation is appropriate, disclosing information on how ASL and Deaf culture were acquired would be an enhancement to the introduction. However, there may be some situations that make it difficult to accomplish this in specific settings such as criminal courts and the emergency room. For those scenarios, interpreters should attempt to take advantage of the first opportunity that arises to quickly make an introduction with their name and organization name without much detail at some point during the assignment. Those introductions can be done upon meeting the Deaf consumers in the waiting room or outside the room and building. If the Deaf consumers engage you into a dialogue, you could share more details such as how you acquired ASL and became an interpreter. Granted, there are some Deaf consumers who may not be interested in an ice-breaking conversation; thus, stating your name and the enlisting entity would suffice. If this pre-interpretation interaction could not take place, find a few seconds at some point during the interpreting event to do so.

The benefits of this practice are twofold. First, this promotes an immediate positive connection between the interpreter and the Deaf consumer(s) involved. The ability to establish rapport is an important soft skill for an effective interpreter.[65] It helps to promote the view that the interpreter is an involved participant in the interpreting process. As mentioned previously, this can also help dissipate the long-standing beliefs and practices of the conduit model.[66] Second, this introductory practice helps tie interpreters to their brand (name and affiliation) and present themselves as professionals. For these reasons, it is essential that interpreters be consistent with their introductory practices with Deaf people. Consistency of this practice is key. By doing so, they establish a positive brand.[67]Additionally, this empowers both Deaf and hearing consumers to provide feedback as needed, either to the interpreter directly or to the organization that dispatched them. Deaf consumers can find an interpreter's contact information in RID if they want to follow up after the situation directly with the interpreter or the enlisting entity.

Unfortunately, many Deaf people leave an interpreted situation without any knowledge of the interpreter's name and/or the enlisting entity. This lack of transparency is oddly common in many interpreting assignments today according to numerous Deaf consumers who have shared their experiences with me, making it practically impossible for Deaf people to share feedback on any aspect of an interpreter's work.

Conclusion and Recommendations

The current landscape in the interpreting profession is one of an uneven power dynamic between the Deaf and interpreting communities. Current practices and actions among interpreters are often conducted with minimal guidance and consultation from Deaf people, unlike the profession's humble beginnings in 1964. Unfortunately, the Deaf community's voice does not ring loud enough in the development of standards and practices.[68] This has further perpetuated culturally insensitive behaviors among many interpreters. The simple practice of making culturally appropriate introductions is sadly not occurring on a regular basis. Additionally, the lack of transparency in identifying the enlisting entity is all too common. These practices oppress and disempower the Deaf community.

The ultimate question for interpreters to consider before beginning a professional interaction with Deaf people is whether they want to be perceived as culturally sensitive and Deaf-centered professionals, or uncaring nameless "machines." When interpreters make the conscious choice not to properly introduce themselves, they are blatantly disregarding Deaf cultural norms, furthering the practice of the conduit model, consequently lacking an effective professional branding of their interpreting services and minimizing any chance of building trust and positive rapport. For these reasons, to establish positive rapport with and earn the trust of Deaf individuals, hearing interpreters must be comfortable practicing the collectivist type of introduction that is common within the Deaf culture.

To further minimize the disconnection between interpreters and the Deaf community, interpreters can and should begin appearing as professionals by wearing an identification badge on assignments and having business cards at the ready. Business cards should include a headshot to help Deaf consumers remember what a specific interpreter looks like. Lastly, business cards can be either from the enlisting entities (i.e. interpreter referral agency) with their names written on them or their own individual cards that include the contact information of the organization that engaged them if this is in line with the protocol of the agency. This would make it convenient for Deaf people to provide feedback or make specific requests for future assignments.

With such recommendations implemented, the process of reunification between the Deaf and interpreting communities can begin. The importance of partnering with Deaf consumers to bridge the gap between the Deaf community and interpreters cannot be overemphasized. In summary, the disconnect between the interpreter and Deaf communities is a result of varied factors, one of which is the inappropriateness of many interpreters in their interactions with Deaf people at the start of an assignment. This small, but significant, step of proper introductions by interpreters will go a long way in building trust and positive rapport with Deaf people.

Notes

1. Jack Hoza, "Saving Face: The Interpreter and Politeness," *Journal of Interpretation* (1999): 39–68; David A. Stewart, Jerome D. Schein, and Brenda E. Cartwright, *Sign Language Interpreting: Exploring Its Art and Science, 2nd ed.* (New York: Allyn & Bacon, 2014); Janice H. Humphrey and Bob J. Alcorn, *So You Want to Be an Interpreter? An Introduction to Sign Language Interpreting, 4th ed.* (Clearwater, FL: H & H Publishing Company, 2007).

2. Terry Janzen and Donna Korpiniski, "Ethics and Professionalism in Interpreting," in *Topics in Signed Language Interpreting,* ed. Terry Janzen (Amsterdam, The Netherlands: John Benjamins Publishing Company, 2005): 165–99; Sherman Wilcox and Barb Shaffer, "Towards a Cognitive Model of Interpreting" in *Topics in Signed Language Interpreting,* ed. Terry Janzen. (Amsterdam, The Netherlands: John Benjamins Publishing Company, 2005): 27–50; Humphrey and Alcorn, *So You Want to Be an Interpreter?*

3. Janzen and Korpiniski, "Ethics and Professionalism in Interpreting"; Wilcox and Shaffer, "Towards a Cognitive Model of Interpreting"; Humphrey and Alcorn, *So You Want to Be an Interpreter?*

4. Lou Fant, *Silver Threads: A Personal Look at the First Twenty-Five Years of the Registry of Interpreters for the Deaf* (Silver Spring, MD: RID Publications, 1990).

5. Stephanie Jo Kent, "Why Bother? Institutionalization, Interpreter Decisions, and Power Relations," in *The Critical Link 4: Professionalisation of Interpreting in the Community. International Conference on Interpreting in Legal, Health and Social Service Settings*, eds. Cecilia Wadensjö, Birgitta Englund-Dimitrova, and Anna-Lena Nilsson (Amsterdam: John Benjamins Publishing Company, 2007): 193–204.

6. Dennis Cokely, "Shifting Positionality: A Critical Examination of the Turning Point in the Relationship of Interpreters and the Deaf Community" in *Sign Language Interpreting and Interpreter Education: Directions for Research and Practice,* eds. Marc Marschark, Rico Peterson, and Elizabeth A. Winston (New York, NY: Oxford University Press, 2005): 3–28.

7. Cokely, "Shifting Positionality"; Anna Witter-Merithew and Leilani J. Johnson, *Toward Competent Practice: Conversations with Stakeholders* (Alexandria, VA: RID Press, 2005); Eileen Forestal,"Foreword" in *Service Learning in Interpreter Education: Strategies for Extending Student Involvement in the Deaf Community,* ed. Sherry Shaw (Washington, DC: Gallaudet University Press, 2013): ix–x; Sherry Shaw, *Service Learning in Interpreter Education: Strategies for Extending Student Involvement in the Deaf Community* (Washington, DC: Gallaudet University Press, 2013).

8. Lorraine Leeson and Susan Foley-Cave, "Deep and Meaningful Conversation: Challenging Interpreter Impartiality in the Semantics and Pragmatics Classroom" in *Translation, Sociolinguistic, and Consumer Issues in Interpreting,* eds. Melanie Metzger and Earl Fleetwood, (Washington, DC: Gallaudet University Press, 2007): 45–68.

9. Kent, "Why Bother?" 200.

10. Kent, "Why Bother?"

11. Cokely, "Shifting Positionality."

12. Kent, "Why Bother?"

13. Cokely, "Shifting Positionality."

14. Andrew Van de Ven, *Engaged Scholarship: A Guide for Organizational and Social Research* (Oxford, United Kingdom: Oxford University Press, 2007).

15. Janzen and Korpiniski, "Ethics and Professionalism in Interpreting."

16. Shaw, *Service Learning in Interpreter Education.*

17. Harlan Lane, Robert Hoffmeister, and Ben Bahan, *A Journey into the Deaf-World* (San Diego, CA: Dawn Sign Press, 1996); Thomas K. Holcomb, *Introduction to American Deaf Culture* (New York: Oxford University Press, 2013).

18. MJ Bienvenu and Betty Colonomos, *An Introduction to American Deaf Culture: Rules of Social Interaction Workbook* (Riverdale, MD: The Bicultural Center, 1992).

19. Anna Mindess, Thomas K. Holcomb, Daniel Langholtz, and Priscilla Moyers, *Reading Between the Signs: Intercultural Communication for Sign Language Interpreters*, 3rd ed. (Yarmouth, ME: Intercultural Press, Inc., 2014).

20. Geert Hofstede, *Culture's Consequences: Comparing Values, Behaviors, Institutions and Organizations Across Nations, 2nd ed.* (Thousand Oaks, CA: Sage Publications, 2001).

21. Edward T. Hall, *Beyond Culture* (New York, NY: Anchor Books, 1976).

22. Mindess et al., *Reading Between the Signs.*

23. Holcomb, *Introduction to American Deaf Culture,* 203.

24. Mindess et al., *Reading Between the Signs.*

25. Pierre Bourdieu, *Language and Symbolic Power* (Cambridge, MA: Harvard University Press, 1991).

26. Charlotte Baker-Shenk, "The Interpreter: Machine, Advocate, or Ally?" in *Expanding Horizons: Proceedings of the 1991 RID Convention* (Silver Spring, MD: RID Publications, 1992): 120–140.

27. Masaomi Kondo, Helen Tebble, Bistra Alexieva, Helle V. Dam, David Katan, Akira Mizuno, Robin Setton, and Ilona Zalk, "Intercultural Communication, Negotiation, and Interpreting" in *Conference Interpreting: Current Trends in Research*, eds. Yves Gambier, Daniel Gile, and Christopher Taylor (Amsterdam: John Benjamins Publishing Company, 1997): 149–66.

28. Holcomb, *Introduction to American Deaf Culture.*

29. Jemina Napier, "'It's Not What They Say but the Way They Say It': A Content Analysis of Interpreter and Consumer Perceptions of Signed Language Interpreting in Australia," *International Journal of the Sociology of Language* 207 (2011): 59–87.

30. Stewart et al., *Sign Language Interpreting: Exploring Its Art and Science.*

31. David Katan, *Translating Cultures: An Introduction for Translators, Interpreters and Mediators, 2nd ed.* (Brooklands, Manchester, United Kingdom: St. Jerome Publishing, 2004).

32. Registry of Interpreters for the Deaf, *NAD-RID Code of Professional Conduct*, 2005, http://www.rid.org/UserFiles/File/NAD_RID_ETHICS.pdf.

33. Naomi Sheneman, "Deaf Interpreters' Ethics: Reflections on Training and Decision-Making," *Journal of Interpretation* 25, no. 1 (2016): Article 8.

34. Baker-Shenk, "The Interpreter: Machine, Advocate, or Ally?"; Hoza, "Saving Face: The Interpreter and Politeness."

35. Richard Clouet, "Intercultural Language Learning: Cultural Mediation within the Curriculum of Translation and Interpreting Studies," *Iberica* 16 (2008): 147–68.

36. Mindess et al., *Reading Between the Signs.*

37. Baker-Shenk, "The Interpreter: Machine, Advocate, or Ally?"

38. Peter Llewellyn-Jones and Robert G. Lee, "Getting to the Core of Role: Defining Interpreters' Role-Space," *International Journal of Interpreter Education,* 5 (2013): 54–72, 56.

39. Janzen and Korpiniski, "Ethics and Professionalism in Interpreting"; Wilcox and Shaffer, "Towards a Cognitive Model of Interpreting"; Humphrey and Alcorn, *So You Want to Be an Interpreter?*

40. Lorna Allsop and Lorraine Leeson, "Professionalism, Philosophy, and Practice," Paper presented at the Association of Sign Language Interpreters (ASLI) Conference, *Newsli* 42 (2002): 4–6; Leeson and Foley-Cave, "Deep and Meaningful Conversation: Challenging Interpreter Impartiality in the Semantics and Pragmatics Classroom."

41. Allsop and Leeson, "Professional, Philosophy, and Practice"; Wilcox and Shaffer, "Towards a Cognitive Model of Interpreting."

42. Wilcox and Shaffer, "Towards a Cognitive Model of Interpreting."

43. Baker-Shenk, "The Interpreter: Machine, Advocate, or Ally?"

44. Baker-Shenk, "The Interpreter: Machine, Advocate, or Ally?"

45. Leeson and Foley-Cave, "Deep and Meaningful Conversation: Challenging Interpreter Impartiality in the Semantics and Pragmatics Classroom," 64.

46. Humphrey and Alcorn, *So You Want to Be an Interpreter?*

47. Stewart et al., *Sign Language Interpreting: Exploring Its Art and Science*; Wilcox and Shaffer, "Towards A Cognitive Model Of Interpreting"; Janzen and Korpiniski, "Ethics and Professionalism in Interpreting"; Humphrey and Alcorn, *So You Want to Be an Interpreter?*

48. Baker-Shenk, "The Interpreter: Machine, Advocate, or Ally?"; Hoza, "Saving Face: The Interpreter and Politeness"; Janzen and Korpiniski, "Ethics and Professionalism in Interpreting"; Jemina Napier, Rachel Locker McKee, and Della Goswell, *Sign Language Interpreting: Theory and Practice in Australia and New Zealand* (Annandale, N.S.W., Australia: Federation Press, 2006).

49. Cynthia Roy, "A Sociolinguistic Analysis of the Interpreter's Role in the Turn Exchanges of an Interpreted Event," PhD diss., Georgetown University, 1989; Cecelia Wadensjö, *Interpreting as Interaction* (New York, NY: Longman, 1998); Melanie Metzger, *Sign Language Interpreting: Deconstructing the Myth of Neutrality* (Washington, DC: Gallaudet University Press, 1999); Franz Pöchhacker, *Introducing Interpreting Studies* (Abdington, United Kingdom: Routledge, 2003).

50. Roy, "Sociolinguistic Analysis of the Interpreter's Role"; Pöchhacker, *Introducing Interpreting Studies.*

51. Roy, "A Sociolinguistic Analysis of the Interpreter's Role"; Metzger, *Sign Language Interpreting: Deconstructing the Myth of Neutrality.*

52. Wadensjö, *Interpreting as Interaction*; Metzger, *Sign Language Interpreting: Deconstructing the Myth of Neutrality*; Kondo et al., "Intercultural Communication, Negotiation, and Interpreting"; Jean-Paul Vinay and Jean Darbelnet, "A Methodology for Translation," in *The Translation Studies Reader, 2nd ed.*, ed. Lawrence Venuti (New York, NY: Routledge, 2004): 128–73.

53. Kondo et al., "Intercultural Communication, Negotiation, and Interpreting."

54. Wilcox and Shaffer, "Towards a Cognitive Model of Interpreting.

55. Cynthia B. Roy, "The Problem with Definitions, Descriptions, and the Role Metaphors of Interpreters," *Journal of Interpretation* 6, no. 1 (1993): 127–54; Robyn Dean and Robert Q Pollard, Jr., "Community Interpreting as a Practice Profession: A Meta-Ethical Analysis," in *Foundations of Interpreting for the 21st Century*, eds. by Len Roberson and Sherry Shaw (Washington, DC: Gallaudet University Press, in press).

56. Dean and Pollard, Jr., "Community Interpreting as a Practice Profession: A Meta-Ethical Analysis."

57. Llewellyn-Jones and Lee, "Getting to the Core of Role."

58. Shaw, *Service Learning in Interpreter Education.*

59. John Williams, "The Basics of Branding," *Entrepreneur*, n.d., https://www.entrepreneur.com/article/77408.

60. Williams, "The Basics of Branding," para 2.

61. MJ Bienvenu, "Third Culture: Working Together," *Journal of Interpretation* 4 (1987): 1–12; Marian Corker, "Deaf People and Interpreting: The Struggle in Language," *Deaf Worlds* 13 no. 3 (1987): 13–20; Jemina Napier and Meg J. Rohan, "An Invitation to Dance: Deaf Consumers' Perceptions of Signed Language Interpreters and Interpreting," in *Translation, Sociolinguistic, and Consumer Issues in Interpreting,* eds. Melanie Metzger and Earl Fleetwood (Washington, DC: Gallaudet University Press, 2007): 159–203.

62. Martin Yate, *Knock 'em Dead: The Ultimate Job Search Guide* (Avon, MA: Adams Media, 2017).

63. Amanda Augustine, "10 Ways to Boost Your Professional Brand," *Ladders,* September 23, 2014. Retrieved from https://www.theladders.com/p/1250/professional-branding-for-career-advancement, para. 5.

64. Janzen and Korpiniski, "Ethics and Professionalism in Interpreting."

65. Marty Taylor, *Interpretation Skills: English to American Sign Language* (Edmonton, Alberta: Interpreting Consolidated, 1993).

66. Roy, "Sociolinguistic Analysis of the Interpreter's Role"; Metzger, *Sign Language Interpreting: Deconstructing the Myth of Neutrality*; Pöchhacker, *Introducing Interpreting Studies.*

67. Williams, "The Basics of Branding."

68. Paddy Ladd, *Understanding Deaf Culture: In Search of Deafhood* (Tonawanda, NY: Multilingual Matters, Ltd., 2003); Cokely, "Shifting Positionality"; Forestal, "Foreword."

Afterword

Carolyn Ball

RARELY HAVE interpreters and interpreter educators been granted the honor of learning from Deaf people regarding their personal experiences while using an interpreter. This book provides the reader with such a gift. Additionally, the essays in this book provide insight into both positive and devastating experiences that occur to Deaf people during interpreted events. Thus, *Deaf Eyes on Interpreting* provides readers with an opportunity for self-reflection and humility, which can encourage interpreters to learn, grow, and understand that it is necessary to collaborate with Deaf people during the interpreting process. If they are able to collaborate, Deaf people will be empowered and the interpreting team will learn to work toward the common goal of inclusion with a collective sense of accomplishment.

This book provides guidance to interpreters and Deaf people (the interpreting team) about how to create such a collaborative and empowering environment in interpreted settings. Each chapter offers valuable advice to benefit the profession of interpreting and encourage it to move forward positively. The ultimate goal of the book is that the interpreting team will both be empowered to work effectively and collaboratively together. Thomas Holcomb describes the interpreting team effort as Deaf-centered, Deaf-friendly, and Deaf-focused and at the same time is mindful of the challenges associated with interpreting as the DEAM approach. Thus, DEAM creates hope; all of the chapters within this book support DEAM and provide evidence that having qualified and caring interpreters is an ongoing quest.

In fact, the quest for DEAM may have begun back in 1947, when Mr. L.A. Elmer wrote an article in the *American Annals of the Deaf* that it is often customary for a group of Deaf and hard of hearing people to attend a conference where an interpreter will interpret the speaker's message from English to sign language. Elmer states, "Deaf people appreciate this courtesy, but sometimes the interpreting is not all that it should be and the reason for it may be the fault of the interpreter or the speaker."[1]

Elmer lists four specific skills that a good interpreter needs to have: a three-track mind, excellent language skills, knowing not to fingerspell everything, and the ability to not sign word for word what is being said in English.[2] He also writes that there are many skilled interpreters, and the Deaf community wishes to have more. However, Elmer mentions that the observations of the Deaf community are that there are specific skills that interpreters need to acquire. Ultimately, the advice provided for interpreters from Elmer is given with "no prejudice," meaning that the Deaf and Hard of Hearing community does not hate or dislike interpreters. In fact, Elmer calls for more qualified interpreters so that Deaf people can, "reap the full benefit of the programs being interpreted by understanding the speakers as they deliver their message."[3] It may be of interest that many of the chapters in this book refer to the same interpreting skills and attitudes listed by Elmer in 1947. Ultimately, the chapters in this book provide the reader with a plan and a hope in which DEAM can be created.

DEAM Creates Hope

Seventy years have passed since L.A. Elmer published his vision of hope for interpreters, and now the research, insights, and advice in this book show that a successful interpreting team can indeed occur. The vital information contained herein will allow the Deaf and interpreting communities to read and discuss the valuable lessons provided in each chapter.

DEAM Removes Barriers

Throughout this book, interpreting scenarios are described in which Deaf people have been marginalized and their professional status compromised while using an interpreter. Regrettably, some interpreters justify the reasons behind their ineffective choices by explaining that they are following the NAD-RID Code of Professional Conduct (CPC). They may in fact be misusing and abusing the code in order to cover or hide their mistakes.

For this reason, it is vital for interpreters and Deaf people to understand that the CPC is not a crutch or a policy to support the lack of quality control by Deaf people. In fact, the CPC states, "It is the obligation of every interpreter to exercise judgment, employ critical thinking, apply the benefits of practical experience, and reflect on past actions in the practice of their profession." The guiding principles in the CPC represent the concepts of confidentiality, linguistic and professional competence, impartiality, professional growth and development, ethical business practices, and the rights of participants in interpreted situations to informed choice. The driving force behind the guiding principles is the notion that the interpreter will do no harm. To reiterate, the interpreter will "do no harm."[4]

Because some interpreters described in this book may justify their unethical behavior by maintaining that they are following the RID CPC, there is an urgent need that the interpreting team understands the CPC in order for the profession to move forward. The CPC is not an excuse for providing poor quality, or for resisting collaborative interpreting.[5]

Moving the Profession Forward

This book has provided insight and examples of how the profession of interpreting and interpreter education can move forward. Above all, the information within these chapters provides insight that Deaf professionals are equal to hearing professionals. Also, the book provides evidence that Deaf people want interpreters to understand that interpreting is a matter of quality control and is an opportunity for the interpreting team to work together. Thus, the chapters in this book provide specific examples of ways that interpreters can work together for the quality assurance of the interpreting process. One recommendation is for the interpreting team to work with Deaf professionals to creatively solve communication needs together. Also,the interpreting team needs to be open to discussion and feedback during the interpreting process.

Furthermore, it is vital that the interpreting team is willing to admit when communication is not happening. Then the interpreting team can communicate and determine the best way to solve the interpreting breakdown.

This book suggests numerous ways to help remove barriers in interpreted situations. For example, it is important for hearing people to understand the meaning of disempowerment and hearing privilege. In addition, it is very important that interpreters and Deaf people establish a true connection during the interpreting process and remember that the interpreting team has a common goal. Even back in 1947 it was recognized that the interpreter's goal should be to create a Deaf-friendly environment. As described in this book, a Deaf-friendly environment includes: (1) finding ways that Deaf people know that they are being understood, (2) knowing that the interpreter will check in with the Deaf person for understanding, (3) seeking feedback, and (4) inquiring about the well-being of the Deaf person.

The world is shifting and the need for quality interpreting for the Deaf Community has increased, as has the desire for the interpreting team to work together. Clearly this book offers insights that trust and collaboration between the interpreting team are vital. In conclusion, there is excitement regarding the future of interpreting and interpreter education that can be found within these chapters. No doubt, great interpreters and interpreter educators will include the Deaf Community by working together. Thus, DEAM will not just be a dream but can become reality.

Notes

1. L.A. Elmer, "What Is a Good Interpreter?" *American Annals of the Deaf* 93, no. 5, (1948): 545–546.
2. Elmer, "What Is a Good Interpreter?"
3. Elmer, "What Is a Good Interpreter?" 545.
4. National Association of the Deaf and Registry of Interpreters for the Deaf, *NAD-RID Code of Professional Conduct* (Silver Spring, MD: Registry of Interpreters of the Deaf), 1. Retrieved from https://drive.google.com/file/d/0B-_HBAap35D1R1MwYk9hTUpuc3M/view
5. National Association of the Deaf and Registry of Interpreters for the Deaf, *NAD-RID Code of Professional Conduct.*

Bibliography

Abbott, Kenneth W. "Trust But Verify: The Production of Information in Arms Control Treaties and Other International Agreements." *Cornell International Law Journal* 26, no. 1 (1993): 1–58.

Adam, Robert, Breda Carty, and Christopher Stone. "Ghostwriting: Deaf Translators within the Deaf Community." *Babel* 57, no. 4 (2011): 375–93.

Allsop, Lorna, and Lorraine Leeson. "Professionalism, Philosophy, and Practice." *Newsli,* no. 42 (2002): 4–6.

Amnå, Erik, and Joakim Ekman. "Standby Citizens: Diverse Faces of Political Passivity." *European Political Science Review* 6, no. 2 (2014): 261–81.

Anderson, Glenn, and Frank Bowe. "Racism Within the Deaf Community." *American Annals of the Deaf* 117, no. 6 (1972): 617–19.

Angelelli, Claudia. "Uh . . . I Am Not Understanding You at All: Constructing (Mis)Understanding in Provider/Patient Interpreted Medical Encounters." In *Investigations in Healthcare Interpreting*, edited by Brenda Nicodemus and Melanie Metzger. Washington, DC: Gallaudet University Press (2014): 1–31.

Angelelli, Claudia V. "Validating Professional Standards and Codes: Challenges and Opportunities." *Interpreting* 8, no. 2 (2006): 175–93.

Angell, Maureen E., Julia B. Stoner, and Debra L. Shelden. "Trust in Educational Professionals: Perspectives of Mothers of Children with Disabilities." *Remedial and Special Education* 30, no. 3 (2009): 160–76.

Aramburo, Anthony J. "Sociolinguistic Aspects of the Black Deaf Community." In *The Sociolinguistics of the Deaf Community*, edited by Ceil Lucas. San Diego, CA: Academic Press, 1989.

Askanius, Tina, and Nils Gustafsson. "Mainstreaming the Alternative: The Changing Media Practices of Protest Movements." *Interface: A Journal for and About Social Movements* 2, no. 2, (2010): 23–41.

Augustine, Amanda. "10 Ways to Boost Your Professional Brand." *Ladders,* September 23, 2014. https://www.theladders.com/p/1250/professional-branding-for-career-advancement.

Bacallao-Pino, Lazaro M. "Social Media Mobilisations: Articulating Participatory Processes or Visibilizing Dissent?" *Cyberpsychology: Journal of Psychosocial Research on Cyberspace* 8, no. 3 (2014): article 1.

Baker, Colin. "Sign Language and the Deaf Community." *Handbook of Language and Ethnic Identity,* edited by Joshua Fishman. New York: Oxford University Press (1999): 122–39.

Baker-Shenk, Charlotte. "The Interpreter: Machine, Advocate, or Ally?" In *Expanding Horizons*, edited by Jean Plant-Moeller. Silver Spring, MD: RID Press (1992): 120–40.

Bakhtin, Mikhail M. *Speech Genres and Other Late Essays*. Austin, TX: University of Texas at Austin, 1986.

Bar-Tzhur, David. "Is Anybody Home? Getting Deaf Feedback." *The Interpreter's Friend*. February 23, 2004. http://theinterpretersfriend.org/misc/home.html.

Bauman, H-Dirksen L., and Joseph J. Murray, eds. *Deaf Gain: Raising the Stakes for Human Diversity.* Minneapolis: University of Minnesota Press, 2014.

Beard, Lillian. *Lillian Beard at RID Opening Ceremonies*. Philadelphia, PA (2009). https://www.youtube.com/watch?v=Py-4B_PHlqQ.

Beaton, Catherine, and Angela Hauser. "Timeliness, Technology, Terminology, and Tact: Challenging Dynamics in Information Technology Environments." In *Deaf Professionals and Designated Interpreters: A New Paradigm*, edited by Peter Hauser, Karen Finch, and Angela Hauser. Washington DC: Gallaudet University Press (2008): 210–33.

Bell, Lee Anne. "Theoretical Foundations for Social Justice Education." In *Teaching for Diversity and Social Justice,* edited by Maurianne Adams et al. New York: Routledge (2016): 3.

Bennett, Jessica. "Hillary Clinton Will Not Be Manterrupted." *New York Times*, September 27, 2016. https://www.nytimes.com/2016/09/28/opinion/campaign-stops/hillary-clinton-will-not-be-manterrupted.html.

Bienvenu, MJ. "Third Culture: Working Together." *Journal of Interpretation* 4, no. 1 (1987): 1–12.

Bienvenu, MJ, and Betty Colonomos. *An Introduction to American Deaf Culture: Rules of Social Interaction Workbook*. Riverdale, MD: The Bicultural Center, 1992.

———. *The Face of ASL*. [DVD] Burtonsville, MD: SIGN Media, Inc., 1991.

Bontempo, Karen, Tobias Haug, Lorraine Leeson, Jemina Napier, Brenda Nicodemus, Beppie van den Bogaerde, and MyrianVermeerbergen. "Deaf Consumers' Perceptions of Signed to Spoken Language Interpretation in Eight Signed Languages." Paper presented at the International Symposium on Sign Language Interpretation and Translation Research. Washington, DC: Gallaudet University, 2014.

Boudreault, Patrick. "Deaf Interpreters." In *Topics in Signed Language Interpreting: Theory and Practice*, edited by Terry Janzen. Philadelphia: Benjamins (2005): 323–56.

———. *The Future of Interpreting: Owning the Process,* 2014. http://www.gallaudet.edu/tedx/presenters/boudreault.html.

Bourdieu, Pierre. *Language and Symbolic Power*. Cambridge, MA: Harvard University Press, 1991.

Boutin, Daniel. "Persistence in Postsecondary Environments of Students with Hearing Impairments." *Journal of Rehabilitation* 74, no. 1 (2008): 25–31.

Bowen-Bailey, Doug, and Trudy Suggs. "To Lead or Not to Lead: Sharing Power in the Field of Interpreting." *RID Views* 31, no. 2 (Spring/Summer 2015): 28–29.

Brasel, Barbara. "The Effects of Fatigue on the Competence of Interpreters for the Deaf." In *Selected Readings in the Integration of Deaf Students at C.S.U.N.* (#1), edited by Harry J. Murphy. Northridge, CA: California State University, 1976.

Bridges, Byron. "How can Interpreters Stay Invisible?" December 30, 2013. https://www.facebook.com/bridgesbyron/videos/10152110551654165/.

Bridges, Byron, and Melanie Metzer. *Deaf Tend Your: Non-manual Signs in ASL*. Pittsburgh, PA: Calliope Press, 1996.

Brown, Brene. *Daring Greatly: How the Courage to Be Vulnerable Transforms the Way We Live, Love, Parent, and Lead.* New York: Avery, 2012: 45.

Bruce, Jackie. "A Comparative Study of Backchanneling Signals between an African American Deaf Speaker and African American and White Deaf Speakers." *Communication Forum*, edited by Elizabeth A. Winston. Washington, DC: Gallaudet University Press (1993): 1–10.

Bug. "Should We Trust Interpreters?" *Fookem and Bug*. Accessed June 1, 2017. http://fookembug.wordpress.com/2007/02/26/should-we-trust-interpreters/.

Cagle, Keith. *1000 ASL Faces*. [CD-ROMs] Austin, TX: Signs of Development, 2000.

Camarota, Steven A., and Karen Ziegler. *S. Immigrants in the United States: Profile of the Foreign-born Using 2014 and 2015 Census Bureau Data.* Washington, DC: Center for Immigration Studies, 2016. https://cis.org/Immigrants-United-States#frontpage.

Campbell, Linda, Meg J. Rohan, and Kathryn Woodcock. "Academic and Educational Interpreting from the Other Side of the Classroom: Working with Deaf Academics." In *Deaf Professionals and Designated Interpreters: A New Paradigm*, edited by Peter C. Hauser, Karen L. Finch, and Angela B. Hauser. Washington, DC: Gallaudet University Press (2008): 81–105.

Castelfranchi, Cristano, and Rino Falcone. *Trust Theory: A Socio-cognitive and Computational Model.* West Sussex, UK: Wiley & Sons, 2010.

Castells, Manuel, Mireia Fernandez-Ardevol, Jack Linchuan Qui, and Araba Sey. *Mobile Communication and Society: A Global Perspective.* Cambridge, MA: MIT Press, 2006.

Cawthon, Stephanie W. "National Survey for Accommodations and Alternate Assessments for Students Who are Deaf or Hard of Hearing in the United States." *Journal of Deaf Studies and Deaf Education* 11, no. 3 (2006): 337–59.

Cerney, Brian. *Relay Interpretation.* Accessed June 1, 2017. http://www.handandmind.org/CerneyDissertation.pdf.

Charmaz, Kathy. *Constructing Grounded Theory: A Practical Guide Through Qualitative Analysis.* London: SAGE, 2006.

Christensen, Christian. "Twitter Revolutions? Addressing Social Media and Dissent." *The Communication Review* 14, no. 3 (2011): 155–57.

Cialdini, Robert. *Influence: The Psychology of Persuasion, Revised Edition.* New York: HarperCollins Publishers, 2007: 220–35.

Claussen, Roger. "Movie Caption Survey." YouTube video, March 18, 2013, 10:08. https://www.youtube.com/watch?v=FQ1JHyP_jYE.

Clouet, Richard. "Intercultural Language Learning: Cultural Mediation within the Curriculum of Translation and Interpreting Studies." *Iberica,* 16 (2008): 147–68.

Cogen, Cathy, and Dennis Cokely. *Preparing Interpreters for Tomorrow: Report on a Study of Emerging Trends in Interpreting and Implications for Interpreter Education.* Boston: National Interpreter Education Center at Northeastern University, 2015.

Cokely, Dennis. "Curriculum Revision in the Twenty First Century: Northeastern's Experience." In *Advances in Teaching Sign Language Interpreters*, edited by Cynthia Roy. Washington, DC: Gallaudet University Press (2005): 1–21.

———. "Shifting Positionality: A Critical Examination of the Turning Point in the Relationship of Interpreters and the Deaf Community." In *Sign Language Interpreting and Interpreter Education*, edited by Marc Marschark, Rico Peterson, and Elizabeth Winston. New York: Oxford University Press (2005): 3–28.

Cokely, Dennis, and Anna Witter-Merithew. "Interpreter Education: History is a Relentless Master." *Street Leverage*, January 21, 2015. http://www.streetleverage.com/2015/01/interpreter-education-history-is-a-relentless-master/.

———. "Interpreter Education: History is a Relentless Master." *Street Leverage*, January 21, 2015. http://www.streetleverage.com/2015/01/interpreter-education-history-is-a-relentless-master/.

Cokely, Dennis, and Charlotte Baker. *American Sign Language: A Teacher's Resource Text on Grammar and Culture.* Silver Spring, MD: T.J. Publishers, 1980.

Cokely, Dennis, and Jennifer Hawkins. "Interpreting in Teams: A Pilot Study on Requesting and Offering Support." *Journal of Interpretation* 14, (2003): 49–94.

Commission of Education of the Deaf. *Toward Equality: Education of the Deaf.* Washington, DC: U.S. Government Printing Office, 1988.

Cook, Amy. "Neutrality? No Thanks. Can a Biased Role Be an Ethical One?" *Journal of Interpretation* 15, (2004): 19–56.

Corker, Marian. "Deaf People and Interpreting: The Struggle in Language." *Deaf Worlds* 13, no. 3 (1987): 13–20.

Creswell, John. *Qualitative Inquiry & Research Design: Choosing Among Five Approaches.* London: SAGE, 2013.

Davis, Jeff. "Code Choices and Consequences: Implications for Educational Interpreting." In *Educational Interpreting: From Research to Practice*, edited by Marc Marschark, Rico Peterson, and Elizabeth Winston. New York: Oxford University Press (2005): 112–41.

Davis, Jeff, and David Supalla. "A Sociolinguistic Description of Sign Language Use in a Navajo Family." In *Sociolinguistics in Deaf Communities,* edited by Ceil Lucas. Washington, DC: Gallaudet University, 1995.

Davis, Jeffrey, Tan Fried, Cindy Herbst, Eileen McCaffrey, Charlotte Toothman, and Tracy S. Clark. "Mentorship: A True Course in Collaboration—the RITC Region IX Mentorship Program." *Mapping Our Course: A Collaborative Venture—Proceedings of the 10th National Convention of the Conference of Interpreter Trainers.* Charlotte, NC: CIT Publications (1994): 129–43.

De Meulder, Maartje. "'Are you friends with the deaf person?' (Net)working with sign language interpreters in academic settings." *Pigs Can Fly: A Weblog by Maartje De Meulder.* July 12, 2017. https://pigscanfly.blog/2017/07/12/are-you-friends-with-the-deaf-person-networking-with-sign-language-interpreters-in-academic-settings/.

Dean, Robyn K., and Robert Q Pollard. "The Application of Demand-Control Theory to Sign Language Interpreting: Implications for Stress and Interpreter Training." *Journal of Deaf Studies and Deaf Education* 6, no. 1 (2001): 1–14.

———. "Community Interpreting as a Practice Profession: A Meta-Ethical Analysis." In *Foundations of Interpreting for the 21st Century*, edited by Len Roberson and Sherry Shaw. Washington, DC: Gallaudet University Press, forthcoming.

Del Vecchio, Silvia, Marcello Cardarelli, Fabiana De Simone, and Giulia Petitta. "Interacting with Participants Outside of Interpretation." In *Signed Language Interpretation and Translation Research*, edited by Brenda Nicodemus and Keith Cagle. Washington, DC: Gallaudet University Press (2015): 24–48.

Delk, Linda. "Interpreter Mentoring: A Theory-Based Approach to Program Design and Evaluation." February 2013.,http://www.interpretereducation.org/wp-content/uploads/2013/03/Interpreter_Mentoring_Theory_of_Change_for_Program_Monitoring_and_Evaluation.pdf.

Dickinson, Jules. *Sign Language Interpreting in the Workplace.* Washington, DC: Gallaudet University Press, 2017.

Distance Opportunities for Interpreters and Teachers. "States that Require or Accept the EIPA: Summary." January, 2015, http://www.unco.edu/cebs/asl-interpreting/pdf/osep-project/eipa-data-summary.pdf.

Doughten, Susan D., Marlyn B. Minkin, and Laurie E. Rosen. *Signs for Sexuality: A Resource Manual for Teachers, Counselors, Interpreters, Parents, and Hearing Impaired Persons Concerned with Deafness and Human Sexuality.* Seattle, WA: Planned Parenthood, 1978.

Downing, Bruce, and Karin Ruschke. "Professionalizing Healthcare Interpreting between Spoken Languages: Contributions of the National Council on Interpreting in Health Care." In *In Our Hands: Educating Healthcare Interpreters,* edited by Laurie Swabey and Karen Malcolm. Washington, DC: Gallaudet University Press (2012): 209–28.

Drolsbaugh, Mark. *Madness in the Mainstream.* Spring House, PA: Handwave Publications, 2013.

Dudis, Paul. "Body Partitioning and Real-Space Blends." *Cognitive Linguistics* 15, no. 2 (2004): 223–38.

Eagly, Alice, and Shelly Chaiken. "The Advantages of an Inclusive Definition of Attitude." *Social Cognition* 25, no. 5 (2007): 582–602.

Edwards, Rosalind, Claire Alexander, and Bogusia Temple. "Interpreting Trust: Abstract and Personal Trust for People Who Need Interpreters to Access Services." *Sociological Research Online* 11, no. 1 (2006). Accessed April 8, 2017, http://www.socresonline.org.uk/11/1/edwards.html.

Elliott, Marlene. *Sign Language Interpreters and the Quest for Cultural Competence.* http://www.streetleverage.com/2013/12/sign-language-interpreters-and-the-quest-forculturalcompetence.

Elliott, Marlene, and Wyatte C. Hall. "Creating Deaf Hearts: Using Popular Education with Interpreting Students." *2014 Conference of Interpreter Trainers*, October 30, 2014.

Elmer, L. A. "What is a Good Interpreter?" *American Annals of the Deaf* 93, no. 5 (1948): 545–46.

Eltantawy, Nahed, and Julie B. Wiest. "The Arab Spring: Social Media in the Egyptian Revolution: Reconsidering Resource Mobilization Theory." *International Journal of Communication* 5, no. 1 (2011): 1207–24.

Erting, Carol J., Robert C. Johnson, Dorothy L. Smith, and Bruce N. Sniders. *The Deaf Way: Perspectives from the International Conference on Deaf Culture.* Washington, DC: Gallaudet University Press, 1996.

Fant, Lou. *Silver Threads: A Personal Look at the First Twenty-Five Years of the Registry of Interpreters for the Deaf.* Silver Spring, MD: RID Publications, 1990.

Floyd, Carol Beth. "Critical Thinking in a Second Language." *Higher Education Research & Development* 30, no. 3 (2011): 289–302.

Forestal, Eileen. "Deaf Interpreters: Exploring Their Processes of Interpreting." Ph.D diss., Capella University, 2011.

———. *Deaf Interpreters: Shaping the Future of the Profession.* Paper presented at StreetLeverage—Live 2014 Conference, Austin, TX. May, 4, 2014. http://www.streetleverage.com/2015/02/deaf-interpreters-shaping-the-future-of-the-sign-language-interpreting-profession/.

———. "Deaf Perspectives in Interpretation Research: A Critical Element Long Overdue." *Signed Language Interpretation and Translation Research*, edited by Brenda Nicodemus and Keith Cagle. Washington, DC: Gallaudet University Press (2015): 1–23.

———. "Foreword." *Service Learning in Interpreter Education: Strategies for Extending Student Involvement in the Deaf Community.* Washington, DC: Gallaudet University Press (2013): ix–x.

Forestal, Eileen, and Stephanie Clark. "The Teaming Model and Transparency for Deaf and Hearing Team Interpreters: Who Owns the Interpretation?" Paper presented at the 2014 Conference of Interpreter Trainers, Portland, OR. October 31, 2014.

Foster, Susan. "Factors Influencing the Academic and Social Integration of Hearing Impaired College Students." *Journal of Postsecondary Education and Disability* 7, no. 1 (1989): 226–35.

Foster, Susan, Gary Long, and Karen Snell. "Inclusive Instruction and Learning for Deaf Students in Postsecondary Education." *Journal of Deaf Studies and Deaf Education* 4, no. 3 (1999): 225–35.

Freed, Rachel. "The Importance of Telling Our Stories." *The Blog: Huffington Post,* November 17, 2011. http://www.huffingtonpost.com/rachael-freed/legacy-telling-our-story_b_776195.html.

Freire, Paulo. *Pedagogy of the Oppressed.* New York: Herder and Herder, 1972.

Fung, Archon. "Deliberation's Darker Side: Six Questions for Iris Marion Young and Jane Mansbridge." *National Civic Review* 93, no. 1 (2004): 49.

Garate, Maribel. "A Case Study of an In-Service Professional Development Model on Bilingual Deaf Education: Changes in Teachers' Stated Beliefs and Classroom Practices." Ph.D diss., Gallaudet University, 2007.

Garrett, Peter. *Attitudes to Language.* Cambridge UK: Cambridge University Press, 2010.

Gee, James P. *An Introduction to Discourse Analysis: Theory and Method.* Abingdon, UK: Routledge, 2014.

Gee, James Paul, and Judy Kegl. "Narrative/story Structure, Pausing, and American Sign Language." *Discourse Processes* 6, no. 1 (1983): 243–58.

Glaser, Barney G., and Anselm L. Strauss. "The Discovery of Grounded Theory: Strategies for Qualitative Theory." *Nursing Research* 17, no. 4 (1968): 364.

Grieve, Rachel, Michaelle Indian, Kate Witteveen, Anne G. Tolan, and Jessica Marrington. "Face-to-Face or Facebook: Can Social Connectedness Be Derived Online?" *Computers in Human Behavior* 29, no. 3 (2013): 604–9.

Gundlach, Gregory T., and Joseph P. Cannon. " 'Trust But Verify?' The Performance Implications of Verification Strategies in Trusting Relationships." *Journal of the Academy of Marketing Science* 38, no. 4 (2010): 399–417.

Hall, Edward T. *Beyond Culture*. New York, NY: Anchor Books, 1976.

Hall, Wyatte C., Thomas K. Holcomb, and Marlene Elliott. "Using Popular Education with the Oppressor Class: Suggestions for Sign Language Interpreter Education." *Critical Education* 7, no. 13 (2016): 1–18.

Harmer, Lisa. "Health Care Delivery and Deaf People: Practice, Problems, and Recommendations for Change." *Journal of Deaf Studies and Deaf Education* 4, no. 2 (1999): 73–110.

Harrington, Tom. *Deaf Statistics*. Washington, DC: Gallaudet University Library, 2014. http://libguides.gallaudet.edu/content.php?pid=119476&sid=1029190.

Harris, Raychelle. "Sign Language as Academic Language." In *The Sage Deaf Studies Encyclopedia*, edited by Genie Gertz and Patrick Boudreault. Thousand Oaks, CA: SAGE (2016): 829–32.

Hauser, Angela, and Peter Hauser. "The Deaf Professional-designated Interpreter Model." In *Deaf Professionals and Designated Interpreters: A New Paradigm*, edited by Peter C. Hauser, Karen L. Finch, and Angela B. Hauser. Washington, DC: Gallaudet University Press, 2008: 3–21.

Hedding, Teri, and Gary Kaufman. "Health Literacy and Deafness: Implications for Interpreter Education." In *In Our Hands: Educating Healthcare Interpreters*, edited by Laurie Swabey and Karen Malcolm. Washington, DC: Gallaudet University Press (2012): 164–89.

Higginbotham, Evelyn Brooks. *Righteous Discontent: The Women's Movement in the Black Baptist Church, 1880–1920*. Cambridge, Mass.: Harvard University Press, 1993.

Hofstede, Geert. *Culture's Consequences: Comparing Values, Behaviors, Institutions and Organizations Across Nations, 2nd ed.* Thousand Oaks, CA: Sage Publications, 2001.

Holcomb, Thomas K. *Introduction to American Deaf Culture*. New York: Oxford University Press, 2013.

Holcomb, Thomas K., and Anna Mindess. *A Sign of Respect: Strategies for Effective Deaf/hearing Interactions* [DVD/Workbook Set]. San Francisco: Eye2eye Productions, 2016.

———. *See What I Mean: Differences Between Deaf and Hearing Cultures*. [DVD]. San Francisco: Eye2eye Productions, 2001.

Howard, Nigel. *Deaf & Hearing Worlds: Enculturation and Acculturation*. Plenary Presentation Conference of Interpreter Trainers. Portland, OR. November 1, 2014. http://www.streetleverage.com/cit-2014-plenary-deaf-hearing-worlds-enculturation-and-acculturation/

Hoy, Wayne K., and Megan Tschannen-Moran. "Five Faces of Trust: An Empirical Confirmation in Urban Elementary Schools." *Journal of School Leadership* 9, no. 3 (1999): 184–208.

Hoza, Jack. "Saving Face: The Interpreter and Politeness." *Journal of Interpretation* 10, no. 1 (1999): 39–68.

———. *Team Interpreting as Collaboration and Interdependence*. Alexandria, VA: RID Press, 2010.

Hsieh, Elaine. "Emerging Trends and the Corresponding Challenges in Bilingual Health Communication." In *Investigations in Healthcare Interpreting*, edited by Brenda Nicodemus and Melanie Metzger. Washington, DC: Gallaudet University Press (2014): 70–103.

Hsieh, Hsiu-Fang, and Sarah E. Shannon. "Three Approaches to Qualitative Content Analysis." *Qualitative Health Research*, 15, no. 9 (2005): 1277–88.

Humphrey, Janice H., and Bob J. Alcorn. *So You Want to Be an Interpreter?: An Introduction to Sign Language Interpreting*. Clearwater, FL: H & H Publishing Company, 2007: 325.

Iezzoni, Lisa, Bonnie L. O'Day, Mary Killeen, and Heather Harker. "Communicating about Health Care: Observations from Persons Who are Deaf or Hard of Hearing." *Annals of Internal Medicine* 140, no. 5 (2004): 356–62.

Jacobs, Rhonda. "Just How Hard Is It to Learn ASL? The Case for ASL as a Truly Foreign Language." In *Multicultural Aspects of Sociolinguistics in Deaf Communities*, edited by Ceil Lucas. Washington, DC: Gallaudet University Press (1996): 83–226.

Jankowski, Katherine A. *Deaf Empowerment: Emergence, Struggle, and Rhetoric.* Washington, DC: Gallaudet University Press, 1997: 147.

Janzen, Terry, and Donna Korpiniski. "Ethics and Professionalism in Interpreting." In *Topics in Signed Language Interpreting,* edited by Terry Janzen. Amsterdam, The Netherlands: Benjamins (2005): 165–99.

Johnson, Robert, Scott Liddell, and Carol Erting. *Unlocking the Curriculum: Principles for Achieving Access in Deaf Education.* Washington, DC: Gallaudet Research Institute, 1989.

Johnson, William L., and Michael Feuerstein. "An Interpreter's Interpretation: Sign Language Interpreters' View of Musculoskeletal Disorders." *Journal of Occupational Rehabilitation* 15, no. 3 (2005): 401–15.

Jones, Bernhardt. "Competencies of K–12 Educational Interpreters: What We Need Versus What We Have." In *Educational Interpreting: How It Can Succeed,* edited by Elizabeth Winston. Washington, DC; Gallaudet University Press (2005): 113–31.

Jones, Bernhardt E., Gary M. Clark, and Donald F. Soltz. "Characteristics and Practices of Sign Language Interpreters in Inclusive Education Programs." *Exceptional Children* 63, no. 2 (1997): 257–68.

Joos, Martin. *The Five Clocks: A Linguistic Excursion into The Five Styles of English Usage.* New York: Harcourt, Brace & World, 1967.

Jurgenson, Nathan. "When Atoms Meet Bits: Social Media, the Mobile Web and Augmented Revolution." *Future Internet* 4, no. 1 (2012): 83–91.

Katan, David. *Translating Cultures: An Introduction for Translators, Interpreters and Mediators, 2nd ed.* Brooklands, Manchester, United Kingdom: St. Jerome Publishing, 2004.

Kent, Stephanie Jo. "Deaf Voice and the Invention of Community Interpreting." *Journal of Interpretation* 22, no.1 (2012): 3.

———. "Why Bother? Institutionalization, Interpreter Decisions, and Power Relations." In *The Critical Link 4: Professionalisation of Interpreting in the Community: International Conference on Interpreting in Legal, Health and Social Service Settings,* edited by Cecilia Wadensjö, Birgitta Englund-Dimitrova, and Anna-Lena Nilsson. Amsterdam, the Netherlands: Benjamins (2007): 193–204.

Kleinfield, Mala S., and Noni Warner. "Variations in the Deaf Community: Gay, Lesbian, and Bisexual Signs." In *Multicultural Aspects of Sociolinguistics in Deaf Communities*, edited by Ceil Lucas. Washington, DC: Gallaudet University Press, 1996.

Klopprogge, Nadia, and Emily Malkin. "Trust But Verify: Confidence and Distrust from Détente to the End of the Cold War." *Bulletin of the German Historical Institute,* 50(2012): 150–55.

Kondo, Masaomi, Helen Tebble, Bistra Alexieva, Helle V. Dam, David Katan, Akira Mizuno, Robin Setton, and Ilona Zalk. "Intercultural Communication, Negotiation, and Interpreting." *Conference Interpreting: Current Trends in Research*, edited by Yves Gambier, Daniel Gile, and Christopher Taylor. Amsterdam: Benjamins (1997): 149–66.

Kurz, Kim Brown, and Elisabeth Caldwell Langer. "Student Perspectives on Educational Interpreting: Twenty Deaf and Hard of Hearing Students Offer Insights and Suggestions." *Educational Interpreting: How It Can Succeed,* edited by Elizabeth Winston. Washington, DC: Gallaudet University Press (2004): 9–47.

Kusters, Annelies, and Maartje De Meulder. "Understanding Deafhood: In Search of Its Meanings." *American Annals of the Deaf*, 158, no. 5 (2013): 428.

Labath, Judith. "Features at Discourse Boundaries in American Sign Language Narratives." *Journal of Interpretation*, 16, no. 1 (2005): 65–78.

Ladd, Paddy. *Understanding Deaf Culture: In Search of Deafhood.* Tonawanda, NY: Multilingual Matters Ltd., 2003.

Lane, Harlan L., Robert Hoffmeister, and Benjamin J. Bahan. *A Journey into the Deaf-World.* San Diego, CA: Dawn Sign Press, 1996.

Lang, Harry G. "Higher Education for Deaf Students: Research Priorities in the New Millennium." *Journal of Deaf Studies and Deaf Education,* 7, no. 4 (2002): 267–80.

———. "Perspectives on the History of Deaf Education." *Oxford Handbook of Deaf Studies, Language, and Education,* edited by Mark Marschark and Patricia Elizabeth Spencer. New York, NY: Oxford University Press (2003): 9–20.

Langer, Elizabeth Caldwell. "Classroom Discourse and Interpreted Education: What is Conveyed to Deaf Elementary School Students." Ph.D diss., University of Colorado at Boulder, 2007.

Lawrence, Shelly. "Interpreter Discourse: English to ASL Expansion." *Mapping Our Course: A Collaborative Venture. Proceedings of the Tenth National Convention of the Conference of Interpreter Trainers*, edited by Elizabeth A. Winston.

Leeson, Lorraine, and Susan Foley-Cave. "Deep and Meaningful Conversation: Challenging Interpreter Impartiality in the Semantics and Pragmatics Classroom." *Translation, Sociolinguistic, and Consumer Issues in Interpreting,* edited by Melanie Metzger and Earl Fleetwood. Washington, DC: Gallaudet University Press (2007): 45–68.

Liang, Ting-Peng, Yi-Ting Ho, Yu-Wen Li, and Efraim Turban. "What Drives Social Commerce: The Role of Social Support and Relationship Quality." *International Journal of Electronic Commerce* 16, no. 2 (2011): 69–90.

Liddell, Scott K. *Grammar, Gesture, and Meaning in American Sign Language.* Cambridge, UK: Cambridge University Press, 2003.

Linck, Jared A., et al. "Working Memory and Second Language Comprehension and Production: A Meta-Analysis." *Psychonomic Bulletin & Review* 21, no. 4 (2014): 861–83.

Llewellyn-Jones, Peter, and Robert Lee. "Getting to the Core of Role: Defining Interpreters' Role Space." *International Journal of Interpreter Education* 5, no. 2 (2013): 54–72.

Lott, Sharon. *Get Grip on Fingerspelling.* Land O'Sky NCRID Workshop. Asheville, North Carolina, 2010.

Lukomski, Jennifer. "Deaf College Students' Perceptions of Their Social–Emotional Adjustment." *Journal of Deaf Studies and Deaf Education* 12, no. 4 (2007): 486–94.

Lummer, Lewis. *Teachers' Perceptions of the Academic and Language Needs of Deaf Immigrant Students: An Exploratory Survey.* Master's thesis. Beaumont, TX: Lamar University, 1999.

Lummer, Lewis, and Cynthia Plue. *Deaf Immigrants' Perspectives of Interpreter Services Panel Session.* Interpreter Workshop Series. Aurora, IL: Waubonsee Community College, 2000.

MacIntyre, Peter D., and Robert C. Gardner. "The Effects of Induced Anxiety on Three Stages of Cognitive Processing in Computerized Vocabulary Learning." *Studies in Second Language Acquisition* 16, no. 1 (1994): 1–17.

Maclaughlin, Dawn, Carol Neidle, and David Greenfield. SignStream™ User's Guide. Version 2.0. American Sign Language Linguistic Research Project, 2000. www.bu.edu/us/asllrp/signstream /index.html.

Major, George. "Sorry Could You Explain That? Clarification Requests in Interpreter Mediated Healthcare Interaction." *Investigations in Healthcare Interpreting*, edited by Brenda Nicodemus and Melanie Metzger. Washington, DC: Gallaudet University Press (2014): 32–69.

Mance, Ina. *Deafblind People and Self-Identity*. Herlev, Denmark: Information Center for Acquired Deafblindess, 2008. http://www.deafblindinternational.org/Docs/Review%20Archive/Deafblind%20People%20and%20self%20identity.pdf.

Manjoo, Farhad. "Exposing Hidden Bias at Google." *New York Times*, September 24, 2014. https://www.nytimes.com/2014/09/25/technology/exposing-hidden-biases-at-google-to-improve-diversity.html.

Marschark, Marc, Harry G. Lang, and John A. Albertini. *Educating Deaf Students: From Research to Practice*. New York, NY: Oxford University Press, 2001.

Marschark, Marc, Patricia Sapere, Carol Convertino, and Rosemarie Seewagen. "Access to Post-secondary Education through Sign Language Interpreting." *Journal of Deaf Studies and Deaf Education* 10, no. 1 (2005): 38–50.

———. "Educational Interpreting: Access and Outcomes." *Sign Language Interpreting and Interpreter Education: Directions for Research and Practice*, eds. Marc Marschark, Rico Peterson, and Elizabeth A. Winston. New York, NY: Oxford University Press (2005): 57–83.

Marschark, Marc, Patricia Sapere, and Rosemarie Seewagen. "Preface." *Sign Language Interpreting and Interpreter Education: Directions for Research and Practice*, edited by Marc Marschark, Rico Peterson, and Elizabeth Winston. New York: Oxford University Press, 2005: v–x.

Marschark, Marc, Rico Peterson, and Elizabeth A. Winston. *Sign Language Interpreting and Interpreter Education: Directions for Research and Practice*. Oxford University Press, 2005.

Mather, Susan A. "Eye Gaze & Communication in a Deaf Classroom." *Sign Language Studies* 54, no. 1 (1987): 11–30.

Matsick, Jes L., and Terri D. Conley. "Maybe I Do, Maybe I Don't: Respectability Politics in the Same-Sex Marriage Ruling." *Analyses of Social Issues and Public Policy* 15, no. 1 (2015): 409–413.

Mayan, Maria. *Essentials of Qualitative Inquiry*. Walnut Creek, CA: Left Coast Press, 2009.

Mayberry, Rachel, and Elizabeth Lock. "Age Constraints on First versus Second Language Acquisition: Evidence for Linguistic Plasticity and Epigenesis." *Brain and Language* 87, no. 3 (2003): 369–84.

Mayberry, Rachel, and Ellen Eichen. "The Long-Lasting Advantage of Learning Sign Language in Childhood: Another Look at the Critical Period for Language Acquisition." *Journal of Memory and Language* 30, no. 4 (1991): 486–512.

McCall, Leslie. "The Complexity of Intersectionality." *Signs: Journal of Women in Culture and Society* 30, no. 3 (2005): 1771–800.

McDermid, Campbell. "Social Construction of American Sign Language—English Interpreters." *Journal of Deaf Studies and Deaf Education* 14, no. 1 (2008): 105–30.

McDermid, Campbell, Lynnette Finton, and Alexis Chasney. "Contextualized Recognition of Fingerspelled Words." *Journal of Interpretation* 25, no.1 (2016): 1–23.

McIntire, Marina L., and Gary R. Sanderson. "Who's in Charge Here? Perceptions of Empowerment and Role in the Interpreting Setting." *RID Journal of Interpretation* 7, no. 1 (1995): 99–109.

McKay-Cody, Melanie. "Well-Hidden People in Deaf and Native Communities." *The Deaf American Monograph Series*, edited by Merv Garretson. Silver Spring, MD: NAD Publications, 1999.

Méndez, Mariza. "Autoethnography as a Research Method: Advantages, Limitations and Criticisms." *Colombia Applied Linguist Journal* 15, no. 2 (June–December 2013): 282.

Mesch, Johanna, and World Federation of the Deaf. "Perspectives on the Concept and Definition of International Sign." May 2010. https://www.diva-portal.org/smash/get/diva2:683050/FULLTEXT01.pdf.

Metzger, Melanie. "Constructed Dialogue and Constructed Action in American Sign Language." *Sociolinguistics in Deaf Communities*, edited by Ceil Lucas. Washington, DC: Gallaudet University Press (1995): 255–71.

——. *Sign Language Interpreting: Deconstructing the Myth of Neutrality*. Washington, DC: Gallaudet University Press, 1999.

Mickelson, Paula L. Gajewski. "Intentional Teaming: Experiences from the Second National Healthcare Symposium." *Journal of Interpretation* 24, no. 1 (2015): 5.

Middleton, Anna. *Working with Deaf People: Handbook for Health Professionals*. Cambridge, UK: Cambridge University Press, 2010.

Mindess, Anna, Thomas K. Holcomb, Daniel Langholtz, and Priscilla Poyner. *Reading Between the Signs*. Boston: Intercultural Press, 2014.

Miner, Annette. "Designated Interpreters: An Examination of Roles, Relationships, and Responsibilities." *Signed Language Interpretation and Translation Research*, edited by Brenda Nicodemus and Keith Cagle. Washington, DC: Gallaudet University Press, 2015: 196–211.

Mitchell, Ross E., and Michael A. Karchmer. "Chasing the Mythical Ten Percent: Parental Hearing Status of Deaf and Hard of Hearing Students in the United States." *Sign Language Studies* 4, no. 2 (2004): 138–163.

MLA Committee on Disability Issues in the Profession. *Disability and Hiring: Guidelines for Departmental Search Committees*. Modern Language Association, 2006. Accessed January 17, 2017. http://mla.devtc.net/Resources/Career-Center/Career-Resources/The-Job-Search-Information-for-Job-Seekers-and-Hiring-Departments/Disability-and-Hiring-Guidelines-for-Departmental-Search-Committees.

Monikowski, Christine. "Language Myths in Interpreted Education: First Language, Second Language, What Language?" *Educational Interpreting: How It Can Succeed,* edited by Elizabeth Winston. Washington, DC; Gallaudet University Press (2005): 48–60.

Monikowski, Christine, and Rico Peterson. "Service-learning Interpreting Education: Living and Learning." *Sign Language Interpreting and Interpreter Education: Directions for Research and Practice*, edited by Marc Marschark, Rico Peterson, and Elizabeth A. Winston. New York: Oxford University Press (2005): 188–207.

Moody, Bill. "Literal vs. Liberal: What is a Faithful Interpretation?" *Journal of Interpretation* 18, no. 1 (2007): 179–220.

——. "What is a Faithful Interpretation?" *Journal of Interpretation* 21, no. 1 (2011).

Morgan, Elizabeth F. "Interpreters, Conversational Style, and Gender at Work." *Deaf Professionals and Designated Interpreters* Edited by Peter C. Hauser, Karen L. Finch, and Angela B. Hauser. Washington, DC: Gallaudet University Press.

Moxham, Tamara. *Deaf Patients, Hearing Medical Personnel: Interpreting and Other Considerations*. Hillsboro, OR: Butte Publications, 2005.

Myers, Mark J., and E. M. Taylor. "Best Practices for Deaf and Hard-of-Hearing Student Success in Postsecondary Education." *JADARA–Rochester NY* 34, no. 1 (2001): 13–28.

Napier, Jemina. "'It's Not What They Say but the Way They Say It.' A Content Analysis of Interpreter and Consumer Perceptions of Signed Language Interpreting in Australia." *International Journal of the Sociology of Language,* no. 207 (2011): 59–87.

Napier, Jemina, Andy Carmichael, and Andrew Wiltshire. "Look-Pause-Nod: A Linguistic Case Study of a Deaf Professional and Interpreters Working Together." *Deaf Professionals and Designated Interpreters: A New Paradigm,* edited by Peter C. Hauser, Karen L. Finch, and Angela B. Hauser. Washington, DC: Gallaudet University Press (2008): 22–42.

Napier, Jemina, and Joseph Sabolcec. "Direct, Translated or Interpreter-mediated? A Qualitative Study of Access to Preventive and On-going Healthcare Information for Australian Deaf

People." *Investigations in Healthcare Interpreting,* edited by Brenda Nicodemus and Melanie Metzger. Washington, DC: Gallaudet University Press (2014): 239.

Napier, Jemina, and Meg J. Rohan. "An Invitation to Dance: Deaf Consumers' Perceptions of Signed Language Interpreters and Interpreting." *Translation, Sociloinguistic, and Consumer Issues in Interpreting,* edited by Melanie Metzger and Earl Fleetwood. Washington, DC: Gallaudet University Press (2007): 159–203.

Napier, Jemina, Rachel Locker McKee, and Della Goswell. *Sign Language Interpreting: Theory and Practice in Australia and New Zealand.* Annandale, N.S.W., Australia: Federation Press, 2006.

National Association of the Deaf. "Advocacy Statement: Use of VRI in the Medical Setting." Silver Spring, MD: National Association of the Deaf, 2008. https://www.nad.org/resources/technology/video-remote-interpreting/advocacy-statement-use-of-vri-in-the-medical-setting/.

———. *Hospitals and Other Health Care Facilities.* Silver Spring, MD: National Association of the Deaf. https://www.nad.org/resources/health-care-and-mental-health-services/health-care-providers/hospitals-and-other-health-care-facilities/.

———. *Legal Rights: The Guide for Deaf and Hard of Hearing People.* Washington, DC: Gallaudet University Press, 2000.

———. *Position Statement Supplement: Culturally Affirmative and Linguistically Accessible Mental Health Services.* Silver Spring, MD: National Association of the Deaf, 2008. https://www.nad.org/resources/health-care-and-mental-health-services/mental-health-services/culturally-affirmative-and-linguistically-accessible-services/.

National Consortium of Deaf-Blindness. *The 2007 National Child Count of Children and Youth who are Deaf-Blind.* Sands Points, NY: *The National Consortium on Deaf-Blindness*, 2008. http://documents.nationaldb.org/products/2007-Census-Tables.pdf.

Newell, William. *Basic Sign Communication: Student Workbook.* Silver Spring, MD: National Association of the Deaf, 1983.

Nicodemus, Brenda. *Prosodic Markers and Utterance Boundaries in American Sign Language Interpretation.* Washington, DC: Gallaudet University Press, 2009.

Nicodemus, Brenda, and Melanie Metzger. *Investigations in Healthcare Interpreting.* Washington, DC: Gallaudet University Press, 2014.

Nielsen-Bohlman, Lynn, Allison M. Panzer, and David A. Kindig. *Health Literacy: A Prescription to End Confusion.* Washington, DC: National Academies, 2004.

Northern California Registry of Interpreters for the Deaf. "Recommendations for Agencies Providing ASL Interpreting Services." Accessed June 5, 2017. https://www.norcrid.org/resources/Documents/Recommendations_for_Agencies_providing_ASL_services.pdf.

Oliva, Gina A. *Alone in the Mainstream: A Deaf Woman Remembers Public School.* Washington, DC: Gallaudet University Press, 2004.

Oliva, Gina A., and Linda Risser Lytle. *Turning the Tide: Making Life Better for Deaf and Hard of Hearing Schoolchildren.* Washington, DC: Gallaudet University Press, 2014.

Olson, Andrea, and Laurie Swabey. "Communication Access for Deaf People in Healthcare Settings: Understanding the Work of American Sign Language Interpreters." *Journal for Healthcare Quality* 39, no. 4 (2017): 191–99.

Padden, Carol. "The Decline of Deaf Clubs in the U.S.: A Treatise on the Problem of Place." *Open Your Eyes: Deaf Studies Talking.* Minneapolis: University of Minnesota Press, 2007.

Padden, Carol, and Tom Humphries. *Deaf in America: Voices from a Culture.* Cambridge, MA: Harvard University Press, 1988.

Patrie, Carol, and Robert Johnson. *Fingerspelled Word Recognition through Rapid Serial Visual Presentation.* San Diego, CA: Dawn Sign Press, 2011.

Pearson, Steven D., and Lisa H. Reake. "Patient's Trust in Physicians: Many Theories, Few Measures, and Little Data." *Journal of General Internal Medicine* 15, no. 7 (2000): 509–13.

Plue, Cynthia. "Deaf Asian/Pacific Island Students: How Can We Enlarge Their Visions and Dreams." *The Deaf American Monograph Series*, edited by Merv Garretson. Silver Spring, MD: National Association of the Deaf, 1998.

———. "A History of Deaf Asians/Pacific Islanders in America." *Deaf Studies VI: Making the Connection.* Conference Proceedings, April 8–11, 1999. Washington, DC: College for Continuing Education, Gallaudet University, 1999.

———. "Multicultural Profiles in the Deaf Community." *Multicultural Review* 12, no. 3 (2003): 48–56.

Pöchhacker, Franz. *Introducing Interpreting Studies.* Abdington, United Kingdom: Routledge, 2003.

Pollard, Robert Q, and Steven Barnett. "Health-related Vocabulary Knowledge Among Deaf Adults." *Rehabilitation Psychology* 54, no. 2 (2009): 182–85.

Pollock, Timothy, and Joyce E. Bono. "Being Scheherazade: The Importance of Storytelling in Academic Writing." *Academy of Management Journal* 56, no. 3 (June 2013): 629.

Quinto-Pozos, David, and Wanette Reynolds. "ASL Discourse Strategies: Chaining and Connecting: Explaining across Audiences." *Sign Language Studies* 12, no. 2 (2012): 211–35.

Ramsey, Claire L. *Deaf Children in Public Schools.* Washington, DC: Gallaudet University Press, 1997.

Ramsey, Franchesca [Chescaleigh]. "5 Tips for Being an Ally." YouTube video: 3:31. https://www.youtube.com/watch?v=_dg86g-QlM0.

Rathmann, Christian, Gaurav Mathur, and Patrick Boudreault. "Amsterdamer Manifest (Amsterdam Manifesto)." *Das Zeichen* 14, no. 54 (2000): 654–65.

Reddy, Michael. "The Conduit Metaphor—A Case of Frame Conflict in Our Language about Language." *Metaphor and Thoughts*, edited by Andrew Ortony. Cambridge: Cambridge University Press (1979): 164–201.

Registry of Interpreters of the Deaf Professional Standards Team. "Team Interpreting." *Standard Practice* Paper. Silver Spring, MD: Registry of Interpreters of the Deaf (2007). Accessed Jan 2, 2017. http://rid.org/about-interpreting/standard-practice-papers/.

Ressler, Carolyn. "Comparative Analysis of a Direct Interpretation and an Intermediary Interpretation in American Sign Language." *Journal of Interpretation* 10, no. 1 (1999): 71–102.

Riahi, Leilani. "Respectability Politics: How 'Activism' Hurts 'Professionalism.'" *Daily Nexus,* University of California Santa Barbara. September 15, 2015. http://dailynexus.com/2015-09-17/respectability-politics-how-activism-hurts-professionalism/.

Richardson, John T. E., Marc Marschark, Thomastine Sarchet, and Patricia Sapere. "Deaf and Hard-of-hearing Students' Experiences in Mainstream and Separate Postsecondary Education." *Journal of Deaf Studies and Deaf Education* 15, no. 4 (2010): 358–82.

Robinson, Brandon Andrew. "Is This What Equality Looks Like?: How Assimilation Marginalizes the Dutch LGBT Community." *Sexuality Research and Social Policy* 9, no. 4 (2012): 327–36.

Ross, Linda L., and Marla C. Berkowitz. "Academic ASL: It Looks Like English, but It Isn't" in *Putting the Pieces Together: Proceedings of the PEPNet Biennial Conference,* edited by Marcia Kolvitz. Knoxville, TN: University of Tennessee (2008): 193–98.

Roy, Cynthia. "Evaluating Performance: An Interpreted Lecture." *New Directions in Interpreter Education: Curriculum & Instruction: Proceedings of the Sixth National Convention of the Conference of Interpreter Trainers*, edited by M. McIntire. Silver Spring, MD: RID Publications (1987): 139–47.

———. "Features of Discourse in an American Sign Language Lecture." In *The Sociolinguistics of the Deaf Community*, edited by C. Lucas. San Diego: Academic Press (1989): 394–408.

———. *Innovative Practices for Teaching Sign Language Interpreters*. Washington, DC: Gallaudet University Press, 2000.

———. "The Problem with Definitions, Descriptions, and the Role Metaphors of Interpreters." 7, no. 1 (1993): 127–54.

———. "A Sociolinguistic Analysis of the Interpreter's Role in the Turn Exchanges of an Interpreted Event." Ph.D diss., Georgetown University, 1989.

Russell, Debra. "Consecutive and Simultaneous Interpreting." *Topics in Signed Language Interpreting: Theory and Practice*, edited by Terry Janzen. Philadelphia: Benjamins (2005): 135–64.

Russell, Debra, and Risa Shaw. "Power and Privilege: An Exploration of Decision-Making of Interpreters." *Journal of Interpretation* 25, no. 1 (2016): 15.

Sandler, Wendy. "Civilization and Prosodic Words in a Sign Language." *Studies on the Phonological Word*, edited by T. Allan Hall & Ursula Kleinhenz. Amsterdam: Benjamins (1999): 223–54.

Santiago, Robert R., and Lisa Frey Barrick. "Handling and Incorporation of Idioms in Interpretation." *Translation, Sociolinguistic, and Consumer Issues in Interpreting*, edited by Melanie Metzger and Earl Fleetwood. Washington, DC: Gallaudet University Press, 2007: 3–44.

Schein, Jerome D. *At Home Among Strangers*. Washington, DC: Gallaudet University Press, 1989.

Schick, Brenda, Kevin Williams, and Haggai Kuppermintz. "Look Who is Being Left Behind: Educational Interpreters and Access to Education for Deaf and Hard-of-Hearing Students." *Journal of Deaf Studies and Deaf Education* 11, no. 1 (2006): 12.

Schweitzer, Maurice E., and Teck H. Ho. "Trust But Verify: Monitoring in Interdependent Relationships." *Experimental and Behavioral Economics*, 13, no. 1 (2005): 87–106.

Scott, George A. "Deaf and Hard of Hearing Children: Federal Support for Developing Language and Literacy." *Report to Congressional Requesters. GAO-11-357*. Washington, DC: U.S. Government Accountability Office, 2011. http://www.gao.gov/assets/320/318711.html.

Sequeiros, Xose' Rosales. "Interlingual Pragmatic Enrichment in Translation." *Journal of Pragmatics* 34, no. 8 (2002): 1069–89.

Shaffer, Laurie, and Wendy Watson. "Peer Mentoring: What is THAT?" *New Designs in Interpreter Education—Proceedings of the 14th National Convention of the Conference of Interpreter Trainers*. Minneapolis/St. Paul, MN: CIT Publications, October 9–12, 2002.

Shalhoub-Kevorkian, Nadera. "E-resistance Among Palestinian Women: Coping in Conflict-Ridden Areas." *The Social Service Review* 85, no. 2 (2011): 179–204.

Shambouger, Nicole. "Navigating Language Variety: ASL/English Interpreters 'Giving Voice' to African American/Black Deaf Signed Language Users." Master's thesis. Monmouth, OR: Western Oregon University, 2015.

Shaver, Debra M., Marc Marschark, Lynn Newman, and Camille Marder. "Characteristics of Deaf and Hard-of-Hearing Students in Regular and Special Schools." *Journal of Deaf Studies and Deaf Education*, 19 (2014): 203–19.

Shaver, Debra, Lynn Newman, Tracy Huang, Jennifer Yu, and Anne-Marie Knokey. "The Secondary School Experiences and Academic Performance of Students with Hearing Impairments. Facts from NLTS2. NCSER 2011-3003." Washington, DC: *National Center for Special Education Research*, 2011.

Shaw, Risa. "Determining Register in Sign-to-English Interpreting." *Sign Language Studies* 57, no. 1 (1987): 295–322.

———. *Meaning in Context: The Role of Context and Language in Narratives of Disclosure of Sibling Sexual Assault*. Cincinnati, OH: Union Institute & University, 2007.

Shaw, Sherry. *Service Learning in Interpreter Education: Strategies for Extending Student Involvement in the Deaf Community*. Washington, DC: Gallaudet University Press, 2013.

Sheneman, Naomi. "Deaf Interpreters' Ethics: Reflections on Training and Decision-Making." *Journal of Interpretation* 25, no. 1 (2016): Article 8.

Shirky, Clay. "The Political Power of Social Media: Technology, the Public Sphere, and Political Change." *Foreign Affairs* (2011): 28–41.

Siple, Linda. "Historical Development of the Definition of Transliteration." *Journal of Interpretation* 10, no. 1 (1997): 77–100.

Smith, Andrea K. "Saving Lives." *Andrea K. Smith, CI, CT, SC: L website.* December 28, 2014. https://www.andreasmithinterpreting.com/saving-lives/.

Smith, David H., and Jean Andrews. "Deaf and Hard of Hearing Faculty in Higher Education: Enhancing Access, Equity, Policy, and Practice." *Disability & Society* 30, no. 10 (2015): 1521–36.

Smith, Jonathan A. ed. "Interpretative Phenomenological Analysis." *Qualitative Psychology: A Practical Guide to Research Methods, 2nd ed.* Thousand Oaks, CA: Sage Publications (2008): 53–80.

Smith, Jonathan A., Paul Flowers, and Michael Larkin. *Interpretative Phenomenological Analysis: Theory, Method and Research.* Thousand Oaks, CA: Sage, 2009.

Smith, Woodruff D. *Consumption and the Making of Respectability, 1600–1800.* New York: Routledge, 2002.

Snidal, Duncan. "The Game Theory of International Politics." *World Politics* 38, no. 1 (1985): 25–57.

Snyder, Thomas D., and Sally A. Dillow. *Digest of Education Statistics 2011.* Washington DC: U.S. Department of Education, National Center for Education Statistics (2012): 61.

Solomon, Caroline, and Jeffrey A. Miller. "Sign Language is Not Performance Art." *The Baltimore Sun*, April 25, 2014. http://articles.baltimoresun.com/2014-04-25/news/bs-ed-media-and-sign-language-20140426_1_american-sign-language-deaf-americans-deaf-people.

Stein, Arthur A. "Coordination and Collaboration: Regimes in an Anarchic World." *International Organization* 36, no. 2 (1982): 299–324.

Steinberg, Annie G., Steven Barnett, Helen E. Meador, Erin A. Wiggins, and Philip Zazove. "Healthcare System Accessibility: Experiences and Perceptions of Deaf People." *Journal of General Internal Medicine* 21, no. 3 (2006): 260–66.

Stewart, David A., Jerome D. Schein, and Brenda E. Cartwright. *Sign Language Interpreting: Exploring Its Art and Science, 2nd ed.* New York: Allyn & Bacon, 2014.

Stinson, Michael, and Gerard Walter. "Improving Retention for Deaf and Hard of Hearing Students: What the Research Tells Us." *Journal of the American Deafness and Rehabilitation Association* 30, no. 4 (1997): 14–23.

Stremlau, Tonya M. *The Deaf Way II Anthology: A Literary Collection by Deaf and Hard of Hearing Writers.* Washington, DC: Gallaudet University Press, 2002.

Struxness, Kevin. *Mouth Morphemes in American Sign Language.* Video. Los Angeles, CA: DeBee Communications, 1996.

Stuard, Victoria L. "Perceptions of Interpreter Qualification by Deaf Consumers and Hearing Interpreters." Ph.D diss., Pepperdine University, 2008.

Suggs, Trudy. "Deaf Disempowerment and Today's Interpreter." http://www.streetleverage.com/2012/12/deaf-disempowerment-andtodays-interpreter/.

Supalla, Ted, Patricia Clark, Sharon Neumann Solow, and Ronice Muller de Quadros. "Developing Protocols for Interpreting in Multilingual International Conferences." In *Interpreting in Multilingual, Multicultural Contexts,* edited by Rachel McKee and Jeffrey E. Davis. Washington, DC: Gallaudet University Press (2010): 197–225.

Swabey, Laurie, and Quincy C. Faber. "Domains and Competencies in Healthcare Interpreting: Applications and Implications for Educators." In *In Our Hands: Educating Healthcare Inter-*

preters, edited by Laurie Swabey and Karen Malcolm. Washington, DC: Gallaudet University Press (2012): 1–26.

Tannen, Deborah. *Talking Voices: Repetition, Dialogue, and Imagery in Conversational Discourse.* Cambridge UK: Cambridge University Press, 2007.

Taube-Schiffnorman, Marlene, and Norman Segalowitz. "Within-Language Attention Control in Second Language Processing." *Bilingualism: Language and Cognition* 8, no. 3 (2005): 195–206.

Taylor, Marty. *Interpretation Skills: English to American Sign Language.* Edmonton, Alberta: Interpreting Consolidated, 2002.

Texas Health and Human Services. "BEI Frequently Asked Questions." Austin, TX: Texas Department of Health and Human Services. Accessed July 14, 2017. https://hhs.texas.gov/doing-business-hhs/provider-portals/assistive-services-providers/board-evaluation-interpreters-certification-program/bei-frequently-asked-questions.

The 2015 Athens Declaration Working Group. "Athens Declaration on Access for Deaf Participants at the International Congress on the Education of the Deaf (ICED)." July 8, 2015. http://www.archipel.uqam.ca/9546/.

The Joint Commission. *Advancing Effective Communication, Cultural Competence, and Patient- and Family-Centered Care: A Roadmap for Hospitals.* Oakbrook Terrace, IL: The Joint Commission, 2010.

Thibeault, A. "Overlap in Filipino Sign Language Discourse." In *Communication Forum,* edited by Elizabeth A. Winston. Washington, DC: Gallaudet University Press (1993): 207–18.

Thumann, Mary. "Identifying Depiction in American Sign Language Presentations." Ph.D diss., Gallaudet University, 2010: 155–57.

Trommlerová, Sofia Karina, Stephan Klasen, and Ortrud Leßmann. "Determinants of Empowerment in a Capability-Based Poverty Approach: Evidence from the Gambia." *World Development* 66, no. 1 (2015): 1–15.

Tuccoli, Tiffany. "*Exploring Hearing Privilege.*" Master's thesis, Gallaudet University, 2008: 23.

U.S. Department of Justice, Civil Rights Division, Disability Rights Division. "Effective Communication." Washington, DC: U.S. Department of Justice, 2014. https://www.ada.gov/effective-comm.pdf.

Unterhalter, Elaine. "What Is Equity in Education? Reflections from the Capability Approach." *Studies in Philosophy and Education* 28, no. 5 (2009): 415–24.

Van de Ven, Andrew. *Engaged Scholarship: A Guide for Organizational and Social Research.* Oxford, United Kingdom: Oxford University Press, 2007.

Vinay, Jean-Paul, and Jean Darbelnet. "A Methodology for Translation." In *The Translation Studies Reader, 2nd ed,* edited by Lawrence Venuti. New York, NY: Routledge, 2004: 128–73.

Wadensjö, Cecilia. *Interpreting as Interaction.* New York, NY: Longman, 1998.

Wadsworth, Yoland. *Do It Yourself Social Research.* Walnut Creek, CA: Left Coast Press (2011): 76.

Walter, Gerard, Susan Foster, and Lisa Elliot. "Attrition and Accommodation of Hearing-Impaired College Students in the U.S." Paper presented at the *Tenth National Conference of the Association on Handicapped Student Service Programs in Postsecondary Education.* Washington, DC, July 23, 1987.

Ward, James, and Diana Winstanley. "The Absent Presence: Negative Space Within Discourse and the Construction of Minority Sexual Identity in the Workplace." *Human Relations*, 56, (2003): 1255–80.

WFD and WASLI. "International Sign Fee Guidelines for WFD Events." https://wfdeaf.org/news/resources/international-sign-fee-guidelines-for-wfd-events-march-2015/.

Wiesman, Lynne, and Eileen Forestal. "Effective Practices for Establishing Mentoring Programs." *A New Chapter in Interpreter Education: Accreditation, Research, and Technology—*

Proceedings of the 16th National Convention of the Conference of Interpreter Trainers. San Diego, CA: CIT Publications (October 18–21, 2006): 183–92.

Wilcox, Sherman, and Barb Shaffer. "Towards a Cognitive Model of Interpreting." In *Topics in Signed Language Interpreting,* edited by Terry Janzen. Amsterdam, The Netherlands: Benjamins (2005): 27–50.

Willemsen, Lotte M., Peter C. Neijens, Fred Bronner, and Jan A. De Ridder. "Highly Recommended! The Content Characteristics and Perceived Usefulness of Online Consumer Reviews." *Journal of Computer–Mediated Communication* 17, no. 1 (2011): 19–38.

Williams, John. "The Basics of Branding." *Entrepreneur*, n.d.

Williams, T. K. "Understanding Internalized Oppression: A Theoretical Conceptualization of Internalized Subordination." Ph.D diss., University of Massachusetts, 2012: 627.

Williamson, Elizabeth. "Interpreters for Deaf Cut Through D.C.'s Political Jargon." *Wall Street Journal,* January 13, 2014. https://www.wsj.com/articles/no-headline-available-1389655017.

Winston, Elizabeth A. "Transliteration: What's the Message?" In *Sociolinguistics of the Deaf Community,* edited by Cecil Lucas. San Diego, CA: Academic Press (1989): 147–64.

Witter-Merithew, Anna. "From Benevolent Care-taker to Ally: The Evolving Role of Sign Language Interpreters in the United States of America." *Gebärdensprachdolmetschen: Dokumentation der MagdeburgerFachtagung: Theorie und Praxis 4*. Hamburg: Verlhörgeschädigte kinder (1999): 55–64.

Witter-Merithew, Anna, and Leilani Johnson. "Market Disorder Within the Field of Sign Language Interpreting: Professionalization Implications." *Journal of Interpretation* 14, no. 1 (2004): 19–55.

Witter-Merithew, Anna, and Leilani J. Johnson. *Toward Competent Practice: Conversations with Stakeholders*. Alexandria, VA: The Registry of the Interpreters for the Deaf, 2005.

Wood, Ruann L. "Bingo! Dealing with the Audience Heckler." *RID Views* 28, no. 4 (2011): 14.

Woodcock, Kathryn, Meg Rohan, and Linda Campbell. "Equitable Representation of Deaf People in Mainstream Academia: Why Not?" *Higher Education* 53, no. 3 (2007): 359–79.

World Federation of the Deaf and World Association of Sign Language Interpreters. "International Sign Fee Guidelines for WFD Events." March 2015. https://wfdeaf.org/news/resources/international-sign-fee-guidelines-for-wfd-events-march-2015/.

———. "International Sign Interpreter Recognition Interim Policy and Guidelines." Last modified March 13, 2015. https://wfdeaf.org/news/resources/international-sign-interpreter-recognition-interim-policy-and-guideline-march-2015/ .

———. "March 2017 Guidelines on Securing and Utilising the Services of Sign Language Interpreters for the UN." Last modified March 21, 2017. https://wfdeaf.org/news/resources/march-2017-wfd-and-wasli-guidelines-on-securing-and-utilising-the-services-of-sign-language-interpreters-for-the-un/.

Yate, Martin. *Knock 'em Dead: The Ultimate Job Search Guide*. Avon, MA: Adams Media, 2017.

Yosso, Tara J. "Whose Culture has Capital? A Critical Race Theory Discussion of Community Cultural Wealth." *Race Ethnicity and Education* 8, no. 1 (2005): 69–91.

Zannirato, Alessandro. "Teaching Interpreting and Interpreting Teaching: A Conference Interpreter's Overview of Second Language Acquisition." In *Translator and Interpreter Training: Issues, Methods and Debates*, edited by John Kearns. London: Continuum (2008): 19–38.

Zimmer, June. "From ASL to English in Two Versions: An Analysis of Differences in Register." *Word* 41, no. 1 (1990): 19–34.

Contributors

Aracelia Aguilar, Advocate, Deaf Hope

Degrees: BS, California State University, East Bay (Criminal Justice)
Educational Background: Deaf program in a public school; transferred to California School for the Deaf, Fremont at 10.
1st Time Sign: SEE at young age, ASL at 10.
CDI: No
Contact info: aracelia@deaf-hope.org

Patrick Boudreault, Associate Professor, Gallaudet University

Degrees: BA, Université du Québec à Montréal (Linguistics); MSc, McGill University (Communication Sciences Disorders); PhD, University of Manitoba (Educational Psychology)
Educational Background: Oral school (elementary); Deaf school (middle school); Public school without interpreting services (high school)
1st Time Sign: At birth, Deaf family
CDI: DI, not certified
Contact info: Patrick. boudreault@gallaudet.edu

Fallon Brizendine, Department Chair and Associate Professor, ASL Interpreting Training program, Austin Community College

Degrees: BA, Gallaudet University (Communication Studies); MA, Gallaudet University (Interpretation)
Educational Background: Kendall, Indiana, and Maryland Schools for the Deaf
1st Time Sign: At birth, Deaf family
CDI: Yes
Contact info: fallon.brizendine@austincc.edu

Justin Buckhold ("Bucky"), Sales at Linguabee

Educational Background: Public school without interpreting services; California School for the Deaf, Fremont (high school)
1st Time Sign: 16 years old
CDI: Yes
Contact info: bucky@linguabee.com

Keith M. Cagle, Professor, Department of Interpretation and Translation, Gallaudet University

Degrees: BSW, Rochester Institute of Technology (Social Work); MA, CSUN (Educational Administration); PhD, University of New Mexico at Albuquerque (Educational Linguistics)
Educational Background: Washington and Oregon Schools for the Deaf
1st Time Sign: At birth, Deaf family
CDI: No
Contact info: keith.cagle@gallaudet.edu

Genie Gertz, Dean, College of Arts and Sciences, Gallaudet University

Degrees: BA, Gallaudet University (Communication Studies); MA, New York University (Human Resources Management and Organizational Development in Higher Education); PhD, UCLA (Cultural Studies with Racial and Ethnic Focus)
Educational Background: Lexington School for the Deaf; private school with interpreting services (high school)
1st Time Sign: Native signer
CDI: No
Contact info: genie.gertz@gallaudet.edu

Susan Gonzalez, Legal Advocate, Deaf Counseling, Advocacy, and Referral Agency

Degrees: BS, University of California Davis (Human Development); MS, San Francisco State University (Special Education); JD, New College of California School of Law; LLM, Golden Gate University School of Law
Educational Background: Public school without interpreting services
1st Time Sign: 23 years old
CDI: DI, not certified
Contact info: susan.gonzalez@dcara.org

Wyatte C. Hall, Postdoctoral Fellow, Clinical & Translational Science Institute, University of Rochester Medical Center

Degrees: BS, Rochester Institute of Technology (Psychology); MA, Gallaudet University (Clinical Psychology); PhD, Gallaudet University (Clinical Psychology)
Educational Background: Public school with interpreting services
1st Time Sign: 5 years old
CDI: No
Contact info: wyatte_hall@urmc.rochester.edu

Raychelle Harris, Associate Professor, Program Co-Director, Master in Sign Language Education Program, ASL & Deaf Studies Department, Gallaudet University

Degrees: BA, Gallaudet University (ASL); MA, McDaniel College (Deaf Education); PhD, Gallaudet University (Education with concentration area in linguistics)
Educational Background: Kendall School and Model Secondary School for the Deaf
1st Time Sign: At birth, Deaf family
CDI: Yes
Contact info: raychelle.harris@gallaudet.edu

Jonathan Henner, Assistant Professor, University of North Carolina at Greensboro

Degrees: BS, Illinois State University (Philosophy); MS, Walden University (Psychology); EdD, Boston University (Developmental Studies in Language)
Educational Background: Public school with interpreting services
1st Time Sign: Signed English at 2 years old and ASL at 11
CDI: No
Contact info: j_henner@uncg.edu

Joseph C. Hill, Assistant Professor, American Sign Language and Interpreting Education Department, National Technical Institute for the Deaf

Degrees: BA, Miami University, Ohio (Systems Analysis); MA, Gallaudet University (Linguistics); PhD, Gallaudet University (Linguistics)
Educational Background: Public school without interpreting services during elementary school, with interpreting services in middle school and beyond
1st Time Sign: 10 years old, Deaf family
CDI: No
Contact info: jchnss@rit.edu

Leala Holcomb, Scholar, National Leadership Consortium in Sensory Disabilities

Position: Scholar
Degrees: BA, Gallaudet University (International Education and Development); MS, National University (Deaf Education); ABD, University of Tennessee, Knoxville (Theory and Practice in Teacher Education)
Educational Background: California School for the Deaf, Fremont
1st Time Sign: At birth, Deaf family
CDI: No
Contact info: lealaholcomb@gmail.com

Tara Holcomb, Advocate, Deaf Hope

Degrees: BA, Gallaudet University (Psychology)
Educational Background: California School for the Deaf, Fremont and Model Secondary School for the Deaf
1st Time Sign: At birth, Deaf family
CDI: No, DI at times
Contact info: tara.holcomb@gallaudet.edu

Thomas K. Holcomb, Professor, Ohlone College

Degrees: BA, Gallaudet University (Psychology); MS, Rochester Institute of Technology (Career and Human Resources); PhD, University of Rochester (Curriculum and Instruction)
Educational Background: Indiana School for the Deaf (K–3); Public school with interpreting services (4–8); Model Secondary School for the Deaf (high school)
1st Time Sign: At birth, Deaf family
CDI: No
Contact info: Tholcomb@ohlone.edu

Tawny Holmes, Education Policy Counsel, National Association of the Deaf, Assistant Professor, Gallaudet University

Degrees: BS, Gallaudet University (Deaf Studies and Sociology); MA, Gallaudet University (Deaf Education); JD, University of Baltimore Law School
Educational Background: Deaf program with interpreters in a public school (K–4); Alabama School for the Deaf
1st Time Sign: At birth, Deaf family
CDI: No
Contact info: tawny.holmes@nad.org

Marika Kovacs-Houlihan, Coordinator/ Associate Professor, ASL Studies, University of Wisconsin-Milwaukee

Degrees: BA, Rochester Institute of Technology (Marketing); MA, University of Wisconsin-Milwaukee (Administrative Leadership)
Educational Background: Deaf program in public school; then mainstreamed with interpreting services (high school)
1st Time Sign: At birth, Deaf family
CDI: No
Contact info: mkh2@uwm.edu

Christopher A.N. Kurz, Associate Professor, Master of Science in Secondary Education for Students Who Are Deaf or Hard of Hearing, National Technical Institute for the Deaf, Rochester Institute of Technology

Degrees: BS, Rochester Institute of Technology (Mathematics); MS, University of Kansas (Deaf Education); PhD, University of Kansas (Foundations)
Educational Background: Deaf program in public school; then mainstreamed with interpreting services (high school)
1st Time Sign: All his life
CDI: No
Contact info: caknsp@rit.edu

Kim B. Kurz, Chair, American Sign Language and Interpreting Education Department, National Technical Institute for the Deaf, Rochester Institute of Technology

Degrees: BS, Rochester Institute of Technology (Social Work); MS, Rochester Institute of Technology (Career and Human Resources); PhD, University of Kansas (Education)
Educational Background: Deaf program in public school; then mainstreamed with interpreting services (5th grade)
1st Time Sign: 9 months old
CDI: No
Contact info: kbknss@rit.edu

Sharon Lott, ASL Coordinator, Eastern North Carolina School for the Deaf

Degrees: BS, Rochester Institute of Technology (Social Work); MS, Rochester Institute of Technology (Career and Human Resources); MA, Gallaudet University (Sign Language Teaching)
Educational Background: Crotched Mts School for the Deaf (elementary/middle school); Austine Schools for the Deaf (high school)
1st Time Sign: 3 years old
CDI: DI, working toward certification
Contact info: sharonjea@gmail.com

Lewis S. Lummer, Senior Lecturer, Deaf Education and American Sign Language, Baylor University

Degrees: AAS, Rochester Institute of Technology (Civil Technology); BA, Gallaudet University (Communication Arts with emphasis on International Studies); MSEd, Lamar University (Deaf Education and Deaf Studies); EdD, Northern Illinois University (Curriculum and Instruction with specialization in Reading)
Educational Background: Public school without interpreting services until 6th grade; Illinois School for the Deaf (high school)
1st Time Sign: At birth, Deaf family
CDI: No
Contact info: lewis_lummer@baylor.edu

Paul W. Ogden, Professor Emeritus, Deaf Studies, California State University, Fresno

Degrees: BA, Antioch College (Computers, Math, Psychology); MA, University of Illinois-Urbana (Educational Psychology); PhD, University of Illinois-Urbana (Educational Psychology)
Educational Background: Public school without interpreting services
1st Time Sign: Some basic signs at 11 years old, 1st class at 24 years old
CDI: No
Contact info: Paulo@mail.fresnostate.edu

Marta Ordaz, Advocate, Deaf Counseling Advocacy & Referral Agency

Degrees: BA, Gallaudet University (Social Work)
Educational Background: Public school without interpreting services; California School for the Deaf, Berkeley (high school)
1st Time Sign: 16 years old at CSD
CDI: No
Contact info: marta.ordaz@dcara.org

John S. Pirone, ASL Program Coordinator/Lecturer, University of Vermont

Degrees: BA, Arizona State University (Interdisciplinary Studies: Communication and Business); MBA, University of Phoenix (Business Administration); EdD, Northeastern University (Higher Education Administration)
Educational Background: Learning Center for the Deaf until 10th grade; mainstreamed with interpreting services in high school
1st Time Sign: 1 year old
CDI: No
Contact info: john.pirone@uvm.edu

Cynthia J. Plue, President and Cofounder, Sign-ology

Degrees: BA, Gallaudet University (Psychology and Communication Arts); MeD, Boston University (Deaf Education); EdD, Lamar University (Deaf Education and Deaf Studies)
Educational Background: Public school without interpreting services
1st Time Sign: 16 years old
CDI: DI, not certified
Contact info: cynthiaplue@gmail.com

Amy June Rowley, Associate Professor and Program Coordinator, California State University, East Bay

Degrees: BA, Gallaudet University (Biology); MA, McDaniel College (Deaf Education with ASL Specialist Certification); PhD, University of Wisconsin, Milwaukee (Urban Education in Curriculum and Instruction)
Educational Background: Public school with and without interpreting services
1st Time Sign: At birth, Deaf family
CDI: No
Contact info: amyjune.rowley@csueastbay.edu

Sam Sepah, Global HR Program Manager, Google

Degrees: BS, Rochester Institute of Technology (Social Science); MS, Rochester Institute of Technology (Human Resources)
Educational Background: Public school with interpreting services; California School for the Deaf, Riverside (high school)
1st Time Sign: Pre-school
CDI: No
Contact info: sepah@google.com

Naomi Sheneman

Degrees: BA, Gallaudet University (Psychology); MA, University of California, San Diego (Bilingual Education); MS, University of Rochester (Educational Administration); PhD, Gallaudet University (Interpretation)
Educational Background: Public school with interpreting services; Model Secondary School for the Deaf (high school)
1st Time Sign: At birth, Deaf family
CDI: Yes
Contact info: naomi.sheneman@gallaudet.edu

Ryan Shephard, Customer Support, Linguabee

Degrees: BA, Gallaudet University (Interpretation)
Educational Background: Maryland School for the Deaf and Model Secondary School for the Deaf
1st Time Sign: At birth, Deaf family
CDI: Yes
Contact info: ryan@linguabee.com

David H. Smith, Associate Professor, University of Tennessee--Knoxville

Degrees: BS, Rochester Institute of Technology (Biology); MS, University of Rochester (Education); PhD, University of Nebraska-Lincoln (Psychological and Cultural Studies)
Educational Background: Public school without interpreting services
1st Time Sign: 18 years old at NTID
CDI: No
Contact info: dsmit147@utk.edu

Trudy Suggs, Owner, T.S. Writing Services, LLC

Degrees: BA, Gallaudet University (Communication Arts and Government); MPA, University of Illinois-Chicago (Public Administration)
Educational Background: Public school with interpreting services; Illinois School for the Deaf (sixth grade)
1st Time Sign: At birth, Deaf family
CDI: Yes

Chad W. Taylor,
Queen Bee, Linguabee

Degrees: BS, Rochester Institute of Technology (Information Technology)
Educational Background: Robarts School for the Deaf, London, Ontario
1st Time Sign: SEE at preschool; ASL at 5 years old
CDI: No
Contact info: chad@linguabee.com

Phyllis Wilcox, Professor Emerita,
University of New Mexico

Degrees: BA, Southeastern Louisiana University (Sociology); MS, Eastern New Mexico University (Special Ed., Emphasis in Deaf Ed.); PhD, University of New Mexico (Educational Foundations)
Educational Background: Public school without interpreting services
1st Time Sign: 21 years old
CDI: Yes
Contact info: pwilcox@unm.edu

Index

Page numbers in *italics* refer to figures.